Countering Cyber Attacks and Preserving the Integrity and Availability of Critical Systems

S. Geetha
VIT Chennai, India

Asnath Victy Phamila
VIT Chennai, India

A volume in the Advances in
Digital Crime, Forensics, and Cyber
Terrorism (ADCFCT) Book Series

Published in the United States of America by
    IGI Global
    Information Science Reference (an imprint of IGI Global)
    701 E. Chocolate Avenue
    Hershey PA, USA 17033
    Tel: 717-533-8845
    Fax: 717-533-8661
    E-mail: cust@igi-global.com
    Web site: http://www.igi-global.com

Library of Congress Cataloging-in-Publication Data

Names: Geetha, S., 1979- editor. | Phamila, Asnath Victy, 1978- editor.
Title: Countering cyber attacks and preserving the integrity and availability
  of critical systems / S. Geetha and Asnath Victy Phamila, editors.
Description: Hershey, PA : Information Science Reference, [2019] | Includes
  bibliographical references.
Identifiers: LCCN 2018052157| ISBN 9781522582410 (hardcover) | ISBN
  9781522582427 (ebook)
Subjects: LCSH: Computer networks--Security measures. | Computer
  crimes--Prevention. | Computer security.
Classification: LCC TK5105.59 .C648 2019 | DDC 005.8/2--dc23 LC record available at https://
lccn.loc.gov/2018052157

This book is published in the IGI Global book series Advances in Digital Crime, Forensics, and Cyber Terrorism (ADCFCT) (ISSN: 2327-0381; eISSN: 2327-0373)

British Cataloguing in Publication Data
A Cataloguing in Publication record for this book is available from the British Library.

All work contributed to this book is new, previously-unpublished material.
The views expressed in this book are those of the authors, but not necessarily of the publisher.

For electronic access to this publication, please contact: eresources@igi-global.com.

Advances in Digital Crime, Forensics, and Cyber Terrorism (ADCFCT) Book Series

ISSN:2327-0381
EISSN:2327-0373

Editor-in-Chief: Bryan Christiansen, Global Research Society, LLC, USA & Agnieszka Piekarz, Independent Researcher, Poland

MISSION

The digital revolution has allowed for greater global connectivity and has improved the way we share and present information. With this new ease of communication and access also come many new challenges and threats as cyber crime and digital perpetrators are constantly developing new ways to attack systems and gain access to private information.

The **Advances in Digital Crime, Forensics, and Cyber Terrorism (ADCFCT) Book Series** seeks to publish the latest research in diverse fields pertaining to crime, warfare, terrorism and forensics in the digital sphere. By advancing research available in these fields, the **ADCFCT** aims to present researchers, academicians, and students with the most current available knowledge and assist security and law enforcement professionals with a better understanding of the current tools, applications, and methodologies being implemented and discussed in the field.

COVERAGE

- Encryption
- Network Forensics
- Data Protection
- Malware
- Cyber Warfare
- Cyber terrorism
- Telecommunications Fraud
- Identity Theft
- Mobile Device Forensics
- Digital Crime

IGI Global is currently accepting manuscripts for publication within this series. To submit a proposal for a volume in this series, please contact our Acquisition Editors at Acquisitions@igi-global.com or visit: http://www.igi-global.com/publish/.

Titles in this Series

701 East Chocolate Avenue, Hershey, PA 17033, USA
Tel: 717-533-8845 x100 ● Fax: 717-533-8661
E-Mail: cust@igi-global.com ● www.igi-global.com

Marimuthu K., *VIT University, India*

Jansi K. R., *SRM University, India*

Grace Mary Kanaga, *Karunya University, India*

Kavitha Devi M. K., *Thiagarajar College of Engineering, India*

Karthikeyan N., *Syed Ammal Engineering College, India*

Kishore R., *SSN College of Engineering, India*

Wahida Banu R. S. D., *GCES, India*

Jennifer Ranjani, *BITS Pilani, India*

Amutha S., *SSN College of Engineering, India*

Sasikala S., *Pavai College of Engineering, India*

Siva S. Sivatha Sindhu, *Shan Security Systems, USA*

Murali Meenakshi Sundaram, *CTS, India*

Vijayakumar V., *VIT University, India*

Table of Contents

Section 1
National Security and Cyber Warfare

Chapter 1

K. S. Umadevi, VIT University, India
Geraldine Bessie Amali, VIT University, India
Latha Subramanian, University of Madras, India

Chapter 2

Kirti Raj Raj Bhatele, BSF Academy, India
Deepak Dutt Mishra, BSF Academy, India
Himanshu Bhatt, BSF Academy, India
Karishma Das, BSF Academy, India

Chapter 3

K. S. Umadevi, VIT University, India
Geraldine Bessie Amali, VIT University, India
Latha Subramanian, University of Madras, India

Section 2
Critical IoT Infrastructure Security

Section 3
Emerging Trends and Methods for Cyber Forensics

Detailed Table of Contents

Section 1
National Security and Cyber Warfare

 K. S. Umadevi, VIT University, India
 Geraldine Bessie Amali, VIT University, India
 Latha Subramanian, University of Madras, India

Security, safety, and privacy are of paramount importance to anyone who likes to crawl on the web. Keeping the best interest of the internet users in mind, India has laid down very solid foundations to safeguard its people from cyberattacks and cyber terrorism. The word "cyber law" encompasses all the cases, statutes, and constitutional provisions that affect persons and institutions who control the entry to cyberspace, provide access to cyberspace, create the hardware and software that enable people to access cyberspace or use their own devices to go "online" and enter cyberspace. Cyber crimes are unlawful acts wherein the computer is either a tool or a target or both. Cyber crimes can involve criminal activities that are traditional in nature, such as theft, fraud, forgery, defamation, and mischief, all of which are subject to the Indian Penal Code.

 Kirti Raj Raj Bhatele, BSF Academy, India
 Deepak Dutt Mishra, BSF Academy, India
 Himanshu Bhatt, BSF Academy, India
 Karishma Das, BSF Academy, India

This chapter provides prerequisites associated with cyber crimes, cyber forensics, and law enforcement. It consists of a brief introduction to the definition of cyber crimes, its classification, challenges associated with it and how it evolved with time, impact on the society, cyber terrorism, and the extent of problem scalability along with focusing on law enforcement aspects associated with the tracking and the prevention from such type crimes. The aspects discussed here include various cyber laws and law enforcement techniques introduced by various countries throughout the world which helps them to fight against cyber crimes. The cyber laws discussed include Australian, Canadian, United States, United Kingdom, and Indian law. This chapter also deals with the digital/cyber forensics, what does digital/cyber forensics mean, its types, and laws/rules revolving around them, like how to collect evidence, jurisdictions, and e-discovery.

Chapter 3

    K. S. Umadevi, VIT University, India
    Geraldine Bessie Amali, VIT University, India
    Latha Subramanian, University of Madras, India

Cybercrime is defined as a crime in which a computer is the object of the crime (hacking, phishing, spamming) or is used as a tool to commit an offense (child pornography, hate crimes). The advancement of technology has made us dependent on internet for all our needs. Internet has given us easy access to everything without moving from our place. Social networking, online shopping, storing data, gaming, online studying, online jobs, every possible thing that man can think of can be done through the medium of internet. However, with the development of the internet and its related benefits, the concept of cybercrimes arose. Cybercrimes are committed in different forms. In a report published by the National Crime Records Bureau, the incidence of cybercrimes under the IT Act has increased by 85.4% in the year 2011 as compared to 2010 in India, whereas the increase in incidence of the crime under IPC is by 18.5% as compared to the year 2010.

Chapter 4

    M. Sivabalakrishnan, VIT Chennai, India
    R. Menaka, VIT Chennai, India
    S. Jeeva, VIT Chennai, India

Smart surveillance cameras are placed in many places such as bank, hospital, toll gates, airports, etc. To take advantage of the video in real time, a human must monitor the system continuously in order to alert security officers if there is an emergency.

Besides, for event detection a person can observe four cameras with good accuracy at a time. Therefore, this requires expensive human resources for real-time video surveillance using current technology. The framework of ATM video surveillance system encompassing various factors, such as image acquisition, background estimation, background subtraction, store, and further process like segmentation, people counting, and tracking are done in cloud environment briefly discussed in this chapter.

Section 2
Critical IoT Infrastructure Security

Chapter 5

 Uma N. Dulhare, MJCET, India
 Shaik Rasool, MJCET, India

The internet of things (IoT) is the network of physical objects accessed through the internet that can identify themselves to other devices and use embedded technology to interact with internal states or external conditions. The IoT is an environment where an object that can represent itself becomes greater by connecting to surrounding objects and the extensive data flowing around it. The number of internet of things (IoT) devices will reach more than 15 billion units by 2021, according to research from Juniper. As businesses and consumers accelerate adoption, we're now on the cusp of an IoT revolution. The chapter walks through the security problems that are seen with IoT devices that continues to highlight how vulnerable these devices are when faced with modern, sophisticated cyber threats. Further, the authors discuss how to solve these security challenges presented by the internet of things.

Chapter 6

 Vetrivelan Pandu, VIT Chennai, India
 Jagannath Mohan, VIT Chennai, India
 T. S. Pradeep Kumar, VIT Chennai, India

Internet of things (IoT) has transformed greatly the improved way of business through machine-to-machine (M2M) communications. This vast network and its associated technologies have opened the doors to an increasing number of security threats which are dangerous to IoT and 5G wireless networks. The first part of this chapter presents instruction detection system (IDS) which detect the various attacks in 6LoWPAN layer. An IDS is to detect and analyze both inbound and outbound network traffic for abnormal activities. An IPS complements an IDS configuration by proactively inspecting a system's incoming traffic to weed out malicious requests. A typical IPS configuration uses web application firewalls and traffic filtering solutions to secure applications. An IPS prevents attacks by dropping malicious packets, blocking offending IPs and alerting security personnel to potential threats. Machine learning (ML)-based instruction detection and prevention system (IDPS) is proposed and implemented in Contiki simulation environment.

Chapter 7

Prachi Sarode, VIT Chennai, India
TR Reshmi, VIT Chennai, India

The internet of things-integrated sensor nodes (IoT-WSN) is widely adopted in variety of applications such as fire detection, gas leakage detection in industry, earthquake detection, vibrating locations on flyover, weather monitoring, and many more wherein highest value is required in time to serve the abnormal areas with highest priority. The query-based information extraction has increased attention of many researchers working on increasing the network lifetime of the IoT-WSN. In resource-constraint IoT-WSN, executing the requests (in the form of queries) in time with minimum energy consumption is the main requirement and focus. The query processing at sink node in collaboration with neighboring nodes and then finding the top-k values for data aggregation is the most challenging job in IoT-WSN. This chapter investigates the various query-based approaches and improvements in the query data availability. The chapter also presents a comparative analysis that gives an idea of different aspects and applications of query-based schemes.

Chapter 8

Muthuramalingam S., Thiagarajar College of Engineering, India
Nisha Angeline C. V., Thiagarajar College of Engineering, India
Raja Lavanya, Thiagarajar College of Engineering, India

In this IoT era, we have billions of devices connected to the internet. These devices generate tons of data that has to be stored, processed, and used for making intelligent decisions. This calls for the need for a smart heterogeneous network which could handle this data and make the real-time systems work intelligently. IoT applications leads to increasing demands in high traffic volume, M2M communications, low latency, and MIMO operations. Mobile communication has evolved from 2G voice services into a complex, interconnected environment with multiple services built on a system that supports innumerable applications and provides high-speed access. Hence the sustainability of the IoT applications do rely on next generation networks. Due to the significant increase in the network components, computational complexity, and heterogeneity of resources, there arise the need for a secure architectural framework for internet of things. For this, the authors propose a secure architectural framework for IoT that provides a solution to the lightweight devices with low computational complexity.

Section 3
Emerging Trends and Methods for Cyber Forensics

Chapter 9

Kirti Raj Bhatele, RJIT, India
Harsh Shrivastava, RJIT, India
Neha Kumari, RJIT, India

Cyber security has become a major concern in the digital era. Data breaches, ID theft, cracking the captcha, and other such stories abound, affecting millions of individuals as well as organizations. The challenges have always been endless in inventing right controls and procedures and implementing them with acute perfection for tackling with cyber attacks and crimes. The ever-increasing risk of cyber attacks and crimes grew exponentially with recent advancements in artificial intelligence. It has been applied in almost every field of sciences and engineering. From healthcare to robotics, AI has created a revolution. This ball of fire couldn't be kept away from cyber criminals, and thus, the "usual" cyber attacks have now become "intelligent" cyber attacks. In this chapter, the authors discuss specific techniques in artificial intelligence that are promising. They cover the applications of those techniques in cyber security. They end the discussion talking about the future scope of artificial intelligence and cyber security.

Chapter 10

Gopinath Palaniappan, Centre for Development of Advanced Computing (CDAC), India
Balaji Rajendran, Centre for Development of Advanced Computing (CDAC), India
S. Sangeetha, National Institute of Technology Tiruchirappalli, India
NeelaNarayanan V, VIT University, India

The rapid rise in the number of mobile devices has resulted in an alarming increase in mobile software and applications. The mobile application markets/stores too have created a fundamental shift in the way mobile applications are delivered to users, with apps being added and updated in thousands every day. Even though research progresses have been achieved towards detection and mitigation of mobile security, open challenges still remain and also keep evolving in this area. Several studies reveal that mobile application markets/stores do harbor applications that are either vulnerable or malicious in nature, leading to compromises of millions of devices. This chapter (1) captures the attack surface of mobile devices, (2) lists the various mobile malware analysis techniques, and (3) lays the ground for research on mobile malware by providing mobile malware dataset resources, tools for malware analysis, patent landscaping for mobile malware detection, and a few open challenges in malware analysis.

Chapter 11

Abijah Roseline S., VIT Chennai, India

Malware is the most serious security threat, which possibly targets billions of devices like personal computers, smartphones, etc. across the world. Malware classification and detection is a challenging task due to the targeted, zero-day, and stealthy nature of advanced and new malwares. The traditional signature detection methods like antivirus software were effective for detecting known malwares. At present, there are various solutions for detection of such unknown malwares employing feature-based machine learning algorithms. Machine learning techniques detect known malwares effectively but are not optimal and show a low accuracy rate for unknown malwares. This chapter explores a novel deep learning model called deep dilated residual network model for malware image classification. The proposed model showed a higher accuracy of 98.50% and 99.14% on Kaggle Malimg and BIG 2015 datasets, respectively. The new malwares can be handled in real-time with minimal human interaction using the proposed deep residual model.

Chapter 12

G. Suseela, VIT University, India
Y. Asnath Victy Phamila, VIT University, India

Due to the significance of image data over the scalar data, the camera-integrated wireless sensor networks have attained the focus of researchers in the field of smart visual sensor networks. These networks are inexpensive and found wide application in surveillance and monitoring systems. The challenge is that these systems are resource deprived systems. The visual sensor node is typically an embedded system made up of a light weight processor, low memory, low bandwidth transceiver, and low-cost image sensor unit. As these networks carry sensitive information of the surveillance region, security and privacy protection are critical needs of the VSN. Due to resource limited nature of the VSN, the image encryption is crooked into an optimally lower issue, and many findings of image security in VSN are based on selective or partial encryption systems. The secure transmission of images is more trivial. Thus, in this chapter, a security frame work of smart visual sensor network built using energy-efficient image encryption and coding systems designed for VSN is presented.

Section 4
Techniques for Countering Cyber Attacks

Chapter 13

Sowmiya B., SRM Institute of Science and Technology, India
Poovammal E., SRM Institute of Science and Technology, India

The information in any real-time application is needed to be digitalized across the world. Since digitalization of data happens, there comes the role of privacy. Blockchain could address the security challenge that happens in the any real sector. There are a few more challenges that prevail in the industry such as integrity in data, traceability of stored records, and interoperability among organizations that share information. This chapter says what blockchain is and applications in which blockchain technology could solve the existing challenges where they lack security, privacy, integrity, and interoperability.

Chapter 14

B. Rajesh Kanna, VIT Chennai, India

This chapter discloses an invention related to methods and systems to provide secure and custom information exchange code for the users of haptic or kinesthetic communication devices in a variety of applications. The proposed information exchange codes are named as "haptic codes," where it maps several touch interactive locations into a single information exchange code. Thus, the proposed haptic code facilitates the representation of different notions to unique information exchange character/digit/symbol. A method has been invented to design eight such codes from the intuitive touch gestures (ITG) of user, each of which uses double-touch on arbitrary location within the touch pad/screen without shifting hand position on every touch. Hand position may or may not be the same after the generation of every ITG. Haptic codes are made secure by incorporating a new cryptographic system, which employs polar graph for encoding and decoding such locations using polar curves as shareable keys. Therefore, haptic codes can be exchanged for secure communication and read by devices that supports to touch.

Chapter 15

Security plays an important role in present day situation where identity fraud and terrorism pose a great threat. Recognizing human using computers or any artificial systems not only affords some efficient security outcomes but also facilitates human services, especially in the zone of conflict. In the recent decade, the demand for improvement in security for personal data storage has grown rapidly, and among the potential alternatives, it is one that employs innovative biometric identification techniques. Amongst these behavioral biometric techniques, the electrocardiogram (ECG) is being chosen as a physiological modality due to the uniqueness of its characteristics which integrates liveness detection, significantly preventing spoof attacks. The chapter discusses the overview of existing preprocessing, feature extraction, and classification methods for ECG-based biometric authentication. The proposed system is intended to develop applications for real-time authentication.

Digital healthcare system, which is undergoing transformation phase to provide safe, swift, and improved quality care, is experiencing diverse problems. The serious threats to the digital healthcare system include misidentification of patients and healthcare-related frauds. Biometrics is a cutting-edge scientific field which overcomes the weaknesses of password-based authentication methods while ensuring a friction-free user experience. It enables unprecedented authentication capabilities based on human characteristics that cannot be replicated by fraudsters. The growing demand for biometrics solutions in digital healthcare system is mainly driven by the need to combat fraud, along with an initiative to preserve privacy of the patient besides with healthcare safety. This chapter examines how biometric technology can be applied to the digital healthcare services.

Foreword

Countering Cyber Attacks and Preserving the Integrity and Availability of Critical Systems is a book about cyber forensics and security edited by S. Geetha and Y. Asnath Victy Phamila. In the age when cybercrime episodes are seen more every day, this book provides in-depth information about cyber attacks, threats, vulnerabilities, cyber forensics and cyber security solutions offering the much –needed awareness.

This book presents ample discussion on various cybercrime, cyber security laws and enforcement, solutions for countering cyber attacks. It provides a discussion of not only Indian but also the global scenario. It is aimed at creating an awareness about the cyber security threats through easy procedures and practices, thereby informing the reader how to keep safe by not becoming a victim of cybercrime. It provides comprehensive treatment of important topic of cyber security to highlight the implications of cybercrime.

The book is designed for IT and legal professionals, students, and individuals who need to increase their awareness and knowledge about cybercrime and cyber security. Each chapter is written by an accomplished expert in his or her field, many of them with extensive experience in cyber security, law enforcement and industry. The author team comprises experts in digital forensics, cybercrime law, information security and related areas.

The book is meticulously compiled and the thought process put into its compilation ensures the key competency - cyber forensics, to tackle the growing risks of cybercrime, as well as for criminal investigation generally and infrastructure protection and security, are well presented. Considering the proliferating pace at which new cyber space technology expands, this book brings contents for researchers and practitioners who regularly face new technical challenges, facilitating them to continuously upgrade their investigatory skills. The book prepares the next generation to rise to those challenges. The material contained in this book can be used by both graduate and undergraduate programs as well.

The editors have done a good job, a trivial exercise that is for the need of the hour, resulting in an inevitable Reference Material in the field of Cyber Security, Cyber Forensics and Solutions!

N. Kamaraj
Thiagarajar College of Engineering, India

Preface

Today's world is highly progressing, and makes a mighty move from an industrial age to an information age. This change envisages Internet as the founding stone in every part of our lives. A serious concern, though, in this development will be ensuring that the complete computer system, the hardware, software, network, communication and transactions happening in this cyber space are secure and free from security attacks. As the world has become more dependent over Internet for most of its operations, we cannot think of a system excluding Internet and Cyber Space. However, it comes with associated risks, particularly when we migrate to a space completely operating with cyber infrastructures facilitating electronic communications. This has opened up the gates for the proliferating services/operations including e-Mail, voice and video over IP, web based systems, mobile based Applications, social networks, etc.,

However, in current scenario, it takes only minutes between connecting into the Internet and being attacked by some other remote machine. The rate of cyber crimes is increasing because of the fast-paced advancements in computer and Internet technology. Crimes involving a computer can range across the spectrum of criminal activity, from child pornography to theft of personal data to corporate espionage to destruction of intellectual property. Crimes employing mobile devices, data embedding/mining systems, computers, network communications, or any malware impose a huge threat to data security. On an extreme case the security attacks are so advanced, that the user is completely unaware of the attack and still continues to use the cyber space, being a victim of the attack. Hence, it is evident that without security, the cyber space holds little value.

Currently the levels of security attacks are highly advanced, seeking solutions addressing significant security challenges, including protecting against host/network attacks, strengthening physical control, and preventing unauthorized access. In internet communications and electronic business, information security is an essential feature, and as of state, there is a pressing need to develop advanced methods to prevent and control these.

It is to be understood that the purpose of enforcing security practices is to secure the organisation's/nation's valuable assets, like information in the form of documents, files, e-mails, images, videos and audios, computer software, hardware, network, servers and other components. By an appropriate choice and application of suitable safety and security strategies, the organisation's/nation's mission of protecting the physical resources, financial resources, legal position, reputation, employees, and all other intangible and tangible assets is ensured. It is commonly misunderstood that security is a thwarting component to the business objective, since the users, mangers and systems are suggested to follow poor cumbersome security policies and procedures. Meticulously chosen security rules, policies and procedures do really support and reinforce the overall business/nation's objectives.

Cyber forensics and investigations have many challenges, starting from effective evidence collection and following prescribed forensic procedures for evidence preservation, custody of evidence chain, managing the digital evidence and data/image authentication and forensics of the hard disk/any storage device, cryptography and cryptanalysis in forensics, steganography and steganalysis and mobile forensics. The interest in cyber forensics and investigations is obvious from the industrial and standardization efforts accomplished in the last years.

Cyber security and cyber forensics share a lot in common. Analyzing a breach may provide new insights over how to prevent such a breach, and to know how those threats and vulnerabilities work, helping out to develop possible solutions and counter measures against those attack vector.

Keeping abreast with the latest developments in cyber security demands enduring commitment, as well as a strong foundation in the principles of cyber security and cyber forensics are two expectations for those security professionals tasked with cyber security. This edited volume strives to address a wide range of perspectives in cyber security, cyber crime and cyber forensics. We have assembled insights from a representative sample of academicians and practitioners.

SECTION 1: NATIONAL SECURITY AND CYBER WARFARE

Digital forensics is a branch of forensic science encompassing the recovery and investigation of material found in digital devices, in relation to computer crime. With the explosion of web technologies and usage of computers and cell phones, the field of digital forensics is consistently growing and there is a huge demand over the last few years. Digital forensics deals with investigating these technological devices and monitoring whether something is hacked or likely to be hacked. The intent of Chapter 1 is to provide a concise overview of the process of collecting forensic evidence and review different methods, tools, and challenges involved in forensic analysis and collection.

Cybercrimes are newer classes of crimes committed using the technology and mainly internet. With the introduction of social media such as Facebook, Twitter, etc., there has been havoc created in the society and the crimes using the internet have risen. Today, the internet is the vital role of the daily life and the society. Cybercrimes is too rampant and finding the potential victims to dupe them and steal their identities on the netizens' accounts for their hacking activity and of course, cyber pornography exploit younger children and minors. The advancement of technology has made us dependent on Internet for all our needs and hence cybercrimes arose. Cybercrime laws, and civil laws applicable to Cyberspace as well, deal with the specific problems that arise when the elements of a crime (or business transaction) are spread out over several different locations because of the nature of the technology and this law is needed too much at this hour. Chapter 2 augments the prerequisites associated with Cyber Crimes, Cyber Forensics and Law Enforcement. Basically, it consists of a brief introduction to the definition of Cyber Crimes, its classification, challenges associated with it and how it evolved with time, impact on society, cyberterrorism, and the extent of problem scalability along with the focus on Law enforcement aspects associated with the tracking and the prevention of such type crimes. Cybercrimes are committed in different forms and Chapter 3 describes cybercrime from different perspectives.

Currently images form an inevitable part of knowledge in the cyber space and every sphere of life has embedded computer vision field. The ability to automatically detect and track objects is of great interest in the field of Security. Tracking a person is a necessary aspect of HCI (Human Computer Interaction), interacting with and within virtual environments, and capturing motion for computer enhanced motion pictures. Smart surveillance cameras are placed in many places such as bank, hospital, toll gates, airports, etc. By tracking various objects, the burden of detection by human sentinels is greatly alleviated. The efficient automatic alarm system is useful for many ATM surveillance applications and it poses many challenging research issues in human abnormal behavior detection approaches. The framework of ATM video surveillance system encompassing various factors, such as image acquisition, background subtraction, storage and further processes like segmentation, counting, and tracking done in cloud environment are briefly discussed in Chapter 4.

SECTION 2: CRITICAL IoT INFRASTRUCTURE SECURITY

The Internet of Things (IoT) is the network of physical objects accessed through the Internet that can identify themselves to other devices and use embedded technology to interact with internal states or external conditions. The number of Internet-of-Things (IoT), devices will reach more than 15 billion units by 2021, according to research from Juniper. As businesses and consumers accelerate adoption, we're now on the cusp of an IoT revolution. The benefits of connected devices are massive and include better data, automation, and increased efficiency.

New approaches to cybersecurity are needed to address access to and deployment of this shared data. Participants need to guarantee each other that there will be no breach with so many moving parts across so many different networks and organizations. Succeeding in the IoT era will depend on defining and deploying not only the right cybersecurity technologies, but also the right policies and operations. The potential of the IoT to yield value for you, your customers, and all of society is vast. We must rethink the cyber security regimes that threaten to limit it. Chapter 5 walks through the security problems that are prevalent with IoT devices and highlights how vulnerable these devices are when faced with modern, sophisticated cyber threats and investigates the ways to solve these security challenges.

Internet of Things (IoT) has changed incredibly the method for business through machine-to-machine (M2M) communications and this has opened the ways to an expanding number of security dangers which are perilous to IoT and 5G remote systems. Chapter 6 exhibits an Intrusion Detection System (IDS) which detect the various attacks in the 6LoWPAN layer. An IDS is to detect and analyze both inbound and outbound network traffic for abnormal activities. An IPS supplements an IDS design by proactively reviewing a framework's approaching movement to weed out vindictive solicitations. A normal IPS arrangement utilizes web application firewalls and activity separating answers for secure applications. An IPS avert attacks by dropping malevolent parcels, blocking insulting IPs and cautioning security faculty to potential dangers. Hence Machine-Learning (ML) based Intrusion Detection and Prevention System (IDPS) is proposed in this chapter and implemented in the Contiki simulation environment.

Latest wireless short-range communication technology is not only targeting reliable data delivery but also addressing the safety and privacy of critical information to some extent. Chapter 7 focuses on query-based delivery models considering the requirements of distinct cases. The data aggregation approach proposed in this chapter contributes with respect to authentication, data freshness, reliable low-cost query, optimum response time, minimum energy consumption, and greater data accessibility. Therefore, the mixture of various technologies together brings the precise extraction of information at right time in the right place for the right decision. In the future, it opens the challenges of data privacy and data integrity in integrated IoT-WSN network.

In this IoT era, we have billions of devices connected to the internet. These devices generate tons of Data that have to be stored, processed and used for making intelligent decisions. This calls for the need for a smart heterogeneous network which could handle this data and make the real time systems work intelligently. IoT applications lead to increasing demands in high traffic volume, M2M communications, low latency, and MIMO operations. Mobile communication has evolved from 2G voice services into a complex, interconnected environment with multiple services built on a system that supports innumerable applications and provides high-speed access. Hence the sustainability of the IoT applications does rely on next generation networks. Due to the significant increase in the network components, computational complexity and heterogeneity of resources there arise the need for a secure architectural framework for the Internet of Things. For this, a secure architectural framework for IoT is proposed in Chapter 8 which provides a solution to the lightweight devices with low computational complexity.

SECTION 3: EMERGING TRENDS AND METHODS FOR CYBER FORENSICS

Cyber Security has become a major concern in the Digital Era. Data breaches, ID theft, cracking the captcha, and other such stories abound, affecting millions of individuals as well as organizations. The challenges have always been endless in inventing right controls and procedures and implementing them with acute perfection for tackling with cyber-attacks and crimes. Fortunately, Artificial Intelligence can be applied to Cyber Security and can protect individuals and organizations from cyber-attacks. In Chapter 9, specific techniques in Artificial Intelligence that have promising applications in Cyber Security and their future scope are explored in detail.

Rapid rise in the number of Mobile devices has resulted in an alarming increase in mobile software and applications. Though research progresses have been achieved towards detection and mitigation of mobile security, open challenges still remain and also keep evolving in this area. Several studies reveal that mobile application markets/stores do harbour applications that are either vulnerable or malicious in nature, leading to the compromise of millions of devices. Chapter 10 captures the attack surface of mobile devices, lists the various Mobile Malware Analysis techniques, and lays the ground for research on Mobile Malware by providing Mobile Malware Dataset resources and related tools.

Malware is the most serious security threat, which possibly targets billions of devices like personal computers, smartphones etc., across the world. Malware classification and detection is a challenging task due to the targeted, zero-day and stealthy nature of advanced and new malware. Malware detection and identification of new malware are some of the cybersecurity challenges. Chapter 11 employs an effective deep learning technique for building intelligent solutions to counter future threats.It explores a novel deep learning model called deep dilated residual network model for malware image classification and the results are compared with various machine learning techniques. The proposed model showed a higher accuracy of 98.50% and 99.14% on Kaggle Malimg and BIG 2015 datasets respectively and the new malware can be handled in real-time with minimal human interaction using this proposed model.

As Visual sensor networks gain more civilian attention, security becomes a major design issue. The VSN is vulnerable and can be demoralized to compromise the network task or to obtain unconstitutional admission to relevant information. The highly sensitive nature of images makes security and privacy in VSNs even more important. Chapter 12 has elucidated the current state and prominence of security concerns in VSN. These networks are inexpensive infrastructure less adhoc networks and found wide application in various domains, especially in surveillance and monitoring systems. The inherent nature of images is self-descriptive. As these networks carry sensitive information of the surveillance region, security and privacy protection are critical needs of the VSN. This chapter discusses about security frame work of smart Visual Sensor Network built using energy efficient image coding systems designed absolutely for low power systems.

SECTION 4: TECHNIQUES FOR COUNTERING CYBER ATTACKS

Nowadays the information in any real-time application is needed to be digitalized across the world. Since digitalization of data happens there comes the role of a word called "privacy". There are few more challenges that prevail in the industry such as integrity in data, traceability of stored records, and interoperability among organizations that share information. Blockchain could address the security challenge that happens in any real time sector. A blockchain is a constantly growing ledger that keeps a permanent record of all the transactions that have taken place, in a secure, chronological and immutable way and can be independently verified and audited by all actors in the network. A new revolutionary way to create a system that is free from attacks or free from reliance on any centralized trusted entity to dictate trust. The blockchain technology would guarantee in helping in critical areas where data need to be preserved and prone from attacks. Chapter 13 projects a study on blockchain and explores the applications in which blockchain technology could solve the existing challenges.

In an Information communication system, coding schemes to represent data or Coding is the vital and fundamental scheme in any information exchange process. It requires language and its characters to be represented as unique code. Code is a unique number associated with every character so as to facilitate the information exchange unambitious between sender and receiver. In Chapter 14, a novel information exchange codes named as "haptic codes", is proposed which maps several touch interactive locations into a single information exchange code. Thus, the proposed haptic code facilitates the representation of different notions to unique information exchange character/digit/symbol. Haptic codes are made secure by incorporating a new cryptographic system, which employs polar graph for encoding and decoding such locations using polar curves as shareable keys. Therefore, haptic codes can be exchanged for secure communication and read by devices that support to touch.

Recognizing human using computers or any artificial systems not only afford some efficient security outcomes but also facilitate to proficiently deliver human services especially in the zone of conflict. In the recent decade, the demand for improvement in security for personal data storage has grown rapidly and among the potential alternatives is one which employs innovative biometric identification techniques. Amongst these behavioral biometric techniques, the electrocardiogram (ECG) is being chosen as a physiological modality due to the uniqueness of its characteristics which integrates liveness detection, significantly preventing spoof attacks. The overview of preprocessing techniques, feature extraction and classification methods for ECG based biometric authentication is presented in Chapter 15 and focuses on the scope of the invention of new methods to develop applications for real-time authentication.

Digital healthcare system which is undergoing transformation phase to provide safe, swift, and improved quality care is experiencing diverse problems and the serious threats to the digital healthcare system include misidentification of patients and healthcare related frauds. Biometrics is a cutting-edge scientific field that enables unprecedented authentication capabilities based on human characteristics that cannot be replicated by fraudsters. Chapter 16 examines how biometric technology can be applied to the digital healthcare services. The growing demand for biometrics solutions in digital healthcare system is mainly driven by the need to combat fraud, along with an initiative to preserve privacy of the patient besides with healthcare safety.

Our intention in editing this book is to offer concepts and various techniques that are employed in *Countering Cyber Attacks and Preserving the Integrity and Availability of Critical Systems* in a precise and clear manner to the cyber security research community. In editing the book, our attempt is to provide frontier advancements in cyber security, cyber forensics and investigation, legal view of the cyber crimes and their punishments, security attacks targeting the web and mobile platform, cloud environment, multimedia – images and videos, network intrusion detection systems, biometric systems, secured infrastructure etc. along with the conceptual basis required to achieve in depth knowledge in the field of cyber security in computer science and information technology. This book will comprise the latest research from prominent researchers working in this domain. Since the book covers case study-based research findings, it can be quite relevant to researchers, university academics, computing professionals, and probing university students. In addition, it will help those researchers who have interest in this field to keep insight into different concepts and their importance for applications in real life. This has been done to make the edited book more flexible and to stimulate further interest in topics

The topics presented are recent works and research findings in state-of-the-art idea of the problems and solution guidelines emerging in Cyber Forensics and Investigations from Law Enforcement Perspective, trends and methods, theoretical and mathematical foundations, thus summarizing the roadmap of current digital forensic research efforts in Countering Cyber Attacks and Preserving the Integrity and Availability of Critical Systems. A wide variety of topics of interest are addressed, from the technical views such as advanced techniques for forensic developments in computer and communication-link environments, to legal perspectives - procedures for cyber investigations, standards and policies, to application perspective, such as image media security, securing critical infrastructure, secure haptic code for information exchange, multimedia forensics, and to user perspective – techniques countering cyber attacks through cyber forensics, malware forensics, authentications, encryptions, forensic procedures, etc.

The prospective audience for this book will be cyber law policy makers, hackers, cyber forensic analyst, academicians, researchers, advanced-level students, technology developers, and global consortiums for security. This will also be useful to a wider audience of readers in furthering their research exposure to pertinent topics in cyber forensics and assisting in advancing their own research efforts in this field.

We have made a sincere effort to keep the book reader-friendly as well as useful to the information security community. A serious look into the cyber attacks, and emerging trends and solutions on how to safeguard oneself in this cyberspace while reaping the maximum benefits out of the cyber space is the prime motive of this book. The book explains with many real world cases and the current best security practices followed globally. At the same time, it enables the readers to identify the possible vulnerabilities in any of their interaction with the cyber space, discover a feasible solution for the trivial as well as non-trivial aspect of the issue. We trust and hope that the book will help its readers to further carryout their research in different directions.

S. Geetha
VIT Chennai, India

Y. Asnath Victy Phamila
VIT Chennai, India

Acknowledgment

Taking up a book project is harder than we thought and more rewarding than we could have ever imagined. None of this would have been possible without the support of our friends, family members, and academic connections.

We would like to acknowledge the help of all the people involved in this project and, more specifically, to the authors and reviewers who took part in the review process. Without their support, this book would not have become a reality.

First, we would like to thank each one of the authors for their contributions. Our sincere gratitude goes to the chapter's authors who contributed their time and expertise to this book. We thank all the authors of the chapters for their commitment to this endeavor and their timely response to our incessant requests for revisions.

Second, the editors wish to acknowledge the valuable contributions of the reviewers regarding the improvement of quality, coherence, and content presentation of chapters. Most of the authors also served as referees; we highly appreciate their double task.

The editors would like to recognize the contributions of editorial board in shaping the nature of the chapters in this book. In addition, we wish to thank the editorial staff at IGI Global for their professional assistance and patience.

Without the support from our Management of VIT, our VC, Pro VC, Dean – SCSE, colleagues, peers and team at VIT, this book would not exist. A sincere thanks to each one of them. A special thanks to Mr. Harish.

We want to thank God most of all, because without God we wouldn't be able to do this.

S. Geetha
VIT Chennai, India

Y. Asnath Victy Phamila
VIT Chennai, India

Section 1
National Security and Cyber Warfare

Chapter 1
Digital Forensics and Cyber Law Enforcement

K. S. Umadevi
VIT University, India

Geraldine Bessie Amali
VIT University, India

Latha Subramanian
University of Madras, India

ABSTRACT

Security, safety, and privacy are of paramount importance to anyone who likes to crawl on the web. Keeping the best interest of the internet users in mind, India has laid down very solid foundations to safeguard its people from cyberattacks and cyber terrorism. The word "cyber law" encompasses all the cases, statutes, and constitutional provisions that affect persons and institutions who control the entry to cyberspace, provide access to cyberspace, create the hardware and software that enable people to access cyberspace or use their own devices to go "online" and enter cyberspace. Cyber crimes are unlawful acts wherein the computer is either a tool or a target or both. Cyber crimes can involve criminal activities that are traditional in nature, such as theft, fraud, forgery, defamation, and mischief, all of which are subject to the Indian Penal Code.

DOI: 10.4018/978-1-5225-8241-0.ch001

INTRODUCTION TO DIGITAL FORENSICS

The field of digital forensics is consistently growing and there is a huge demand over the last few years, since the usage of computers and mobiles is exponentially growing. Digital forensics deals with investigating these technological devices and monitoring whether something is hacked or likely to be hacked. The end user might not be aware or interested in knowing about these dangers. A deleted photo or a video from your mobile phone or computer in the hands of a hacker is a serious issue. Hence this field is constantly growing to cope with the possible threats. Along with growing demand for new technology in mobile industries, the malware or spyware are also growing. These malware or spyware are capable of monitoring user activities including text messages, emails, phone calls, user locations and so on. As per McAfee report on mobile threats – 2018, one of the most significant threats is Android Grabos. Android Grabos pushes unwanted apps into unsuspected pay per download scam. It was estimated that by the time Google play store identified and removed nearly 144 apps around 17.5 million smart phone users had already downloaded these apps (McAfee mobile threat report, 2018). Including Apple all the app stores are affected by malwares and they remove the dead apps if it poses a security and/or privacy threat to the user without any disclosure of information.

EVOLUTION OF DIGITAL FORENSICS

Modern electronic computer has evolved from the late of the 1900s. As per the history of computing project 1947 considered as the starting of the industrial era of computing and still, we are in the mid of it. Digital forensics has a much shorter history. Industries, research centers, universities needed a large infrastructure set up to meet their requirements, till 1980s computers were used by their appliances only. A textbook "Crime by computers" authored by Donn Parker in 1976 describes the investigation and prosecution carried out using computer data and information (Pollitt, 2010). It further adds that system administrators are solely responsible for securing the networked system and data contained in it. Several organizations like Department of Defense, Internal Revenue Service (IRS) and Federal Bureau of Investigation (FBI) created groups and trained the volunteers of law enforcement to assist the investigators to gain the information by assessing logs and other data from the networked system. But during the 1990s, Cliff Stoll's highlighted how the government agencies shillyshallied in conducting the investigation procedure (Pollitt, M, 2010).

The rise of IBM PCs paved the way for many computer hobbyists. It further resulted in the formation of the first organization on digital forensics named The

International Association of Computer Investigative Specialists (IACIS) (Allen, W.H., 2005). IACIS is a voluntary association, composed of computer forensic professionals from around the world who are dedicated to promoting the standards, professionalism, and ethics in digital forensics. The digital forensics had its own limitations and geographical boundaries. It couldn't function as the traditional forensics science lab. Since, the hackavist functions across the boundaries some agencies including IRS, U.S Secret service, FBI, U.S Air Force office created their own agency based on their culture, training and other procedures.

Digital forensics was still continuously growing and had numerous key factors behind its growth. During 1990s computers became ubiquitous and without the internet usage, the entire functionality came to a standstill. The need for digital forensics grew stronger and deeper. In response to the huge crime rate involving digital devices in both commercial and private sector, various agencies/bodies started publishing their guidelines.

The European lead a global contract called an indenture on Cybercrime, which came into action by 2004 with the intention of reuniting national level legal procedures, investigations, and co-operation. 43 countries including US, Canada, Japan, UK and many other European nations' signed the policy. In 2005, ISO published a standard (ISO 17025) for general requirements for the competence of testing and calibration laboratories.

DIGITAL FORENSICS PROCESS

Forensics science is the use of science in the field of criminal identification and enforcement of civil law for the criminal. Forensics scientists gather information, protect and examine the evidence observed during the investigation. While some of the scientists carry out the field study by visiting the respective place others remain in the laboratory for analyzing the evidence brought by them.

Digital evidence is the digital footprint left by the criminals in terms of data stored and/or transmitted using digital devices to address the critical elements used during the crime. Some of the requirement of forensics includes inappropriate use of computer systems, identification of malicious files, theft of ID, assets, documents, and so on. Forensics here explores the nature of the evidence that satisfies and proves the guilt of the criminal.

Digital forensics (aka Digital Forensic Science) is a branch of science that deals with the investigation of crime using digital devices. The aim of this process is to preserve any evidence in its original form, identifying and validating the digital information for the purpose of reconstructing past events. It requires rigorous standards to stand up to cross-examination in court.

Digital Forensics (aka Digital Forensic Science) is a part of science that deals with the examination of crime using digital devices with the aim of safeguarding any proof in its unique form, discovering and proving the information in order to reconstruct the past events. It needs to go through rigorous protocols and standards to confront cross-examination in the court.

NIST presents the basic process of Digital forensics using following steps [Figure 1]:

- **Data Retrieval:** The First stage in digital forensics is the detection and retrieval of the source of information relevant to the crime which depicts the nature of the crime, clue about the personnel involved in it and data residing location.
- **Data Reliability:** The process of checking the reliability of electronically relevant information and documenting the various details collected in the previous stage.
- **Data Collection:** Next stage is gathering digital information about the crime scene in terms of images, copies or printouts etc.
- **Review of Evidence:** A detailed analysis of the crime based on the evidence gathered in the previous stages is done.
- **Report Findings:** Using the outcome of the analysis, the report is generated using the technologies and proven methods so as to prove the relationship between the gathered information and crime committed.

Figure 1. Phases in digital forensics

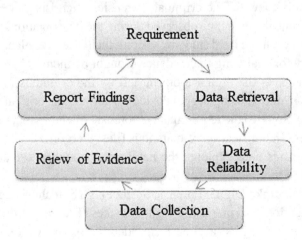

Applications of Digital Forensics

Digital forensics is used to convalesce and infer the data in order to recollect past events. It is very difficult for the organizations to deal with circumstances when they suspect that representatives misuse their PCs by doing actions that are against organization's regulations. The same scenario is applicable for those who suspect that their neighbors are committing crimes through computers or mobile phones. If not taken care in a legal and moral way, examining someone else can be exceptionally risky. In addition to this, you put yourself in danger of violating the law, of humiliating a worker or unjustifiably blaming them. For each situation where you speculate misusing computers by somebody, it is of most extreme significance that you utilize methodologies that are both compelling and lawful.

Digital forensic science is one of the best investigative procedures that an organization or individual can use while examining someone who's indulged in illegal activities. Basically, advanced crime investigation is a part of measurable science relating to prove the evidences found in PCs, cell phones, storage media, cloud administrations and web-based facilities. In a perfect world, advanced criminology means to look at a proof in a forensically critical method with the expectation of recognizing, saving, removing, recuperating and introducing actualities fact about the data.

By utilizing the best expert or licensed personnel, recording the Chain of Custody of proof, and using approved tools and strategies to ensure that activities have been legitimately reviewed, digital forensic sciences guarantees substantial outcomes. With the data revealed, a customer can efficiently investigate any proof and also set it up for presenting to the court or people. The adoption of the approach for this procedure, at last, relies upon how you mean to utilize the proof revealed by the digital forensic team

Criminal Investigation

Criminal investigators carry out various tasks to uncover enormous information that can be used to convict crimes and sue offenders (Swanson, C. R., Chamelin, N. C.,& Territo, L., 2003). As per the Bureau of Labor Statistics (BLS), a criminal investigator works with people, law implementation officials, and organizations to discover and inspect the associated information. Criminal investigators and private detectives may offer security to famous personalities and administrators. The job of digital forensics in the offense has advanced to proof of vindication in a court which is considered as a basic step to show how the evidence is protected and accumulated. The FBI uses IT specialists to get authentic proof in their examinations and these offenses. It can be straightforward hacking, reconnaissance or even bank jiggery-pokery. The FBI presently utilizes digital forensics as a standard tool to examine crime. It utilizes digital equipment such as cell phones, tablets, and hard disks to gather the evidence anticipated in order to showcase the crime.

There are four foremost investigation categories accomplished by the digital forensic investigators. They are criminal forensics, intelligence gathering, electronic discovery and Intrusion Investigation. The first three resemble each other, and they differ only in judicial decree adopted, digital evidence and format of the report.

- **Criminal Forensics**: It is a part of a more extensive investigation led by law enforcement and different authorities. It makes reports that facilitate the investigation and will be submitted as appropriate evidence to the court. It focuses on forensically stable data extraction and creating report/proof in basic terms.
- **Intelligence Gathering**: This sort of investigation is frequently connected with the crime, however in connection with intelligence to track, stop or distinguish criminal proceedings.
- **Electronic Discovery**: This is similar to "criminal forensics". eDiscovery, in particular, has its own limitations, typically in connection to the extent of any investigation. Security laws and human rights legislation regularly influence electronic disclosure.
- **Intrusion Investigation:** The last type of investigation is not like the previous three. It is initiated as a response to identify hackers who access their company assets. Intrusion investigation is induced as a reaction to identify the entry points for performing these attacks. Intrusion investigation frequently happens "live" (i.e. progressively) and inclines vigorously on network forensics.

CIVIL LITIGATION

Civil litigation matters are any court or administrative procedure that validates a will, family law, and criminal issues. This incorporates contracts suit, and equity procedures by methods of injunctive consolation demands, petitions in help of cases or judgments, and innumerable alternative issues that the only solution presents itself similar to a court or body organization and individuals from the firm appear in State Courts of each level like Supreme Court, judicature, District Division and so on. Legal advisors routinely appear under the watchful eye of the Federal Courts. Models of civil litigation contain employee claims, partner issues; contract litigation etc., common prosecution legal advisors speak to offended parties and respondents including people, associations, investors and companies in the following kinds of cases:

- Disputes related to business
- Administration matters
- Criminal discharges
- Preliminary and permanent injunctions
- Real estate litigation

Intelligence

Knowledge is perceived as the well-timed, exact and usable result of sensibly processed data with regard to the criminal justice framework and the data identify the crime and the situation in which it arises. For instance, using a sequence of offenses, a suspicion about where the criminal survives or when he/she will commit the next offense can be inferred from the existing information. These conclusions offer a piece of information which can be further considered for operative procedures like surveillance or patrols. This interpretation can be considered as the core procedure for incorporating the entire information from the core to scratch in implementing the intelligence.

The investigation includes heterogeneous intellect results using various calibers, for example, criminology, computer science, psychology, forensic science, and financial matters. Perception on inadequate data may result in exhaustive discussion on those areas where interpretations are deliberately examined and debated, with the point of giving intelligence through all well-grounded criminal examination techniques. However, a significant amount of effort is spent in concluding the formalities; the correctness of the result may vary with respect to the real context based on the investigation.

Various conclusions derived by the other domains experts are frequently viewed as a supplement to the examination procedure and added into the investigation by incorporating through appropriate investigative frameworks. Moreover, the investigation procedure needs more of common sense since it is rarely formalized. Criminal intelligence ought to be considered as an area that gives strategies and procedures that help the combination of various procedures and methods of a particular learning, the aftereffect of which is to structure better the thinking forms utilized over the span of investigation and to convey adequately the outcomes to the associates.

Different Types of Digital Forensics

Digital forensics is a highly evolving field and can be applied to numerous sub-disciplines. In this section, the various resources used for digital data communication and their usage for committing crime are elaborated.

- **Computer Forensics**: The resources used for communication includes computers, laptops, mobile phone, storage devices, etc. Computer Forensics deals with the collection of various evidence to support the investigation as per legal measures from the above-mentioned entities.
- **Network Forensics**: To enable communication among the communicating entities the digital devices must be connected to the Internet. The appropriate usage of virus, worm, malware, and bots could identify the vulnerabilities in the devices which might lead to security breaches. Network Forensics includes monitoring the data traffic through the network, logging them for future purpose and analysing them for discovering the attacks, intrusions or any other misbehaviour.
- **Mobile device Forensics**: Capturing the digital evidence from mobile phones, SIM cards, Personal Digital Assistants, Global Positioning devices, tablets and gaming consoles in support of the crime.
- **Digital Image Forensics**: Digital Image Forensics explores the procedure of information gathering from digitally acquired images to substantiate the current state of crime using the metadata associated with these images.
- **Video/Audio Forensics**: While handling the evidences, it deals with the procedure of proving that the video or audio files are genuine and discover the authenticity of the acquired data.
- **Memory Forensics**: The process of retrieving the proof of evidence from RAM of a functioning computer called as live acquisition.
- **E-mail Forensics**: E-mail comprises sender, receiver, date and time and the content. This investigation involves collecting the metadata about the origin, IP of the email server and authentication.

DIGITAL FORENSICS AND EVIDENCES

The main aim of digital forensics is to diagnose, gather, document and deduce the digital data using computer to support investigation for legal purposes. Ken Zatyko, former director of Defense Computer Forensics lab gave eight steps to validate digital evidence (Nelson, B., Phillips, A., & Steuart, C,2014).

1. **Search Authority**: Preliminary stage in a forensic process is to collect the evidences by a legal authority. The legal authority can conduct the search in various forms and grab the data. Due to large amount of data stored in computer, the authority must identify the right data in a much-controlled situation related to the evidence to be inspected. They are expected to work closely with the prosecutor to resolve the inquiries that arise during the examination.

2. **Chain of Custody**: It is the process of maintaining, controlling and transferring the real evidences collected in chronological order by an authenticated person. Since the evidence must be produced in the court to convict persons of crimes, it must be handled more cautiously. It carries out the integrity check by answering the following questions:

    a. What is the evidence?
    b. How did you have it?
    c. When did you have it?
    d. Who handled it?
    e. Why the person did handle it?
    f. When and where it was stored?

3. **Imaging/Hashing Function:** Hashing techniques are used to verify the source with the hashed values. This help in securing complete evidence found in the disk. Any data collected as evidence must not be tampered or altered before submitting to the court.

4. **Validated Tools**: The data submitted to the court must be entirely competent and/or reliable. Hence, this phase deals in utilizing appropriate tools and techniques to validate the acquired information and affirm the reliability.

5. **Analysis**: Since digital evidences play a crucial role in crime analysis, the secured images or data is analysed by trained professional. Using prior experience, their understanding, existing tools and software, the professionals carry out their analysis.

6. **Repeatability**: To verify the already produced proof of evidence relevant to the crime at later stage based on the requirement, the procedures must be repeated. Quality assurance protocols are also adopted to ensure the reproducibility of the data.

7. **Reporting**: The forensics analysts must document their observations on to the evidence so that it can be used wherever it is required.

8. **Possible Expert Presentation**: Last stage, forensic analyst will present to the court or other spectators.

Digital Evidences

Digital or electronic evidence is any data stored or communicated in digital form which is considered to be probative that involved with a court case may use at trial(Granja, F. M., & Rafael, G. D. R, 2017). The court will decide whether the proof is important, regardless of whether it is legitimate or not before accepting the evidence. In the event that it is rumor and whether a duplicate is satisfactory or the first is required (Casey, E, 2011). The utilization of digital evidence has grown enormously for the past few decades as courts have permitted the use of e-mails, photos, ATM logs, word documents, SMS histories, files about account information, spreadsheets, web access related documents, databases, history of memory utilization, backups, printouts, Global Positioning System tracks, logs from a hotels e-locks, video, audio files, etc.,

In United States numerous courts have applied the Federal Rules of Evidence to digital evidence corresponding to conventional reports, though there is a noticeable difference like lack of standardization and procedures. Since the digital data is huge in volume, expensive, easy to modify, duplicate, available and so on. Considering these facts, some courts find it difficult to authenticate and prove rumor content. In December 2006, the Federal Rules of Civil accepted firm new principles demanding the conservation and reveal digital evidence. Five Rules that must be followed by Evidence:

- **Admissibility**: It must have the relevant to the crime to be utilized in court or somewhere else.
- **Authenticity**: Evidence must be relevant to the crime.
- **Completeness**: Alternative suspicious evidences collected as a part of the reported crime.
- **Reliability**: The reported evidence is genuine and valid.
- **Believable**: The evidence collected is flawless, gives a good understanding and highly acceptable.

In criminal law, the prosecution must present the entire set of evidence and doesn't matter either it supports the prosecution or the defendant. To support the prosecution following are categories of Evidence supported by Digital Forensics:

- **Best Evidence**: Digital evidence claimed by the trial at the first as principal evidence of the crime. Normally, these evidences are documented.

- **Secondary Evidence**: Secondary evidences are those which are not highly reliable but a strong source i.e. inculpatory. These are not documented but mostly oral in nature.
- **Direct Evidence**: To authenticate the document produced as evidence, the next source to prove the crime is by using eyewitness called an examination in chief which is used to substantiate the incident by it.
- **Conclusive Evidence**: Conclusive Evidence will be evidence that can't be repudiated by some other evidence. It is highly firm as to overbear some other evidence to be conflicting. The evidence plays a major role in enabling the fact finder to draw a conclusion immediately.
- **Circumstantial Evidence**: Circumstantial evidence is proof that depends on a deduction to interface it to a finish of certainty. On the other hand, direct evidence supports the truth directly — i.e., without the requirement of any extra proof or derivation. All alone, Circumstantial evidence takes needs some more clarification regarding the crime. A clarification including Circumstantial evidence turns out to be more probable that have been ignored. Circumstantial evidence enables another attempt for a trier of certainty to construe that a reality exists.
- **Corroborative Evidence**: Corroborative evidence is proof that supports the primary evidence to prove the clue. In criminal law, Corroborative evidence is utilized to maintain the declaration of observers.
- **Opinion Evidence**: Opinion evidence refers to proof of what the observer considers, accepts, or interprets with respect to actualities, as recognized from individual learning of the certainties themselves. In precedent-based law purviews, the general principle is that an observer should affirm regarding what was watched and not to give a feeling on what was watched. Be that as it may, there are two special cases to this standard: master proof and non-master opinion given by laymen which individuals in their day by day lives reach without conscious reasoning.

Forensics Investigation Tools

Digital Forensics is a critical part of computer science in connection with computer and Internet related violations. Prior, Computers were just used to deliver information yet now it has extended to all devices identified with advanced information. The objective of digital forensics is to perform crime examinations by utilizing evidences collected from digital devices to discover who was the in charge of that specific crime. For better research and examination, engineers have made numerous computer legal forensic tools. Police departments and examination offices select the tools dependent on different components including budget and availability of the specialists in the group.

Though a lot of tools used for digital forensics, in this article a few of effective and highly utilized are mentioned below:

1. **Digital Forensics Framework**: Digital Forensics Framework is a platform is an open source and can be used by both forensic experts as well as non-experts. It explores the chain of custody, provides access to local and remote source of information, Windows and Linux based OS to recover even the hidden files, access to meta data related to the files.

2. **Open Computer Forensics Architecture (OCFA):** OCFA is yet another popular open source forensic distributed platform developed on Linux using PostgreSQL. In order to automate the digital forensics process, Dutch National Police Agency developed OCFA.

3. **CAINE (Computer Aided Investigative Environment):** CAINE is a platform for integrating the existing software for forensics in a user-friendly manner based on Linux.

4. **X-Ways Forensics**: X-Way is a resource friendly environment assures that it consumes fewer resources. It helps the forensics professionals and investigators to interact in the workflow to find the solution.

5. **SANS Investigative Forensics Toolkit or SIFT**: SFIT is a VMWare appliance preconfigures using necessary tools to accomplish the following modules: support file system, Evidence image creation, software for analysing. It is completely built on Ubuntu and competent enough with all the latest forensics technologies in terms of plugins and capabilities.

6. **EnCase:** It is a shared technology developed to support various modules to support digital forensic process, analytics for security, recovering content from seized hard drives. It helps in completely gathering information from various devices and extract possible evidences.

7. **Registry Recon:** As the name indicates registry in a system comprises wealthy information. This is a computer forensics tool used to recover the registry data from windows-based system. It helps in identifying the external devices connected to the computer.

8. **The Sleuth Kit (TSK):** TSK comprises set of tools and library files for Unix and Windows based system to perform forensic analysis. It provides memory access through command line argument as well.

9. **Llibforensics**: It is a python-based framework developed for digital forensics where some of the bottlenecks were fixed using C.

10. **Volatility**: One of tool used for memory forensics resulting an organizations data loss, accessing various functions and associated services as well as malware analysis. Basically, developed using Python and supports Windows, Mac and Linux.

11. Other than these WindowsSCOPE, The Coroner's Toolkit, Oxygen Forensic Suite, Bulk Extractor, Xplico and so on to support the digital forensics in recovering data from memory, imaging, providing support for file system, accessing metadata, e-mail, mobile, Operating System, networks database and so on.

Digital Forensics in Law Enforcement

Digital evidence examination models are sufficient today in the online networking, Television from the Law and Order establishment to Court TV's Forensic Files. Since, we have expected from TV, there is a trace of legitimacy in the misrepresentation of the realities. Forensic science is merely utilization of technology to examine and find the truth for a criminal case or civil court. Physical and medical proofs (e.g., blood, DNA) are all acknowledged in court and in addition the heart and mind of the law authorization network and people in general. Less outstanding, yet considerably known is the job of digital forensics and investigation.

The Internet is a noteworthy issue for legal investigations and jurisdiction. Crimes such as phishing, identity theft and further activities enabled by Internet are enabling the commitment of crime internationally. The discussion of child pornography generally shut down in the U.S. by the postal administration, is uncontrolled on the Internet. Because of the global reach of the Internet, Luring, bullying, stalking and other child sexual exploitation activities increased dramatically. Since laws vary from one country to another country, a crime in one country might not even be illegal in another.

The Internet is absolutely changing crime scene examination. On account of the dynamic nature of the Internet, a webpage on the Internet used to execute a crime on one day may be remarkable or missing the next day. Access to the Internet is relatively unavoidable in the industrialized countries so a criminal can get entrance from a device at another location each time they logon; while it may be anything other than hard to exhibit a particular device was used to get associated with a given server at a given date and time, it may be hard to show whose fingers were on the · console. Moreover, Internet access and capacity gadgets are getting less in size, more affordable, quick access and more adaptable reliably.

Computers can yield evidence of a broad variety of criminal and other criminal activities; criminals carrying out network-based violations are not using any and all means the main ones who store information on computers! Various culprits involved in murder, kidnapping, sexual assault, extortion, drug dealing, auto theft, espionage and terrorism, gun dealing, robbery/burglary, gambling, economic crimes, confidence games, and criminal hacking keep up documents with implicating proof on their PC. At times the data on the computer is vital in recognizing a suspect and once in a while the computers yield the most condemning proof.

As of late, the examination of a single system archive gave a key bit of information in the catch of the BTK killer in Wichita, Kansas, in March 2005 (Siegel, L. J. & McCormick, C. R.,2010). The BTK killer's 30-year serial killer splurge spend was passed on to an end by an immaterial oversight on his part. As a habit, the BTK killer sent a letter to a Wichita TV opening about his adventures using email. Police investigated the record and found the primary name of the author (Dennis) and the association name (Christ Lutheran Church) using the metadata (properties) of the document. A simple search using the above information retrieved, The Church's Web site shows that Dennis Rader is president of the congregation at Christ Lutheran Church. Police went to the church with a warrant to search through the system and found a floppy disk that Rader had given to the church pastor with the arrangement for an upcoming church council meeting; the disk moreover contained the BTK letter. Until this time, Dennis Rader's name was a part of thousands of names of students however he was never suspected. Computers may likewise contain essential data for knowledge gathering purposes. Despite the fact that the utilization of the Fourth Amendment is to some degree diverse when gathering proof as opposed to criminal or against fear monger insight, the advanced examination process and instruments are the equivalent.

Relevant Laws

India is increasingly gaining global attention for an instance, recently India has been nominated as a topmost nation from where spam is originating. Considering spam, it is very clear that cybercrime is increasingly on the rise in India. The Indian government has short to put into place a legal reason for regulating cybercrime and consequently, various kinds of provisions have been incorporated. It is easy to remember that India does not have a dedicated law for cybercrime, but yet Indian legislature thought it fit to have a chapter on the cybercrime in India's mother legislation that deals with the data and information in the electronic form. This is India's technology act 2000 not only the chapter 11 specific cybercrime in India and their respective punishments but also this particular legislation has an amendment in the Indian penal code in such a manner so as to meet various offences under the Indian penal code in sync with the requirements of the digital platforms.

In case, if an attacker wants to steal a source code or a set of documents then they may be alerted because of this activity itself the cybercrime under Section

65 of the information technology act 2000 as well as punishable with 3 years of imprisonment and Rs. 5000 fine. Earlier the information technology act has specially made hacking as crime under Section 66 but then 2008 amendments deleted hacking and came up with much more broader computer related offences. If they do various activities on any computers with or without authorizations, they all come within the ambit of these offences, provided they are done either dishonestly or fraudulently. For example, if they access without the permission of the owner or any person in charge of computers or computer networks, access the system, download, copy or extract data, introduced any damage, disturb the working of the computer system or otherwise diminish the value and the utility of information residing in a computer resource. All these activities are considered as criminal activities, it is punishable under act 66 and 43 with 3 and 5 years of imprisonment says Mr. Pavan Duggal, is the Founder & Chairman of International Commission on Cyber Security Law. India has got a long duration of cultural development and consequently. Indian law has taken a very nuanced stand on obstinacy, so Sec 67-A of the IT act makes it an offence, if you publish or transmit in electronic form to public, is tend to deprave and encrypt the minds of those who likely to see, read and hear the same.

But the Indian law does not focus pornography, but it accepts anything which is likely to the current minds of those who are likely to see read or hear the content then Obscenity law followed in England will be applied under Section 63 of the Criminal Justice Act 2008. Further transmission of messages appears to be sexually explicit is prone to Section 67A is punishable with 5 years of imprisonment and fine. Earlier India was not much concerned about child pornography although because it is covered under the broader events or pornography. Further to be noticed, capturing the images of a private part of a person without that person's knowledge or consent under circumstances where the concerned person has an expectation of privacy is again considered as an offence and punishable for 3 years imprisonment with Rs. 5 Lakh fine.

Misuses of digital signature for fraudulent activities are considered as an offense under Section 72. For example, if you transmit any information using a computer resource which is grossly offensive having menacing character considered as a separate offense under Section 66 a punishable with three years' imprisonment and fine. Further if you transmit information that you know is false but has been said but has been done for the purposes of causing annoyance, inconvenience, hatred, ill-will or enmity that is further an offense under Section 66 as you steal somebody's identity and the law is not going to spare you three years imprisonment and fine.

Cybercrime are the illegal acts which are committed in a very refined method by using either the computer as a device, an objective or both for committing a crime. The crimes encompassed in the IT Act 2000 are as follows (B.M.Gandhi, 2017):

- Damaging computer resources.
- Hacking the stand alone or networked system.
- Dissemination of obscene data in electronic form.
- Directions to subscribe to prolong services for decrypting data
- Accessing a secure system
- A penalty for data distortion, breach of privacy, integrity and confidentiality, leaking Digital Signature Certificate
- Publication for fake purpose
- Any act to apply for crime either inside or outside India
- Seizure

Laws Under IT Act 2000: Penalties and Offenses

- Section 43 expresses whichever demonstration of abolishing, modifying or theft of sensitive information in a computer or networked system and erasing data with the intention of harming information or data without the approval of proprietor of system is at risk. They must pay some proportional amount as fine in terms of recovery charges to the system owner/admin for damages. It includes security breaches enabling unlawful gain of information about a person or an organization and affecting them.
- Section 66 states that an individual or a group of people with immorality or falsely leading to hack a system must be imprisoned 3 years with fine of Rs. 5,00,000 or both.
- Section 66A expresses every unreceptive data by means of disgrace character or data known as false however communicated with a motive of causing the disturbance, distress, risk, dislike or unlawful terrorizing to deceive the beneficiary is at risk for penitentiary up to 3 years with (or) without fine.
- Section 66 under B, C, D for deceitfully or falsely utilizing or conveying data or Identity theft is liable to 3 years quod or 1,00,000 fine or both.
- Section 66 for Breach of protection by communicating a picture of a private zone is impunited with 3 years' penitentiary or 2,00,000 fine or both
- Section 66 F on an act through digital medium affecting unity, sincerity, security and sovereignty of India by cyber terrorism is at risk forever quod.
- Section 67 states distributing profane data or quod imprisonment up to five years or punishment of Rs. 10,00,000 or both.

The world first computer specific law was sanctioned in the year of 1970 by the German State of Hesse as 'Data Protection Act, 1970' with the advancement of digital technology. With the rise of innovation, the exploitation of innovation has additionally extended to its ideal level and then required strict statutory laws to direct the criminal exercises in the digital world and to secure technical advancements. It is under these conditions Indian parliament passed its "INFORMATION TECHNOLOGY ACT, 2000" on 17th October to have its thorough law to manage the innovation in the field of e-governance, e-commerce, e-banking and punishments and disciplines in the field of digital crimes.

CURRENT CHALLENGES IN DIGITAL FORENSICS

Cyberattacks have a notable impact on socioeconomic factors on individuals, national as well as international level. Due to requirement of sophisticated life style demanded by human beings, the tremendous growth of cloud computing, Internet

Table 1. Effect of IoT and cyber physical systems in digital forensics

Property	Relation to Digital Forensic Investigation	Exemplary Challenges
Density of device deployment	Influences the resolution of events that took place in a physical environment	Reconstruct physical events on the basis of unevenly deployed devices. This can also vary according to the considered environment.
Device Type	Influences the type of information.	Provision of computer aided, evidence driven and court proof frameworks for the reconstruction of events. Such software should be able to take into account a mixed/ increasing set of devices, for instance by means of a plug-in architecture.
Device location	Influences physical accessibility of the device for a digital forensic investigation and influences which area of a physical environment was covered by the device.	Develop a cost benefit analysis to determine whether IoT devices located in hard to reach areas are worth accessing. One idea is to use databases that point our device properties useful for forensics investigations and additional details such as the accuracy of on-board sensors.
Recording history	All available information on an IoT device can be recorded locally or in the cloud. Local storage is usually limited; thus, the number of recorded sensor values/ actuators states is kept under a certain threshold.	Automatic integration of IoT devices into the reconstruction process of physical events. This requires fetching the recording history of sensors and correctly placing it within the time frame of the event to be reconstructed. It could entail the support of visual analytics tools capable of handling devices that provide data with inconsistent or inaccurate timing and spatial positions.
Device interfaces	The interfaces used to access evidences highly influence the amount of information that can be retrieved. Some types of information might be provided by certain interfaces while others are. In several cases, interfaces might be undocumented by the vendor.	Provision of a unified meta-interface for IoT forensics covering a large spectrum of different devices and low-level interfaces of several vendors. This can likely be adequately addressed by larger community projects.

of things and its various applications resulted more focus on forensics and table below presents their impact [Table 1, 11].

According to Fahdi et al., the challenges of digital forensics can be categorized into three parts (Al Fahdi, M., Clarke, N. L., &Furnell, S. M, 2013).

1. Technical challenges like Varying media formats, Cipher Protocol Suites, steganography, anti-forensics, live data acquisition and analysis.
2. Legal challenges include Jurisdictional and privacy issues and a lack of standardized and procedure for international legislation.
3. Resource challenges – e.g. volume of data, time taken to acquire and analyse forensic media.

Digital forensics deals with a specialized field of forensics in handling digital data which is handled by a variety of sources. It is generated by digital devices with heterogeneous architecture with hardware and software to provide the full-fledged functionality. To enable communication amongst these devices it uses number of protocols, cryptographic algorithms, storage places with different policies, different vendor offering services and so on. Advancements in the technology facilitate a comfortable lifestyle but invites variety of issues. So as a forensic analyst, to find the origin of a data, storage place, and data in the transit network, other connected systems a variety of tools are required (Luca C, Steffen W & Wojciech M (2017).

1. **The Large Volume of Data:** The growth of the Internet of Things results 5 quintillion bytes of data generated per day. According to Cisco, by 2020 nearly 30 billion devices would be connected to the network. There are varieties of data being used like structured, unstructured and semi structured and rich in context. In addition, these data are stored in various locations hence collecting clues about the nature of the data and location about its storage would be difficult task for the analyst.
2. **Lack of Standards:** Digital forensics analyst needs to handle huge variety of hardware and software resources. As discussed earlier, they need to collect, analyze and determine the fact about the data. Though there are variety of tools available for analysis more of task specific, the research community agree on the outcome with less probability of success.
3. **Heterogeneous Devices and Network:** Network of systems is basically created for resource sharing. But it started welcoming the attackers/hackers for introducing various malwares to disturb the smooth functionality as well as to access the data without the user concern. The recent advancement in the networks and distributed systems includes cloud computing technologies and Internet of things (Conti, M., Dehghantanha, A., Franke, K., & Watson, S.

2018). Cloud introduced too many ambiguities in handling the data by storing it in different location and hiding the details behind. Since it handles huge amount of data as mentioned earlier new data handling, mining, classification methods are used to reduce the complexity. Internet of things facilitates any communicating entity can be connected to the internet with less privacy and security. But in most of the cases, these devices were not properly identified, and documented procedures were limited and hence it attracts more researchers. Digital/ Electronic evidence is extremely volatile. Once the evidence is contaminated it cannot be reverted. The process of manipulation of the evidence is irretrievable. But the court acceptance on evidence is based on its best principle. With computer data, printouts or other output readable by sight, and bit stream copies adhere to this principle.

The quick pace of improvement and nature of digital forensics bring various security and crime investigation challenges. In this article, real security and legal issues with possibly encouraging alternative solution are swiftly exhibited. Papers incorporated into this uncommon issue offer various perspectives of forensic, security and legal sciences challenges with creative provisions that makes equipped towards secure and forensically stable investigations.

REFERENCES

Al Fahdi, M., Clarke, N. L., & Furnell, S. M. (2013). Challenges to digital forensics: A survey of researchers and practitioners attitudes and opinions. *Proceeding in IEEE conference in Information Security for South Africa*, 1-8. 10.1109/ISSA.2013.6641058

Allen, W. H. (2005). Computer Forensics. *IEEE Security and Privacy*, *3*(4), 59–62. doi:10.1109/MSP.2005.95

Casey, E. (2011). *Digital evidence and computer crime: Forensic science, computers, and the internet*. Academic Press.

Conti, M., Dehghantanha, A., Franke, K., & Watson, S. (2018). *Internet of Things security and forensics: Challenges and opportunities*. Academic Press.

Gandhi, B. M. (2017). *Indian Penal Code* (4th ed.). Eastern Book Company.

Granja, F. M., & Rafael, G. D. R. (2017). The preservation of digital evidence and its admissibility in the court. *International Journal of Electronic Security and Digital Forensics*, *9*(1), 1–18. doi:10.1504/IJESDF.2017.081749

Luca, C., Steffen, W., & Wojciech, M. (2017). The Future of Digital Forensics: Challenges and the Road Ahead. *IEEE Transactions on Security and Privacy, 1*, 12-17.

McAfee. (2018). *Mobile threat report*. Author.

Nelson, B., Phillips, A., & Steuart, C. (2014). *Guide to computer forensics and investigations*. Cengage Learning.

Pollitt, M. (2010). A history of digital forensics. *Proceedings of International Conference on Digital Forensics*, 3-15.

Siegel, L. J., & McCormick, C. R. (2010). *Criminology in Canada: Theories, patterns, and typologies*. Nelson Education.

Swanson, C. R., Chamelin, N. C., Territo, L., & Taylor, R. W. (2003). *Criminal investigation*. Boston: McGraw-Hill.

Chapter 2
The Fundamentals of Digital Forensics and Cyber Law

Kirti Raj Raj Bhatele
BSF Academy, India

Deepak Dutt Mishra
BSF Academy, India

Himanshu Bhatt
BSF Academy, India

Karishma Das
BSF Academy, India

ABSTRACT

This chapter provides prerequisites associated with cyber crimes, cyber forensics, and law enforcement. It consists of a brief introduction to the definition of cyber crimes, its classification, challenges associated with it and how it evolved with time, impact on the society, cyber terrorism, and the extent of problem scalability along with focusing on law enforcement aspects associated with the tracking and the prevention from such type crimes. The aspects discussed here include various cyber laws and law enforcement techniques introduced by various countries throughout the world which helps them to fight against cyber crimes. The cyber laws discussed include Australian, Canadian, United States, United Kingdom, and Indian law. This chapter also deals with the digital/cyber forensics, what does digital/cyber forensics mean, its types, and laws/rules revolving around them, like how to collect evidence, jurisdictions, and e-discovery.

DOI: 10.4018/978-1-5225-8241-0.ch002

INTRODUCTION: CYBER CRIME

Cybercrimes are described as crimes committed using a computer network. It is illegal behaviour directed by means of any electronic operations. If taken exactly, each term suffers from one or more insufficient. Mainly cybercrimes or virtual crimes are may be seen as focusing exclusively on the Internet. The terms such as 'digital', 'electronic or 'high-tech' crime may be seen as so broad as to be meaningless.

For example, 'hi-tech crime' may go afar networked information technology to include other 'hi-tech' developments such as nanotechnology and bioengineering. Terms should not, however, be approached mainly, but rather as usually descriptive terms which importance the role of technology in the commission of a crime. Although it is still the case that no one term has become truly prevalent, with many being used interchangeably, 'cybercrime' has been adopted in this chapter for a number of reasons. First, it is mainly used in the literature. Secondly, it has found its way into common usage. Thirdly, it accents the importance of networked computers. Fourthly, and most importantly, it is the term adopted in the Council of Europe Convention on cybercrime.

Evolution of Cyber-Crime

All know that the radical change in transportation of persons and goods affected by the introduction of the automobile, the speed with which it moves, and the ease with which malevolent persons can avoid capture, has greatly encouraged and increased crimes. In 1920s automobile is equally opposite of digital technology today. There also have been negative aspects of these developments. The convenience and ease provided through electronic banking and online sales also form a ground for the commitment of frauds. Electronic communication such as email has helped us to communicate farther away it also has generated issues like stalking and harassment. Due to a greater need for computers and digital networks, we have grown entirely dependent on them. Technology has made itself a tempting target; either for the purpose of gaining important and various types of information or for the objective of causing disruption and damage (Clough, 2010).

The Challenges of Cybercrimes

The societies we live in nowadays have grown extremely dependent on science and technology, and ironically most of us don't know much about it. For the commission of a Cybercrime, there is a requirement of three factors: a motivated criminal or a group of motivated criminals, the presence of opportunities to perform the heist and absence of individuals who can prevent them from doing so. On the account of all these three chapters, the digital environment tends to provide fertile grounds for the commitment of such offences. Though there will a description of its impact and protection measures ahead it would not be wise to not summarise some of the key features of digital technologies which help the criminals to initiate the crime and also tries to prevent the law from enforcing protection from such commitments (Clough, 2010).

1. **Scale:** The most traditional forms of communication in the world of computer and computer networks, the Internet allows all the users around the world to communicate with many people, cheaply and easily. According to the recent reports around1.6 billion people in the world are currently using the Internet, which is approximately equal to 24 per cent of the world's population; this could also provide unprecedentedly large pools of potential offenders and victims.

2. **Accessibility:** Computers were a large utilized device, primarily by government, research and financial institutions. The capability to commit computer crimes was widely limited to those with access and expertise. Nowadays, technology is prevalent throughout the world and is increasingly getting easy to use, and thus ensuring that it is available for both the criminals and the victims. In 2007–08, 67% of Australians had access to a computer at home, while in 2006, 70% had used the Internet and 82% a mobile phone (Australian Bureau of Statistics, 2007-08; Australian Government, 2008). In 2003, 64% of Canadian households had at least one member who used the Internet regularly and in 2006, 67% of households reported having a mobile phone (Canada Statistics, 2007). In 2003, 75% of adults in the UK had a mobile phone, while in 2007 61% of households could access the Internet from home. The ubiquitous 'Internet cafe' also provides a ready source of connectivity. For those activities that may be beyond the skills of the individual, the Internet provides easy access to those who will do it for you or tell you how. Offenders, who might otherwise be isolated in their offending, can now find like minds, forming virtual communities to further their offending.

3. **Anonymity:** Anonymity is an obvious advantage for an offender, and digital technology facilitates this in a number of ways. Offenders may deliberately obscure their identity online by the use of proxy servers, spoofed email or IP addresses anonymous e-mailers. Simply opening an email account which does not require identity verification provides a false identity. Confidentiality may be protected by the use of readily available encryption technology, while traces of digital evidence may be removed using commercially available software. The networked nature of modern communications in itself means that data will routinely be routed through a number of jurisdictions before reaching its

destination, making a tracing of communications extremely difficult and time sensitive. Accessing wireless networks, with or without authorisation, may obscure the identity of the actual user even if the location can be identified.

4. **Portability and Transferability:** Central to the power of digital technology is the ability to store enormous amounts of data in a small space, and to replicate that data with no appreciable diminution of quality. Storage and processing power which would once have occupied rooms will now fit into a pocket. Copies of images or sound may be transmitted simply and at negligible cost to potentially millions of recipients. The convergence of computing and communication technologies has made this process a seamless one, with the ability to take a digital image with a mobile phone and then upload it to a website within seconds.

Magnitude of Problems

The lack of consensus as to the meaning of 'cybercrime' means that it may not be included within official crime statistics. Even where there is a specific cybercrime, it may be concealed within other statistics. For example, unauthorised access to a computer under the computer misuse Act is recorded as 'other fraud' in the British Crime Survey. Many so-called 'cybercrimes' are in fact existing offences that are facilitated by technology. Consequently, although the offence itself, such as stalking, will be recorded in crime statistics, the use of technology by offenders may not. However, care must also be taken in incorporating the use of computers within crime statistics. For example, in the United States, the Uniform Crime Reporting Program allows reporting crime officers to indicate whether a computer was the object of the crime or was used to perpetrate the crime. While this is a useful development, it may skew results as theft of laptops or other computers is therefore included within 'computer crime' statistics.

Access to an Unauthorized Computer System

Access to an unauthorized computer may be obtained simply by logging on without permission. At the more sophisticated level, it may involve hackers using networks to gain remote access, sometimes via computers in a number of jurisdictions. Such hacks may be 'user level', where the hacker has the same access to the system as an ordinary user of the system, or 'root level' or 'god' access, where the hacker has the same rights as the system administrator and can view or modify data at will. The rapid pace with which software is developed means that 'bugs' in software are inevitable, with hackers seeking to exploit these vulnerabilities before they are rectified. The reasons for gaining unauthorised access to computers are as varied as the data found in those computers. Nonetheless, some categorisation of offender motivation is important in further refining precisely what conduct falls within the broad umbrella of unauthorised 'accesses to a computer.

Access to Information

Unauthorized access of data includes obtaining confidential commercial or government information (e.g. trade secrets, intellectual property and defence secrets) or personal information (e.g. medical records, credit card or social security numbers or credit history).

For example, in, in the USB. Levine6, the defendant and others used decryption software to gain access to the database of a corporation that was a repository for customer information for other companies and downloaded more than 1 billion personal records.

Data Modification

In data, modification defendant accesses the data in a computer. They only not wish to access the data in a computer, but they delete valuable data or alter that data. In US Middleton the defendant, a former employee of an ISP, used a program called 'Switch User' to switch his account to that of the company's receptionist. He then used his unauthorised access to create, delete and modify accounts, alter the computer's registry and delete the entire billing system and two internal databases. Modification of data may also be used to obtain a financial or another advantage, for example by increasing a line of credit.

Malicious Software

Malicious software, usually known as malware, is any software that conveys harm to a computer system. Malware can be in the form of viruses, Trojans, spyware, worms and bot.

Virus

It is a type of software developed by an attacker such that it spreads in a computer system by modifying software programs and inserting its own malicious code in the program. It usually comes in the form of a .exe file. So most of the times, it can stay hidden in the computer system without being detected. It can cause small disruptions in a computer or sometimes be a part of the big denial of service attacks.

Worm

The worm-like virus quickly spreads in other computer systems by creating a replica of self. It usually depends on a computer network to spread itself. They depend on security loopholes of a computer network to spread. They harm a network in many ways like consuming the network bandwidth.

Trojan

Trojan is used by an attacker to access the personal information of a user. They usually come in the form of an email attachment or a link. When the user clicks on the particular malicious link, a connection is established between the attacker and user's computer. In this way, an attacker can gain access to the user's computer and steal user information. Ransomware attacks are carried out using Trojan. Unlike Virus and worms, they do not replicate themselves.

Spyware

These are used to track a user web activity to display appropriate pop-up advertisements. They are generally used to "spy" on user's activity. They can be used for malicious purposes such as taking a user's bank account and credit card information, changing settings of user's computer thus decreasing the browsing speeds. To deal with it, there is various "anti-spyware software" in the market these days.

Bot

More than half on web traffic on the internet is made up of bots. These are software that is used for performing repetitive and automated tasks on the internet usually faster than human speeds. Servers are varying of them. Servers usually have a "robots.txt" file stating rules of a bot's behaviour on a server.

Denial of Service Attacks

Denial of Service attack impairs the use of a particular computer resource like network bandwidth, application resources, system resources etc. It does so by flooding the server/computer resource with a large number of malicious requests such that the authorized user finds it difficult to access that particular resource. Now we will see how each resource gets affected by Denial of Service attack: -

1. **Network Bandwidth:** Usually a small network within an organization is connected to a wider higher bandwidth internet. In the case of a DDOS attack, a large amount of malicious traffic is directed towards the target server of the organization, which inhibits the authorized user from accessing it.
2. **System Resources:** Example of this type of attack is SYN spoofing and poison packet. In the case of SYN spoofing the attacker fills the table that is used to manage TCP connections with a large number of requests. This prevents the authorized user from accessing these tables. Poison Packet is used to take advantage of a bug in the system's network handling software to take down the system. The classic ping of death and teardrop attacks directed at older Windows 9x systems were of this form.
3. **Application Resources:** In this case, the attacker attacks a particular application like a web server. The attacker fills the application resource with a large number of requests, which prevents the authorized user from accessing that resource. For example, in the case of a database server, the attacker will generate a large number of costly queries that will increase the load on the server. This type of attack is known as a cyber slam. Another alternative is to make a request that sets off a bug in the server program that can cause it to crash.

CYBER LAW AND LAW ENFORCEMENT

In the prospect of cybercrimes, the meaning of 'Computer' is generally described to be central i.e. it mostly revolves around some globally accepted meaning (Clough, 2010). Even being a common word, it can have different versions of definitions depending on the context it is described and also on the audiences it addresses. Due to advancement in technology nowadays even domestic appliances come with some computational powers and that of mobile phones have become comparable to once called highest processing systems the 'Mainframes'. These aspects are considered as the challenges to the definition of 'Computer' when they are expressed as laws for protection from cybercrimes. To solve those challenges, we have come with two responses:

- Leaving the term 'Computer' undefined as is done in the case of Australia, Canada and the United Kingdom
- Provision of a comprehensive definition of the term 'Computer' as is done in the case of the United States and India.

For further assistance in the regard of defining the term 'Computer', the Cybercrime Convention is referred while undertaking any of these approaches. This convention defines a 'Computer System' rather than a 'Computer'. The convention defines a computer system as "any device or group of interconnected devices which are working under the command of a program and performing processing of data". This definition neither advocates for a comprehensive definition nor an undefined term.

Definition of the Computer in Cyber Law of Australia, Canada and the United Kingdom

In Australia, Canada and the United Kingdom the definition of the term 'computer' is considered as undefined under the suggestion of law reform agencies. The Law Commission recommended this on the basis that defining the term would likely be both under-inclusive, because it may not be up-to-date to the latest technological advances and over-inclusive, because it may include household appliances, calculators, watches and the like. The Commission also rejected the possibility of leaving the term undefined and actually specified certain items which were not computers which were used for such intended purposes (Clough, 2010).

The Australian Committee even though being partly influenced by the law commission's recommendations, they were less optimistic about the fact that this issue was more manageable before the first proposal of this recommendation. Due to the increasing computerisation of household appliances, there was a constant threat of over-criminalisation. So, it was proposed by the Law Commission and the MCCOC (Model Criminal Code Officers Committee) that let the problem of over-criminalisation be addressed by the scope of the offence, rather than defining the 'computer'. If the limits of offences were described properly then the issue of over-criminalisation will be dealt with. The only scenario of over-criminalisation that may occur would be a result of broadly limited offences, for such cases the decision is purely under the hands of the prosecutor.

The provision defined under Canadian act, it does not define the term 'computer' as such rather it defines a 'computer service' or 'computer system'. The definition of 'computer service' includes the storage, retrieval and processing of data. The definition of 'computer system' says that it is a device or group of interconnected or related devices which contains computer programs and other data and works in accordance with the computer programs. Thus, simply in the Canadian provisions, the term is left undefined is given its ordinary meaning as known to the world i.e. under the Canadian provision it does not possess a technical meaning through the term data does possess a technical meaning.

The United Kingdom's provisions are defined by the Law Commission and do consist of all possible aspects of keeping the term 'computer' undefined though not completely undefined as it describes such devices which do not fall under the prospect of being a device of crime. The UK provisions are somewhat similar to both the Australian and the Canadian provisions. The difference between them occurs in the way of defining various terms associated with the computer systems. For example, we know that in the Canadian provision there is a proper technical definition of the word 'data' whereas in the UK provision it is defined by its traditional definition and not a technical definition (Clough, 2010).

Definition of the Computer in Cyber Law of the United States and India

In the United States, the CFAA (Computer Fraud and Abuse Act) draw contrast to other jurisdictions, by giving away a precise and well-defined definition of the term 'computer' – An optical, electrochemical, magnetic, electronic or any other a fast processing device which can perform arithmetic, logical and storage operations on the data or works along with any such device (Clough, 2010). The definition was designed as such it can be broad spectrum i.e. it may cover future technological advancements, but it also possessed the threats of over and under-inclusion which were also observed by the CFAA. This act defines a computer and not a computer network. But still, the definition covers the communication facilities connected to the computer i.e. it covers the routers and other network associated devices.

The Indian definition of the term 'computer' is similar to the definition as described by the CFAA under the United States cyberlaw. Additional to this the Indian act further elaborates the term mentioned under this act, being the likes of a computer system, computer networks, data, etc. The major difference we can see between the acts of United States and Indian act is that the United States prosecution takes into account the dictionary definitions of the terms coming under the definition and then imparting the judgements on the basis of definition and the extent of crimes. The Indian act simply defines each and every term for the ease of jurisdiction.

Access Offences

Access offences under the Cybercrime Convention mean unauthorised and unsupervised access to whole or any part of the computer system (hardware, software, storage devices etc.). Access offences can be as simple as computer trespassing or can be as complex as hacking usually undertaken without the permission of the owner and could be protected by some security. We can visualise access into two perspectives – 'internal' and 'external'. The internal perspective says that access is believed as getting 'inside' the system whereas the external perspective is of the view that even an alteration in the computer is term as access whether a success or failure.

Australia

The Australian provision tends to define access as displaying of data, moving, copying of data and execution of particular functions which involves data and processing (Clough, 2010). This definition may seem to be exhaustive but it's a broad-spectrum definition. Any operation involving data using computer whether successful or not is considered as access. In Australia, an access is considered as an access offence when the data in the computer is unauthorised because it is not caused by the person who is entitled the owner of that system.

Canada

The Canadian provision says that an access to the computer is considered as access offence when a person directly or indirectly obtains any computer service or uses a computer system with the specific intent of committing an offence under the impression of someone else. Or simply, Canadian act says that when an access to someone else's computer is made 'fraudulently' or without the colour of righteousness.

India

According to the Indian provision when someone intentionally tries to gain unauthorised secure access or gain access to a protected system containing sensitive or confidential or personal information directly or indirectly via the computer systems is termed as access offences in India.

United Kingdom

According to United Kingdom's provision access offences are referred when someone uses or causes a computer to perform a task or operation which makes it secure or enable access to the individuals or bodies the access that did not have access to that system. In the UnitedKingdom, any access to a system is considered as unauthorised when that person does not have the access of controlling the program that the owner of that system is entitled to and do not have the consent of the authorised owner of that system.

United States

In the United States provision, there is no specific definition of 'access' is generally considered as its original meaning of gaining entry into something or the ability to make the use of something thus here the information or data has no relation to access. Since data alteration is not considered in this provision, then if someone makes an unsuccessful access, he/she is partly guilty for attempting but not for an access offence. In the UnitedStates, the word unauthorised also has its normal meaning and is considered as unambiguous thus, no need of defining.

Data Impairment

Introduction

Data Impairment is related to as such offences under the Cybercrime Convention which relates to intentional or without right damage, deterioration, alteration, suppression or deletion of computer data. These offences are defined to prevent computer data from intentional damages, proper utilisation of computer data and integrity protection. There are some norms by the Cybercrime Convention defined which separates data alteration by programs designed by system administrators and data alterations by offenders.

Legislative Provisions

Australia

Australian federal provisions are divided into two categories – offences related to the modification of data and offences related to communication impairment. In the modification of data, a person is guilty if there is an unauthorised modification of data or the owner knows there is a modification of data. While the other offence says that the person is guilty if there is communication impairment or the owner knows there is communication impairment.

Canada

According to Canadian provisions, this offence is known as 'mischief in data' and the person is guilty if the data is altered or destroyed, the data is left meaningless or useless, or obstructing the use of data and programs as per the owner's desire (Clough, 2010).

India

When someone intentionally or knowingly reveals, destroys or modifies or intentionally or knowingly causes another to reveals, destroys or modifies some computer program, source code or data which is necessary to kept and maintained by the authorised body or person, for the time being, is considered guilty for data impairment.

United Kingdom

According to the Computer Misuse Act, a person is found guilty if he/she attempts unauthorised operations of impairing computer operations, hindering the access to a particular program or data and damaging the reliability of data or program.

United States

The principal federal offence related to computer damage is separated into three aspects (Clough, 2010). The first aspect deals with intentional transmission of program information or data. The second and third aspects both deal with intentional unauthorised access where damage or damage and loss are caused either recklessly or accidentally. Not only this, each of such offence must be proved to be unauthorised and the damage or loss should be caused.

Conduct Causing Impairment

Australia

The Australian provision has defined the impairment conducts in a very simple manner. It just requires the defendant to cause unauthorised modification. As with unauthorised access, there is a need of impairment process being either directly or indirectly done by the operation of a computer.

Canada

The Canadian provision does not specify a particular offensive conduct other than those prohibited results included in it. There is no reference to the computer but the act focuses entirely on data. Though the section protects electronic data it is broad enough that it may cover a computer or a computer network. Even the physical damage to data is considered as an offence.

India

In the Indian provision, any act of intentional alteration or deletion or transmission of information or data from a computer or unauthorised access to a secured system falls under the categories of the conduct of data impairment.

United Kingdom

The United Kingdom provisions say that any activity related to the computer that falls under the 'unauthorised act' which says any action that one takes involving the use of the computer (Clough, 2010). This act made sure that one now doesn't have to prove that there has been an unauthorised modification rather has to prove an unauthorised action against or with a computer.

United States

The provision of United States says that the conduct of impairment can be categorised as – first is the transfer of information, data, program, or codes and the second is intentional access to a protected system.

Exploitation of Devices

Introduction

The offences we have discussed must require some extent of technological knowledge to be committed. But there is also another type of offence which is termed as 'computer misuse' or 'exploitation of devices' which does not require any technical knowledge but some data like passwords of secured systems which can later be shared to others for the commitment of crimes. Though these conducts could be prosecuted like general fraud and incitement crimes there is an arguable need for laws against offences which are involved in the trafficking of items which facilitates computer offences.

Provisions

Australia

The Australian provisions have divided this type of offences into two categories – possession or control of data and produce, supply and obtain data. The first category is referred as an offence for a person to have possession of data with the intention of that data being used by another person and the second category says that it is an offence for producing, supplying and obtaining of the data to be used by another person.

Canada

The Canadian provisions have separate offences related to passwords and other tangible devices which are an offence related to fraudulently and unauthorised usage, possession, sharing, trafficking and allowing another user to access that computer system and then the user can use that computer to commit their offences. It does not consider unsuccessful access attempts as offences and along with this one can also use this provision to argue against the security concerns of that particular computer system.

India

In accordance with the Indian provisions, any individual found liable for forging, making, or sharing information like passwords and security codes to others for the purpose of performing a computer offence is termed as a crime. Not only is this if a person forges an identical device through which that one can perform financial transactions also termed as a viable offence.

United Kingdom

Until the year 2004, there existed no such provision in the United Kingdom (Clough, 2010). But in 2004 due to new additions in Cybercrime conventions made the United Kingdom come up with its own provisions on these types of crimes. The provision says that if an individual makes, adapt, and offer any article (program or data in electronic form) with the intention of assisting or committing an offence are found to be guilty.

United States

The United States had such offences into two relevant types – first is access devices, the devices which can solely or along with other devices be used for the purpose of obtaining money, services etc. the individuals found in the possession and usage of such devices are guilty. Second is the counterfeiting and unauthorised access, this provision says that any individual found to be using a device which is a counterfeit i.e. a fake but identical device for obtaining money and other services are found to be guilty.

Fraud and Related Offences

1. **Fraudulent Sales Online:** Online good sale always has risk on both sides, a merchant who don't want to release goods until get paid and the buyer who doesn't want to pay before delivery, a greater level of trust required. In online transactions, cards are not present and some of its security features are not present like signature and chip technology.
2. **Advance-Fee Schemes:** Here, the victim is persuaded to pay a fee in advance for receiving some service or benefit which turns out to be a lie. Despite their notoriety and questionability, a significant number of people become a victim of it every day.
3. **Fraudulent Investment:** With little efforts, anyone can create an authentic looking website encouraging high returns for investors. Most people look on the Internet to discover investment opportunities, those fake sites about fraudulent investments can be spread very quickly.
4. **Identity Crime:** It is a generic term used for offences where the accused uses a false identity to perpetrate the crime. This crime can be drug trafficking, tax evasion, money laundering. Identity fraud is another form of identity crime where a false identity is used for getting money whereas Identity theft is conjecture of an existing identity.
5. **Phishing:** It is a combination of technological development and social engineering; its fundamentals are to create a fake email or website to collect personal, financial and sensitive information.
6. **Card Skimming:** It's a process where a legitimate credit card data is captured and copied; this is done by exploiting the vulnerabilities of magnetic tape-strip technology present on the card. It can be done using a card skimmer which is small and easy to conceal. It can be used when the card is out of sight in any store or restaurant also it can be placed into the ATM card slot.

Cyber- Crime Against a Person

1. **Grooming:** Grooming is the process of befriending a child by a (potential) abuser in an attempt to gain a child's trust and confidence, enabling them to get the child agrees to abusive activity (Gillespie, 2002). Internet and electronic communication have provided offenders with significantly increased opportunities where they are virtually enabled to communicate privately with children in their homes, whereas in past, only family members, trusted friends or teachers had private access to children.

2. **Cyberstalking:** Stalking may be described as a way in which one individual perpetrates on another continuous unwanted intrusion and communication, to such extent that the victim fears for her or his safety (Purcell, Pathe & Mullen, 2004). Cyber stalking is simply, the use of the Internet, e-mail, and other electronic communication devices to stalk another person (Deirmanjian, 1999) (Ellison & Akdenis, 1998). Technology helps to overcome traditional obstacles such as anonymity, direct line of communication to the victim, pseudo-anonymity to offending, both physical and psychological also encourage this offending behaviour.

3. **Digital Voyeurism:** Due to the hike in miniaturization and ready availability of digital technology like a recording device with the ability of easy reproduce and upload has led to an increase in voyeurism (Oxford English Dictionary). This involves a person covertly observing or in case recording another person, generally in private places.

DIGITAL FORENSICS

If there involve a computer in a crime or even if there is a computer in the vicinity of the crime scene, it is very much likely to have an evidence on that computer. Computer and its content's usefulness or credibility of that evidence will be corrupted if entertain untrained or inexperienced computer forensics specialist. You should take the services of someone who is likely to call to testify in court to explain in what she or he organized the computer or its data to gather the evidence, moreover the court only acknowledge the individual's own level of training and expertise, and it is also recommended that he or she has the tendency to stand up to the scrutiny and all the pressure of cross-examination.

Digital Forensics in Law Enforcement

Sometimes it is impossible for a (computer) forensics expert to separate the legal issues around the evidence from actual aspects of digital forensics such reliability, authenticity, and completeness along with its ability to convince the court. From the time of evidence collection till presented at the court, it must NOT be altered or damaged and must fully account for. Hence, it must meet the appropriate evidence laws.

There is more legal term than just technical ones. For example, these days remote are targeted and compromised with malicious events while investigating this kind of crime can raise an international issue as the electronic evidence, either to prevent, investigate or prosecute a crime outside the country. In that case, Law enforcement must seek assistance from different country's law enforcement authorities. Protecting the evidence or request for one can come under mutual legal assistance agreements; consistency with all legal system is an ability to create an assurance in the integrity of evidence.

Types of Law Enforcement Digital Forensics Technologies

1. **Preservation of Evidence:** Computer evidence is very sensitive can be altered or erased by any number of times. Computer forensic specialist must be known to bit stream backup theories to ensure the safeguard of all storage levels that may have evidence. For instance, there is Safe Back software (can be purchased from New Technologies, Inc.) which used to create mirror-image (bit-stream) backup files of a hard disk drive or partition. Safe Back is an industry standard self-authenticating digital forensics tool that is used to create evidence-grade backups of hard drives which cannot be altered or change to alter the reproduction it.

2. **Trojan Horse Programs:** It is clear that protection of the computer evidence is must before processing a computer, and there are programs that can destroy data and modify the operating system thus, a digital forensics expert has the ability to avoid such destructive programs and traps that can be placed with the intention of destroying data and evidence or they can use for getting sensitive information, passwords, and network logons.

3. **Computer Forensics Documentation:** It is important to maintain the documentation of forensic processing methodologies and findings, it is so because it without proper documentation will be tough for anyone to present finding during computer security risk assessments and internal audits and also when audit finding become an object of any lawsuit or crime investigation.

4. **File Slack:** In hidden storage areas random memory dump can happen and a computer forensics investigator must know the techniques and automated tools that are used to study file slack. This data is a serious security leak concerning passwords, network logins, email, database entries or word processing documents. An investigator (digital forensics) must have the ability to handle slack and he should proficient in probing file slack and documenting their findings, along with that he should able to eliminate the security risk.

5. **Data-Hiding Techniques:** Sensitive data can easily hide using any techniques; there is a possibility that the diskettes hid within diskettes or a complete computer hard disk partition hidden. Digital Forensics investigator should have knowledge of tools that can help in detecting such anomalies. For instance, AnaDisk, Anadisk Diskette Analysis Tool was created in 1991 to identify the

floppy diskette anomalies. It works at a very low level but makes maximum use of floppy diskette hardware (River, 2005).

6. **E-commerce Investigation:** Due to the growth in World Wide Web activities and the activities of computer users, there is a recent forensic tool Net Threat Analyzer by New Technology Inc. It is available free of cost (though not available to the public). This software scans a computer's disk drives and other storage areas to search the past internet browsing and email activities are done through specific computers. Someone can hide their browser history from finding their supervisors, but Net Threat Analyzer goes back where things are easier to find.

7. **Dual Purpose Programs:** These programs are expected to perform multiple process and tasks simultaneously, which include delayed tasking and a digital forensics investigator should have hands-on experience with this kind of programs.

8. **Text Search Techniques:** This specialized search techniques and tools which were developed by New Technologies Inc to find targeted strings of text in files, file slacks, unallocated file spaces ad Windows swap files. Text Search Plus software is such an example and being a computer forensics investigator, one should have known about it. For example, Text Search Plus was created for speed and accuracy in security reviews that's why it is widely used by classified government agencies or corporations that support those agencies. Text Search Plus is quick in scanning hard disk drives, zip disks for a keyword or any kind of pattern of texts.

9. **Fuzzy Logic Tools Used to Recognize Unknown Text:** To deal with identification of relevant evidence and unknown strings of text New Technology Inc has developed a new tool which provides valuable leads as for how a subject computer was used; an investigator should fully understand these methods and techniques. For instance, Intelligent Forensic Filter, a utility to make quick sense of nonsense data in an analysis of ambient data sources like page file/ window swap or data associated with erased files).

10. **Disk Structure:** The knowledge of how to modify a structure or hide data in incomprehensible areas of a hard disk drive requires a good knowledge of computer hard disks and how evidence resides at different levels within the structure of the disk (River, 2005).

11. **Data Encryption:** Digital forensics separates the good encryption from bad encryption. Moreover, it includes password-recovery software regarding Lotus, Microsoft Word, PKZIP files. A computer forensics investigator should familiar with the use of software to crack security related with different file structures.

12. **Data Compression:** One must know how compression works and how can compression can hide or disguise the sensitive data. Also, a forensic investigator should know how to break password-protected compressed files.

13. **Erased Files:** Recovering previously erased files is another perk in digital forensics which can be done by using a DOS program or manually using data-recovery techniques.

14. **Internet Abuse Identification and Detection:** There is specialized software that can identify how a targeted computer has been used on the internet, this is a focus on the computer forensics issues tied with data that most computer never realizes exist.

15. **Boot Process and Memory Resident Programs:** The operating system can be modified to change data or destroy it at the whim of the person who set up the system. These techniques can be used for capturing keyboard activity from any computer user.

Rules and Software of Forensics

A good forensics investigator should always follow some rules:

1. One should try to examine as little as possible on original evidence. Instead, the examination should be performed on duplicate evidence.
2. Never tamper with the evidence and keep a check on the rules of evidence
3. Always care evidence with care and prepare a chain of custody
4. Make sure to document changes in evidence, if any.

In any typical investigation, the computer forensics examiner must follow some sequence of the process, which starts right from accessing the case, asking questions to relevant peoples and documenting the results in order to identify the crime and location of evidence. Computer Forensics revolves around two types of computer: the one which used for committing a crime, and other which was the target of the crime.

Chain of Custody: Preservation of Evidence

Integrity must be maintained by the preserve Identification of the evidence. A chain of custody is an accurate document of the movement and possession of particular evidence; it includes all the time into consideration right from taking the evidence into custody until its delivery to the court. It is a very important piece of the document as it actually proves that the evidence was stored in a legally accepted location and it documents who is in custody and controls the evidence during the forensic testing phase.

1. **Collection:** The process of collecting data includes finding evidence then collecting relevant data from it, preparing an Order of Volatility, removing all external areas of alteration, and last preparing a chain of custody. After collecting data, one should create an MD5 hash of the evidence, it advisable to do a preliminary assessment of the search for evidence. Once the assessment is concluded, collect and seize the equipment used to commit the crime and document the item collected like disks, flash drives or CDs and DVDs etc. A photograph of the crime scene should be taken before confiscating evidence. It is not necessary to seize the whole system sometimes it can result in over collection of data thus in some cases, only relevant data should be collected.

2. **Examination:** Digital forensics investigator must trace, filter and extract hidden data during the process because sometimes evidence cannot stay for long some evidence are volatile because it either needs a consistent power supply for storage or some evidence keeps changing its contained information. An investigator must look into the registers, cache, ARP cache, Routing tables, process tables, and kernel statistics and modules. An order of recovery of system data according to the volatility can be:

    a. **Virtual Memory:** Swap space or paging files
    b. **Physical disk:** A Physical hard disk of the system
    c. **Backup:** Offline backup media. Sometimes data are not available on the system, but it was there before, and it is in the last backup.

3. **Analysis:** Analysis of the Data mostly depends on the collection of digital evidence and how it was copied. A duplicate copy should be used for all the analysis in order to protect the original evidence from alteration which is the first rule of forensics. Analysis can be done using various forensic analysis tools like Access Data, Encase etc.

Law for Evidence Gathering

It is important for the Law enforcement or the digital forensics professionals to know about the laws for gathering evidence. If laws are not followed, then some criminal can walk on the streets freely or someone's innocence can't prove. The forensic investigator must have knowledge of the status of the particular jurisdiction of where the crime happened as well. For example (USA jurisdiction), Electronic Communication Privacy Act (ECPA) of 1986 affects the digital forensics.

ECPA majorly have three titles which are:

1. Wiretap Act, A warrant is required to intercept the communications.
2. Stored Communication Act (SCA), it protects the privacy of an individual's content of files stored by the service provider.

3.   Pen Warrant Act, it asks the government to get a court order if it needs to install or use a pen register or a trap-and-trace (it stores call information related to the number dialled not the actual communications (DeFranco, 2013).

Many of these laws need a warrant but there can be an exception to the warrant and that is called Plain View Doctrine. Thus, a digital evidence admissible to the court if and only if the investigator has a proper warrant for the same context or it has to be in plain view doctrine.

E-Discovery

In the lawsuit, if an electronic artefact like spreadsheet, e-mails, audio/video or a document is requested is Electronic Discovery or E-discovery (DeFranco, 2013). E-discovery is different than the digital forensics. E-discovery is acquiring a readily available to access on storage device while in Digital forensics analysis goes deep down because maybe information acquired cannot be accessible due to encryption, deletion, damage, web activity etc. The E-discovery is usually sent to the legal team to analyze whereas in digital forensics first the digital forensic professional analyze the results than hand over to legal team.

SUMMARY

This chapter discusses the fundamental introduction of cyber crimes and how it is defined that is type of crimes that uses a computer system or group of computer systems or computer networks to cause a criminal offence against an individual, group of individuals, computers or group of computers or computer networks, how did it evolved that is how the advancements in science and technologies allowed different criminals to take their activities onto the cyber space, challenges of cybercrime that is the challenges a criminal requires before initiating the crime it involves motivation, proper operational conditions, absence of individuals which can prevent its operations and proper knowledge of systems they intend to attack, the magnitude at which it can cause problems to victims because at different countries there is a different definition which makes it difficult to prosecute a cyber crime and most cyber crimes due to this remains unprosecuted, what is unauthorised access to a computer system what can one do when he/she gets the unauthorised access to that computer system and when someone gets the unauthorised access to the system they have accesses to the information which can be personal, professional or public and one can do any operation on them. One can also modify the data present in those computer systems as they please which could further to lead to financial gains or so. After this the chapter further elaborates the topic when it discusses what are malicious software and their types that is what is malicious software (software with malicious intent), malicious software can be of following types- viruses, worms, spyware, Trojans and bots. The next topic is the denial of service attacks that are such attacks which do not let users access particular sites that they want to access and thus stops the operations such as financial transactions and so. Cyber terrorism or terrorism did through computers, here the terrorist can hack the military systems of a target country and can also cause digital damages by disabling various security systems of that system it can be initiated through encryptions, steganography and many more. The topic which we arrive is now cyber laws and its enforcement in which we can define cyber laws as laws designed for the protection of individuals from cybercriminals. Here we first discuss how the term 'computer' is defined in these laws of countries like Australia, Canada and the United Kingdom which preferred to keep the term undefined and then the definition of the term 'computer' in the United States and India which have developed an exhaustive definition of the term. The next is access and access offences here we also discuss the definition of access and access offences in Australian, Canadian, United Kingdom, the United States and Indian provisions. Our next aspect is then the data impairment its definition and its provisions along with conduct which causes impairment amongst countries like India, Australia, Canada, United Kingdom and the United States. The next topic we discuss is misuse of computer and other such devices/data (especially passwords and access codes) which leads to computer misuse in this the person having such information does commits the crime but rather supplies it to criminals to initiate criminal activities, and discusses different provisions provided by the United States, United Kingdom, India, Canada and Australia. Then the discussion focuses on topics such as frauds and its related offences which involve crimes like identity thefts, online frauds, fraudulent emails, spoofing etc. and then the cybercrimes that can be performed against a person i.e. crimes like child pornography, cyberstalking, digital voyeurism, grooming (digitally befriending children and then training them in doing unsolicited tasks). Then we discuss our final topic that is Digital forensics the field of forensics whose objective is to extract evidence from the computer systems on which and through which the crimes are committed. Where we will discuss the roles of digital forensics in law enforcement, i.e. how digital forensics can help the law in catching the criminals by providing the required evidence to the court for prosecution of offences. It also discusses the different types of law enforcement technologies which are associated with digital forensics like preservation of evidence, Trojan horse programs, Computer forensics documentation etc. Then there is a discussion of rules and regulations of digital forensics that is under which a digital forensic research is done and the software using which one can perform the operations that fall under the aspects of digital forensics which are a chain of custody, collection, examination and analysis. Then in the final topics what we discuss are the laws for evidence gathering that a cyber forensics researcher has to follow and thus gather evidence under such norms which can then be later represented into the court for prosecution under the required conditions that court requires. Then the final discussion moves to e-discovery (electronic discovery) which is referred to as the requesting of electronic artefacts like spreadsheets, e-mails etc. and how it is different from digital forensics as it has more access to storage and information which are inaccessible to forensic researchers and thus e-discovery analysis is undertaken by legal team and have higher level of access than forensic experts.

REFERENCES

Clough, J. (2015). *Principles of Cyber Crimes.* Cambridge University Press.

DeFranco, J. F. (2013). *What Every Engineer Should Know About Cyber Security and Digital Forensics.* CRC Press. doi:10.1201/b15581

Deirmenjian, J. M. (1999). Stalking in cyberspace. *The Journal of the American Academy of Psychiatry and the Law, 27,* 407–413. PMID:10509940

Ellison, L., & Akdeniz, Y. (1998, December). *Cyber-stalking: The Regulation of Harassment on the Internet. Criminal Law Review,* 29–48.

Finch, E. (2001). *The Criminalisation of Stalking: Constructing the problem and Evaluating the solution.* London: Cavendish Publishing. doi:10.4324/9781843142638

Finch, E. (2002). Stalking: A Violent Crime or a Crime of Violence? *Howard Journal, 41*(5), 422–433. doi:10.1111/1468-2311.00256

Gillespie, A. A. (2002). Child protection on the Internet - challenges for criminal law. *Child and Family law Quarterly Journal,* 411-412.

Household Use of Information Technology. (2007-08). *Australian Bureau of Statistics.* Retrieved from http://www.abs.gov.au

Offences, C. (2001). *Model Criminal Code Officers Committee.* Retrieved from https://catalogue.nla.gov.au/Record

Online Statistics of Communication and Digital Economy. (2008). *Australian Government archive.* Retrieved from http://www.archive.dbcde.gov.au/2008

Purcell, R., Pathe, M., & Mullen, P. E. (2000). *Stalkers and Their Victims*. New York: Cambridge University Press.

Purcell, R., Pathe, M., & Mullen, P. E. (2004). Stalking: Defining and prosecuting a new category of offending. *International Journal of Law and Psychiatry, 27*(2), 157–169. doi:10.1016/j.ijlp.2004.01.006 PMID:15063640

Residential Telephone Service Survey. (2007). *Statistics Canada*. Retrieved from http://www.statcan.gc.ca

Vacca, J. R. (2005). *Computer Forensics (Computer Crime Scene Investigation)*. Hingham, MA: Charles River Media.

Chapter 3
An Indian and Global Perspective on Cybercrime

K. S. Umadevi
VIT University, India

Geraldine Bessie Amali
VIT University, India

Latha Subramanian
University of Madras, India

ABSTRACT

Cybercrime is defined as a crime in which a computer is the object of the crime (hacking, phishing, spamming) or is used as a tool to commit an offense (child pornography, hate crimes). The advancement of technology has made us dependent on internet for all our needs. Internet has given us easy access to everything without moving from our place. Social networking, online shopping, storing data, gaming, online studying, online jobs, every possible thing that man can think of can be done through the medium of internet. However, with the development of the internet and its related benefits, the concept of cybercrimes arose. Cybercrimes are committed in different forms. In a report published by the National Crime Records Bureau, the incidence of cybercrimes under the IT Act has increased by 85.4% in the year 2011 as compared to 2010 in India, whereas the increase in incidence of the crime under IPC is by 18.5% as compared to the year 2010.

DOI: 10.4018/978-1-5225-8241-0.ch003

INTRODUCTION

Any sort of crime committed using a computer either as the object of the crime or as a tool to commit the offense is called cybercrime. In 2015 consumers in the UK reported a loss of more than 1.7 billion pounds due to cybercrime. This is way more than other serious crimes like illegal drug trafficking. This sharp increase in crime is due to the growth in e-commerce and online banking. In the last few years alone there have been hundreds of millions of cases of credit card theft; cases of compromise in Social Security Numbers and health care records. Crimes like these are committed by hackers who exploit the vulnerabilities in software which are sometimes caused by naive mistakes made by the people while using the software.

People committing cybercrime cannot be pinned down to a specific class of individuals. They may belong to any race, religion or sex. It could be a teenager from high school who just wants to impress his girlfriend or even a member of a terrorist group. Countries are now not only equipping their regular armies to fight crime but also their cyber army. In fact, the next world war might not be fought with weapons but with computers which could be used to shut down national water supplies, energy grids, and transportation systems.

By Google Security Princess Parisa Tabriz, an attacker can infect someone's computer in two ways. The first way is to deceive the person into installing a program on their computer. Many viruses are often disguised as security updates. The second way is to use the vulnerability in the software already installed in the system. In such a case the attacker doesn't even need permissions to install a virus. Once the virus is installed then the system's data is compromised. The attacker can then steal sensitive data like bank account details etc. He can also remotely monitor and control the computer. He can even create a digital army with millions of computers and plan a full-fledged attack and even take down websites. This kind of attack is called a Distributed Denial of Service attacks (DDoS).

A denial of service is when hackers overwhelm a website with too many requests. Most of the websites are ready to handle a large number of requests. But if the requests are in the order of billions and trillions then the servers will be overloaded and they stop responding. Hackers also send out a large number of spam emails which deceive the user into giving their sensitive information. Information such as passwords to bank accounts can be collected from unsuspecting users by making them logging into their bank accounts. This is called a phishing scam. Hackers then use the newly obtained passwords to steal money from bank accounts.

Types of Cybercrimes

To secure yourself you have to think about the distinctive manners by which your computer can be compromised and your protection encroached. This section doesn't provide an exhaustive list, yet will give an idea about loopholes in the systems and security frameworks, which can be abused by attackers, and furthermore their conceivable intentions in doing so. To begin with, the list of crimes the system is prone to be mentioned below but not limited to:

- Identity theft and invasion of privacy
- Internet fraud
- ATM skimming
- Wire fraud
- Internet Piracy and File sharing
- Data diddling
- Hacking
- Cyberbullying and Cyberstalking
- Cyber defamation
- Cyber Terrorism

Identity Theft and Invasion of Privacy

Identity theft is the act of fraudulently identifying the user identity in order to gain access towards one's personal information like credit card information, banking and/or financial information to gain access towards it. Using banking information, criminal can purchase, transfer amount from victim's account to any other account or any other financial assets.

Identity theft is a very serious crime as the hacker can use the social security number and buy a house, car, or even take a loan. The main issue with identity theft is that it takes months before the victim realizes that his information has been compromised. By the time the victim realizes it might become too late as the criminal would have taken off before that. Victims have to report their concerns immediately in order to bring the situation under control.

The following are the steps that have to be followed in order to get the credit back on track [Council, E. B., 2012). Creative industries, Wall Street Journal.].

Step 1 - File an Initial Fraud Alert: As soon as the victim suspects of an identity theft, he/she should file an initial fraud alert with the credit agency. They will then check the credit report. Doing so they can monitor the credit so that if any criminal has tried to take out a loan and if it is in the final stages of approval, the agency can stop it. Criminals will not then attempt to open a new account in the name of the victim. There are three major credit reporting agencies, Experian, Equifax or TransUnion. These three reporting agencies work together, therefore it doesn't matter which one the victim approaches. The reporting agency will then notify the other two as well. For more protection, the victim can put a credit freeze on file with all three credit reporting agencies.

Step 2 - Initiate a Credit Freeze: When the victim initializes a credit freeze with the reporting agencies, no bank or Credit Card Company can view the credit report of the victim. No potential creditor or business can look at the credit report without the permission of the victim. This makes it harder for the hackers to open a new account or take out a loan in the victim's name. A credit freeze can be initiated by anyone for free or for a very small fee depending upon the rules of the state. The victim has to inform the three reporting agencies of the credit freeze. After the credit freeze, the victim has to go through the credit report carefully to check for any transaction that he did not initiate. If any transaction seems suspicious the federal agency has to be reported and an identity theft fraud has to be filed. This will help in removing the information from the credit report so that the creditors do not approach the victim to collect the debt.

Step 3 - File an Identity Theft Report: Filing an identity theft report is s two-stage process. First, a report has to be filed with the Federal Trade Commission. FTC is the government body that protects the consumers from identity theft. The report can also be filed online. Once the report is filed an affidavit will be issued for further reference. The second stage is to file a report at the local police precinct. This can be done either online or in person. The police report and the FTC report together is the proof for filing the Identity Theft Report.

Step 4 - Contact Credit Bureaus and Business: Each fraud that the victim has identified in the credit report have to be disputed. Generally, one can dispute claims by making phone calls to each and every lending agency and dispute the transaction. This process needs a lot of bookkeeping with respect to the time, date, person spoken to etc for future reference. FTC also provides with checklists that the victim can use in order to dispute the claim

Step 5 - Place an Extended Fraud Alert: The victim can also file an extended fraud alert. It is free and lasts for seven years. Two free copies of the credit report will be given which will help in monitoring the credit for any fraudulent transactions. In addition to the three big credit agencies, local small companies will also help in monitoring and reporting fraudulent activities. These agencies will file fraud alerts with them as well. It is a challenge to get your credit score back after an identity theft. Guarding the social security number very carefully can help a person avoid identity theft in the future.

Internet Fraud

- **Internet Fraud:** Internet fraud is a sort of committing fraud using the Internet. As indicated by the FBI's 2017 Internet Crime Report, the Internet Crime Complaint Center (IC3) got around 300,000 complaints exploited people over $1.4 billion in online fraud during 2017(Internet Crime Report, 2017). As per an investigation led by the Center for Strategic and International Studies (CSIS) and McAfee, cybercrime costs the worldwide economy as much as $600 billion, which converts into 0.8% of worldwide GDP. Internet fraud is the utilization of Internet applications or programming methods using Internet access to swindle unfortunate casualties or to generally exploit them. Internet crime plans steal millions of dollars every year from exploited people and keep on plaguing the Internet through different strategies. A few prominent strategies are:
- **Credit Card Fraud:** Credit card scam covers a wide range of stealing and fraud committed using payment cards like credit or debit card, as a fake source of funds in a transaction. The reason might be to buy goods without paying or to get unapproved assets using others account. Worldwide credit card fraud has been rising every year, particularly during the past decade. In 2016, losses topped $24 billion dollars. Nearly half of those losses took place in the United States alone. Since the credit card information is highly sensitive and always at a risk of theft. There are various ways of avoiding credit card fraud.
  - Shred the credit billing documents before tossing them away
  - Don't give out your credit card information
  - Be careful of e-mails even if the email is genuine because they may be phishing emails.
  - Review your bank statements each month to check for any unauthorized charges.
  - Report lost or stolen credit cards instantly.
- **Data Breach:** One's personal information is spread across many websites throughout the internet from online banking credit reports e-commerce tax returns and healthcare accounts your personal information may be at risk of loss or theft. Identity and endpoint security is critical to an organization because most business and organizations that help to transact with have elaborate security programs to protect your personal information. But this doesn't stop cybercriminals from trying to steal your data due to vulnerabilities in software these cyber criminals can infiltrate and steal not only your data.

But potentially thousands of other people's information to data breaches and data theft affects millions of people around the world and is on the rise. Many companies have suffered a massive data breach leading to layoffs, lawsuits, and fraud. Once these cybercriminals have your personal information they can completely drain your bank account funds.

A data breach can also result in identifying theft allowing someone else to use credit cards with your name potentially damage your credit history. In some cases, data breaches can results in blackmail, if the victim is a member of a questionable site or has the information they don't want to be made. Public individual users may be targeted with specifically designed malware that can delete or steal information off of a personal computer while data breaches can severely impact individuals business and government organizations are usually at a larger risk.

Even employees can steal and sell personal information to third parties who use it for criminal purposes protect yourself against data breaches by changing your passwords often and using a password manager that generate secure passwords like Kaspersky Password Manager. Ensure that any sensitive information that is kept in the cloud is well protected and encrypted with the latest security software. Finally, make regular backups of important data on a separate system such as an external hard drive or cloud to minimize the risk of losing vital information if a data breach does occur.

The top 10 data breaches reported are

1.   A Korean credit bureau reported in 2014 – An employee of Asian credit institution pulled one of the largest cases of identity theft in history for over a year and a half a hacker secretly copied personal data from over 20 million people which are nearly 40% of the country's entire population

2.   United States Office of Personnel Management – More than 22 million current and former federal employees records were stolen during 2015 breach which experts believe was carried out by hackers connected to the Chinese government. This breach was undetected for nearly a year. The hackers gained access to the federal network by using contractor stolen credentials. They then escalated their privileges and then planted a malware backdoor.

3.   Ashley Madison, the most sensational stated that this dating site for extramarital affairs had the records of 37 million customers stolen by the hacking group the impact team who demanded the shutdown of Ashley madison.com. The high profile leak of this sensitive data led to public embarrassment and in two cases possible suicides.

4.   Home depot malware installed in cash registers across 2,200 North American stores of this home improvement company siphon credit card over 256 million customers. The September 2014 attack is believed to have been perpetrated

by the same group of Russian and Ukrainian hackers responsible for the data breaches of Target and PF changes.

5. The second largest health insurance in the United States was hacked in February of 2015 with personal information from as many as 80 million customers were compromised. Investigators believe hackers gained access to Anthems network via a watering hole attack in 2015 that obtained an administrators login credentials which were undetected for almost a year.

6. The personal information from TJX companies about 94 million shoppers was lost in the largest breach in the history of retail when hackers infiltrated the parent company of Marshalls t.j.maxx and home goods.

7. PlayStation network parent company Sony was the unfortunate target of three separate hacks in three years which saw more than 23,000 Sony online entertainment users credit card info stolen in 2011 and the embarrassing hijacking of sensitive email scripts and social security numbers from their TV division. But a hack to their video game platform resulted in the breach of over 77 million user accounts.

8. Target over 70 million credit and debit cards were stolen from this popular retailer after a high profile hack in December of 2013. Investigators believe the data was obtained from illegal software installed on physical readers at Target stores.

9. Heartland payment systems in 2009, new jersey based payment processing company fell victim to the largest credit card scam in American history over a hundred and thirty million credit and debit card numbers were siphoned via Plantin malware. Heartland paid over a hundred million to credit card companies to settle claims while Albert Gonzalez was sentenced to 20 years for orchestrating the hack.

10. eBay in early 2014, the personal information of 145 million customers were compromised when hackers used login credentials from a small number of employees they accessed a database containing names, addresses, birthdays, phone numbers and passwords.

- **Malware/Spyware:** Malware is a malicious code designed to function in ways that mistreat or harm the user. An app running slowly, homepage changes or redirects you to other web pages are all warning signs that the computer might be infected by malware. Some of the highly reported malicious software are viruses, worms, spyware, Trojans, Browser hijacking, adware, Ransomware etc.
  - A virus is a program that is created to damage the system.
  - Worms infect computers via a network and slow down the system tremendously.

- ○ Spyware is a program that collects information from the victim's computer without the victim's knowledge
- ○ Trojan horse allows the other malware into the victim's computer
- ○ Browser hijacking is a modification of a web browser setting which may replace the existing home page, error page or search page on its own.
- ○ Adware is software that creates pop-up advertisements on the user's screen without proper permission.
- ○ Ransomware is a malicious code that blocks access to a victim. It demands some amount to be paid to regain the access.

To keep your system safe, you have to read messages and warning messages carefully before clicking on them. Other than these, the highly reported attack includes E-Mail Account Compromise, Denial of Service and so on.

ATM Skimming

Automatic Teller Machines are believed to be foolproof, high security and adopt the latest technology. Not only ATMs are vulnerable to hacking, but they can also be physically modified with minimal effort in a manner that can be difficult for the customer to detect. The way skimming works is the attackers place a card scanner on top of the little slot provided for the customer to enter their payment card. These skimmers allow the cards to pass the ray through them and steal numerous data during a legitimate transaction. This is not known to the victims until they come across their bank statement which may be received after a month or so. These skimmers are available in the black market which is designed similar to titled international banks ATM card swiping slots. To access a bank account, one need the account number and 4-digit PIN number, the frauds fix small cameras on the ATM to capture data entered by the victim. Some scammers even use a number pad which is overlaid on the existing number pad on the ATM. Most recent skimmers use GSM/Bluetooth to transmit the stolen information wirelessly making it simple for the scammers. To keep your data safe, check the following areas for any suspicious tampering:

- Light diffuser area
- Speaker area
- ATM side fascia
- Card reader entry slot
- ATM keyboard area

Wire Fraud

Wire fraud is a misconduct in which an individual creates a scheme to deceive or obtain incorrect illustration or assurances. This illegal activity is carried out through electronic communications or a regional communications capability. Two of the broadest federal criminal statutes are to the mail fraud and wire fraud. Any fraudulent activity that uses the US mail or wires will be converted into a crime. It's almost impossible in today's day and age to engage in any kind of activity without using the mails or the wires. Internet cyber thieves gained access to the company's email and bank accounts using keylogging malware. They monitor these accounts until they were able to mimic the owner and authorized an employee to transfer funds into a fraudulent bank account costing billed for them over seven hundred and fifty thousand dollars. To prevent a similar attack on your business follows these steps:

- Never provide confidential information in an email
- Require in-person or phone authorization for wire transfers
- mandate multiple sign-off policies on transactions
- Consider a social engineering test to identify weaknesses and
- Train employees to stay alert for any red flags that set off warning bells so they know to verify authenticity before they click send.

Internet Piracy and File Sharing

Peer to Peer file sharing technology is changing our society. The origin of peer to peer systems date back to the late 90s when the revolutionary Napster arrived with the original file-swapping service. The new program received tons of crust and sparked a debate that had never existed. Movies, computer software, and music are all different forms of intellectual property/products of human intelligence. While using file-sharing services, the web users can find and download files from hard drives of other person's computers. File sharing is often carried out through peer to peer networks or server-based networks. File sharing and movie and/or music partisan nowadays we're so accustomed to living on the internet. Most of the actions we carry out whether for story workshop in entertainment or other activities depend on it since they are done online.

However, despite the success we get from it we never said they will commit the crime of piracy. We access documents that don't belong to us with online files for example music. The media entertainers tend to open the file because it became their property so they use it for their income without giving credit to the original author because they think that the client who requires it is not willing to pay the amount which is requested. So we need to consider some of the disadvantages we face because Isis has a positive side for those who practice it and also a negative side.

The computer files could end up in the wrong hands when an unethical or non-professional user installs the p2p file-swapping program on their computer and they don't know how to really set up the access rights properly. They may be sharing all of their personal identifying information without their knowledge. In 2007, Mr. Robert Siciliano, Boston computer expert could explore personal information using BearShare (Musiclab, B, 2006) by using keywords like passwords, taxes, credit cards etc within five minutes. Robert is able to locate thousands of sensitive information files immediately available for download. He was able to collect Credit card information including expiration dates, online passwords, and secure bank rounding numbers to liquidate a victims bank account.

Data Diddling

The unauthorized modification of data before or during their input to a computer system is called Data diddling also called false data entry. It is the technique of modifying data for fun and profit (Gunjan, V. K., Kumar, A., & Avdhanam, S., 2013). Examples are forging, altering documents or counterfeiting documents like modifying grades, changing credit rating, altering security clearance information etc. When an offender modifies documents stored in digital form, the offense committed may be fake. In this case, computers are the objective of illegal activity; it can also be used as tools to commit forgery.

A new generation of falsified modification or forging arose when electronic color laser photocopiers came to the market. These devices are highly capable of high-resolution photocopying; changing the documents, and even for making fabricated documents without the advantage of an original, and they can produce high-quality documents which are indistinguishable from the original documents other than experts. These schemes need very little knowledge about the computer to execute. Forged documents, invoices and stationery can be produced. Such forgeries are difficult to detect by the normal person.

Hacking

Hacking is gaining access or gathering information for an unauthorized source of information by an unauthenticated skilled person called hackers. At the beginning of digital age, hackers were nerds who just wanted to experiment with the emerging technologies. Steve Wozniak was one such hacker who then went on to co-found Apple computer. The era of playful innocence ended soon after computers and networks became more commonplace. Now the individual hackers are classified based on their intentions namely white hat, black hat, and grey hat.

- White hat hackers are security researchers and penetration tester. These security professionals are often paid by the company whose task is to hack with permission and identify vulnerabilities in the system. Some white hat hackers reported massive security flaw for e.g. Dan Kamisky discovered a flaw in DNS that could have crippled huge parts of the Internet (Hacking I., 1983).
- Grey hat hackers, don't have malicious intentions. They act without the permission of their targets. How they handle the data acquired depends upon their own moral code. Grey hat hacking incidents have helped the FBI access data which will not be possible otherwise.
- Black hat hackers are those who hack without permission of their targets and they do it for their own benefits. They do know that their act is against the law and that their profit will be at someone else's expense.

There are other categories of hackers like hackavist whose actions inspire impassioned arguments or government spy agencies includes the National Security Agency(NSA). Some black hats have even had their talents recognized by major IT and private security firms who have ended up offering them jobs as long as the hacker trades in his or her black hat for a white hat. Now a day there are varieties of ways in getting into consulting rather than committing cybercrimes. Different types of hacking are Email hacking. Computer hacking, Server hacking, Web application hacking and so on.

Cyberbullying and Cyberstalking

Cyberbullying is any kind of aggressive, intentional act that is being carried out by a group or individual on an individual who is unable to defend himself. The attackers use electronic forms of contact, repeatedly and overtime against a victim. Social websites and forums are generally the most common medium for these attacks. It can arise through chats, email, pictures, videos and so on. The offender's intention is to

- Harass the victim by repeatedly sending offensive messages and threats,
- Denigrate the victim through spreading rumors, posting gossips or false information to damage their reputation or disrupt their friendship or relationships,
- The attacker impersonates as the victim and can post material that can damage that person's reputation.

- Outing /Trickering is the act of sharing someone's secrets and intimate private information. This information can be potentially embarrassing to the victim. The attacker can even talk the victim into sharing his private information and then leaking them.
- Intentionally Excluding/ Isolating someone from an online group

A study reports that girls were more likely to be victims of verbal or relational assaults, while boys were more likely to be physically bullied. As the kids become bigger this old-school bullying changes to cyberbullying (Smith, P. K., Mahdavi, J., & Carvalho, 2003). Research says that one in four teens will be cyberbullied. Due to teens carrying smartphones with them all the time, cyberbullying is on the rise. The long-term effects of cyberbullying have not been studied yet.

A report released by the Boston Children's Hospital says that kids who were victims of bullying at any stage of their life will experience the harmful effects forever. It might be in the form of mental disorders, low self-worth, depression, poor social life etc. Another report says that victims developed higher levels of C-reactive protein, a biomarker which has been linked to higher cardiovascular risks. The case with cyberbullying is much more serious than normal old school bullying, as teenagers have more difficulty processing and dealing with cyberbullying than classic bullying simply because online is more solitary. The victim is on his own and friends will not come to help.

Cyberbullying not only affects kids. Even climate scientists, weathermen get a lot of hate emails and intimidating letters every time they publish any results. The journalist also experience bullying on a regular basis,

Cyberstalking affects victims the same way as cyberbullying but most of the time it doesn't end with as extreme cases as cyberbullying. To protect a victim from cyberbullying and Cyberstalking

- Victims should always know that bullying is nothing to be ashamed of
- Try to ignore minor teasing and name calling if you can avoid it
- Keep a record of all the messages sent so that way it's easier to verify what went on and who the bully was.
- Reach out always to a teacher, friend or a trusted adult so that they can help.

Cyber Defamation

Cyber defamation is the act of publishing or broadcasting a false statement of fact that seriously harms someone's reputation (Wood L. A., 2001). Applies to printed statements and spoken statements, both online as well as offline. Online defamation is also called as slander or libel. An example of online defamation is, an offender posted a tweet saying Professor Samuel stole a College bus and used it for a family vacation this summer. The offender may be right or wrong; if right then they may be probably seriously harmed and defamed Professor Samuel's reputation. But Professor Samuel must show five things before he successfully sues for defamation.

1.   The victim must submit a proof of the published defamatory statement. The broadcasted or published statement must occur in online, newspaper, websites, blogs, tweets, Yelp reviews, YouTube videos and elsewhere considered to be the common sources of defamation.
2.   In addition to submission of proof, the person suing must also prove that he or she has been individually identified
3.   Evidence produced must be sufficient; reliable, trustworthy and unbiased.
4.   Suing person must show that the defamatory statement is an assertion of fact an opinion if a statement contains the only opinion it cannot be defamatory
5.   First amendment requires that in order for defendants to be held for defamation, the person suing must show at a minimum that the reporter/editor acted unreasonably.

Public officials or figures must prove that the person who claims he has been defamed may even have to show that defendants knew what they said was false or that they acted with reckless disregard for the truth.

Cyber Terrorism

When a computer is used to instill fear and disruption in the minds of individuals it is called Cyber terrorism. Some cyber terrorists spread computer viruses, and other often threatens people electronically (Lewis, J. A., 2002). The various types of cyber terrorism include Information theft, Credit Card Number Theft, Electronic Cash and Hacking. While thinking about the word cyber terrorism, normally the thoughts of terrorist attacks, explosions or some types of physical activities that causes the death of innocent people to strike a stunning blow. On the contrary Cyber terrorism is used to gain access to confidential data or financial information. Cyber terrorism is an act of sabotage which can bring a loss of critical infrastructure. Computers are used for storing and processing information which is manipulated to cause the attacks by the attackers. Because it is cheap, difficult to track and can affect a large number of people from anywhere in the world.

There are numerous ways hackers can get into a system as discussed in the previous section like a virus, Trojan horse, email etc.,

Direct Impact of Terrorism

- The decline in sales
- Slow networks and irregular access for users
- The cost associated with recovery
- Increase in the insurance premium due to the lawsuit
- Theft of intellectual property
- Nonavailability of communications during emergency

The Indirect Impact of Terrorism

- Loss of trust and integrity in the financial systems, government, and computer industry
- Spoilt relationships globally
- Anxious business partner relationships internationally as well as domestically.

The Solution to Cyber Terrorism

- Identify and take legal action against the Perpetrators
- Always ensure that the best security practices like firewall, browser safety are followed.
- Be Proactive using encryption, Pop up blocker
- Deploy vital security applications
- Stricter cyber laws
- Increase security awareness
- Encourage research and development
- Establish business stability and disaster recovery

CYBER CRIME: ONE OF THE BIGGEST THREATS TO GLOBAL SECURITY

Cybersecurity matters are of the essence as cybercrime is borderless and has targeted not only individuals but companies, industries, and government. Cybercrime is one of the biggest threats to global security. Global State of Information Security Survey 2017 reports that organizations worldwide are working to develop digital infrastructure to manage these threats. 59% of companies worldwide say they have to increase spending on Cybersecurity as their business have been digitalized. Russian companies are lagging because only 48% of the companies have ramped up their cyber protection.

The Internet of things has an impact on the cybersecurity landscape. Just less than half of companies worldwide say they will invest in a security strategy dedicated to the Internet of Things this year. But some of the strategies start at ground level with company workers. 56% of the companies worldwide currently require their employees to complete privacy training and assessment where Russian businesses are closely in line with that number. When a company uses cybersecurity to protect itself from hackers, it not only gives the company a competitive advantage but also helps build brand trust. But even with an increase in preventive measures, cybercrime remains a hazard. Last year five industries worldwide including telecoms and media reported there is an increase in information security incidents despite their continuous investments in security. As cybersecurity and privacy practices evolve in line with technological advances, what can be done in order to address cyber threats around the world?

Cyber Crime Growing Global Threat

With each click of a mouse credit card and identity theft to child pornography is increasing exponentially. Criminals are always on the lookout for new ways to victimize millions of people. Once such notable case is that of Jeremiah Mondello from Oregon. He pleaded guilty to selling counterfeit computer software of legitimate programs authorities say he stole financial information from unsuspecting neighbors and used it to set up fraudulent accounts to sell the software earning more than four hundred thousand dollars for himself when we confronted him/his response was how did you catch me how did you figure it out. Senior agent Michael goldfrey is with a cybercrime center of the US immigration and customs Enforcement Agency says Mondello tapped into the signal coming from a neighbor's wireless internet router conducted electronic surveillance at the scene that identified the suspect is being located at the residence. The unsecured access point he was connecting to be located across the street at a neighbor's residence. The investigation actually identified other residences with unsecured wireless access points a wireless router with encryption disabled that he was connecting to throughout the neighborhood. Godfrey says that the Internet has given the criminals the speed and ease to create an international border free crime zone. This is especially useful in trading stolen financial and personal information because this information is very valuable. It only lasts for a short period of time before the victims either cancel their accounts, changes their passwords you know or close their credit card numbers once they realize that they have been a victim and so this information is valuable to these criminal organizations and its transmitted around the world within minutes if not hours.

Investigators say that if people are aware of the threats lurking and if they would apply common sense while using the Internet many online crimes can be prevented.

Captain Tim Evans of the Virginia State Police is part of a task force that works on preventing child sexual exploitation online if an individual doesn't know the person in their real life that their friends down the street or another family member or someone that they specifically know then they should respond to him. He or She couldn't strike up conversations or strike up internet relationships law enforcement agencies have benefited from advances in technology as they fight cybercrime. Computer software giant Microsoft has provided some agencies with a USB device that helps extract evidence from a computer but both captain Evans and Special Agent Godfrey say criminals constantly adapt their techniques and those folks who are out on the internet and some of them are technically adaptive. All they need is to know what they want so that they will pursue the technological challenges in order to circumvent the law enforcement efforts. The biggest threat the young kids in today's generation are much smarter than who have been working in this technological field. Because they could sit and spend a lot of time to learn this stuff to write viruses and spread through peer to peer programs. Godfrey and Evans say that cybercrime needs more resources as the internet grows and changes and both acknowledge the battle is as infinite as the digital world.

In 1994, a group of criminals headed by a brilliant programmer from St. Petersburg, Russia hacked into the network of a major US bank and stole almost $400,000. Unlike a typical bank robbery, these guys did not use masks nor gun. They were not even in the same place as the bank. This robbery was through the use of technology. Late in July of 1994, several banks started noticing that money that added up to $400,000 was missing. They filed a complaint with the FBI immediately. The criminals, in this case, had targeted the firm's cash management system. This system allowed the clients to move their funds into other bank accounts. The hackers used this loophole to hack the telecommunication network and compromise the client's user ids and passwords.

Cyber Crime in India

No one is safe from cyber-crime. The case of the famous Bollywood actor Sharukh Khan is an example of how hackers can dupe even very well informed and powerful personalities. Three individuals were detained by the Giridih district police on account of cyber-crime charges. The criminals Bajrangi Kumar Mandal and Ajay Kumar Mandal belonged to a small village in Giridih. They had allegedly made many fraudulent calls to bank account holders, in this case, Mr. Khan, and have looted their hard earned money from their bank accounts. Mr. Khan had lost more than 75 lakhs. The police confiscated seven mobile phones which gave critical information regarding the transactions.

A constable serving at the Oshiwara police station lost 1 lakh rupees of his hard earned money. He was a victim of cyber-crime. Constable Gokul Devare lost the amount in 10 fraudulent transactions. He started receiving messages from the bank about the transactions which he doesn't know about. Before Mr. Gokul could react in a matter of minutes almost one lakh rupees was deducted from his bank account. He has filed a complaint with the local police. These two cases in India show that hackers do not distinguish between rich or poor, educated or uneducated etc.

Case Study: Handling Child Pornography - India vs. the United States

The kidnap and a missing case of a 10-year-old boy from Brentwood, Maryland in 1993 unveiled the more horrific trend of sexual exploitation of children via computers. After receiving the complaint about the boy's disappearance, the FBI agents and Maryland police personnel went door to door enquiring the neighbors. They found two suspicious men who had been befriending the boys in the neighborhood, giving them gifts and even taking them out on vacations. The FBI then discovered that these two suspects were paedophiles and have been sexually abusing the boys for many years. They have also used the Internet to share obscene pictures of boys to other paedophiles. They were sharing child pornography with other paedophiles. Although they did not have enough evidence to link the disappearance of the boy with these two criminals, they were able to uncover the bigger network that targeted children.

The CBI took serious action and have ordered a worldwide inquiry in a child pornography case here in India. They have approached nearly 40 countries for the details of mobile phone owners who had indulged in sharing child pornography in a WhatsApp group. They had illicitly shared images and videos which are inappropriate and harmful. It was shocking for the agency who had approached the countries through Interpol to discover that the child pornography group consisted of 234 members. It had 66 Indians, 56 Pakistani, 29 US nationals and the remaining were from 37 other countries.

On February 22nd, 2018 the CBI claimed that they have busted the child pornography racket and its an alleged leader. The criminal Nikhil Verma from Uttar Pradesh was interrogated regarding the case and uncovered some crucial details. They discovered that the WhatsApp group called "KidsXXX" had 119 members not only from India, Pakistan, and the US but also from China, Sri Lanka, Mexico, New Zealand, Kenya, Brazil, Afghanistan, and Nigeria. They confiscated laptops, mobile phones and hard discs from the criminals. The Supreme Court of India on June 26th, 2018 made a strong judgment against the Internet giants like Google, Facebook, Yahoo, Microsoft, and instant messaging application WhatsApp, for disregarding Supreme Court's order to provide details of the complaints they have received in

India regarding online child pornography. It lashed out on them on their subsequent failure to disclose steps taken to control the circulation of child pornography on their platforms, the Supreme Court has imposed a fine of INR 100,000 (USD 1491 approx.) on each company. This all began with a complaint (PIL) sent on January 2015. Hyderabad based NGO Prajwala stated that "videos of sexual violence were being circulated in abundance via internet and WhatsApp", along with two rape videos on YouTube via a pen-drive.

Based on the NGO's letter the idea of maintaining a national sex offenders' register was initiated which will contain details of persons convicted for offenses like eve-teasing, stalking, molestation and other sexual assaults. The NGO had also suggested that the Ministry of Home Affairs (MHA) should have a tie-up with YouTube and WhatsApp to ensure that such offensive videos are not uploaded, and the culprits punished.

NEXT GENERATION OF DEFENCE

In 1995, the Secret Service formed the New York Electronic Crimes Task Force (ECTF). USA Patriot Act in 2001 mandated that the established task force should work nationwide to prevent, detect and deter the electronic crimes including terrorist attacks against critical infrastructure and financial payment systems. Similarly, European Electronic Crime Task Force was formulated by an agreement in 2009 along with US ECTF. As discussed earlier, Data breach at TARGET occurred during the holiday season where hackers stole 10 million and above data of the shoppers. A report says that a 46% drop in the profit for TARGET when compared to the previous year. The Federal Bureau of Investigation (FBI) is also fighting against the hackers' activities but it is understaffed justice program and watchdog says that the bureau is finding and hiring enough qualified personnel.

REFERENCES

Gunjan, V. K., Kumar, A., & Avdhanam, S. (2013, September). A survey of cybercrime in India. In *Advanced Computing Technologies (ICACT), 2013 15th International Conference on* (pp. 1-6). IEEE.

Hacking, I. (1983). *Representing and intervening* (Vol. 279). Cambridge, UK: Cambridge University Press. doi:10.1017/CBO9780511814563

Lewis, J. A. (2002). *Assessing the risks of cyber terrorism, cyber war and other cyber threats*. Washington, DC: Center for Strategic & International Studies.

Musiclab, B. (2006). *P2P Application.* Retrieved from http://www. bearshare. com

Smith, P. K., Mahdavi, J., Carvalho, M., Fisher, S., Russell, S., & Tippett, N. (2008). Cyberbullying: Its nature and impact in secondary school pupils. *Journal of Child Psychology and Psychiatry, and Allied Disciplines, 49*(4), 376–385. doi:10.1111/j.1469-7610.2007.01846.x PMID:18363945

Wood, L. A. (2001). Cyber-Defamation and the Single Publication Rule. *BUL Rev., 81*, 895.

Chapter 4
Smart Video Surveillance Systems and Identification of Human Behavior Analysis

M. Sivabalakrishnan
VIT Chennai, India

R. Menaka
VIT Chennai, India

S. Jeeva
VIT Chennai, India

ABSTRACT

Smart surveillance cameras are placed in many places such as bank, hospital, toll gates, airports, etc. To take advantage of the video in real time, a human must monitor the system continuously in order to alert security officers if there is an emergency. Besides, for event detection a person can observe four cameras with good accuracy at a time. Therefore, this requires expensive human resources for real-time video surveillance using current technology. The framework of ATM video surveillance system encompassing various factors, such as image acquisition, background estimation, background subtraction, store, and further process like segmentation, people counting, and tracking are done in cloud environment briefly discussed in this chapter.

DOI: 10.4018/978-1-5225-8241-0.ch004

INTRODUCTION

Pedestrian detection is a vital and important task in several smart video surveillance systems. It offers the essential evidence for the semantic understanding of the video footages for video content analysis. It is a new technology for analyzing the video which includes video analytics, text analytics, and audio analytics. From this video, analytics has more challenging and gives a better understanding of the semantics of the video. Video Analytics utilizes numerical calculations to the screen, break down and oversee huge volumes of video. It carefully investigates video inputs; changing them into clever information which helps in making choices.

Video analytics applications can keep running at the inside (on servers or DVRs at the focal observing station), at the 'edge' (incorporated with cameras) or as a mix of both. The 'edge' arrangements are perfect to find live investigation. Focal continuous preparing can come up short on steam in view of the no. of cameras in the system, preparing power and the system data transmission; while in the 'edge' arrangement, each camera has committed handling. Clients with constrained transmission capacity on their systems can settle on an investigation arrangement at the 'edge', so just data on suspicious episodes gets sent through the system; and thus, doesn't go through system transfer speed.

Some run of the mill utilization of Video Analytics in security and surveillance includes, Security Access Point Monitoring, Intrusion Detection/Perimeter Protection, License Plate Recognition, Object Removal, Camera Tampering, Abandoned Object. Current video analytics solutions do work, however, in a compelled domain is a major limitation of video analytics.

Figure 1. Overview of background subtraction methods

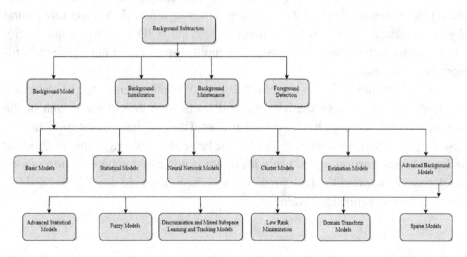

Various approaches have been proposed for object tracking. Modeling the object, the suitability of object representation for tracking, selection of features from images are the key requirements of an object tracking algorithms. The choice is made based on the environment in which tracking is performed and the use for which tracking is performed. The significance of object tracking is realized in various activities like motion-based recognition, automated surveillance, video indexing, traffic monitoring, medical applications, industrial applications etc.

Pedestrian detection can be implemented in video analytics techniques which can extract the people from the real-world environment with cost-effective and accurate. It has unlimited potential outcomes in any application territories. An obvious application in surveillance. The quantity of camera in broad daylight places, for example, railway station, shopping centers, and roads develop every year on account of security. And also used in cars, mobile device, flying drone. The immediate reaction in the reason for an occurrence anyway required the manual perception of the video stream which is as a rule financially infeasible. This implies these cameras are for the most part used to catch confirm material after the episode.

In real time pedestrian detection system comprise the techniques like part-based detection, motion-based detection, holistic detection, detection using multiple cameras, patch-based detection for extracting the people from a video scene. Each technique has their own limitations. Holistic detection method uses the mechanism of template matching with the trained model. The drawback is a new template or environment change not handled by this method. Part based detection method based on a collection of part models application detect the object. But the difficulty is detection parts from a video sequence more challenging. Patch based detection is similar to template match but here template is a small block to store in the codebook. Motion-based detection is used to detect foreground object from a video sequence. To perform this process lot of techniques are their background subtraction is one among them. The limitation is to get better background model to detect foreground object. Detection using multiple cameras has to get a 3D view of an object. So, it easily detects the object. But it required more storage and a high processor for processing the data.

Among these methods, motion-based detection is optimal and effective detection strategies used in most of the research and application development area of the current era. This technique has been used in most of the computer vision applications. Based on the technique, a lot of methods have been developed from that method the background subtraction can use in a lot of application in computer vision related development and provide a better result in less execution time. So, this method has used in many real-time applications.

Background subtraction is a technique used for detecting the foreground object. It ascertains the distinction between the present current and background picture. In the event that the distinction is not as much as the threshold then it is background or else the pixel is foreground. These techniques give the complete feature data for pedestrian detection and object recognition. But it has a major limitation or drawback in illumination changes in the dynamic scene. The technique can be updated by using the background model. In the background model, the system can be updated more frequently so illumination variation is captured. Now researchers are devoted to developing a robust background model to prevent falseness in motion detection caused by scene changes. To update the background model either pixel based, block based or region-based background model. The speed and accuracy of background subtraction depend on the result of the background model algorithms. If the frame has no moving object, then it is a pure background image. But in the real-world prediction of the pure background image is very hard. Still, it is a more tedious job for most of the applications to extract the pure background image.

Pixel-level calculations just utilize highlights assembled at each single pixel position. These techniques are quick, yet they don't utilize any sort of between pixel connections. There have been numerous recommendations in the writing for these sorts of techniques; among them, Gaussian Mixture Models (Stauffer and Grimson, 1999), Running Gaussian Averages (Wren et al., 1997), and Median Filtering (McFarlane and Schofield, 1995) have been of uncommon pertinence and have begun countless frameworks.

Block level-based methodologies separate a picture into squares and figure square related highlights to depict the background. Block level methodologies are generally heartier against commotion than pixel-level methodologies, then again, they give courser identifications of the foreground protests and are computationally costly. Some case of these sort of methodologies are the Local Binary Pattern surface (LBPS) created method in (Heikkilä et al., 2004) and the Normalized Vector Distance created a method in (Matsuyama et al., 2000).

Region level-based techniques isolate a picture into an arrangement of locales which are then named background or foreground. There is an extremely set number of absolute districts level-based techniques since finding significant locales in a picture by methods for spatial consistency criteria can be computationally costly. In this way, region level-based methodologies are generally joined with another sort of approach which is utilized to decide the areas took after by the locale characterization itself. However, there are a few cases of simply region level-based techniques as the one introduced in (Huang et al., 2004), which depends on the Partial Directed Hausdorff distance, and others only just projected in (Yu et al., 2007), where the author suggests displaying foreground and background region by techniques for Spatial-Color Gaussian Mixture Models.

Most of the computer vision application has foreground segmentation to be an initial stage. The arrangement of foreground area locales for human discovery is generally acquired, by computing the contrasts between the present frame and the background picture. On the off chance that the extra precision gave by square insightful methodologies isn't justified, pixel-wise methodologies are ideal. They produce more stable segmentations in the presence of the illumination condition. Investigating a video scene is troublesome on the grounds that numerous people are eloquent and distinctive lighting condition. The segmentation of the foreground object can be able to identify the difference of toys, photos, and humans. Most edge recognition techniques take a shot at the presumption that an edge happens where there is an intermittency in the sharp intensity gradient or intensity in the picture. The most significant attribute for people detection is edge detection which includes clear edges, discontinuation, and fake edges.

Background modeling is the most important process in computer vision applications. For detecting the foreground region, background model act as a vital role to identify the foreground mask. If the model is well formed, then the system gets clear foreground edges. The edge is clear then the algorithm can easily extract the feature point from an image and then classified. Pixel-wise background subtraction is most recommendable for foreground detection. The system based on background subtraction has high computation time but less execution time. Because nowadays the system processor has more core chips. If the data are independent, then it can be processed faster rather than dependent data of the block-based approach.

Robust and efficient object detection is currently unavailable. Researchers have proposed many techniques to address the problems of detecting and recognizing people in video data. The limitations that branch from using background subtraction algorithms are, binary detection and relatively simple features with these methods, the entirety of the person being detected needs to be visible.

FUNDAMENTAL ELEMENTS IN VIDEO TRACKING

The efficient and reliable automatic alarm system is useful for many ATM surveillance applications. There are basically two kinds of crimes possible in ATM sectors. The violent crime leaves the question to our lives such as killing and robbing, the little-deprecated nonviolent crime involves fraudulent actions of thieving ATM cards or passwords. Apart from the crime, sometimes human may be affected by abnormal behavior such as heart attack, fits and so forth. ATM Video monitoring systems present many challenging research issues in human abnormal behaviors detection approaches. The architecture for the surveillance-based video monitoring system is shown in figure 3.

Figure 2. Architecture flow diagram

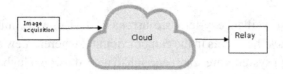

Figure 3. ATM video surveillance system architecture

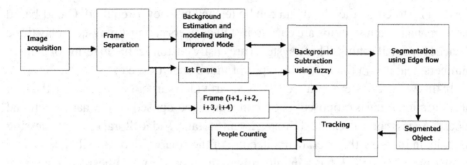

The rest of this Chapter is organized as follows: In Section 2.1, the way to perform image acquisition can be explained. In section 2.2, present the cloud architecture for surveillance. In section2.3, present the background estimation and subtraction from the video sequence. Edge detection for image segmentation is used to detect a region of interest to be discussed in Section 2.4. In Section 2.5, the author discussed here people counting and tracking the peoples. Experimental analysis and performance of each module can be discussed in section 3. Then, in Section 4, here conclusion along with how this framework work in ATM scenario has discussed.

Image Acquisition

A day and night camera is a security camera that can see the picture during the day hours when there is enough sunlight, and during the night in total darkness or minimum illumination. A day and night camera has special lenses that allow infrared emission produced by infrared LEDs and reflected from objects to go through and reach a CCD or CMOS chip inside the camera. A day and night camera can have infrared LEDs mounted on its housing or can accept the emission, produced by an infrared turret. Day and night cameras often have modifications in their digital signal processor (DSP) that compensates for the difference in illumination between day and night modes. HDR technology may also be used in more expensive models to compensate for the difference in illumination between shaded and lighted areas of surveillance.

Cloud Architecture

Traditional ATM surveillance systems are just analog devices with limited functionality to monitor and track the events in the camera vicinity, whereas new age cloud-based video management systems are smart enough to record, store, playback, and analyze the captured events in real-time and later. Cloud-based Video Surveillance systems are equipped with high-quality IP cameras, which provide a high-quality image with better fps for the system network. Storage is never an issue with these systems as all the data is stored on the cloud and can be fetched whenever required. Cloud-based video management systems are easy to install as users can just plug-and-play these devices for small setups. These systems are easily customizable in terms of camera numbers, features in the software, types of video analytics, etc.

In this work, a system architecture for smart video surveillance based on the idea of cloud computing is proposed. The architecture is composed of five main functional blocks: Access control, Context Broker, Event Storage, Video Storage, and Processing module, in Figure 1 the overall architecture of the smart video surveillance system is presented, each block has a unique role in the process of synthesizing data from real-time video stream into a human understandable format.

Access control: The role of this module is to establish a secure connection between the user and the system, while it prevents strangers from gaining access. In other words, here's where the system grants predefined specific permissions to each user according to its role. The implementation was made using the KeyRock GE, which is an identity manager, developed by FIWARE, that takes care of a variety of tasks related to cybersecurity, such as users' access to the network and services, private authentication from users to devices, user profile management, etc.

Context Broker: To implement this module we use the Orion Context Broker (OCB) from FIWARE. The OCR component is a context information manager; thus, it enables the creation, update and deletion of entities, it is also possible to register subscriptions in order for other applications (context consumers) to retrieve the latest version of all the variables that constitute an entity when some event occurs. This component can be seen as the moderator that carries out the communication process between the other modules, so that, once a module has defined the entities it will send and receive, the OCB takes care of the rest.

Event Storage: This module persists the data related to the context information, this information might be an alarm from the system or a simple notification. By saving this information, we can retrieve it for later analysis. In order to implement this block, we have used two GE, Cygnus and Cosmos. The first one is in charge of the data persistence, it handles the transfer of information from a given source to a third-party storage, serving as a connector, which is a great feature that increases the flexibility of the system and its scalability if required. While the second one provides a means for BigData analysis, so their users avoid the deployment of any kind of infrastructure.

Video Storage: This block is employed to store raw video data so that users have access to the video related to an event detected/stored according to the processing module.

Processing module: This block is conformed by two submodules: Kurento and Computer Vision Filters. The Kurento sub-module provides video streaming from IP cameras through the Kurento Media Server (KMS). The KMS is based on Media Elements (ME) and Media Pipelines. Media Elements are the modules that perform a specific action on a media stream by sending or receiving media from other elements, while a Media Pipeline is an arrangement of connected ME's, that can either be a linear structure (the output of every ME is connected to a single ME) or a non-linear one (the output of an ME might be connected to several ME's). The ME's used in the implemented processing module were four: WebRtcEndpoint, PlayerEndpoint, Vision Filters, and RecorderEndpoint. The Media Pipeline implemented for our architecture prototype, i.e., the logic arrangement in which we connected the four ME. In this pipeline, we get the video stream with the PlayerEndpoint through a rtsp URL, after that, the output goes to the computer vision filters, then, the output of this ME is sent to the WebRTCEndpoint, after that, the processed video is ready to be visualized. Additionally, by using the RecorderEndpoint we are able to store video from the PlayerEndpoint and thus, we will give the user the capability to play stored videos any time in the future.

Video management system (VMS) has required an Infrastructure as a Service (IaaS) which may be a fully federated architecture, billing management & tenant management – based on a private, public or hybrid cloud architecture.

VSaas service is liable to provide security to their cloud storage as huge video data of all of their clients is stored on the cloud. VMS service providers can ensure the

Figure 4. Cloud architecture

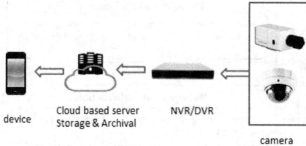

security of the data in the cloud by installing Checksum algorithms such as SHA1, CRC, MDS etc. These algorithms verify the data from time to time and notify the user in case of any attempt to tamper the same. Video Management System server connection can be secured using HTTPS communication protocol. The connection through HTTP is secured by transport layer security or SSL (Secured socket layer).

Estimation and Subtraction of the Background From Video Objects

The aim is to build a preliminary step for an automatic background estimation and subtraction, which accepts different types of image sequences. The block diagram of the author methodology is shown in Figure 5.

The author method consists of the following stages: Background estimation, and background subtraction.

Background Estimation

Tracking a moving object is a confronting task in the field of computer vision. The conventional approach evolves in finding the changes between the current and background image. People counting include background estimation, background subtraction, segmentation, and tracking. To estimate the background in real time is the first important step for many video surveillance applications. Background extraction surface has lots of challenges in handling low-resolution color, foreground, and complex background element details. Recently, researchers have come up classical algorithms for background Estimation, including algorithms with parameters of mean, median and mode, stable interval determinants and change detection. In addition, there are some highly complex methodologies are used in the background estimation algorithm, a few among them are a mixture of the Gaussians model,

Figure 5. Block diagram of background estimation and subtraction method

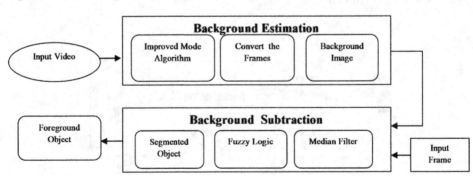

approximated median filtering, progressive background estimation method, and group-based histogram approaches /histogram but they are complex to implement in real time video surveillance. These complex methods deal only with non-moving pixels and also take a long time for creating the background model.

A unified approach commonly applicable to all types of images is applied to achieve handling of moving pixels in the frame. To design a common framework for background estimation from a sequence of images, an appropriate method should be chosen for calculating the pixels. Differentiating the background and foreground elements in any scene of a video is known to be a background estimation process. When the improved mode algorithms are applied to any scene on the video, two steps are to be performed. Step one is to convert the scene of the video into frames and step two is to perform background estimation automatically on the frames.

Current approaches for estimating the background consider the pixel to be a non- moving object. The motivation for the improved mode algorithm is to use the distinguishing pixel to separate the unchanging background and the moving object. The frame differentiation method categories the pixels into two: a static background and the moving objects, and then it calculates the unchanged background pixels through the mode algorithm.

In the Frame difference algorithm, whenever an object moves in the video, it's grey level will change significantly. $I_n(x, y)$ is the value of the pixel at (x, y) in frame $t=t_n$. Likewise, $I_{n+1}(x, y)$ is the value of the pixel at (x, y) in frame $t=t_{n+1}$. The simple difference image $D(x, y)$ between these two frames is:

$$D(x,y)=\mid I_{n+1}(x,y) - I_n(x,y)\mid \forall(x,y)\in[1,N]X[1,M] \tag{1}$$

Where N×M is the image frame dimension. Applying a suitable threshold T on $D(x, y)$ results in a binary image, which classifies all the pixels into two classes: static background and moving objects.

$$BW_n(x,y)= \{ \ 0=\text{unchanged background if } D(x,y)<T \tag{2}$$

1=moving object otherwise

After image binarization, applying the opening and closing of the mathematical morphology on $BW_n(x,y)$ results in a devoicing image and still saves the result in $BW_n(x,y)$.

$$B\_back_n(x,y) = \{ \ 1 \text{ if } BW_n(x,y)=0 \tag{3}$$

0 otherwise

B_back$_n$(x, y) is taken to mark the value of the pixel at (x, y) whether it is valid or not. If the value is available, then B_back$_n$(x, y) =1; this implies that the value of the pixel at (x, y) can be used in the calculation of the mode algorithm. Otherwise, B_back$_n$(x, y) should be equal to 0(a flag of unavailable value), and it should be avoided in the calculation.

The Mode Algorithm is used in 2-D image sequences. For every pixel at (x, y), the corresponding point values in the previous N frames are: $B_{t-N}(x,y), B_{t-N+1}(x,y), B_{t-N+2} \cdots$ $B_{t-2}(x,y), B_{t-1}(x,y)$ the sequence of values through the mode algorithm is calculated and the background value of the current image is taken as the result. The computing formula of the background value is:

$$B(x,y)=\text{mode}(I_{t-N}(x,y), I_{t-N+1}(x,y) \ldots I_{t-2}(x,y), I_{t-1}(x,y)) \tag{4}$$

To eliminate the deficiency of the mode algorithm, an improvement is done on it. This method can eliminate the deficiency in the mode method. The computing formula of the new method is:

$$BG(x,y)=\text{mode}(B_{t-N}(x,y)X \; \alpha_{i-N}, B_{t-N+1}(x,y) \; \alpha_{i-N+1}, \; B_{t-N+2}(x,y)X\alpha_{t-N+2} \ldots B_{t-2}(x,y)$$
$$x\alpha_{t-2}, B_{t-1}(x,y)x\alpha_{t-1}) \tag{5}$$

$\alpha_n = \{1$ if B_back$_n$(x,y)=1

0 otherwise

Where α_n determine the pixel (moving or background). The background can be estimated from this formula. And then proceed to the background subtraction model.

Background Subtraction

Background subtraction is a general term for a process which aims to separate foreground objects from a relatively stationary background. This process generates a foreground mask for each frame. The background image is subtracted from the current frame. Background view excludes the foreground; it is obvious that foreground objects are projected out after the comparison on the background image in the video. This approach is applied to each frame, to achieve the moving object tracking.

So, the author designed to estimate the background from a sequence of frames, and a pure background image is obtained. Using this background image, the current frame is subtracted to get a segmented foreground image. To design a common framework for background subtraction from current images, appropriate methods should be chosen for subtracting. The major contributions of the background estimation/subtraction method are as follows:

- Background estimation using the improved mode algorithm for getting a pure background.
- Background subtraction using a fuzzy based system for getting the foreground mask by separating the foreground from the background.

Detection is achieved in some approaches using only background subtraction, and by predicting the background intern using the next update interval. In these approaches, the background is not estimated but detected. Here, the background image was generated by the improved mode algorithm. In the standard background method, it is hard to determine whether a pixel is actually a moving object or not. Illumination variations occur in the scenes which generate a false classification of the image pixels. The fuzzy logic inference system acts multiple information sources together for decision- making. To determine the foreground object, the proposed binarization of the fuzzy background subtraction is done, after passing through the median filter. The method detects moving objects even if their gray level is similar to the background gray level. In addition, it can remove small noise because of the median filter.

In the adaptive background modeling and classification scheme, the image data in the past frames are used to compute the joint distribution of the images to build a background model. Based on the background model, the image block is classified as the foreground or the background. If a new object is introduced into the background or a background object is moved, before it is updated, this object will be classified as a foreground object and hence becomes part of the silhouette. To solve this problem, high-level knowledge about the object motion is utilized to guide the adaptive update of the background model.

The prime thing is the need for a methodology to detach the objects which are moving. Which is a challenging task due to the lack of automated reasoning on which is, and which is not, the target object, referenced from the video sequence?

Sophisticated object recognition and identification algorithms can be deployed. Which are computationally intensive and not robust, an effective yet simple algorithm for object segmentation is designed. Fuzzy logic inference used for object segmentation for this system. Suppose one is working on frame n and the object in frame $n - 1$ has been correctly extracted. Let the foreground image region in frame n be O_n, which might contain the human body and moving objects. The fuzzy logic inference system is based on the following observations:

1. If an image block in O_n belongs to the object, it should have a high possibility of finding a good match in O_{n-1}. The sum of absolute difference (SAD) is used to measure the "goodness" of matching.
2. If any of the blocks in its neighborhood have good matches in O_{n-1}, it is highly possible that this block also belongs to the object.
3. If this block is far from the predicted position of the object centroid, the possibility that this block belongs to the object is low.
4. SAD in motion matching. For each block in O_n, the best match in frame $n-1$ is found.

The SAD between this block and its best match form the first feature variable is the distance between the new block and the predicted object centroid.

This algorithm is based on image differencing techniques. It is mathematically represented using the following equation:

$$D(t) = \frac{1}{N} \sum \left| I(t_i) - I(t_j) \right| \tag{6}$$

where N is the number of pixels in the image used as a scaling factor, $I(t_i)$ is the image I at time i, $I(t_j)$ is the image I at time j and D(t) is the normalized SAD for that time.

In an ideal case, when there is no motion

$$I(t_i) = I(t_j) \tag{7}$$

and $D(t) = 0$. However, noise is always present in images and a better model of the images in the absence of motion will be

$I(t_i) = I(t_j) + n(p)$ (8) where n(p) is a noise signal.

The value D(t), which represents the normalized SAD is used as a reference for comparing the threshold value. To estimate the membership functions of these features, a set of membership functions are defined from these distribution data. A fuzzy inference system has the following parameters:

Rule 1: If SAD is medium, AND the Neighborhood is small, THEN the Object is low
Rule 2: If SAD is high, AND the Neighborhood is small, THEN the Object is high
Rule 3: If SAD is high AND the Neighborhood is high, THEN the Object is high

According to the above rules, if an object is recognized to be in the foreground, it uses the fuzzy inference system to detach the moving objects and will erode the object from misclassification. The proposed binarization of the fuzzy background subtraction, after performing morphological operations and neighborhood information, would find out the missing parts. The moving images are subjected to morphological operations. noise reduction is a trivial step considered like pre-processing of results. Median filter usage eliminates the effect of input noise with an extremely large value of magnitudes. The motion across the boundary is also removed. This removal is done to avoid ambiguity in recognizing the moving object.

At last, the targeted object is fitted in the block. If there is no moving object in the scene, then this object can be taken to be an optimal object for background subtraction. Let the pixel coordinates of the reference background image and the scene image at the frame, be gray levels.

Algorithm: Background Estimation/Subtraction

From the current image, the automatic background estimation starts by processing the estimated background as in the following steps: According to the discussion given above, the various steps are:

Step 1: A movie is taken and converted into a number of successive frames (images).

Step 2: Two frames are obtained at fixed intervals from the video and saved in $I_n(x, y)$ and $I_{n+1}(x, y)$. For the purpose of simple calculation and real-time speed, these two frames should be converted into grey images.

Step 3: Using $I_n(x, y)$ and $I_{n+1}(x, y)$ the frame difference image can be obtained as $D_n(x, y)$. And then, the opening and closing operation of the mathematical morphology on $D(x, y)$ is applied and the computed result using equation 2 is saved in $BW_n(x, y)$.

Step 4: According to the value of pixels in $BW_n(x, y)$, the pixels are classified into either background moving objects or unchanging objects. According to equation 3, make a flag as the pixel whether it is the moving objects or background. If the flag value is 1, it implies that the pixel belongs to a moving object and it's unavailable in mode calculation; otherwise its background is available. These values of the flag are saved in $B\_back_n(x, y)$.

Step 5: If n reaches the maximum set up, the procedure goes on to step 6; else the procedure should go to step 1.

Step 6: $B_n(x, y)$ should be calculated including the video and saved as $B(x, y, z)$, namely, the values of the background of all frames. Through the steps above, the background image can be estimated accurately. As a result of the pixels of moving objects being removed, even if the pixel background value just emerges once, it can be estimated accurately by the new method.

Step 7: The estimated background should be subtracted from the current image and the resulting image is filtered.

Step 8: Fuzzy based background subtraction is applied and the segmented foreground image is obtained from the input image.

Step 9: The resulting foreground image is compared with the ground truth image and the accuracy of the detected image using different metrics, is evaluated.

Step 10: The fuzzy based background subtraction method is compared with the other methods.

This algorithm was implemented in MATLAB and various metrics have been evaluated from the test results. These data set images have been gathered from the sites of several research groups.

- EC Funded CAVIAR Project, IST 2001
- For sequences belonging to Toyama et al. (1999), the ground truth is available as a binary detection mask for one reference frame
- http://perception.i2r.a-star.edu.sg/bk_model/bk_index.html

Edge Detection for Image Segmentation

Image segmentation is one of the widely studied problems in image processing and has found its application directly or indirectly in the task, such as object detection, object tracking and recognition, content-based image retrieval, and medical image analysis. The strength of many image processing and computer vision problems depends on the spotting of the meaningful edges. Edge detection refers to the process of identifying and locating sharp discontinuities in an image.

Most edge detection methods work on the assumption that an edge occurs where there is a discontinuity in the intensity function or a very steep intensity gradient in the image. The discontinuities are abrupt changes in pixel intensity, which characterize the boundaries of objects in a scene. In typical images, edges characterize the object boundaries and are therefore useful for segmentation, registration, and identification of objects in a scene. There are many techniques used for edge detection; some of them are Canny edge detection, Marr–Hildreth algorithm, Sobel Operator, Prewitt, LoG.

In this book, it is decided to apply the enhanced edge flow method. The major contributions of the improved edge flow vector detection systems are as follows:

- An effective segmentation technique based on an edge field computed directly from the images.

- The flow field can be computed from various image features, including color, texture and intensity edges.
- A new edge function that is more precise than the commonly used gradient magnitude, based on the scalar potential of the edge flow field.

EDGE FLOW

On the contrary, the detection and localization of edges (or more general sense for image boundaries) are computed indirectly. First, by identifying a flow direction at each pixel location that points to the closest boundary, followed by the detection of locations that encounter two opposite directions of the edge flow. Since any image attributes such as color, texture and their combination are useful to define the edge flow, this scheme serves as a general framework for shouldering different types of image information in boundary detection.

Enhanced Edge Flow Method

In this topic, the processing steps of the enhanced edge flow vector approach are presented. The algorithm consists of six stages of image acquisition: Gaussian Kernel Smoothing, Gabor filtering and Smoothing, Edge Flow vector, Edge Detection, and post-processing. Figure 6 shows a process flow of the human motion detection algorithm. In the detailed description of each stage is given below.

The problem of achieving a robust tracking is solved by designing a rule base, using the erroneous and sparse data from the image processing algorithms.

Image Acquisition and Frame separation

Image acquisition is to get the frames of the image which is taken by a camera or by the various cameras. Before the work starts, a video is subsampled into a sequence of images. Which is called frame separation and it is done by the frame grabber.

Gaussian Kernel Smoothing

For each data point in the time series, a kernel function is applied by some of the efficient smoothing algorithms. This process is called Kernel smoothing which will be categorized under weighted moving average class. In that time series, all the points are weighted, and they are used to compute the result of the kernel function. This function should have the following properties.

Figure 6. Block diagram of the enhanced edge flow method

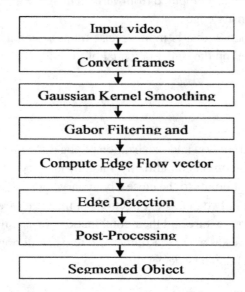

- The kernel functions are usually symmetric
- Kernel values should be non-negative integers
- These values are decreased from maximum to zeros

To find the object's nature or noise this might be observed by Gaussian probable form. Gaussian kernel smoothing technique is used often for image processing. This is used to remove the image noise that image is smoothened by a Gaussian filter like techniques.

Gabor Filtering and Smoothing

To find the illusory boundaries or to build n edge flow field Gabor filter approach is used. The complex Gabor filtered image can be written as

$$O(x,y)=Re(x,y)+Im(x,y) \tag{9}$$

Where $Re(x,y)$ and $Im(x,y)$ represent the real and imaginary parts of the Gabor filtered output, respectively. The phase of the filtered image can be expressed as

$$\phi(x,y)=atan[Im(x,y)/Re(x,y)] \tag{10}$$

The Gabor filter is basically a Gaussian (with variances sx and sy along x and y-axes respectively) modulated by a complex sinusoid (with center frequencies U and V along x and y-axes respectively) and described by the following equation:

1 -1 x ^ y ^

$$G(x,y) = \text{------------} * \exp\left(\left[\text{----}\{(\text{----}) \, 2+(\text{----}) \, 2\}+2*pi*i*(Ux+Vy)\right]\right) \tag{11}$$

2*pi*sx*sy 2 sx sy

Where

I : Input image

Sx & Sy: Variances along x and y-axes respectively

U & V : Centre frequencies along the x and y-axes respectively

G : is the output filtered image

Edge Flow Vector Method

To detect the boundary, combine the various edges energies and their probabilities to get a single edge to flow field.

Consider

$$E(s, \theta)=\sum\nolimits_{a\in A}E_a\left(s,\theta\right).w\left(a\right)\, and \sum\nolimits_{a\in A}W\left(a\right)=1 \tag{12}$$

$$P(s, \theta)=\sum\nolimits_{a\in A}P_a\left(s,\theta\right).w\left(a\right) \tag{13}$$

where $E_a(s, \theta)$. a $P_a(s, \theta)$ represent the energy and probability of the edge flow computed from the image attribute a, a. $\in$ {intensity/colour, texture, phase}. $w\left(a\right)$ is the weighting coefficient associated with the image attribute a or each of the RGB color band, the edge flow intensity is calculated by using the texture information is the combined color for boundary detection. Compute the flow direction also. Each location of the image contains, $\{[E(s, \theta), P(s, \theta), P(s, \theta+\pi)]|_{0\leq\theta<\pi\}}$. To maximize the sum of probabilities of the corresponding half plane, identify the continuous range of flow directions:

$$\Theta(s) = \arg\max_{\theta} \left\{ \sum_{\theta \leq \theta' < \theta + \pi} p\left(s, \theta'\right) \right\} \tag{14}$$

The edge flow vector is then defined to be the following vector sum:

$$\vec{F} \cdot \vec{F}\left(= \sum_{\Theta(s) \leq \theta < \Theta(s)+\pi} E(S, \theta) \cdot \exp\left(j^{\theta}\right)\right) \tag{15}$$

Where $\vec{F}(s)$ is a complex number with its magnitude representing the resulting edge energy, and the angle representing the flow direction.

The edge flow vector properties are given as follows:

- Points of the vectors are naturally towards the nearest edge.
- The magnitude of the vectors is small away from the edges and increases near the edges.
- The flow vectors from opposite directions cancel each other on the edges.

Identify the directional flow of each pixel location which points the closest boundary that is pursued by the location detection to concern the edge flow application direction.

At each location of the image, there are some direction changes in its attributes like texture, color and phase discontinuities which are to be identified and integrated for predictive coding model that is used by edge flow method.

Edge Detection

The development of optimal edge detectors has most emerging research for detecting an edge, which leads to the best trade-off between the localization performance and detection. An approach is to scheming such edge operator is to find the filter which can reduce the performance with a high opinion to the three divisions: good localization, unique response, and good detection to a single edge. On hand algorithms (Canny 1994) the first derivative of a Gaussian is approximated for the optimal detector. This filter is used to convolving the image; the edge detection is correspondent to discover and the appropriate direction for the maxima in the gradient magnitude of a Gaussian-smoothed image. Another important issue in edge detection is to Detecting and combining edges at many scales and multiple resolutions. (Witkin, 1983) initiated the scale-space technique which entails to generating coarser resolution images, and then Gaussian smoothing kernel for convolving the novel images.

Post-Processing

A number of image regions can be identified by connecting the disjoint boundaries until to get closed contours to obtain before that boundary detection can be recognized.

After that compute the edge flow of an image, the edge flow can be computed with help of boundary detection and repeat iteratively propagating method to find a frame where two conflicting directions of flows come across each other. At each position, the local edge flow is broadcasted to its neighbor in the direction of the flow, if they also have the same flow path. The steps are

1. Set n=0 and $\vec{F}_0(s) = \vec{F}(s)$

2. Set the initial Edge flow $\vec{F}_{n+1}(s)$ at time n+1 to zero

3. At each image location, identify the neighbor $s' = \left(x', y'\right)$ which is in the direction of the edge flow $\vec{F}_n(s)$

4. Propagate the edge flow if $\vec{F}_n(s').\vec{F}_n(s) > 0$: $\vec{F}_{n+1}(s') = \vec{F}_{n+1}(s') + \vec{F}_n(s)$ otherwise the edge flow stays at its original location $\vec{F}_{n+1}(s) = \vec{F}_{n+1}(s) + \vec{F}_n(s)$

5. If nothing has been changed, stop the iteration. Otherwise, set n=n+1 and go to step 2 and repeat the process.

Once the edge flow proliferation reaches a steady state, detect the image borders by recognizing the positions where the non-zero edge flows to be coming from two contrasting directions. Let the edge signals $V(xy)$ and H(xy) be the vertical and horizontal edge maps between the image pixels, and let

$$\vec{F} = h((x,y),v(x,y)) = (\text{re}(\vec{F}(s), Im(\vec{F} s))) \tag{16}$$

Then, the edge signals V(x,y) and H(x,y)will be turned on, is equivalent to, the two neighboring edge flows point at each other. Its energy is distinct to be the summation of the ledges of that two edge flows towards it before this edge signal is on. Summarizing:

- Turn on the edge V(x,y) if and only if H(x-1,y) >0 and H(x,y)< 0; then V(x,y)= H(x-1,y) –H(x,y) (17)
- Turn on the edge H(x,y) if and only if V(x,y-1)>0 and V(x,y)<0 then H(x,y)=V(x,y-1)-V(x,y) (18)

After detected the edge signals, Edge signals $V(x,y)$ and $H(x,y)$ can be identified by an average of the energy of connected edges to form boundaries.

A number of image regions can be identified by connecting the disjoint boundaries until to get closed contours to obtain before that boundary detection can be recognized. A half circle with its center located at the unconnected end of the contour is called a neighborhood. The basic approaches for linking the boundaries are recapitulated to pursuing.

- For each open contour, link a neighborhood search size comparative to the length of the contour.
- Within the half, the circle is identified by the nearest boundary element.
- If the boundary element is identified, then a smooth boundary segment gets to attach the unwrap contour to the nearest boundary element.
- Repeat this process few times (typically 2-3 times), till the contour is completely closed.

In the end, a region merging algorithm is used to merge similar regions, based on a measurement that evaluates the sizes of the regions, the percentage of the unique boundary between the two adjacent regions and the distances of region texture and color features. This algorithm sequentially reduces the total number of regions can be reduced by sequentially applying this algorithm at each time, by inspection if the user's ideal number has been drawn near.

Tracking and People Counting System

Moving object tracking is one of the difficult tasks in computer vision problems, such as human-computer interactions, visual surveillance etc. On especially in monitoring large scale environments such as security sensitive areas and the public has become an important task in video surveillance. An object of interest would be identified and then monitored or tracked kind of operations performed in this field of video surveillance.

A numerous method for tracking an object and to handle or overcome the problem in tracking such as occlusion (Bird et al., 2005), and noise in surveillance videos, but required the robust tracking method for an improvement. From the video, sequence frames are split for performing Tracking objects and it consists of two main steps: from each frame background object can be separated and find a relationship between objects in successive frames to trace them.

This chapter describes the novel and secure tracking framework for counting people for ATM surveillance. A novel human motion detection algorithm that identifies moving blob regions by using a fuzzy rule-based classification scheme, In addition, this chapter also discusses the integration of background estimation, subtraction and edge flow-based segmentation with this person counting framework, to build a complete people tracking system and also based on the people count relay unit arise the alarm.

Tracking and Counting System Architecture

This system consists of five stages; image acquisition, RGB to HSV conversion, BitXOR operation, preprocessing and blob identification. Figure 7 shows the proposed people counting algorithm and its process flow. The detailed description of each stage is given below.

Image Acquisition and Segmentation

In any motion-based vision application, as a common preliminary step is Image acquisition, image frames are obtained from stationary or multiple cameras, or moving the camera. Before the actual processing begins, the frame grabber is used to sample the image from the video at the certain frame rate.

Usually, a video sequence can be a low frame rate (< 10 *fps)* or *a* high frame rate (10-30*fps)* that can be maintained by the threshold. Based on the type of video system used, then only a suitable segmentation method can be implemented. Later than the image acquisition, Background subtraction for image segmentation can be performed, based on the frame rate of the video sequences.

Frame Segmentation

For high frame rate sequences, the RGB color model can be converted to HSV model then identify the moving object by subtraction of adjacent frame. Since variation is very small in consecutive frames for the change of motion. A fixed time interval technique is used to find a current frame and the next acquiring frame distance by $D(x,y,t)$, so frame rate can be reduced for background subtraction where the change is 1 *fps*. The normal calculation of the frame rate motion is bigger. The desired motion region from the stationary background can get from this method. Illumination changes, reflection, and noise like error may occur during the video acquisition process.

Figure 7. Tracking and counting system architecture

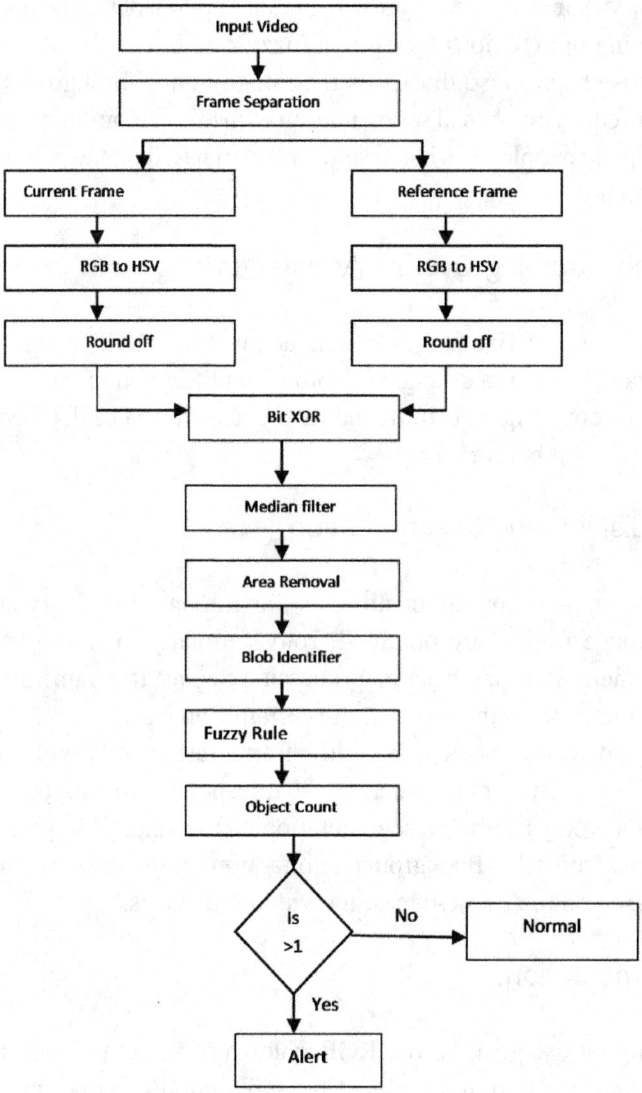

Preprocessing

After frame segmentation, perform the morphological operations for getting the complete contour of the object then blob Identification and prepare the blob identification for moving object.

Morphological Operations

To remove the noise in the image, the median filter can be used and is a nonlinear *digital filtering* technique. By using this noise reduction technique is used to improve the result and also typical pre-processing step. The result of input noise values with extremely large magnitudes can be eliminated by the median filter. The refresh rate of moving object in the video sequence can be high to eliminate the boundary of ambiguity regions of belonging to the possible moving region.

Fuzzy Classification

In the ultimate stage, the extracted major blob can be classified by using proposed fuzzy rule base classification. The candidate regions for uncertainty creates reasonable extrapolation of movements, and guess pattern of the model using a rule set, these problems are solved by using knowledge base. The regions with a bigger distance preferred by the rule and stop the tracking from finding near the head, avoid detection of the head.

At the time of tracking in the pointer section, due to imperfect tracking results; i.e., the illumination level in the observed environment changes or gets occluded or region disappears are leads to appear error. During tracking the model is updated to estimate value the movements to prevent data loss or occlusion, to decide the situation in the subsequent frame. If another application is the overhead tracking of individuals and groups by date of image processing as shown in figure 8. The rule-based approach describes or used to find motion detection, luminance-level segmentation, and blob analysis. The process is as follows: minimum of five frames used find motion and also to identify the argument for tracking at different luminance level. Hence objects can be tracked.

Figure 8. Silhouette of the user shown with search regions

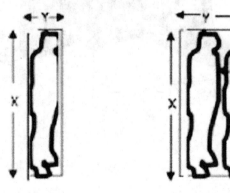

To preserve the object in frame *n* while detaching blocks are established by fuzzy logic inference that communicates to non-human artifacts. The proposed method for the bounding box of the human body in frame *n+1* from the statistics of the earlier frames is guessed. The proposed system is based on the following studies:

1.   The training of each and every silhouette is identified
2.   The bounding box is calculated for each and every individual.
3.   The person entering the focused screen is taken as object and proceeds with a unique identifying number until the object leaves the frame.
4.   Continuous monitoring of the width and height of the silhouette is done.
5.   Counting is done as to whether there is a new unique identifier number entering.
6.   Counting memory of the unique identifying number is resized and fuzzy is processed.
7.   Width & height are the inputs of the silhouette for the bounding boxes.

The 6 rules given below, are used in the fuzzy logic and are exemplified in Figure 8 and the set of membership functions for these rules are illustrated in figure 9 in a MATLAB implementation. The fuzzy rule is based on three input variables (*X*, *Y*, and Z) and one output variable Count.

Figure 9. Surface viewer of the fuzzy system

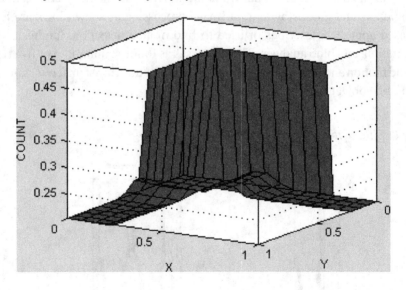

Figure 10. Membership functions of 6 rules of the fuzzy logic inference system

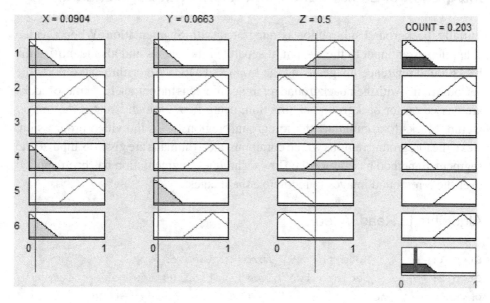

1. If (X is CONSTANT) and (Y is CONSTANT) and (Z is FALSE) then the (COUNT is ONE)
2. If (X is VARYING) and (Y is VARYING) and (Z is TRUE) then the (COUNT is TWO)
3. If (X is VARYING) and (Y is CONSTANT) and (Z is FALSE) then the (COUNT is ONE)
4. If (X is CONSTANT) and (Y is VARYING) and (Z is FALSE) then the (COUNT is ONE)
5. If (X is VARYING) and (Y is CONSTANT) and (Z is TRUE) then the (COUNT is TWO)
6. If (X is CONSTANT) and (Y is VARYING) and (Z is TRUE) then the (COUNT is TWO)

Where X = width, Y = height, Z = holes

CASE STUDY

This section deals with the integration of various factors, such as Background Subtraction, Segmentation, Tracking and counting system together, to produce a complete people counting system for videos.

Integration of Background Subtraction With Segmentation

Initially, background subtraction is integrated with Segmentation. When a video is applied as an input to the system, it separated the frames and also identifies the background reference image, using the Improved Mode Algorithm and reports the various frames with their background reference image as the output. Later these blocks are passed on for background subtraction, using fuzzy, which isolates the image/picture blocks to accumulate the foreground regions as of the video progression. Next, the foreground regions which communicate to humans are given as input to the segmented method based on edge flow techniques Segmentation has been applied over the foreground images to recognize the images.

Algorithm to Read Video

Step 1:   Read the AVI format video file.

Step 2:   Declare two global variables row and columns, which store the

          Width and Height values of video frames respectively.

Step 3:   for i = 1 to No of_Frames in steps of 1 with an interval of 4 frames

•   Read each frame of the video clip and store it.

•   Store the video frames into img_1d

•   Increment variable k which stores the total number of frames in img_1d.

        end for

Step 4:   for i = 1 to frame_cnt$k$ Convert images obtained in step 3 from RGB to gray format and store.

Automatic Background Extraction

A set of successive frames is a pre-condition for carrying out the background extraction process automatically. This process initially starts with two successive frames as already described in the algorithm. The output of the background extraction method is the background reference image.

Algorithm Background Subtraction Using Fuzzy

Step 1:   Read the input, background reference image, and ground truth image.

Step 2:   Convert the input, background reference RGB image to a Gray image.

Step 3:   Subtract the input, background reference image and store the result.

Step 4:   Apply the fuzzy rule.

Step5:   Subtracted image should be evaluated through fuzzy.

Step 6:   Apply median filter and store the result.

Step 7:   Stop.

Algorithm for Segmentation Using the Edge Flow Vector

Step 1:   Read the input image

Step 2:   compute the number of rows and columns using the size function

Step 3:   Remove the lonely Pixels from the input image

Step4:   Read the ground truth image

Step 5:   Find the number of connected objects in the input image

Step 6:   Measure the properties of the image regions (blob analysis)

Step 7:   Remove the unwanted area using the area properties.

Setp8:   Find the number of connected objects in the input image after the blob analysis.

Step 9:   Display the resulting image.

Step10:   Stop.

Integration of Background Subtraction With Segmentation and Tracking and Counting System

A complete people counting system has a tracking and counting system. This tracking and counting system are integrated with Background subtraction and Segmentation. In this integration, the segmented output will be the input of the people counting system. Then, the blobs are calculated, and the human emergence models in every frame are updated until they occlude each other or merge into a group. The performance of the people counting framework has been evaluated by integrating the background subtraction and segmentation results, which are shown in Figures 12.

Table 1 shows the number of objects in the video sequence in each frame. Figure 11 shows the graphical representation of the objects in the video sequence. Then implement the fuzzy-based rule for the occluded frame. Based on precise human body location prediction, the algorithm uses a huge temporal modernize window size unit in its frames for image blocks inside the bounding box, while using a relatively small size for those outside. The most common interaction patterns are observed in test cases that formerly led to tracking errors. The fuzzy-based system can resolve these cases, and continuously track the user's body. In comparison, it is evident that improved one's given a better result than the other methods. An increase in tracking ability was spotted after adaption using the fuzzy method, failure rate also improved than in conventional tracking. To make a solid comparison using numbers is an unclear way.

A repetitive target detection scheme and motion prediction technique can use propose an algorithm and their results are shown that do not rely on spatial immediacy. Figure 12 shows the people segmentation, tracking and counting results, and Figure 12(a) shows the Original frame. Figure 12 (b) our proposed extraction method can identify the background image. Figure 12 (c) shows the Ground truth. Figure 12(d) shows the fuzzy-based background subtraction. Figure 12(e) shows the Edge flow vector people segmentation Figure 12(f) gives the results for tracking with blobs. The people segmentation algorithm shows good performance. The fuzzy permutation of motion-based tracking has improved the tracking performance under different

Table 1. Number of people appearing in each frame

F1	F2	F3	F4	F5	F6	F7	F8	F9	F10	F11	F12	F13	F14	Total
1	2	0	2	1	0	2	0	2	2	1	3	2	2	20

Figure 11. Results of people appearing in each frame

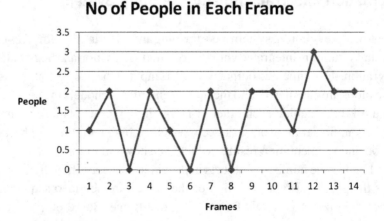

Figure 12. Open results and processing steps for background estimation, background subtraction, people segmentation, tracking, and counting. (a) Original frame (b) Background image generated by our proposed extraction method c) ground truth (d) Fuzzy based background subtraction. (e) Edge flow vector people segmentation (f) Tracked image with occlusion

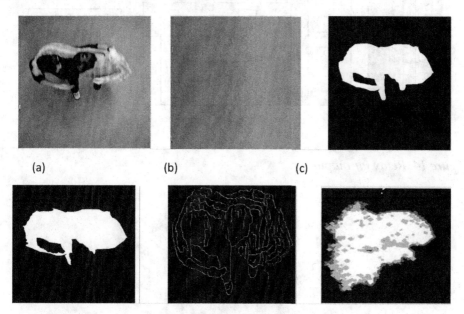

Table 2. Comparison of fuzzy people counting and other methods

	Ground Truth	Barandiaran et al (2008)	Antic et al(2009)	Proposed
In+Out	11+10	11+9	10+10	11+9
TP	21	19	20	20.5
FP+FN	0+0	1+2	0+1	1+1
Precision	1.00	0.95	1.00	1.00
Recall	1.00	0.90	0.95	0.97
F-Score	1.00	0.92	0.97	0.99

luminance. In complex luminance and environment with modeled backgrounds, our method allowed tracking where it was not possible before, as well as in critical first application cases.

A relay is an electrically operated *switch*. Many relays use an *electromagnet* to mechanically operate a switch, but other operating principles are also used, such as solid-state relays. Relays are used where it is necessary to control a circuit by

Figure 13. Comparison of the performance measures for the people counting system

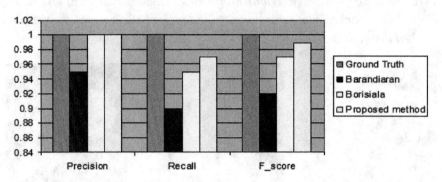

Figure 14. Relay for output

a separate low-power signal, or where several circuits must be controlled by one signal. The first relays were used in long distance *telegraph* circuits as amplifiers: they repeated the signal coming in from one circuit and re-transmitted it on another circuit. Relays were used extensively in telephone exchanges and early computers to perform logical operations.

In this study, the performance of people counting has been improved. Based on the people count the relay trigger the alarm. So, this framework can be used for real-time ATM video surveillance. On account of ATM has a lot of anomalies action to be performed in ATM centers, so this framework can be used to track and identify those anomalies things. The Way framework used to identify anomalies is as per the law in ATM center has to permit one person at a time if more than one person entered into the center means. It's against the law so framework identifies, track and raise the alarm to the administrator.

CONCLUSION

Video surveillance is getting more importance in various critical applications like Automatic monitoring of ATM Systems, Unmanned auditing activities, several security-based solutions and so forth. In the case of ATM Systems, by analyzing the video streams, we can determine the count of people inside the ATM facility at any time to track any abnormal events. Also, several types of research are currently carried out in video processing for crowd detection and tracking of abnormal events in the crowded places. Hence through automatic analysis of these video streams. In the future, we can anticipate solutions which would alarm the control person, in case of any abnormal events in the public places.

Also, in the course of recent decades, significant efforts have been made in video analysis prompting the improvement of numerous propelled innovations. In addition, the development in the Internet, online networking, and video capture devices, combined with the needs of security applications, has prompted the demand for storage of video streams. Inspection of such a huge volume of video streams is opening up new research issues, which will likely call for novel solution strategies. As opposed to completely self-ruling applications, the meeting of man and machine may be the future trend in many video processing solutions.

REFERENCES

Antic, B., Letic, D., Culibrk, D., & Crnojevic, V. (2009). K-means based segmentation for real-time zenithal people counting. *16th IEEE International Conference on Image Processing (ICIP)*. 10.1109/ICIP.2009.5414001

Barandiaran, J., Murguia, B., & Boto, F. (2008). Real-Time People Counting Using Multiple Lines. *Ninth International Workshop on Image Analysis for Multimedia Interactive Services*, 159-162. 10.1109/WIAMIS.2008.27

Bird, N., Masoud, O., Papanikolopoulos, N., & Isaacs, A. (2005). Detection of Loitering Individuals in Public Transportation Areas. *IEEE Transactions on Intelligent Transportation Systems*, 6(2), 167–177. doi:10.1109/TITS.2005.848370

Brown, L. M., Senior, A. W., Tian, Y., Connell, J., Hampapur, A., Shu, C., ... Lu, M. (2005). Performance Evaluation of Surveillance Systems under Varying Conditions. *Proc. IEEE PETS Workshop*, 1-8.

Canny, J. (1986). A Computational Approach to Edge Detection. *IEEE Transactions on Pattern Analysis and Machine Intelligence,* 679-698.

Graevenitz, G. (2007). Biometric authentication in relation to payment systems and ATMs. *DuD Datenschutz Und Datensicherheit*, 681-683.

Piccardi, M. (2004). Background subtraction techniques: A review. *IEEE International Conference on Systems, Man and Cybernetics (IEEE Cat. No.04CH37583)*.

Sivabalakrishnan, M., & Manjula, D. (2009). An Efficient Foreground Detection Algorithm for Visual Surveillance System. *International Journal of Computer Science and Network Security, 9*(5), 221–227.

Sivabalakrishnan, M., & Manjula, D. (2010). Adaptive Background subtraction in dynamic environments using fuzzy logic. *International Journal on Computer Science and Engineering, 2*(2), 270–273.

Sivabalakrishnan, M., & Manjula, D. (2010). Human Tracking Segmentation using color space conversion. *International Journal of Computer Science Issues, 7*(5), 285–289.

Sivabalakrishnan, M., & Manjula, D. (2010). RBF Approach to Background Modelling for Background subtraction in Video Objects. *International Journal of Computer Science and Research, 1*(1), 35–42.

Sivabalakrishnan, M., & Manjula, D. (2010). Fuzzy Rule-based Classification of Human Tracking and Segmentation using Color Space Conversion. *International Journal of Artificial Intelligence & Applications IJAIA, 1*(4), 70–80. doi:10.5121/ijaia.2010.1406

Sivabalakrishnan, M., & Manjula, D. (2010). Adaptive background subtraction using fuzzy logic. *IJMIS International Journal of Multimedia Intelligence and Security, 1*(4), 392–401. doi:10.1504/IJMIS.2010.039239

Sivabalakrishnan, M., & Manjula, D. (2011). Novel Segmentation Method using improved edge flow vectors for people tracking. *Journal of Information and Computational Science, 8*(8), 1319–1332.

Sivabalakrishnan, M., & Manjula, D. (2011). Background extraction using improved mode algorithm for visual surveillance applications. *IJCSE International Journal of Computational Science and Engineering, 6*(4), 275–282.

Sivabalakrishnan, M., & Manjula, D. (2012). Performance analysis of fuzzy logic-based background subtraction in dynamic environments. *Imaging Science Journal*, *60*(1), 39–46. doi:10.1179/1743131X11Y.0000000008

Toyama, K., Krumm, J., Brumitt, B., & Meyers, B. (1999). Wallflower: Principles and practice of background maintenance. *Proceedings of the Seventh IEEE International Conference on Computer Vision*, 255-261. 10.1109/ICCV.1999.791228

Witkin, A. (1983). Scale-Space Filtering. *Proceedings 8th International Joint Conference*, 1019-1022.

Zhang, X., Zhou, L., Zhang, T., & Yang, J. (2014). A novel efficient method for abnormal face detection in ATM. *2014 International Conference on Audio, Language and Image Processing*. 10.1109/ICALIP.2014.7009884

Section 2
Critical IoT Infrastructure Security

Chapter 5
IoT Evolution and Security Challenges in Cyber Space:
IoT Security

Uma N. Dulhare
MJCET, India

Shaik Rasool
MJCET, India

ABSTRACT

The internet of things (IoT) is the network of physical objects accessed through the internet that can identify themselves to other devices and use embedded technology to interact with internal states or external conditions. The IoT is an environment where an object that can represent itself becomes greater by connecting to surrounding objects and the extensive data flowing around it. The number of internet of things (IoT) devices will reach more than 15 billion units by 2021, according to research from Juniper. As businesses and consumers accelerate adoption, we're now on the cusp of an IoT revolution. The chapter walks through the security problems that are seen with IoT devices that continues to highlight how vulnerable these devices are when faced with modern, sophisticated cyber threats. Further, the authors discuss how to solve these security challenges presented by the internet of things.

DOI: 10.4018/978-1-5225-8241-0.ch005

INTRODUCTION

Human beings were given capable and inquisitive minds, so they endlessly seek better ways of doing things. This kind of drive, along with an inborn curiosity and a strong drive to unlock the secrets of nature, has created a steady stream of technical innovations over the ages. These ground-breaking efforts have focused on the means for endurance, comfort, and accumulation of wealth--with the hierarchy of needs extending from physical basics of existence to higher-level wants associated with self-actualization. A principal push of innovation today carries on toward technological advances that enhance the productivity of labour and free humans of tasks done more economically by machines. A great insatiable appetite for convenience, comfort, and entertainment products and services, as well as for means to overcome natural barriers like geography and travel time, creates a regular pull on technology. The pull is especially strong in areas relating to the quality of life, and there have been many technological innovations to meet that require. But the opportunities are far from exhausted.

Between society's hottest demands on technology is good for the means to handle the huge amount of information made by modem life. This kind of information explosion stems from complex business practices, new residential services, substantially increased record keeping through comprehensive data bases, and the globalization of our advanced society. The information technology has evolved over many years to help a growing portion of the work force devoted to the generation.

Every baby given birth to today under western culture has a life span of around 100 years, which means it will be alive in 2110. It can practically impossible to predict in greater detail life in 2110. However, what we can endeavour to speculation centred on existing drifts is that humans will still inhabit the planet, as drive animals, and we will be combined by simple natural being premeditated naturally in lab, and of course, machines. Equipment will roam the planet, working in factories, taking our children to college, delivering babies, cleaning the streets, and other such tasks, which will make them seemingly indispensable to us (Parag et al, 2016).

We how to start how superior these machines will be a century from today. Some might continue as dumb machines like the methods we have now, assiduously screwing on the caps of Coke containers. Or they might be humanoid robots that look like us and nurse our elderly parents. The cumulative erudition of Technology from the steam engine and encounter of electricity to telecommunications, the Internet and biotechnology is seen as a haphazard confluence of the breakthroughs of geniuses -- or it might be seen as an evolutionary pattern.

Technology, spawns' new generations of products by using existing components, a phenomenon this individual calls combinatorial evolution. The change in 'species' can thus be quite significant in a short period of time. The evolution of technology becomes faster when we have huge number of components being developed leading to massive permutations of latest technologies. The technology eco-system becomes surviving with increasing likelihood with the passage of time.

Gradually we are shifting into an era were technology can be merged together to create endless possibilities of output that could help lead a sustainable life and opening a door of fresh possibilities to the world. This will have a huge impact on health and make things smarter and more manageable. Technology, once a means of development, is becoming a biochemistry.

With this anywhere/anytime gain access to the Internet, businesses have created web applications that answer common needs of shoppers. These applications can do everything from tracking food portions to sending massive numbers of information in a mouse click.

Perhaps the most obvious difference in the Net today is to be able to be personable in this kind of impersonal setting. Social networks have changed the way people build relationships one another. Now, the way people hook up with one another has changed to a more superficial setting online. Even if artificial, this form of communication has assisted people stay closer to the other person when they would have otherwise lost contact.

Face-to-face conversations are much easier too. There are no geographic boundaries that exist yesterday as people have started using the latest technologies to perform video / audio conferencing for communication. Rather, companies can engage with consumers in a more human manner, people can speak to people face-to-face without the need for costly travel and calling people around the globe is faster and easier.

By means of so many new machineries infusing the way people entree information and entree one another, the onwards thrust looks auspicious for forthcoming technological advances.

Discover not a single aspect of the human experience that hasn't been handled by technology. Everything from industry, to medicine, to how we work has been fundamentally reshaped by the technologies which come about in the second fifty percent of the 20th hundred years.

Technology can also change the human in conditions of his or her characteristics and abilities. Wish to be smarter? You can create a Nootropic. Want to perceive the world with more detail and more information? Put on Google Glasses. Want to get more robust or maybe more physically agile? There are medicines or robotic exoskeletons. Technology has moved away from simply making our lives more convenient, now it has the potential to change every factor of what we are as humans.

As more prevailing systems are stacked onto the other person and advanced into something superior, consumers and businesses alike can imagine seeing more opportunity with impending technology. Technology will be quicker, possess the ability to accomplish more, and everything will develop more modernized to make getting work, easier. Good devices, such as cell phones and tablets, will continue to evolve to work better together. These machines will share data automatically limiting the need for human involvement.

More people and companies will use cloud services for his or her business, or store everything online rather than on a solitary device. This has gigantic potential to replace the way business is done, the fact that traditional office appears, and exactly how people interact with companies regularly.

The more technology continues to evolve, the more the world will change, creating new habits, and forming new ways of working together.

INTERNET OF THINGS

The Internet of Things (IoT) recognizes the use of smartly linked devices and systems to leverage data accumulated by embedded sensors and actuators in machines and other physical objects. IoT is expected to propagate rapidly within the coming years and this convergence will unleash a new dimension of services that increase the quality of life of consumers and productivity of enterprises, unlocking a possibility that the GSMA calls the 'Connected Life' (Zhang et al, 2014).

For consumers, the IoT provides the potential to deliver solutions that drastically improve energy efficiency, security, health, education and many more aspects of daily life. For businesses, IoT can underpin alternatives that improve decision-making and productivity in manufacturing, selling, agriculture and other industries ("Understanding the IoT", 2014).

Figure 1. Evolution of technology

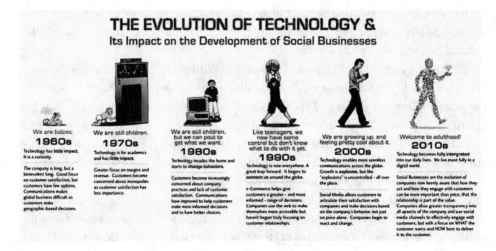

Figure 2. IoT evolution

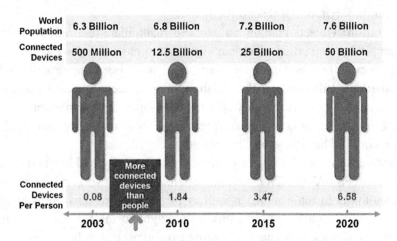

IoT is rapidly evolving. Generally, there is a need to understand challenges in obtaining horizontal and vertical software balance and the key fundamentals required to attain the expected 50 million linked devices in 2020. From a technical point of view, the Net of Things is not the consequence of a single-story technology; instead, several contrasting technical developments provide capacities that taken together help to bridge the space between the virtual and physical world (Mattern et al, 2010). These capacities include:

1. **Communication and Cooperation:** Objects have the ability to network with Internet resources or even with each other, to use data and services boost their state. Cellular technologies such as GSM and UMTS, Wi-Fi, Wireless Bluetooth, ZigBee and various other wireless networking standards presently under development, particularly those relating to Wireless Personal Area Networks (WPANs), are of primary relevance here.
2. **Addressability:** Within an Internet of Things, items can be located and addressed via discovery, look-up or name services, and hence remotely interrogated or configured.
3. **Identification:** Things are uniquely identifiable. RFID, NFC (Near Field Communication) and optically readable pub codes are examples of technologies with which even passive objects which do not have built-in energy resources can be determined (with the help of a "mediator" such as an RFID reader or mobile phone). Identification permits objects to be associated with information associated with the particular object and that can be retrieved from a server, provided the mediator is linked to the network

4. **Realizing:** Objects accumulate information of their surroundings with sensors, record it, forward it or react directly to it.

5. **Actuation:** Objects contain actuators to manipulate their environment (for example by converting electrical signals into mechanical movement). Such actuators can be used to remotely control real-world operations over the internet.

6. **Embedded Information Processing:** Smart objects feature a processor or microcontroller, plus memory space. These types of resources can be taken, for example, to process and interpret sensor information, or give products a "memory" of how they have been used.

7. **Localization:** Smart things are aware about their physical location or can be located. GPS NAVIGATION or the mobile telephone network are best appropriate technologies to achieve this, as well as ultrasound time measurements, UWB (Ultra-Wide Band), radio beacons (e. g. neighbouring WLAN basic stations or RFID visitors with known coordinates) and optical technologies.

8. **Customer Interfaces:** Smart objects can communicate with people in an appropriate manner (either directly or indirectly, for example using a smartphone). Progressive interaction paradigms are relevant here, such as real user interfaces, flexible polymer-based displays and voice, image or gesture recognition methods.

CYBER SECURITY

Although IoT is usually entering day ever more, security risks per IoT are generally growing and tend to be changing immediately. In today's environment of "always on" technology not enough safety measures awareness for users, cyberattacks are not any longer an issue of "if" nevertheless "when." Cyber criminals will work on new methods for getting in the security with established agencies, accessing patio furniture from IP to help individual site visitor information they are this process to enable them to cause hurt, disrupt delicate data together with steal intelligent property.

On a daily basis, their attacks are more sophisticated together with harder to help defeat. Consequently, ongoing progress, we are unable to tell exactly types of threats might emerge following year, with five a long time, or in a decade's time; we can only say these threats are going to be even more dangerous as compared to those with today. We are usually certain that will as old options for this pressure fade, new options will emerge to look at their position. Despite the following uncertainty in truth, because from it we should instead be crystal clear about the species of security equipment needed.

Effective cybersecurity is usually increasingly complex to produce. The standard organizational outside is eroding together with existing safety measures defences are generally coming with increasing demand. Point options, in certain antivirus software programs, IDS, IPS, patching together with encryption, remain an important factor control with regard to combatting todays referred to attacks; nevertheless, they become less effective after a while as cyber-terrorists find new ways of circumventing equipment.

IoT communicates information to people and systems, such as state and health of equipment (e.g. It's on or off, charged, full or empty) and data from sensors that can monitor a person's vital signs ("An Introduction to the IoT", 2015).

Evolution of Cyber Security Challenges

The interconnectivity of folks, devices together with organizations with today's electronic digital world, opens up a completely new taking part in field with vulnerabilities — connection points the location where the cyber criminals can usually get in. The over-all risk "landscape" in the organization should be an integral part of a probably contradictory together with opaque galaxy of real and probable threats that nearly always come with completely unanticipated and surprising threat personalities, which may have an on the rise, effect ("Cybersecurity", 2015).

Speed With Change

From this post-economic-crisis environment, businesses switch fast. Innovative product roll-outs, mergers, purchases, market improvement, and opening paragraphs of innovative technology are generally rising: these modifications invariably possess a complicating influence on the potency and breadth of organization's cybersecurity, and also its particular ability to remain pace.

Facilities

Finding loopholes to help enter any sort of network are going to be easier for almost any attacker since you will have so many ways of attack. Traditionally closed down operating technological know-how systems get increasingly ended up given IP addresses that could be accessed on the surface, so that will cyber perils are producing their way to avoid of the back-office environment systems together with into fundamental infrastructures, which include power age bracket and vehicles systems and also other automation solutions.

Cloud Computing

Cloud computing has become a 2010 prerequisite about IoT in the very conception of its evolution. The cloud gives a platform about IoT to help flourish, nevertheless, there are nevertheless many conflicts which we are up against today in regard to cloud safety measures or info security inside cloud. Organizations are frequently discovering way too late that will their fog up provider's principles of security would possibly not correspond on their own. The current events with "CelebGate" together with Amazon's IAAS compromise are the live samples of such anomalies. These are the incidents that create led that critics to help call a lot of these services since single issue of hack into, instead on the single issue of storage space.

With Substantial Data also getting in picture, you will have an enormous number of data produced for any service providers additionally. With that plethora with data that they can have, the storage space servers should be updated together with secured on a regular basis. There are going to be an improve in dangers for connection links way too, since that sensors together with devices are going to be communicating sensitive e-mail address on a regular basis on that channels.

With data stashed away on these cloud solutions, there is in addition an associated risk of improve in spam as being the cloud machines are pretty much moved collected from one of geographic location even to another within minutes, above the condition. Hence, there is absolutely no IP-specific clog possible

Budding Entry to Mobile Items

Smart phones have previously become an important part of our activities; we rely on them to maintain significant info, such since our property address, credit-based card details, personalized photos/videos, e-mail balances, official paperwork, contact numbers together with messages. The internet stored with our devices include the places that him and i visit frequently and then a "pattern" that uniquely pinpoints us, so anyone that can hack into all of these devices can usually get into some of our lives easily.

The losing a sole smart device but not just means have an effect on information, but increasingly this also leads for a loss with identity (identity theft). The online market place knows virtually no monopoly and therefore all devices cannot have that same firmware and software running on these. Hardware with different companies may not support the other and consequently it might trigger interoperability factors of items.

The improve in may be devices is usually a problem as being the vulnerabilities quite possibly associated using will distribute very immediately. With 1000s of vendors across the country, it might be very difficult for any network engineers to help patch a lot of these vulnerabilities, especially with 1000s of new outages to bring up to date daily — IoT multi-level engineers will now take over tenfold items communicating on their servers outside of the network. Organized cyber criminals are able to sell computer with Trojan viruses or backdoors now installed inside them, and thanks to these vulnerabilities, they might hunt many other victims and generate a botnet from it. These items, scattered everywhere in the world, will be ideal for a DDOS breach on several servers, considering sensors don't get anti-viruses and any junk e-mail.

Governance Together With Compliance Factors

Increasing personal space legislation can be a trend that will likely might continue soon. As agencies design IoT safety measures controls, these may restrict personal anticipation of personal space. A well-formed IoT policy will include defined, crystal clear expectations with privacy-impacting measures, bearing in your mind that legislation varies in confident geographical districts

SECURITY CHALLENGES WITH IoT

Internet of Things increases significant challenges that can stand in the form of recognizing its potential benefits. Media headlines about the hacking of Internet-connected devices, monitoring concerns, and personal privacy fears currently have captured open public attention. Technical difficulties continue to be and new insurance policy, legal and development troubles are emerging. Internet of Things (IoT) starts opportunities for wearable devices, kitchen appliances, and software to talk about and communicate home elevators the Internet. Considering that the distributed data contains a sizable amount of personal information, conserving information security on the distributed data can be an important concern that can't be neglected. The security issues of the Internet of Things (IoT) are immediately related to the extensive program of its system. You start with introducing the structures and top features of IoT security,

From a functional perspective, it pays to think about how precisely IoT devices hook up and converse in conditions of the complex communication models. In March 2015, the Internet Architecture Panel (IAB) released a guiding architectural doc for networking of smart items (RFC 7452),39 which describes a platform of four common communication models employed by IoT devices. The debate below presents this construction and points out key characteristics of every model in the platform (Zhao et al, 2013).

Device-to-Device Communications

The device-to-device communication model signifies several devices that straight hook up and talk between each other, rather than via an intermediary software server. The unit communicate over various kinds of sites, including IP systems or the web. These device-to-device systems allow devices that abide by a specific communication process to connect and exchange announcements to attain their function. This communication model is often found in applications like home automation systems, which typically use small data packets of information to talk between devices with relatively low data rate requirements.

Device-to-Cloud Communications

Inside a device-to-cloud communication model, the IoT device links directly to an Internet cloud service as an application company to switch data and control subject matter traffic. This process frequently takes good thing about existing communications systems like traditional wired Ethernet or Wi-Fi contacts to establish a link between these devices and the IP network, which in the end attaches to the cloud service.

Device-to-Gateway Model

Within the device-to-gateway model, or even more typically, the device-to-application-layer gateway (ALG) model, the IoT device attaches via an ALG service as a conduit to attain a cloud service. In simpler conditions, which means that there is software operating on an area gateway device, which operates as an intermediary between your device and the cloud service and security and other operation such as data or standard protocol translation.

Back-End Data-Sharing Model

The back-end data-sharing model identifies a communication structures that permits users to export and assess smart subject data from a cloud service in combo with data from other resources. This architecture helps "the [user's] desire to have granting usage of the uploaded sensor data to third gatherings. This approach can be an expansion of the sole device- to-cloud communication model, which can result in data silos where "IoT devices publish data and then a single program service agency A back-end posting architecture allows the info collected from solitary IoT device data channels to be aggregated and examined.

Five key IoT concern areas are evaluated to explore a few of the most pressing issues and questions related to the technology. Included in these are security, privacy, interoperability and specifications; legal, regulatory, and protection under the law; and rising economies and development

Security

Within the development of any IoT request security and evaluation frameworks play an important role. To assist you create more secured and episode evidence internet of things empowered devices and applications we've discussed top security concerns you should dwelling address.

A general Internet of Things topology is seen in Figure 3. Security must be tackled throughout these devices' lifecycle, from the original design to the functional environment:

1. **Secure Booting:** When electric power is first released to these devices, the authenticity and integrity of the program on these devices is confirmed using cryptographically made digital signatures. In quite similar way a person signs

Figure 3. A generic internet of things topology

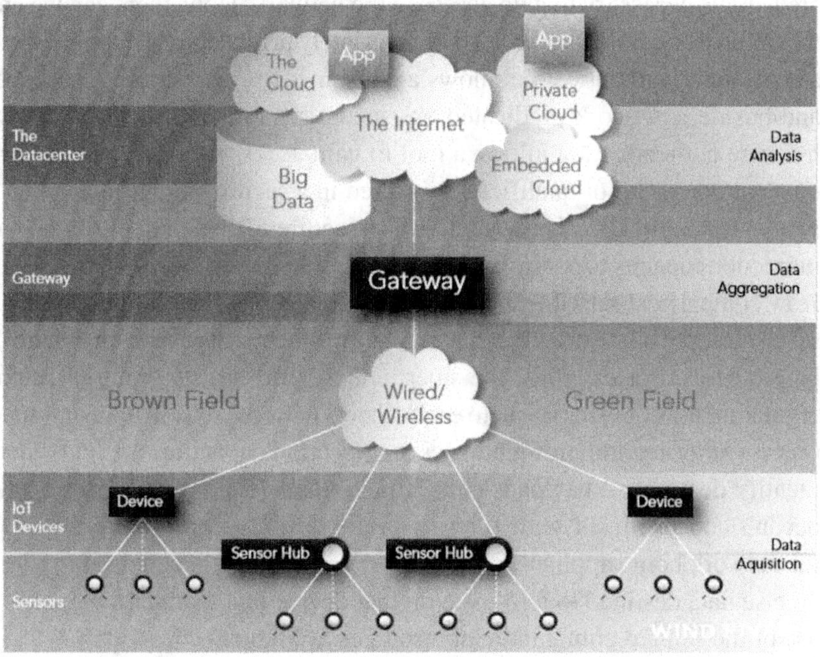

the or a legal record, a digital personal attached to the program image and confirmed by these devices means that only the program that is authorized to perform on that device, and agreed upon by the entity that certified it, will be packed. The building blocks of trust has been proven, however the device still needs coverage from various run-time dangers and malicious motives.

2. **Access Control:** Next, different varieties of resource and gain access to control are applied. Essential or role-based gain access to controls included in the operating-system limit the privileges of device components and applications so they gain access to only the resources they have to do their careers. If any part is compromised, gain access to control means that the intruder has as nominal access to other areas of the machine as is possible. Device-based gain access to control systems are analogous to network-based gain access to control systems such as Microsoft Working Directory website: even if someone were able to steal corporate qualifications to gain usage of a network, jeopardized information would be limited by only those regions of the network certified by those particular qualifications. The basic principle of least privilege dictates that only the little access necessary to execute a function should be approved in order to reduce the potency of any breach of security.

3. **Device Authentication:** When these devices are connected to the network, it will authenticate itself prior to obtaining or transmitting data. Deeply inlayed devices often don't have users seated behind keyboards, ready to source the credentials necessary to gain access to the network. How, then, can we ensure that those devices are determined appropriately prior to authorization? Equally as consumer authentication allows a consumer to gain access to a corporate and business network predicated on customer name and security password, machine authentication allows a tool to gain access to a network predicated on a similar group of qualifications stored in a secure storage space.

4. **Firewalling and IPS:** These devices also require a firewall or profound packet inspection capacity to control traffic that is destined to terminate at these devices. How come a host-based firewall or IPS required if network-based devices are set up? Deeply inlayed devices have unique protocols, unique from organization IT protocols. For example, the smart energy grid has its group of protocols regulating how devices speak to each other. That's the reason industry-specific process filtering and profound packet inspection capacities are had a need to identify destructive payloads concealing in non-IT protocols. These devices needn't concern itself with filtering higher-level, common Internet traffic-- the network home appliances should care for that--but it can need to filter the precise data destined to terminate on that device in a manner that makes best use of the limited computational resources available.

5.   **Updates and Areas:** After the device is functioning, it'll start acquiring hot areas and software revisions. Providers need to rotate out areas, and devices need to authenticate them, in a manner that does not take in bandwidth or impair the useful safety of these devices. It's a very important factor when Microsoft delivers changes to Windows(R) users and ties up their notebooks for quarter-hour. It's quite another when a large number of devices in the field are executing critical functions or services and are reliant on security patches to safeguard against the unavoidable vulnerability that escapes in to the wild. Software changes and security areas must be provided in a manner that conserves the limited bandwidth and intermittent connection of embedded device and absolutely removes the opportunity of compromising efficient safety ("Security in the IoT", 2015).

IoT Security-Hardware Issues

From the starting the internet of things hardware has being the situation. With all the current hype and quick involvement in IoT devices chipmakers like ARM and Intel are reinforcing their processors for additional security with every new era but the sensible scenario doesn't seem to be to ever before closing that security difference.

The problem has been modern structures of the potato chips made designed for the IoT devices, the costs will rise making them expensive. Also, the intricate design will demand more battery which is obviously difficult for IoT applications. Affordable wearable IoT devices won't use such potato chips meaning there may be dependence on better approach (Singh et al, 2016).

IoT Security Solution-Testing Hardware

The ultimate way to lessen the hardware security difficulties of internet of things is to obtain stringent testing construction in place. Listed below are our top picks for secured assessment of hardware.

Device Range

Coverage network of the IoT device is paramount. You should be very specific about the number metrics for the application or device.

For instance, if you work with Zigbee technology to enable your device's network you will need to calculate just how many repeaters you'll need within the establishment to provide communication range for your device. Nevertheless, you cannot blindly put a variety of repeaters much like increasing variety of repeaters the capability of one's body lessens. Therefore, device range assessment will permit you to find that great place where you can increase the number without achieving the breaking point.

Latency and Capacity

Capacity is the bps (bytes per second) managing swiftness of your network while latency denotes the full total time used for data copy between the software endpoints.

Designers always look for ways to increase capacity and latency of the IoT applications to boost performance. Problem is both these factors are inversely proportionate, increasing one degrades the other. Data extensive devices and applications should be thoroughly tested for latency and capacity balance.

Manufacturability Test

It is rarely that you'll build you IoT device from scuff by yourself. More often than not, you'll be using part and module created by others in the application. Examining these modules by yourself for proper working is vital.

Manufacturers always do the set-up line testing on the end nevertheless, you should also validate the same. Also, when you put all the modules collectively on a mother board testing is necessary to be sure there are no mistakes unveiled because of soldering and wiring. Manufacturability assessment is essential to ensure the application works as it is supposed to.

Developing Secured IoT Applications

The security alternatives reviewed above should be integrated totally to ensure proper working with safety.

IoT technologies remain immature to a huge amount and being little paranoid about their security is definitely helpful. Before you begin with development of any IoT software it's important that you do research and become informed approximately you can. There will be trade-offs like more security for poor UI but as stated before you will need to discover that sweet spot.

Also, you shouldn't be in the dash to bring your product on the market without proper planning permanent support. IoT devices are cheap so chances are incredibly high that manufacturers don't pay enough focus on provide security revisions and patches. This isn't an ecological development model for internet of things.

As an IoT software developer always avoid risks. Security breaches are almost destined to happen, and you ought to be equipped for them. You should prepare yourself with a leave intend to secure maximum data in case there is an attack.

Last rather than least always take effort to instruct customers and employees on latest IoT security dangers and solutions.

Privacy

As the Internet of Things becomes more wide-spread, consumers must demand better security and personal privacy protections that don't leave them susceptible to corporate security and data breaches. But before consumers can demand change, they need to be educated -- which requires companies to become more transparent (Bannan et al, 2016).

By far the most dangerous part of IoT is the fact that individuals are surrendering their privateers, piece by piece, without knowing it, because they're unacquainted with what data has been collected and exactly how it has been used. As mobile applications, wearables and other Wi-Fi-connected consumer products replace "dumb" devices on the marketplace, consumers will never be able to buy products that don't possess the capability to track them. It really is normal for consumers to upgrade their kitchen appliances, and it probably does not eventually them that those new devices may also be monitoring them.

After an electric Frontier Groundwork activist tweeted about the unsettling similarity of the Samsung Smart Television online privacy policy -- which warned consumers never to discuss sensitive issues near to the device -- to a passing from George Orwell's 1984, popular criticism brought on Samsung to modify its online privacy policy and clarify the Smart TV's data collection techniques.

But most people do not read level of privacy policies for each and every device they buy or every software they download, and, even if indeed they attempted to accomplish that, most would be written in legal dialect unintelligible to the common consumer. Those same devices also typically include similarly unintelligible conditions of use, such as required arbitration clauses forcing them to stop there to be listened to in court if they're harmed by the merchandise. Because of this, the personal privacy of consumers can be jeopardized, and they're left without the real remedy.

Increased commercial transparency is frantically needed, and you will be the building blocks of any successful answer to increased personal privacy in the IoT. This transparency could be completed either by industry self-regulation or governmental legislation requiring companies to get informed and important consent from consumers before collecting data.

Businesses can self-regulate by expanding and implementing industry-wide guidelines on cybersecurity and data minimization. When companies accumulate user data, they need to take responsibility for guarding their users; if indeed they do not need to be in charge of the data, they need to avoid collecting it to begin with.

These guidelines would make huge progress in guarding the personal privacy of consumers, nevertheless they aren't enough. Companies must be legally obliged to the assurances they make with their customers. The usage of pre-dispute required arbitration clauses in conditions of use have grown to be standard in many market sectors. These clauses refuse consumers there to pursue a cure in a judge of legislation, usually without their knowledge, because they're buried in indecipherable small print.

The Buyer Financial Cover Bureau has discovered that arbitration clauses' club on class activities further hurts the general public interest because lawsuits often generate promotion about a corporate and business practice, and, without them, consumers may well not get access to that information. The firm has therefore suggested prohibiting necessary arbitration clauses for some consumer financial loans and services.

The Section of Education in addition has proposed a guideline that could prohibit the utilization of pre-dispute compulsory arbitration contracts by for-profit universities, giving students who've been exploited the to sue their colleges. The Government Trade Commission should think about proposing an identical rule that could prohibit the utilization of pre-dispute required arbitration contracts by companies that sell IoT products.

Because this is such a sophisticated problem, involving many sectors and implicating various level of privacy concerns, a satisfactory solution will demand contribution by consumers, businesses and the federal government. Consumers must demand to really know what data is accumulated and exactly how it can be used. Establishments should develop best personal privacy routines that match their customers' goals.

Interoperability and Expectations

A fragmented environment of amazing IoT specialized implementations will inhibit value for users and industry. While full interoperability across products and services is not necessarily possible or necessary, buyers may be hesitant to buy IoT products and services when there is integration inflexibility, high possession complexity, and matter over supplier lock-in ("IoT, an Overview", 2015).

Standards will offer lots of benefits. Expectations can offer guarantee to their associates that if indeed they implement the requirements, their products and services will continue steadily to operate within given parameters with one another. Technical interoperability is usually a goal of industry specifications. The broader the group of given hardware, software and marketing communications protocols a typical support, the broader the interoperability it may enable.

Central challenges elevated by the proliferation of IoT interoperability specifications are the following:

- Device manufacturers understand a market advantages in creating an amazing ecosystem of appropriate IoT products that limit interoperability to the people devices within the manufacturer's products. By preserving the proprietary mother nature of the systems, developers ply more control over an individual experience. These "walled backyards" are compared by interoperability followers as impediments to user choice because they probably deter users from changing to alternative products. Some also claim that they create impediments to creativity and competition, restricting competitors' ability to build up new products appropriate for the standardized facilities.

- One of IoT's key attractions is the power of linked devices to transfer and acquire data to and from cloud services, which may perform powerful analytic functions. Having less a consistent, program and OS-agnostic standard regulating the collection, control and writing of such data may inhibit the power of users to gain access to the originating data, proceed to other companies or perform their own analyses.

- Device manufacturers understand a market benefits in building an amazing ecosystem of suitable IoT products that limit interoperability to the people devices within the manufacturer's products. By keeping the proprietary characteristics of the systems, developers ply more control over an individual experience. These "walled backyards" are compared by interoperability followers as impediments to user choice because they probably deter users from changing to alternative products. Some also claim that they create impediments to development and competition, restricting competitors' ability to build up new products appropriate for the standardized system.

- One of IoT's principal attractions is the power of linked devices to transfer and get data to and from cloud services, which may perform powerful analytic functions. Having less a consistent, system and OS-agnostic standard regulating the collection, control and showing of such data may inhibit the power of users to gain access to the originating data, proceed to other companies or perform their own analyses.

- The insufficient a pre-existing and proven standard that IoT device manufacturers might use to evaluate technological design dangers in the development process improves development costs.

- In the lack of standardization, coders face the behemoth activity of growing integrations with legacy systems, and customers will be confronted with the task of configuring multiple specific devices across a variety of standards. Furthermore, product designers may be dissuaded from producing new products anticipated to uncertainty concerning compliance with future benchmarks.

- End users may be discouraged from purchasing products where there is integration inflexibility, construction complexity or matter over merchant lock-in, or where they dread products may be outdated scheduled to changing benchmarks. The issues posed by too little uniform connectivity benchmarks for product development and industry progress are apparent in the competing, incompatible benchmarks for devices with a low-range and medium-to-low data rate (i.e., ZigBee, Bluetooth and LTE Category 0).
- Shortage of guide and architectural models that look at the various needs for interoperability and standardization could also have adverse repercussions for the sites with which IoT devices hook up, since terribly designed sensor sites might use disproportionate bandwidth, and become greedy consumers of available electricity.

On the other hand, well-defined device interoperability expectations may encourage invention as disruptive technology emerge, provide efficiencies for IoT device manufacturers and generate monetary value as "things" become cheaper, smarter and better to use. Obstacles to access may be decreased. Moreover, interoperability helps the power of users to choose the devices suitable to the user's needs within an environment where different devices can discuss and converse data between one another. Nevertheless, such quarrels continue to be counterbalanced by companies recognized competitive and monetary features of building amazing systems for market domination in the IoT

Legal, Regulatory and Rights

The use of IoT devices poses a variety of problems and questions from a regulatory and legal point of view, which need thoughtful awareness. In some instances, IoT devices create new legal and regulatory situations and concerns over civil protection under the law that didn't can be found prior to the unit. In other situations, the unit amplify legalities that already been around. Further, technology is evolving much more speedily than the associated insurance policy and regulatory conditions.

The number of legal, regulatory and protection under the law issues from the Internet of Things is wide-ranging. IoT devices create new legal and plan problems that didn't recently exist, plus they amplify many obstacles that already are present. For example, availability requirements for IoT devices for people that have disabilities offer new troubles due to the launch of new varieties of IoT devices, while left over appropriate for existing accessibility benchmarks and rules.91 Alternatively, the enormous size of cordless IoT devices and the air frequency (RF) noises and disturbance they produce can be an example of just how IoT devices amplify the prevailing difficulty of regulating the utilization of the RF variety.92 Legal and regulatory concerns of intellectual property issues, environmental issues (e.g. removal of devices), and legal possession of devices (e.g. will devices be held or rented) are appearing issues as well for IoT devices.

Combined with the complexities of deciding the correct regulatory or insurance plan approaches for IoT problems, you have the added difficulty of

deciding where within an IoT system structures is the greatest destination to achieve the required outcomes. If the regulatory control buttons be located on these devices, on the stream of the info, on the gateway, on an individual, or in the cloud where data is stored? The answers to these questions among others rely upon the perspective taken up to analyse the problem. Regulatory evaluation of IoT devices is progressively more viewed from an over-all, technology neutral perspective legal zoom lens, such as consumer coverage regulations. Examining legal implications of IoT devices from the point of view of avoiding unjust or deceptive procedures against consumers can help inform decisions of privateers and security amongst others.

Lastly, the image resolution of problems in this space, and their effects, have to be considered with regards to the guiding Internet World concepts that promote the capability to hook up, speak, innovate, talk about, choose, and trust.

SHIELD AGAINST CYBER CRIME

Organization may currently have strong IT regulations, processes and systems, but could it be prepared for what's coming? Early alert and diagnosis of breaches are decisive to being in circumstances of readiness, and therefore the emphasis of cybersecurity has altered to threat cleverness. Most organizations know that we now have threats for his or her information and functional systems, as well for their products --the step beyond is to comprehend the nature of these threats and exactly how these express themselves.

A business in circumstances of readiness to cope with cyber-attacks inhabits a totally different mind-set, views the world in different ways and responds in ways the cyber thieves wouldn't normally expect. It needs behaviours that are thoughtful, considered and collaborative. It discovers, prepares and rehearses. No corporation or authorities can ever forecast or prevent all (or even most) problems; nevertheless, they can reduce their appeal as a goal, increase their resilience and limit destruction from any given harm.

Circumstances of readiness includes:

- Developing and putting into action a cyber danger intelligence technique to support proper business decisions and leverage the worthiness of security
- Defining and\encompassing the organizations lengthened cyber security ecosystem, including associates, suppliers, services and business sites.
- Taking a cyber economical way understanding your essential belongings and their value, and making an investment specifically in the security
- Using forensic data analytics and cyber danger intelligence to investigate and anticipate where in fact the likely dangers are via and when, upping your readiness
- Ensuring that everyone in the business understands the necessity for strong governance, end user settings and accountability

Organizations may well not have the ability to control when information security occurrences occur, nevertheless they can control the way they react to them -- growing detection features are an excellent location to start. A well-functioning security businesses center (SOC) can develop the center of effective diagnosis.

Managing cyber dangers matching to business priorities should be the concentrate of the SOC. By correlating business-relevant information against a secure baseline, the SOC can produce relevant reporting, permitting better decision-making, risk management and business continuity. An SOC can permit information security functions to answer faster, work more collaboratively and reveal knowledge better.

Follow Leading Cybersecurity Procedures

By leveraging-industry leading tactics and implementing strategies that are adaptable and scalable, organizations will be better outfitted to cope with incoming (sometimes unexpected) challenges with their security infrastructure.

As technology advancements and companies continue steadily to innovate on the approaching years, organizations using the IoT should constantly examine the security implications of implementing these progresses. A steady and agile multi-perspective risk of security assessment methodology will measure the organizations risk coverage. The benefits of appropriate methods and regular evaluation can help organizations become smarter and make their workers more alert to the problems that IoT poses for the complete enterprise.

- **Know Your Environment, Inside and Out**

In depth, yet targeted, situational recognition is crucial to understanding the wider threat scenery and exactly how it pertains to the business. Cyber threat cleverness may bring this knowledge -- it features both exterior and internal resources of risk, and includes both present and future, while learning from days gone by.

- **Continuously Learn and Develop**

There is nothing static -- not the thieves, not the business or any part of its operating environment -- which means pattern of continual improvement remains. Turn into a learning firm: research data (including forensics), maintain and explore new collaborative associations, renew the strategy regularly and progress cybersecurity capabilities.

- **Be Confident in Your Occurrence Response and Turmoil Response Mechanisms**

Organizations that are in circumstances of expectation regularly rehearse their incident response functions. This includes warfare gaming and stand top exercises, to enacting complex event scenarios that basically test the organization's functions.

- **Align Cybersecurity to Business Goals**

Cybersecurity should turn into a standing boardroom concern -- a quite crucial item on the plan. The organization's authority should comprehend and discuss how cybersecurity permits the business enterprise to innovate, open up new channels to advertise and manage risk. To reach your goals, the info security function needs management support in providing the correct income to aid and develop better security safety, to market cybersecurity understanding within the labour force, and sponsor co-operation with business peers.

Move from Security as an Expense, to Security as an Advantage

Security is usually situated as an obligatory cost -- an expense to pay to be compliant, or an expense to pay to lessen risk. But moving to a style of security as risk and trust management indicates looking after security as a company enabler; for example, handling consumer data gain access to leverages the value of the info rather than concentrating on the coverage of the info itself. Actually, this change means enabling the introduction of even more expanded networks of sites, of more and new kinds of collaboration and freedom, and of home-based business models. "Security as an advantage" should be considered a mainstay of the business enterprise.

CASE STUDY

Ecolab Uses Cloud Computing to Save Freshwater on The Ground

Freshwater accounts for only 2.5 percent of the world's total normal water source, and demand because of its use keeps growing combined with the global inhabitants. The United Countries' "World Drinking water Development Statement 2015" predicts that within 15 years, demand for freshwater will outpace source by almost 40 percent, resulting in serious concerns for two-thirds of the world's people. Microsoft is collaborating with Ecolab to utilize cloud-based processing and the web of Things (IoT) to help establishments worldwide find answers to the challenge of drinking water scarcity (Edson et al, 2016).

Nalco Water, the key water procedure within Ecolab, is dealing with Microsoft to build up solutions for drinking water management that get and analyse huge levels of data about their drinking water usage. Because they build on Microsoft Azure, Nalco Drinking water can use cloud processing and advanced analytics to make solutions on the much larger size and with more deeply analytical features than previously. Sensors will take data from in-plant monitoring equipment, which is transferred instantly to a secure cloud storage space program built on Microsoft Azure and Azure IoT Collection. Machine learning provides insights and brains that employees can respond on using familiar information management tools such as Microsoft Dynamics 365, Microsoft Office 365 and Microsoft Ability BI. Businesses may then use that information to modify their business procedures to lessen, reuse and recycle drinking water to attain net-zero water utilization.

By the finish of 2016, Nalco Water's goal for the cooperation is to give a suite of thorough, end-to-end service delivery alternatives for Ecolab's worldwide customer foundation that bridge process monitoring and control, cloud system for data management and analytics, mobile applications, and hardware.

With Azure, "Suddenly, intricacy and size are no more obstacles," says Christophe Beck, leader of Nalco Drinking water. "We are able to get any data, everywhere, and transfer that information across the world very swiftly. We are able to now harness the energy of this program to serve a lot more customers, measuring a lot more flows at a lot more plants than we're able to even get pregnant of before."

Fathym's IoT Enabled Weathercloud Enhances Drivers Safety During Bad Weather

Wherever your home is, you're probably all too aware that bad weather can have a significant impact on resident safe practices and city costs. And until just lately, municipalities afflicted by local street and climate didn't have quick access to the info they had a need to do anything apart from respond to weather patterns after they occurred. Now, because of recent developments in the web of Things (IoT), areas can make faster, more enlightened decisions predicated on hyper-local street weather data, increasing road security and increasing inexpensive efficiencies - turning city representatives into city heroes (Lee, 2016).

Every year, dangerous street conditions cause 7,400 fatalities and 700,000 injury, while businesses and municipalities spend $2.3 billion on snow and snow control businesses. By access microclimate information regarding current highway conditions, municipalities will not only keep their individuals safer but also possibly save thousands of us dollars, if not large numbers, by being better with resources.

Figure 4. WeatherCloud application on mobile device

For instance, in Fairbanks, Alaska, the state's Office of Travel needed ways to make important decisions such as whether to de-ice the highways as a snowstorm technique or as the surprise is going on. Fairbanks considered IoT solutions company Fathym, which developed WeatherCloud, a complex weather traffic monitoring solution built on Azure IoT Hub that delivers a far more complete knowledge of real-time street weather.

Fathym considered Azure IoT after formerly building its solution on Amazon.com Web Services (AWS). To permit a remedy as advanced as WeatherCloud, Fathym had a need to put into practice an IoT offering with best-in-class overall flexibility and acceleration of deployment.

"Microsoft Azure and Azure Service Textile has allowed us to make out a complete ecosystem of IoT microservices," said Matthew Smith, CEO of Fathym. "We expect that scalability is likely to be a major gain even as we move out our treatment for additional clients and having Microsoft Azure IoT as our deployment program is perfectly received by our clients, potential customers and strategic associates. The efficiency and velocity of development on the system as well as the scalability means cost benefits and overall flexibility that are incredibly welcome to your company."

WeatherCloud happens to be being employed by multiple organizations like the National Middle for Atmospheric Research, the Alaska, Utah, Iowa and Colorado Departments of Travel and the Meteorological Service of New Zealand to assist in improving maintenance, commuting, and routing functions by providing correct, hyper-local street conditions. With Fathym's individualized dashboards, city representatives can view current highway conditions, future forecasts, and arranged alerts predicated on incoming data, assisting metropolitan areas maintain safer streets and make more proper and cost-efficient decisions regarding their weather-related response systems. These alternatives decrease the impact of dangerous and costly streets by allowing city representatives to make more educated decisions about whether to deploy expensive belongings to ensure that individuals receive the help they want when and where they want it.

"We'd a freezing rainfall event move around in from the Southwest. I travelled off the info I had formed from only the WeatherCloud detectors to select a plan of action. We were proactive and averted any incidents. Fantastic Results." -- Daniel Schacher, Area Superintendent, Alaska Section of Transportation

Commercial fleets using the technology can also save thousands of dollars by access near real-time highway condition information. The WeatherCloud solution helps reduce delays created by bad weather with more exact weather forecasting and real-time fleet re-routing features.

Figure 5. WeatherCloud data

The WeatherCloud solution is a superb exemplary case of how companies are accelerating their digital change in ground breaking ways with Azure IoT alternatives. It also features the immediate impact of migrating from AWS to Azure, which empowered Fathym to level, grow, and enhance their businesses.

Zion China Uses Azure IoT, Stream Analytics, and Machine Learning to Evolve Its Intelligent Diabetes Management Solution

People throughout the world more and more use their cellular devices to keep track of health signals and article the leads to their doctors. Zion China, a specialist of mobile medical care and telemedicine services, is an integral part of this tendency. The Beijing company is rolling out progressive health monitoring and evaluation tools that accumulate data on blood sugar levels, diet, exercise, and medication for every single patient and producing personal advice to help patients take care of their health. Its programmers recognized that as the business's installation basic grew, the pure level of real-time data provided a scalability and data management problem. They collaborated with Microsoft to consider good thing about the scalability of the Azure IoT Collection, Machine Learning, Stream Analytics, SQL Databases, and Microsoft Vitality BI while also bettering analytics and data security ("Zion China Uses Azure", 2017).

In the centre of why Zion China built this solution is the fact "China presently has 130 million people who've been identified as having diabetes," says Vincent Yang, CEO of Zion China. "It really is our objective to help these patients and their own families control this chronic disease."

Zion China's original technological solution, E-Followup, was based on traditional BI with data sourced from on-premises and different devices or cloud storage space. In this proposal, they wished to achieve these technological and business goals:

1. Design and architect a good, fast, and cost-effective way to consistently nourish data from devices to the cloud

While wearing these devices, a user will create more than 3,000 readings of blood sugar in a 7-day period, once every three minutes. At exactly the same time, the device gathers data on the user's daily food diet, exercise, medication, insulin, and other information. High-frequency data transmitting, and huge amounts of data storage area have grown to be a specialized problem. The recently designed architecture resolved the ingest of data from the devices into Azure to create a robust solution.

2. Optimise the analytic collection, moving from BI evaluation to proactive prediction to get insights from data easier

Before, despite having a data analytic product, doctors put in 4 hours or even more on each data evaluation to recognize the impact of varied factors on an individual and discover the correlation between your data. Users and doctors need to see data in a number of cases, such as webpages, mobile apps, tablets, and so forth. Zion China requires a tool that may be modified to multiple devices and is not hard to build up and experienced in data examination and presentation.

3. Persist data storage space for future use and ensure data security

Zion China would like to ensure that the persisted stored data, despite having all private information removed, is stored in an extremely secure manner.

Solution to Controlling Significant Data Volumes

Xi Wang, Microsoft Complex Evangelist, says, "For just about any given patient, E-Followup transmits huge quantities of data as time passes. Making that transmitting better and enhancing the capability to scale the storage space and research of the info, required a fresh architecture."

The Microsoft China team caused Zion China to re-architect the perfect solution is:

- Adding IoT Hub to leading end to provide real-time data transmitting from device to cloud.
- Using Azure Machine Understanding how to create proactive prediction on glucose and patient data.
- Using Transparent Data Encryption in Azure SQL Databases to secure data.
- Using Ability BI and Electric power BI Embedded for easier visualization of insights.

Key technological components contained in the solution are:

- **IoT Hub:** The info will be safely moved from the dedicated blood sugar data device to a mobile iPhone app via Bluetooth. The mobile software (iOS and Google android) will firmly transfer the info to IoT Hub through AMQP and HTTPS and the patient's private information is removed prior to the data copy. Try IoT Hub with a laboratory.

Figure 6. Zion China architecture

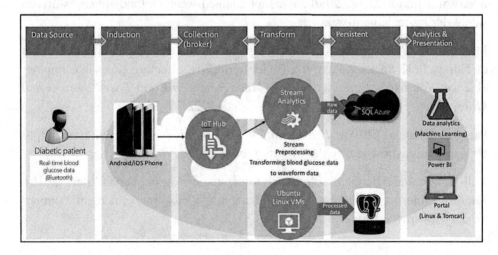

- Stream Analytics steps ingested data instantly on IoT Hub and channels useful data for examining onto SQL Databases. Get started doing stream analytics
- SQL Databases provides high-end security features that may be easily configured to ensure data security. Understand how to set-up, manage, and migrate directories using SQL DB
- Azure Machine Learning fundamentally increases the complete solution's analytic and prediction level. Create your own data knowledge experiment.
- Microsoft Electric power BI brings visualization of the info understanding to users. Read getting began with Microsoft Vitality BI Embedded

REFERENCES

An Introduction to the Internet of Things (IoT). (2013). Lopez Research LLC. Retrieved from https://www.cisco.com/c/dam/en_us/solutions/trends/iot/introduction_to_IoT_november.pdf

Bannan. (2016). *The IoT threat to privacy*. Retrieved from https://techcrunch.com/2016/08/14/the-iot-threat-to-privacy/

Edson. (2016). Ecolab uses cloud computing to save freshwater on the ground. *Microsoft Internet of Things*. Retrieved from https://blogs.microsoft.com/iot/2016/04/05/ecolab-uses-cloud-computing-to-save-freshwater-on-the-ground/#XMQgmhjSRmdtDQ7B.99

Lee. (2016). Fathym's IoT-enabled WeatherCloud enhances driver safety during inclement weather. *Microsoft Internet of Things*. Retrieved from https://blogs.microsoft.com/iot/2016/12/09/fathyms-iot-enabled-weathercloud-enhances-driver-safety-during-inclement-weather/

Mattern, F., & Floerkemeier, C. (2010). From the Internet of Computers to the Internet of Things. In K. Sachs, I. Petrov, & P. Guerrero (Eds.), Lecture Notes in Computer Science: Vol. 6462. *From Active Data Management to Event-Based Systems and More*. Berlin: Springer. doi:10.1007/978-3-642-17226-7_15

Parag & Khanna. (2016). *The Evolution of Technology*. Retrieved from http://bigthink.com/hybrid-reality/the-evolution-of-technology

Rolls-Royce and Microsoft collaborate to create new digital capabilities. (2016). Microsoft Internet of Things. Retrieved from https://customers.microsoft.com/en-us/story/rollsroycestory

Singh. (2016). *IoT Security-Issues, Challenges and Solutions*. Retrieved from https://internetofthingswiki.com/iot-security-issues-challenges-and-solutions/937/

Understanding the Internet of Things (IoT). (2014). *Connected Living, GSMA*. Retrieved from https://www.gsma.com/iot/wp-content/uploads/2014/08/cl_iot_wp_07_14.pdf

Zhang, Z. K., Cho, M. C. Y., Wang, C. W., Hsu, C. W., Chen, C. K., & Shieh, S. (2014). IoT Security: Ongoing Challenges and Research Opportunities. *2014 IEEE 7th International Conference on Service-Oriented Computing and Applications*, 230-234. 10.1109/SOCA.2014.58

Zhao, K., & Ge, L. (2013). A Survey on the Internet of Things Security. *2013 Ninth International Conference on Computational Intelligence and Security*, 663-667. 10.1109/CIS.2013.145

Zion China uses Azure IoT, Stream Analytics, and Machine Learning to evolve its Intelligent Diabetes Management Solution. (2017). *Microsoft Internet of Things*. Retrieved from http://customers.microsoft.com/en-us/story/zionchina

Chapter 6
Network Intrusion Detection and Prevention Systems for Attacks in IoT Systems

Vetrivelan Pandu
VIT Chennai, India

Jagannath Mohan
VIT Chennai, India

T. S. Pradeep Kumar
VIT Chennai, India

ABSTRACT

Internet of things (IoT) has transformed greatly the improved way of business through machine-to-machine (M2M) communications. This vast network and its associated technologies have opened the doors to an increasing number of security threats which are dangerous to IoT and 5G wireless networks. The first part of this chapter presents instruction detection system (IDS) which detect the various attacks in 6LoWPAN layer. An IDS is to detect and analyze both inbound and outbound network traffic for abnormal activities. An IPS complements an IDS configuration by proactively inspecting a system's incoming traffic to weed out malicious requests. A typical IPS configuration uses web application firewalls and traffic filtering solutions to secure applications. An IPS prevents attacks by dropping malicious packets, blocking offending IPs and alerting security personnel to potential threats. Machine learning (ML)-based instruction detection and prevention system (IDPS) is proposed and implemented in Contiki simulation environment.

DOI: 10.4018/978-1-5225-8241-0.ch006

INTRODUCTION

Internet of Things (IoT) is a smart system which associates everything to the web to exchange data with concurred conventions. Intrusion Detection System (IDS) is utilized to screen the activity specifically hub and system. It can go about as a second line of protection which can guard the system from interlopers. Interruption is an undesirable or noxious movement which is destructive to sensor hubs. IDS recognizes the system parcels and decide if they are gatecrashers or authentic clients. There are three segments of IDS: Monitoring, Analysis and identification, Alarm (Shanzhi et al., 2014). The checking module screens the system's traffics, examples and assets. Examination and Detection is a center part of IDS which distinguishes the interruptions as indicated by determined calculation. Caution module raised an alert if the interruption is identified.

Background

IoT is a quickly developing advancement that will significantly change the manner in which people live. It tends to be thought of as the following enormous advance in Internet innovation (Tejas et al., 2017). The changing working condition related to the Internet of Things speaks to impressive effect to the attack surface and risk condition of the Internet and Internet associated frameworks (Jun et al., 2014).

Data science is an interdisciplinary field about procedures and frameworks to extricate learning or experiences from information in different structures, either organized or unstructured, which is a continuation of a portion of the information investigation fields, for example, measurements, machine learning, information mining and learning revelation, and prescient examination (Khan et al., 2016).

As constrained remote detecting and activating gadgets are logically incorporated with the Internet interchanges foundation, the significance of recognizing and managing attacks against its security and strength shows up as a principal necessity. This coordination is turning into a reality, because of an institutionalized correspondences stack being intended for the IoT, enabled by conventions, for example, the 6LoWPAN adjustment layer, RPL (IPv6 Routing Protocol for Low Power and Lossy Networks), and the Constrained Application Protocol (CoAP). Other protocols could also be considered at the application layer, such as MQTT (Message Queuing Telemetry Transport) (B. Andrew et al., 2014), but our focus in CoAP is motivated by its support of low-energy wireless local communication environments, machine-to-machine (M2M) communications between constrained sensors and actuators and other external Internet devices, and its direct compatibility with HTTP.

6LoWPAN has been generally utilized as an adaption layer between the standard IPv6 convention and IEEE 802.15.4 connection layer. In this manner, empowers the asset constrained gadgets to viably transmit data by means of the standard IPv6. In the 6LoWPAN system, RPL has been acquainted as a steering convention with manage restricted memory, control and so forth. RPL makes Destination Oriented Directed Acyclic Graph (DODAG) and empowers the hubs to forward the bundles upwards to their folks or descending to their youngsters. In any case, in such constrained condition, RPL has restricted help for security benefits and are presented to inner attacks. There are three fundamental attacks that focusing on the RPL convention in IoT in particular hi surge, sinkhole, and wormhole attacks. There are two surely understood 6LoWPAN-IDS usage, in particular, SVELTE and Pongle's IDS (Pongle et al., 2015).

IoT paradigm permits measures to be detected and prepared at continuously making an immediate cooperation stage between digital physical frameworks. Such a methodology prompts enhanced productivity in the age and use of information prompting financial advantages. Research led by Cisco reports there are as of now 10 billion gadgets associated, contrasted with the total populace of more than 7 billion and it is trusted it will increment by 4% continuously in 2020. These sorts of attack incorporate changing critical information substance or robbery of secret information. Past and ongoing works utilizing Artificial Neural system interruption recognition framework on KDD99 informational collection (N.T.T. Van et al., 2015) demonstrate a promising execution for interruption discovery. IoT danger can be grouped into DoS, Malware, Data Breaches.

DETECTION OF HELLO FLOOD ATTACK AND SYBIL ATTACK

This section contains the depiction of proposed answer for recognition of Hello surge attack and Sybil attack. These methodologies have a few constraints as far as computational overhead. Accordingly, these methodologies are heavyweight so it isn't appropriate for IoT. There is no unified methodology accessible to recognize surge attack and Sybil attack in IoT. To beat these impediments, a lightweight way to deal with recognize hi surge attack and Sybil attack in IoT arrange (Shyam 2015) was proposed. Our proposed framework is intended to recognize Hello surge attack and Sybil attack in IoT condition. The design of IDS is depicted in Figure 1, in which all sensor hubs are associated with web utilizing IPv6 fringe switch (6BR) (M. Hossain et al., 2015). The position for IDS framework utilizes hybrid breed approach, in which Centralized module on 6BR (GIDS) and Distributed module (NIDS) on the sensor hubs which coordinates with one another to distinguish attacks.

Figure 1. Architecture of IDS

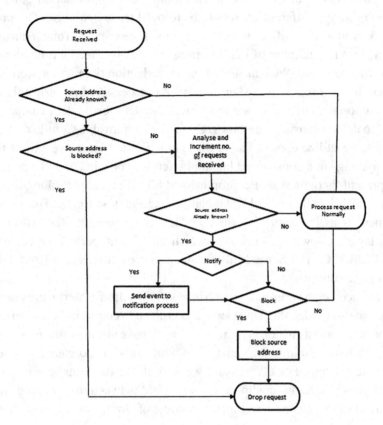

The concentrated module identifies the welcome surge attack and circulated module distinguishes the Sybil attack and assailant (P.Pongle et al., 2015).

DENIAL-OF-SERVICE ATTACK

A Denial-of-Service attack is an attack which can be utilized to impact the association of system, making it difficult to reach to its planned clients. DoS attack is acknowledged by flooding the objective with activity or sending it data to triggers an accident. It is a standout amongst the most mainstream digital attack techniques in the security of the system (Alessandro et al., 2016). Casualties of DoS attack are frequently the web servers of prominent associations, for example, managing an account, business and media organizations The conduct of every Node must encourage the spread and recovery of legitimate blocklist Packages all through the system (A.K. Kyaw et al., 2015).

The framework is in Contiki OS. The same size of information bundles was transmitted through different sensors hubs to outskirt switch hubs. The proposed framework is looked at different measurements, for example, Total Transmission Energy, add up to a number of bundles transmitted, organize lifetime and vitality devoured by every hub. We considered the reproduction time as a system lifetime and system lifetime is a period when no course is accessible to transmit the parcel.

This proposed analysis is done in Contiki's system test system Cooja that has appeared to deliver sensible outcomes. Cooja runs deployable Contiki code. In our recreations, we utilize copied Tmote Sky hubs. By and large, we expect that the 6BR is anything but a constrained hub and it tends to be a PC or a PC; be that as it may, at present there exist no PC proportional 802.15.4 gadgets, along these lines we run the 6BR locally i.e. JNI (Java Native Interface) on Linux. The convention arrangement is as, as Radio interface cc2420 is utilized, at RDC (Radio Duty Cycling) layer sicslowmac is utilized, which is 802.15.4 perfect. Over this layer, in MAC CSMA (Carrier Sense Multiple Access) conventions is utilized. UDP is a transport layer convention.

As referenced in the presentation a fringe switch helps in interfacing one system to another. In this model, the fringe switch is utilized to course information between an RPL arrange and an outside system. Till now we have just made the RPL organize. Presently we have to mimic the situation in which this RPL organize is associated with an outer system. For this reason, we will utilize the Tunslip utility gave in Contiki. In this precedent tunslip makes a scaffold between the RPL organize and the nearby machine. Because of this the conduct of Border switch may changes.

INTRUSION DETECTION SCHEME USING DATASETS

Intrusion discovery alludes to the methodology of examining and breaking down the occasions happening in a framework to recognize malevolent practices. The interruption recognition process includes identifying an arrangement of terrible activities that bargain accessible assets. In a years ago, there is a genuine requirement for new information science strategies for investigation of the complex attack in the Internet of Things condition (Zarpelao et al., 2017). Current strategies experience the ill effects of assessment, correlation, and arrangement which start from the shortage of satisfactory openly accessible system follow informational collections. Likewise, openly existing datasets are either obsolete or created in a controlled domain. Information science includes different logical strategies, for example, machine learning, man-made brainpower, and information digging that is helpful for separating highlights from informational collections. There are numerous methods which can use to distinguish obscure new attacks (Zawoad. et al., 2015).

Four Categories of Attacks

- Denial of Service (DOS) Attack
- Users to Root (U2R) Attack
- Remote to Local (R2L) Attack
- Probing Attack

1. **Denial of Service (DOS) Attack:** In this attack, the aggressor makes registering or memory assets occupied to permit the authentic demand, or prevent the entrance genuine from claiming clients to the framework. The DOS includes attacks, for example, 'arrive', 'smurf', 'neptune', 'unit', 'back' and 'tear'.
2. **Users to Root (U2R) Attack:** In this kind of attack, the aggressor begins with access to an ordinary client account on the framework and can abuse some weakness to acquire root access to the framework. The U2R includes attacks, for example, 'loadmodule', 'rootkit', 'buffer_overflow' and 'perl'.
3. **Remote to Local (R2L) Attack:** In this attack, the assailant sends parcels to the framework over a system however who do not have a record on that framework and adventures a weakness to increase nearby access as a client of that framework. The R2L contains attacks, for example, 'warezclient', 'imap', 'multihop', 'guess_passwd', 'warezmaster', 'spy' 'ftp_write', and 'phf'.
4. **Probing Attack:** In this classification, the aggressor endeavors to assemble data about the system of PCs for the obvious reason for bypassing its security.

FRAMEWORK FOR INTRUSION DETECTION AND PREVENTION WITH COAP

1. **Message Layer model in COAP:** CON (confirmable), NON (non-confirmable), ACK (Acknowledgement), RST (Reset)
2. **Reliable Message Transport:** Keep retransmission until getting ACK with a similar message ID. Utilizing default timeout and diminishing tallying time exponentially when transmitting CON, if beneficiary neglect to process the message, it reactions by supplanting ACK with RST.
3. **Unreliable Message Transport:** Transporting with a NONtype message. It shouldn't be ACKed, however, needs to contain message ID for overseeing if there should arise an occurrence of retransmission. In the event that beneficiary neglect to process the message, the server answers RST.

Figure 2. Processing of communication and security (Sensing device)

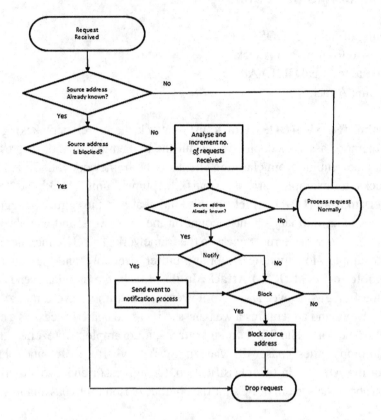

At whatever point a detecting gadget sends a notice to the 6LBR, the notice message transports a sign of the sort of demand got and of the root IP address of the demand as appeared in Figure. 2. After accepting the warning, the 6LBR (J. Nieminen et al., 2015) chooses if an activity must be activated, as indicated by the security arrangement nearby as appeared in Figure 3.

Communications might be secured by means of encryption, either at the system layer utilizing IPSec or at the vehicle layer utilizing DTLS (I.Butun et al., 2014). In Figure 6 we show, at the best, the arrangement for security messages started at a detecting gadget and at the base those began at the 6LBR.vAs for security messages started at a detecting gadget, the IP record field stores a situation to a vector holding structures which contain an IP address, the number of particular solicitations gotten by the sensor from each source IP address and a fag demonstrating climate correspondences from that source address is as of now blocked or not. The record asks for field demonstrates the sort of demand gotten by the constrained gadget (that hence has propelled the age of the security warning message).

Figure 3. Processing of communication and security (6LBR)

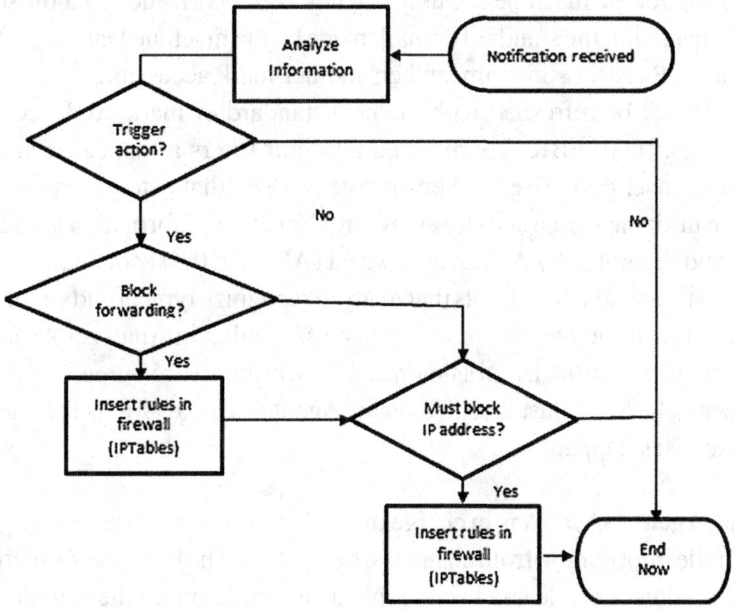

Upon receiving the notification, the 6LBR (J. Nieminen et al., 2015) decides if an action must be triggered, according to the security policy at hand as shown in Figure. 3.

Finally, in the *num requests* field, we transport the number of requests received, so far, by the sensing device, which is of type *index request* and have been received from the source IP address identified by *ip index*. Regarding the security notification messages originated at the 6LBR, *ip to block* is used again as an index to a position in a vector maintained in the memory of the destination sensithe ng device, storing information about the blocked origin device. This information, together with the identification of the type of request, allows for the exchange and updating of the information required for the security management module in each device to be able to detect and act upon received 6LoWPAN and CoAP communications.

INTRUSION DETECTION SYSTEM FRAMEWORK (IDSF-6BR) FOR 6LoWPAN

IDSF-6BR is a hybrid breed based IDS that connected both inconsistency and mark based IDS in the plan. Brought together location framework is actualized in IDSF-6BR where every one of the information will be steered to 6BR gadget for identification of potential attacks. IDSF-6BR uses 6LoWPAN pressure header as the component for the machine learning calculation to learn and order the sort of the attacks. At that point, the standard or mark made by the machine learning calculation is put at the 6BR. After some time, when another mark accessible for the directing attacks, 6BR will be refreshed with the new standard or mark produced from the new highlights. IDSF-6BR is partitioned into four layers as appeared in Figure 4. The principal layer comprises of Sensor Agents (SA) that catches pressure header information utilizing Cooja activity analyzer. The caught information is additionally examined and separated by Aggregator Agent (AGA) in the second layer. The AGA extricates just particular highlights that ready to recognize typical and strange system exercises. This is trailed by the information class naming in Analyzer Agent (ANA) layer. At this layer, information is named either ordinary, hi surge, sinkhole or as wormhole attack. At the last layer, Actuator Agent (ACA) cautions the client if any noxious exercises happen.

- **Sensor Agent (SA):** SA is in charge of catching system movement by gathering got bundle information from all hubs in the system. The bundle information gives a deliberation of crude and heterogeneous information. In the examination, we utilize Cooja movement analyzer to catch the radio message and spare as the parcel catch (pcap) document.
- **Aggregator Agent (AGA):** This layer features the principle commitment of this paper which is finding the critical highlights that can be utilized to separate among ordinary and anomalous exercises. To play out this errand, a trial that contains ordinary and strange exercises are arranged. At that point, the pcap documents for these two exercises are sifted to choose the information that just identified with 6LoWPAN convention.
- **Analyzer Agent (ANA):** Three routing attacks in IoT to be specific, hi surge, sinkhole and wormhole attack are arranged at this layer. The noteworthy highlights of the attacks as decided from AGA layer are decided for further examination. Their parcel number is plotted against time to contemplate the conduct of each attack and an arrangement of the guideline is then conceived. Next, classes marked as ''Normal'', ''Hello Flood'', ''Sinkhole'' and ''Wormhole'' are made dependent on the amended guideline. To arrange each attack as indicated by the characterized classes, we look at six machine calculations by means of WEKA apparatuses to locate the best performing calculation. The calculations are MLP, SVM, J48, Naïve Bayes, Logistic, and Random Forest.
- **Actuator Agent (ACA):** This agent will execute an activity by giving a caution to the clients. It has basic conduct that reacts to the ANA procedure by

contrasting them and an edge esteem (S.Shamshirband et al., 2014). On the off chance that the outcome from the ANA procedure surpassed the limit esteem, a caution will trigger.

SOFT COMPUTING: ARTIFICIAL NEURAL NETWORK (ANN) LEARNING

The IoT network is made out of 5 hub sensors. Four of the hubs are going about a customer, and one is going about as a server transfer hub for information scientific purposes. The movement is caught by means of a system tap dodging adjustment of the live activity. The server hub recognizes the information sent by the sensor hubs and answers with information dependent on the got information. This enables the sensor hubs to adjust their conduct and respond to happening occasions as appeared in Figure. 5 (Left). With regards to this examination, the attack is from an outside interloper. The attack is appeared in Fig. 6 (Right). The assailants just focus on the server hub, as it is the one breaking down, logging and reacting to the sensors hubs (M.A. Alsheikh et al., 2014). The ANN-based test set-up appears in Figure 5.

The DoS attack was performed utilizing a solitary host, sending more than 10 million parcels. While the DDoS attacks were performed by up to 3 has to send more than 10 million bundles each at wire speed flooding the server hub. The parcels sent amid the DoS/DDoS attacks are UDP bundle created by a custom content in C. As

Figure 4. The framework of the IDSF-6BR

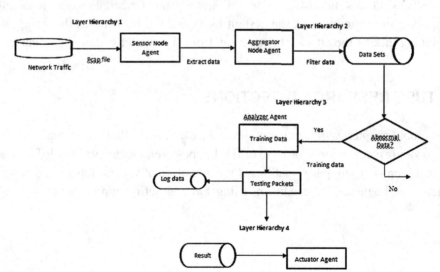

Figure 5. The experimental architecture of artificial neural network

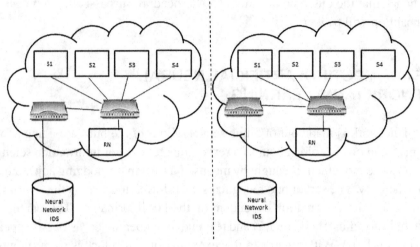

the server hub progresses toward becoming un-responsive the sensors hubs are not ready to adjust their conduct, at last prompting a blame on the observed framework (X. J. A. Bellekens et al., 2014). The location of the attack is in this manner vital, permitting the reaction group to keep away from interruption of the sensor system and certification the solidness of the system.

The system was prepared with 2313 examples, approved with 496 examples and 496 test tests. The system yield right reaction esteems fall under two classifications: This model exhibits that the ANN calculation actualized can effectively distinguish DDoS/DoS attacks against genuine IoT arrange movement. Besides, it enables enhancing the soundness of the system by notice the reaction to the group at a beginning time of the attack, staying away from significant system disturbances.

FUTURE RESEARCH DIRECTIONS

This book chapter will bring out layer-wise security challenges and solution provisioning mechanism in order to fulfill the end-to-end security in any IoT system. Also, this chapter will pave a pathway for exploration of various intrusion detection schemes and defending mechanisms using soft computing approaches.

CONCLUSION

The IoT is a smart network which interfaces physical articles to the web with the end goal of correspondence. There is no arrangement accessible to distinguish Hello surge attack and Sybil attack in IoT organize. Considering the potential utilization of the IoT it is essential that 6LoWPAN systems are ensured against inside and outside interruptions. This work presumes that lightweight IDS framework is essentially intended for asset constrained sensor hubs and ready to recognize Denial of Service attacks of two kind bundle transfer and exemplification. Generally, concentrated modules are utilized for doing substantial preparing and Lightweight modules keep running on sensor hubs causing sparing of vitality on sensor hubs. In this article, we address the structure of a design for appropriated interruption recognition and response in Internet incorporated CoAP detecting conditions and depict its usage and the exploratory assessment of its adequacy in identifying and responding to attacks, and additionally its effect on the central assets of constrained remote detecting stages. Concentrating all the more nearly on the application-layer, we intend to distinguish further attacks against the ordinary task guidelines of the CoAP convention. An IDS to distinguish directing attacks specifically, hi surge, sinkhole and wormhole attacks and additionally their blend is proposed. The IDSF-6BR uses 6LoWPAN pressure header as highlights. The 6LoWPAN pressure header comprises of 77 data with respect to the steering subtle elements. From this data, we utilized BFS-CFS and GS-CFS seeking calculations to choose the most critical data as info highlights into a machine learning calculation. This outcome in five highlights being chosen which are goal port, setting identifier, goal setting identifier, next header, and example. It could distinguish effectively extraordinary kinds of attacks and indicated great exhibitions as far as obvious and false positive rate.

REFERENCES

Alrajeh, N. A., Khan, S., & Shams, B. (2013). Intrusion detection systems in wireless sensor networks: A review. *International Journal of Distributed Sensor Networks*, *9*(5), 167575. doi:10.1155/2013/167575

Alsheikh, M. A., Lin, S., Niyato, D., & Tan, H. P. (2014). Machine learning in wireless sensor networks: Algorithms, strategies, and applications. *IEEE Communications Surveys and Tutorials*, *16*(4), 1996–2018. doi:10.1109/COMST.2014.2320099

Bellekens, X. J., Tachtatzis, C., Atkinson, R. C., Renfrew, C., & Kirkham, T. (2014, September). A highly-efficient memory-compression scheme for GPU-accelerated intrusion detection systems. In *Proceedings of the 7th International Conference on Security of Information and Networks* (p. 302). ACM. 10.1145/2659651.2659723

Butun, I., Morgera, S. D., & Sankar, R. (2014). A survey of intrusion detection systems in wireless sensor networks. *IEEE Communications Surveys and Tutorials*, *16*(1), 266–282. doi:10.1109/SURV.2013.050113.00191

Cady, F. (2017). *The Data Science Handbook*. John Wiley & Sons. doi:10.1002/9781119092919

Chen, S., Xu, H., Liu, D., Hu, B., & Wang, H. (2014). A vision of IoT: Applications, challenges, and opportunities with China perspective. *IEEE Internet of Things Journal*, *1*(4), 349–359. doi:10.1109/JIOT.2014.2337336

Hossain, M. M., Fotouhi, M., & Hasan, R. (2015, June). Towards an analysis of security issues, challenges, and open problems in the internet of things. In *Services (SERVICES), 2015 IEEE World Congress on* (pp. 21-28). IEEE. 10.1109/SERVICES.2015.12

Jun, C., & Chi, C. (2014, January). Design of complex event-processing ids in internet of things. In *Measuring Technology and Mechatronics Automation (ICMTMA), 2014 Sixth International Conference on* (pp. 226-229). IEEE. 10.1109/ICMTMA.2014.57

Khan, M. A. (2016). A survey of security issues for cloud computing. *Journal of Network and Computer Applications*, *71*, 11–29. doi:10.1016/j.jnca.2016.05.010

Kumar, S. N. (2015). Review on network security and cryptography. *International Transaction of Electrical and Computer Engineers System*, *3*(1), 1–11.

Kyaw, A. K., Chen, Y., & Joseph, J. (2015, November). Pi-IDS: evaluation of open-source intrusion detection systems on Raspberry Pi 2. In *Information Security and Cyber Forensics (InfoSec), 2015 Second International Conference on* (pp. 165-170). IEEE.

Mehare, T. M., & Bhosale, S. (2017). *Design and Development of Intrusion Detection System for Internet of Things*. Academic Press.

Nieminen, J., Savolainen, T., Isomaki, M., Patil, B., Shelby, Z., & Gomez, C. (2015). *Ipv6 over bluetooth (r) low energy* (No. RFC 7668).

OASIS Standard. (2014). *MQTT version 3.1. 1*. Retrieved from http://docs. oasis-open. org/mqtt/mqtt/v3

Pongle, P., & Chavan, G. (2015). Real time intrusion and wormhole attack detection in internet of things. *International Journal of Computers and Applications, 121*(9).

Sforzin, A., Mármol, F. G., Conti, M., & Bohli, J. M. (2016, July). RPiDS: Raspberry Pi IDS—A Fruitful Intrusion Detection System for IoT. In *Ubiquitous Intelligence & Computing, Advanced and Trusted Computing, Scalable Computing and Communications, Cloud and Big Data Computing, Internet of People, and Smart World Congress (UIC/ATC/ScalCom/CBDCom/IoP/SmartWorld), 2016 Intl IEEE Conferences* (pp. 440-448). IEEE.

Shamshirband, S., Amini, A., Anuar, N. B., Kiah, M. L. M., Teh, Y. W., & Furnell, S. (2014). D-FICCA: A density-based fuzzy imperialist competitive clustering algorithm for intrusion detection in wireless sensor networks. *Measurement, 55,* 212–226. doi:10.1016/j.measurement.2014.04.034

Van, N. T. T., & Thinh, T. N. (2015, November). Accelerating anomaly-based IDS using neural network on GPU. In *Advanced Computing and Applications (ACOMP), 2015 International Conference on* (pp. 67-74). IEEE. 10.1109/ACOMP.2015.30

Zarpelão, B. B., Miani, R. S., Kawakani, C. T., & de Alvarenga, S. C. (2017). A survey of intrusion detection in Internet of Things. *Journal of Network and Computer Applications, 84,* 25–37. doi:10.1016/j.jnca.2017.02.009

Chapter 7

Study on Query–Based Information Extraction in IoT–Integrated Wireless Sensor Networks

Prachi Sarode
VIT Chennai, India

TR Reshmi
VIT Chennai, India

ABSTRACT

The internet of things-integrated sensor nodes (IoT-WSN) is widely adopted in variety of applications such as fire detection, gas leakage detection in industry, earthquake detection, vibrating locations on flyover, weather monitoring, and many more wherein highest value is required in time to serve the abnormal areas with highest priority. The query-based information extraction has increased attention of many researchers working on increasing the network lifetime of the IoT-WSN. In resource-constraint IoT-WSN, executing the requests (in the form of queries) in time with minimum energy consumption is the main requirement and focus. The query processing at sink node in collaboration with neighboring nodes and then finding the top-k values for data aggregation is the most challenging job in IoT-WSN. This chapter investigates the various query-based approaches and improvements in the query data availability. The chapter also presents a comparative analysis that gives an idea of different aspects and applications of query-based schemes.

DOI: 10.4018/978-1-5225-8241-0.ch007

INTRODUCTION

Wireless Sensor Network (WSN) Cao and Wang (2004) is an application specific network consisting of sensor nodes that senses data, do some computation and communicate the information. However, Sensors nodes are energy constrained, which pose many research challenges to create an energy efficient networks which comprises various types of traffic models and data delivery models. Recent work focuses on query-based data delivery, event-based data delivery, continuous data delivery, and hybrid-based data delivery models. There are many applications using Internet of Things integrated WSN (IoT-WSN) where sensor nodes join internet dynamically, use it to collaborate and accomplish their tasks. This integration requires many investigations and analysis to resolve the architectural issues. The Figure 1 given below shows IoT architecture layers and their integration with other private networks. The IoT-WSN is used in variety of applications such as Fire detection, Gas leakage detection in industry, earthquake detection, and vibrating locations on flyover, weather monitoring and many more wherein highest values is required in time to serve the abnormal areas with highest priority. This study focuses on query-based delivery models considering the requirements of distinct cases. The job of sink node is to find the highest value(s) from specific region of the sensor network by broadcasting the control query message to all the neighbor nodes. Generally, after reception of query message, the sensor nodes report the updated highest top-k value(s) to its parent node after an authentication process. In most of cases for processing the data, sink node will be require only part of the information instead of whole event data of a particular region. Henceforth the authentication process assures the data shared is reliable and the adopted query-based data aggregation reduces the overheads of the network and thereby contributes to prolong the network life. So, the scheme assures reliability, timeliness and efficiency in data aggregation at various levels in underlying network configuration.

Figure 1. IoT architecture layers

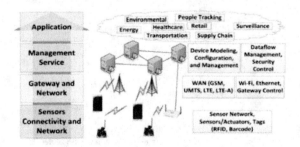

The necessary information is requested using various types of queries such as: Top–k query, query with identifier, Location aware query and cluster centered query. Consequently, this study focuses on top-*k* query wherein it tries to find: 1) highest k values from sensor nodes 2) highest readings of 'K' nodes from all the connected sensor nodes. The sensor nodes consume more power during packet transmission rather than receiving or performing any computational work. There are mainly two approaches to reduce the energy consumption in sensor nodes; 1) turning off transducer for a period of time. 2) to reduce the bulk data communication during network processing. Therefore, sending only the specific information required is the need of most of the critical applications in real world scenarios which indirectly reduces the energy consumption of contributing sensor nodes of the network. The figure 2 shows a typical query-based information gathering in IoT-WSN. It shows a user sending a query with precise information to the sink node. Sink node processes the requested query and broadcast to other sensor nodes instructing to extract required information. Sensor nodes answer the query by applying appropriate top-k query approaches, data aggregation techniques and filtering schemes. After receiving response, it is sent back to the requested user.

LITERATURE SURVEY

In this study review article, the different types of information retrieval schemes for Query based IoT-WSN are studied to understand their contribution to optimize the prolong network life. Cheng and Li and Yu (2012) proposed a scheme which provides highest sensed value(s) and location of sensor nodes. Traditional algorithm

Figure 2. Query processing in IoT-WSN

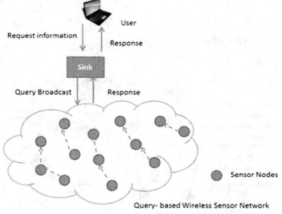

sends top-*k* value which belongs to one area only. Hence it is insufficient to identify the polluted or abnormal region. In the current scheme, user decides largest sensed values-'k' and their location-'D' values. Problem of Query processing is identified as NP-hard and proposed two different algorithms are based on Greedy approach and accordingly regions are partitioned. Greedy algorithm is useful when there is a need to get large number of highest values from small region. Second approach is more suitable when sensor region is large and highest value requirement is less. LAP-(D, K) centralized greedy scheme is evaluated and theoretically proved that required ratio bound is much larger than distributed greedy algorithm. Distributed greedy algorithm consists of sub two algorithms 1) Marking Algorithm for Sensor (selects candidate to send their values). 2) Result Collecting Algorithm transmits the sensed values and location of 'k' candidate sensors. All 'selected' tag sensors transmit their values and location using spanning tree method. Sensed values and their location are forwarded towards sink using spanning tree scheme and values are aggregated at every parent in the tree. Sensor marking algorithm runs at every node in the network. Firstly, Sink gives call to sensor marking algorithm and result collecting algorithm. Broadcast messages are more which consume more energy for transmission and receiving. In the second approach, partition-based algorithm sensor region divided into 3 hexagon regions. The main motto behind choosing hexagon for partition is hexagon strategy has maximum edges as compared with any other polygon which covers the maximum space. Ratio bound is directly proportional to number of colors chosen for hexagon. Whole network is divided into hexagon network. Hexagon is called as cluster. Each cluster has cluster head. 1) Cluster head of all same color cell form spanning tree (ST) rooted at sink. 2) Every sensor node in cluster is candidate tuple from its child and calculate threshold eights using linear algorithm. 3) Cluster heads in spanning tree omits the candidate tuple and transmits few cells to sink. The performance of the algorithm is examined in three ways: 1) Indoor sensor network consists of fifty Telos B motes. 2) Simulated 200 sensors on Tossim Simulator. 3) On testbed with varying density regions. Analysis and experimental setup results show that proposed algorithm gives better performance in terms of preciseness and cost of energy.

Jiang et al. (2012) focuses on multidimensional sensor data with multidimensional top-k queries. Dominant graph layered architecture is developed to build relationship in-between different data stored in multi-dimensional sensors wherein data points shares the parent child relationship in-between k_{th} and $(k+1)_{th}$ layers. The data points *d* in k_{th} layer dominates the *d* data points $(k+1)_{th}$ layer. This multidimensional Top-k framework is built on network layer. Overall the network is divided into two parts: Base Station network and Sensor network. Two types of messages flow in network: data flow and control flow. Data flow is mainly concerned with the Sensor network and Control flow with both types of networks. Individual sensor node prepares the "Dominant graph" based on result set received from sink. As a response to the Query process each node receives RS_i top-k result from its child nodes which then is aggregated and sent back to the parent node. This process is repeated until it reaches the sink. Using control flow base station sends global top-k information (filter) over network. The Top-k extraction algorithm relayed on sensor nodes combines the top-k responses RS_i from its children along with its own results and forward to its parents. Sink also builds its DG to respond query to user and periodically floods its top-k results into network to collects top-k values to complete its view. It has been observed that nodes send useless data to the sink over the routing tree which may not be a part of the top-k query result. So, enhanced scheme sends all data points in RS_{sink} to individual nodes which filter out non top-k results. It introduces filtering technique to filter out data points which are dominated by at least *(k-1)* other data point. If filter is not updated in consecutive iterations for a particular time period, then it fails to filter out the non-top-k nodes (data points) called as conservative filter. Counter variable is used with every filter. Its high value indicates that filter updating algorithm works properly at every node. The framework is also compatible with additional modules like data aging and approximate queries which provides latest information and helps to reduce the communication cost. By applying above framework simulations results showed that the communication cost was reduced by 90 percent compared to the centralised scheme.

Liao and Huang (2012) demonstrate the scheme of data storage for top-k query to an increase network life time and decrease the cost of query. Proposed work illustrates the novel approach of Grid top-k query algorithm with storage scheme compared with existing FILA top-k query algorithm. Wireless sensor network is configured with grid topology. Dimension of each grid depends upon quantity of sensor nodes and their rate of sampling. If sampling rate is high and there are large numbers of sensor nodes, then grid dimension is considered high. Every sensor node is assigned unique id and aware of its geographical location. The sensing values are normalised to fit into the range of 0 to 1. Each grid is having Grid Head (GH) which is located at the centre part of grid, stores the sensed data and sensor ID. Grid to Grid communication happens in snake style order. According to sub range values assigned to grid head, every sensor node data is forwarded to its desired GH. Each grid maintains value of *count$_{ID}$* which maintains the entries of sensed data in the grid GID. Grid Top-k algorithm at sink, queries the highest rank grid head for top-k values if k<*count$_{ID}$* at a grid it will immediately respond to query with its top-k values if not then, it adds its *count$_{ID}$* into query packet. Also, it decreases the values of 'k' by *count$_{ID}$* and forwards query packet to next lower grid dimension. Procedure of forwarding query packets to lower rank grid is repeated until sink gets the all top 'k' sensed values. Each sensor node in network has to store data at grid head after some unit interval time with fixed data transmission frequency. The performance of Grid top-k algorithm is evaluated by varying sensor nodes and area of sensor network. Total power consumption is computed on the basis of storage cost and Query cost. Due to hop distance the cost of storage is influenced between sensor node and its Grid head to store the data. Query cost depends on both frequency of query and hop-distance. Simulation results show: 1) Top-k of Grid algorithm performance is better than FILA Top-k algorithm due to data traffic is distributed over network which reduces the hotspot. 2) Network life time decreases due to addition of sensor nodes which in turn increases storage cost of sensor node. 3) Network life time is directly propositional to sensor network dimension. As count of Grid Head increases it becomes easy to store and distribute information and also the problem of hotspot is addressed. But after increasing network dimension which increases cost of query and further surpasses the storage cost which result in reduction of network lifetime.

Malhotra and Nascimento and Nikolaidis (2011) proposed Exact top-k, in order to reduce the query reply time and network overheads the query filtering algorithm is proposed. Unlike FILA, EXTOK has less overheads, no hop communication restriction and does not rely on any underlying topology. Initially, after reception of request from user sink node disseminate query to its neighbor nodes and request all neighbor nodes to do the same. It is repeated until all connected nodes receive the requested query. In order to reduce the message overheads, the SPT and DST tree structure are taken into design consideration for building the tree to maximize the network life. EXTOK prolongs the network life compared to FILA approach. FILA filter uses round structure considering two bounds i.e. lower bound and upper bound. It updates these two values in each round by finding top-2 values using aggregation scheme. Few issues of EXTOK like violation of filter rule at certain situations are not properly addressed as well as accuracy of returning value is less because it produces approximate results after every round. These issues are taken into consideration in EXTOK top-k algorithm. It uses synthetic and real data sets. In each round, its execution starts from leaf node and ends with root node. It works similarly to TAG approach. TM node updates and forwards value(s) to sink and then it checks whether updated value is greater than or equal to given threshold value. If it exceeds then only updates the top k results. In EXTOK, overheads of message transmission, query reply time, and power utilization are less but filter is required at every node which demands aggregation.

Tang, et al. (2014) discussed top-k queries in wireless sensor network leveraging hierarchical grid index based on spatial queries to achieve certain goals. Proposed novel top-k query algorithm and filtering technique divides sensor network into hierarchical grid index. Each child node sends the sensed information to its parent node after every periodic time interval. Parent node decides the range of values and also keeps the information related to owner (child) of top-k value. However, top-k value is being transmitted in every round in-between sink and head nodes. In the first iteration, all sensor nodes transfer their values to the grid heads (GH) and then GHs transfer top-k values with location of sensor node to Parent Node (PN). Furthermore, Parent Nodes evaluate top-k value and returns to root node. Therefore, sink node communicates with root node to find the actual result. During the iteration, top-k value holding nodes become temporal node (TM) and other becomes filter node (F). Root node stores top-k values and lowest value from i.e l_v is broadcast in the network during second iteration. If sensed value is greater than stored desired value, then only it reports to its GH. However, filter value is broadcasted to only its GH in each round. Filter broadcast approach consumes less power compared with traditional approaches. Also, for the next top-k values requirement values will be compare with only TM-grid or F-grid instead of whole sensor network which increased query response time.

Zhu *et al.* (2015) discussed the top-k query-based approaches in duty-cycled WSN (D-WSN), D-WSNs with data replication and connected kc-neighborhood (DRC-WSN) and Always-on WSNs (A-WSN) to find out the highest value of set sensor nodes. The scheme mainly focuses on query data availability and to reduce the cost of query in terms of query reply time and overall power consumption. It is in analyzed with respect to various parameters such as number of neighbors, total number of sensor nodes, and connected Kc neighborhoods (CKN). CKN sleep scheduling algorithm gives the guarantee of reliable switching in-between "asleep" and "awake" states of every node in order to retain the connected multi-hop sensor network. The various models such as network model, interference model, transmission saturation model, and energy model are designed for improvising the system in terms of query cost and data accessibility. Initially, sleep scheduling CKN approach replicates the data of randomly selected K_r one-hop neighbors and then performs the actual communication. The performance analysis illustrates three different types of network configurations such as D-WSN, DRC-WSN, and A-WSN. The DRC-WSN has better query data accessibility as compared to DC-WSN network but the query cost is almost same.

Considering the factor of number of sensor nodes, A-WSN has always more total power consumption and query reply time than of DRC-WSN and D-WSN because sensors are always in "awake" state. Whereas, top 'k' query in DRC-WSN basically achieves reasonable tradeoff in-between query data availability and cost of query measured with A-WSN and D-WSN. Furthermore, increasing K_r will eventually increase the total energy consumption, query data accessibility and query response time for DRC-WSN and D-WSN. Analysis describes that an increase in the value of 'N' will decreases the query data availability of DC-WSN and DRC-WSN but increases the total power consumption and reply time of DC-WSN, DRC-WSN and A-WSN. Finally, it is observed that the use of DR approach in D-WSN with CKN sleep scheduling algorithm forms the DRC-WSN which achieves the best tradeoff of query data availability and cost of query as compared to A-WSN and DC-WSN sensor network.

The various aspects and limitations in resource constraint Q-WSN shows the vital part of retrieving specific information in limited time period. Achieving the target top-k desired results should be independent of any underlying topology in Q-WSN. The current literatures mainly target only on homogenous wireless sensor network. Efficient execution of top-k depends upon the minimum number control packets and data packets to get desired value(s). Minimizing a tradeoff in-between energy consumption and reliable execution of query is an important concern in the sensor network. After reviewing it is observed that few parameters need to be taken into design consideration such as network connectivity, topology configuration, sensor nodes, and sensor network dimension, filter technique, data aggregation, data storage, and data replication. Network configuration is an important aspect in Q-WSN. For example, in grid configuration, if the number of nodes and dimensions of the grid is high then grid head or storage node has to store more values which may indirectly affects the query cost. In case of hierarchical grid configuration, parent node should equip with well filtering technique and time to time filter updates to avoid unnecessary data transmission in network. To keep network connected at all the time in duty cycled wireless sensor network, it is necessary to have some provision to replicate data and to awake sensor node(s). Handling, execution, and getting desired values are the considerable factors to increase the overall performance of the top 'k' query which in turn contributes to attain the QoS parameters of the configured query-based sensor network. To achieve the data accessibility, parameters such as, less query cost, fast query response and improve the network lifetime are needing to be considered cautiously while retrieving of accurate information.

DISCUSSIONS

The section presents the prior work of top-k approach in integrated IoT-WSN and put forth their applicability. It covers many distinct areas where finding the maximum sensor reading is important like in earthquake detection, fire detection, finding highest water level in tank, weather temperature, gas leakage, vibration level of flyover, manufacturing industry, healthcare service industry, Transportation Logistics, Mining, and firefighting and many more. Finding the highest value in time is a crucial task in most of the applications. Therefore, in our survey, we have identified the usage scenarios where IoT can work in association with WSN to address the problem. In this review article, you might have noticed that the focus is given more on an integrated approach using sensor technology. Following query-based information extraction techniques would be used to bring the automation to address the problem of finding the highest reading are as follows and disscussed by Kakad and Sarode and Bakal (2012).:

- Top-k query
- Exact top-k query i.e. EXTOK
- Data replication for top-k query
- Data storage scheme for top-k query
- Continuous top-k data collection queries
- Insight top-k query in duty-cycled WSN
- Location-aware peak value, and many more

The above-mentioned techniques will bring improvements in the query data availability and will help to reduce the cost of the query with respect to query response time and energy consumption. Moreover, to get access to event information and the alive connection is essential. In this regard, IoT plays the crucial role in bringing life to most of applications devices who report the readings. There are various applications of IoT from which key applications areas of IOT are manufacturing industry, healthcare service industry, Transportation Logistics, Mining, and firefighting. IoT solutions are very important in mining services. It is very common to have a different kind of accidents in mines. It is important to collect data to provide early warning before any disasters or accidents will happen. In mining monitoring air quality inside the mine, detecting the presence of different types of poisonous gases is a need. Fluctuation of oxygen level is very regular problems in mines. So, all these things can be not only needed to monitor but by the help of top k query, we can vastly identify locations as well as top k alarming values which may help to prevent accidents.

In firefighting application where RFID tag embedded things deployed in the building or forest fire detection so that emergency services can provide. If we can observe carefully all the above applications these are having lots of challenges have to take care such as Identification of object, managing a huge amount of data and enabling the infrastructure with data storage. Also, the most important concern is with security and privacy which an elaborate as information security on data privacy protection. Things can be tracked and monitored and get connected with the internet so there is a chance of an attack on personal and private data.

In the manufacturing industry, achieving the tight and stressful deadlines is truly crucial job nowadays. To balance the three important things, namely, time, cost, and quality are essential to prevent the big loss and to improve the profit. The main challenging task is to collect the data timely to take the decision promptly with high accuracy. Currently, most of the manufacturers have implemented Industry 4.0 standards specifically covering the data mining and Internet of Things. Traditional systems lag in terms of getting access to data and delivering it on time. Therefore, manufactures fails to achieve their customer demands. To overcome this problem, data aggregation and analysis become the necessity of the production line. Smart machines are used nowadays to meet the real-time deadlines, reduction in the production line, improvising the quality of the product, mining the data set, and effective use of data aggregation approach with communication capability to the internet. Identifying the affected location within time automated maintenance facility through IoT infrastructure reduces the production loss and minimizes the repairing time which results into higher profit with a greater level of quality product.

Healthcare sector is nowadays costlier than ever, world population is aging and number diseases are on a rise. The most part of the population is older people. It is noticed that they are suffering from chronic diseases. Though we have technology still we cannot reduce aging or from long persisting diseases. Traditional hospital procedures take a lot of time to diagnose the patient and also leads to higher bills. Currently, medical facilities are become hospital-centric instead of patient-centric. Therefore, it is need of connectivity among machine to machine and machine to human to improve communication to diagnose the patient's health. It will lessen the need for hospitalization. To save the life of a patient in the critical condition, IoT can use to monitor a patient's health remotely in the emergency situation like heart attack, diabetic, asthma attack, lower oxygen level, etc. The smart medical device can deliver the information to smartphone application using sensing technology. Medical devices equipped with sensor technology should be used to collect and deliver the information. In addition, body sensor network is useful to continuous delivery of vital signs. Moreover, gathered data can be analyzed and remotely shall prescribe the medicine so that human life could be saved without wasting time locate the patient. Top-k values of different events can be captured with the effective use of wireless technology like BLE, ZigBee, WI-Fi, Z wave, etc. to reliable delivery. Therefore, aggregating the data at the patient location is essential instead of forwarding unnecessary information to the hospital. In this application, data aggregation approach with IoT enabled sensing technology plays a vital role to serve the critical information and patient tracking timely. Location-aware peak reading is important in the case to name a few like high blood pressure, sugar level, and body temperature where data freshness is required. In this regard, data accessibility shall be achieved with adequate topology to aggregate the data. Despite delivery, the every vital sign reading, the communication model could be developed to deliver only abnormal reading which is needed to diagnose the patient by aggregating the values at various data points.

Currently, human kind is experiencing the various societal problems like water pollution, environmental sudden changes, and air pollution. To handle these problems without technology is almost impossible. However, having effective technology does not indicate the solution to a problem unless it can tackle it safely and accurately in time. Thus, the study focuses on the essential extraction of information with minimum energy consumption with the highest level of data freshness. Furthermore, the reduction of query cost is directly proportional to the reduction in overall data overheads into the network. For instance, sudden changes in environmental increase large packets into the network which results into maximum energy consumption. Therefore, to decrease the cost of the query, the data handling approach need to be inculcated appropriately. The selection of topology depends upon the design of the data aggregation model to handle the data accuracy and freshness.

Table 1. Classification and analysis of top-k query techniques

Method	Communication Pattern	Type of Query	Scheme Used	Target Outcome	Applications
Insights of Top-k Query in Duty-Cycled Wireless Sensor Networks	Tree base topology	Top-k query	CKN sleep scheduling algorithm, top-k query approach	High data accessibility, Query cost (includes query response time and energy consumption)	Healthcare, Earthquake detection, Environmental monitoring system
Top-k Queries in Wireless Sensor networks Leveraging Hierarchical Grid Index.	Hierarchical Grid Index	Spatial top-k	Hierarchical Grid Index construction Top-k Query Routing Top-k Filter	Reduces communication costs and energy consumption	Internet of Things (IoT) for collecting sensory data
A General Framework for Efficient Continuous Multidimensional Top-k Query Processing in Sensor Networks	Dominant graph data structure (Layered architecture among nodes with parent-child relationship)	Top-k query on multidimensional data	The Multidimensional Top-k Framework (Dominant graph) Distributed Top-k Extraction Algorithm Filter Construction Filter Update Data Aging Approximate Queries	Reduce communication cost by 90 percent Better performance for top-k query on multidimensional data	Data processing and information retrieval
An Efficient Data Storage Scheme for Top-k Query in Wireless Sensor Networks.	Grid topology	Top-k, Location based query	Grid network formation Data storage at grid Top-k query algorithm	Reduce query cost and prolong network life time	Environmental monitoring system
Location Aware Peak Value Queries in Sensor Networks	Hexagon pattern grid topology	Top-k, Location based query	LAP-(D,k) Distributed Greedy Algorithm Sensor Marking Algorithm Result Collecting Algorithm. Region Partition based Algorithm	High accuracy to query response With very low query cost	Water pollution monitoring
Exact Top-k Queries in Wireless Sensor Networks	Dominating Set Tree (DST)	Top-k, Location based query	DST Construction EXTOK's Top-K Queries	Save 80% of communication cost Low energy consumption Increase network life	Highest temperatures values in a building or patch of forest, the points of most intense vibration in a bridge

CONCLUSION

This chapter presents the prior work of top-k approach in integrated IoT-WSN and put forth their applicability. It covers many distinct areas where finding the maximum sensor reading is important like in earthquake detection, fire detection, finding highest water level in tank, weather temperature, gas leakage, vibration level of flyover, manufacturing industry, healthcare service industry, Transportation Logistics, Mining, and firefighting and many more. Latest wireless short-range communication technology is not only targeting reliable data delivery but also addressing the safety and privacy of critical information to some extent. To summarize the integrated IoT-WSN technology, it has been observed that the proposed data aggregation approach contributes with respect to authentication, data freshness, reliable low-cost query, optimum response time, minimum energy consumption, and greater data accessibility. Nowadays it becomes a heart of the short-range wireless network, specifically for IoT networks. The data aggregation approaches achieve three main goals, namely, authorized data injection, minimize data transmission overheads and maintain data freshness with minimum query cost. The IoT sensing devices have equipped the ability of communication to the internet. Therefore, the mixture of various technologies together brings the precise extraction of information at right time in the right place for the right decision. In the future, it opens the challenges of data privacy and data integrity in integrated IoT-WSN network. Hence, we conclude with putting the tagline that *"Integrated Wireless sensing technology is the heart of internet of things network instead of the subset"*.

REFERENCES

Cao, P., & Wang, Z. (2004). Efficient top-k query calculation in distributed networks. In *Proc. of ACM PODC*. ACM. 10.1145/1011767.1011798

Chen, B. (2010). *Energy Efficient Top-K Query Processing in Wireless sensor network. Canberra, ACT, Australia, October 26 30, Toronto*. Ontario, Canada: ACM.

Chen, B., Liang, W., & Yu, J. X. (2010). *Online Time Interval Top-k Queries in Wireless Sensor Networks. Management*. MDM.

Cheng, J., Jiang, H., Liu, J., Liu, W., & Wang, C. (2011). On Efficient Processing of Continuous Historical Top-k Queries in Wireless Sensor Networks. *IEEE Trans. Vehicular Technology, VOL., 60*(5), 2363–2367. doi:10.1109/TVT.2011.2148203

Cheng, S., Li, J., & Yu, L. (2012). Location Aware Peak Value Queries in Sensor Networks. *Proceeding IEEE INFOCOM*, 486-494. 10.1109/INFCOM.2012.6195789

Cho, Y., Son, J., & Chung, Y. D. (2008). POT: An Efficient Top-K Monitoring Method for Spatially Correlated Sensor Readings. *Proc. Fifth Workshop Data Management for Sensor Networks (DMSN '08)*, 8-13. 10.1145/1402050.1402053

Ge, T., Zdonik, S., & Madden, S. (2009). Top-k Queries on Uncertain Data: On Score Distribution and Typical Answers. SIGMOD'09, 375-387.

Hara, T., Hagihara, V., & Nishio, S. (2010). Data Replication for Top-k Query Processing in Mobile Wireless Sensor Networks. *IEEE International Conference on Sensor Networks, Ubiquitous, and Trustworthy Computing*, 115-122. 10.1109/SUTC.2010.25

Ilyas, I., Beskales, G., & Soliman, M. (2008). A Survey of Top-k Query Processing Techniques in Relational Database Systems. ACM Computing Surveys, 40.

Jiang, H., Cheng, J., Wang, D., Wang, C., & Tan, G. (2012). A General Framework for Efficient Continous Multidimensional Top-k Query Processing in Sensor Networks. *IEEE Transactions on Parallel and Distributed Systems*, 23(9), 1668–1680. doi:10.1109/TPDS.2012.69

Jiang, H., Cheng, J., Wang, J., Wang, C., & Tan, G. (2011). Continuous Multi-Dimensional Top-k Query Processing in Sensor Networks. *Proceedings - IEEE INFOCOM*.

Jiang, H., Jin, S., & Wang, C. (2010). Parameter-Based Data Aggregation for Statistical Information Extraction in Wireless Sensor Networks. IEEE Trans. *Vehicular Technology, VOL.*, 59(8), 3992–4001. doi:10.1109/TVT.2010.2062547

Kakad, Sarode, & Bakal. (2012). A Survey on Query Response Time Optimization Approaches for Reliable Data Communication in Wireless Sensor Network. *International Journal of Wireless Communications and Networking Technologies, 1*(2), 31-36.

Kakad, S., Sarode, P., & Bakal, J. (2013). Analysis and Implementation of Top k Query Response Time Optimization Approach for Reliable Data Communication in Wireless Sensor Networks. *International Journal of Engineering and Innovative Technology*, 3(2), 201–211.

Kaswan, A., Tomar, A., & Jana, P. K. (2018). An efficient scheduling scheme for mobile charger in on-demand wireless rechargeable sensor networks. *Journal of Network and Computer Applications, 114*, 123–134. doi:10.1016/j.jnca.2018.02.017

Liang, W., Chen, B., & Xu, J. (2008). Response Time Constrained Top-k Query Evaluation in Sensor Network. *14th IEEE International Conference on Parallel and Distributed Systems*, 575-782. 10.1109/ICPADS.2008.65

Lianh, W., Chen, B., & Yu, J. X. (2010). *Top-k Query Evaluation in Sensor Networks Under Query Response Time Constraint*. Canberra, Australia: School of Computer Science, Australian National University.

Liao, W., & Huang, C. (2012). An Efficient Data Storage Scheme for Top-k Query in Wireless Sensor Networks. *IEEE Network Operations and Management Symposium (NOMS)*, 554-557.

Liu, X., Xu, J., & Lee, W. C. (2010). A Cross Pruning Framework for Top-k Data Collection in Wireless Sensor Networks. *Proc. Int'l Conf. Mobile Data Management.* 10.1109/MDM.2010.41

Mai, H., & Kim, M. (2011). Processing Continuous Top-k Data Collection Queries in Lifetime-Constrained Wireless Sensor Networks. ICUIMC'11, Seoul, South Korea. doi:10.1145/1968613.1968631

Malhotra, B., Nascimento, M., & Nikolaidis, I. (2011). Exact Top-k Queries in Wireless Sensor Networks. IEEE Transactions on Knowledge and Data Engineering, 23(10). doi:10.1109/TKDE.2010.186

Niedermayer, J., Nascimento, M., & Renz, M. (2010). Exploiting Local Node Cache in Top-k Queries within Wireless Sensor Networks. ACM GIS '10, 434-437. doi:10.1145/1869790.1869855

Re, C., Dalvi, N., & Suciu, D. (2007). Efficient Top-k Query Evaluation on Probabilistic Data. ICDE. doi:10.1109/ICDE.2007.367934

Silberstein, A., Braynard, R., Ellis, C., Munagala, K., & Yang, J. (2006). A sampling-based approach to optimizing top-k queries in sensor networks. *Proc. ICDE*, 68–80.

Tang, J., Wang, Z., Sung, Y., Du, C., & Zhou, Z. (2014). Top-k Queries in Wireless Sensor Networks Leveraging Hierarchical Grid Index. *Eighth International Conference on Innovative Mobile and Internet Services in Ubiquitous Computing*, 381-386. 10.1109/IMIS.2014.51

Wu, M., Xu, J., Tang, X., & Lee, W. C. (2007). Top-k Monitoring in Wireless Sensor Network. *IEEE Transactions on Knowledge and Data Engineering, 19*(7), 962–976. doi:10.1109/TKDE.2007.1038

Yeo, M., Seong, D., Park, J., Ahn, M., & Yoo, J. (2013). An energy-efficient sequence-aware top-k monitoring scheme in wireless sensor networks. *International Journal of Distributed Sensor Networks*, 1–13.

Zhu, C., Yang, L., Shu, L., Leung, V., Hara, T., & Nishio, S. (2015). Insights of Top-k Query in Duty-Cycled Wireless Sensor Networks. *IEEE Transactions on Industrial Electronics*, *62*(2), 1317–1328. doi:10.1109/TIE.2014.2334653

Chapter 8
Lightweight Secure Architectural Framework for Internet of Things

Muthuramalingam S.
Thiagarajar College of Engineering, India

Nisha Angeline C. V.
Thiagarajar College of Engineering, India

Raja Lavanya
Thiagarajar College of Engineering, India

ABSTRACT

In this IoT era, we have billions of devices connected to the internet. These devices generate tons of data that has to be stored, processed, and used for making intelligent decisions. This calls for the need for a smart heterogeneous network which could handle this data and make the real-time systems work intelligently. IoT applications leads to increasing demands in high traffic volume, M2M communications, low latency, and MIMO operations. Mobile communication has evolved from 2G voice services into a complex, interconnected environment with multiple services built on a system that supports innumerable applications and provides high-speed access. Hence the sustainability of the IoT applications do rely on next generation networks. Due to the significant increase in the network components, computational complexity, and heterogeneity of resources, there arise the need for a secure architectural framework for internet of things. For this, the authors propose a secure architectural framework for IoT that provides a solution to the lightweight devices with low computational complexity.

DOI: 10.4018/978-1-5225-8241-0.ch008

INTRODUCTION

The novel communication frameworks Next Generation Networks (NGN) is the one that transports all information and services by packets. One of the next generation networks is the Internet of Things. The term Internet of Things has emerged from the concept of a network of objects. These devices are capable of sensing the various factors of the environment and collecting the data. It is one among the next generation networks which are going to interact without human intervention. IoT framework has various heterogeneity levels and desired connectivity among the billions of uniquely identifiable objects. A variety of applications such as healthcare, industrial surveillance with a number of techniques such as intelligent sensors, wireless communication, networks, data analytics, and cloud computing are developed. The biggest obstacles in IoT is security which can be of any type such as communication network security, application security, and general system security.To provide a solution to security issues of IoT we need to develop a secure architectural framework for IoT which encompasses the different network layers. The rise of new applications and wireless devices on fixed and mobile terminals led to the need of secure network architecture. (Massimo, 2016). The communication among the networks devised a strategic evolution of growth of the information to be communicated on the Internet. IoT includes light weight devices such as sensors and actuators. The security threats to IoT includes authentication failure and leakage of data. Since every device is light weight the solutions should also be simple. Traditional security mechanisms like Firewalling, Intrusion Detection and Prevention Systems are deployed at the Internet edge. Those mechanisms are used to protect the network from external attacks which are not sufficient to secure the Internet. IoT architecture does not provide enough security for the wireless network.

Security is the process of protecting a device or an object against all kinds of active and passive attacks. It also prevents from physical damage and unauthorized access of data thus providing authentication and authorization. Leakage of information is also to be prevented thus ensuring confidentiality and data integrity. Ensuring IoT security is not different from other networking environments. It requires to maintain the communication and data management inside and outside the network.

In the rest of the part section 2 describes the different types of protocols of IoT. Section 3 describes the security requirements of IoT which includes the various goals of security. Section 4 describes the lightweight security framework for IoT which addresses all the above described protocols and security requirements to be incorporated in the IoT architecture which is described in section 5. Section 6 focuses on the applications of IoT which can use the described architecture. Section 7 concludes the chapter with enhancement of future work for the architectural framework.

PROTOCOLS FOR IoT APPLICATIONS

Though many of the already available protocols can be used for IoT Applications, they still could be too heavy for most of the applications. Hence the introduction of specific protocols which could support low power devices and work in constrained networks. Let's discuss some of the protocols that can be specially used for IoT.

Constrained Application Protocol (CoAP)

It was developed by IETF CoRE - Constrained RESTful Environments working group - RFC 7252. CoAP shares the REST model with HTTP and hence it is a good choice for Low battery power devices and constrained networks. It is used to work on microcontrollers with so low as 10KiB of RAM and 100KiB of Code Space. CoAP packets are much smaller than HTTP TCP flows. Packets are simple to generate, and it also can be easily parsed without consuming extra RAM in constrained devices. CoAP follows the Client/Server model. It employs a two-layer structure. The bottom layer is the message layer which deals with UDP and asynchronous switching. Then the request/response layer concerns communication method and deals with request/response message. Request and response messages may be considered as confirmable or non-confirmable. If the message is confirmable then it must be acknowledged by the receiver with an ack packet. If it is non-confirmable then they are fire and forget. CoAP runs over UDP, not TCP. It provides connectionless-mode of communication between client and server. It also provides UDP broadcast and multicast features. In an IoT network, CoAP could be used to provide resource discovery service. Security has also been dealt with using CoAP Protocol using DTLS parameters.

MQ Telemetry Transport (MQTT)

MQTT is open source protocol for Constrained, Low Bandwidth, and High Latency Network. It is a Publish/Subscribe messaging protocol. It is message oriented where each message is a chunk of data. It follows the Client/Server model for communication where the client is a sensor and the server are also referred as a broker. Every message is published to an address it is called topics. Every client subscribed to a topic receives every message published to the topic. The topics are hierarchical like a filing system. It is used to support light weight message transfer between constrained networks. Since it is bandwidth efficient, it helps to reduce the resource requirements in a massive IoT network. It also ensures the reliability of the network due to the QoS features it provides. It does not support multicast. In application-level quality of service, it supports three quality of service levels they are fire and forget, delivered at least once and delivered exactly once.

AMQP (Advanced Message Queue Protocol)

AMQP is a message-oriented protocol and it is an open standard to exchange messages between applications. It provides features such as routing and queuing. The key factors of this protocol are open, interoperable, secure and reliable.

STOMP (Simple/Streaming Text Oriented Messaging Protocol)

Stomp is a text-oriented messaging protocol and it is very easy to use. In this protocol, the clients are connected to a message broker to exchange messages.

SECURITY REQUIREMENTS FOR IoT

Security and privacy issues play a major role in the development of IoT. The real-time external environmental data that is collected by devices or objects is transmitted inside a wireless medium of gateways and access points. There are many critical factors that make IoT data to be hacked. The types of attacks such as physical attack, active and passive attack and wireless information attack can affect the network communication and data management of IoT network.

Security Goals

The security goals that need to be accomplished for IoT architecture are explained in detailed as follows:

Data Integrity

It is a security goal which enables the devices or the objects or the nodes to ensure that the data in transmission is not altered by any kind of unauthorized users. In IoT data are collected from external stimuli and are transmitted to the server through gateways or access points. It has to be ensured that the data that is originated is the one that has been delivered. It also provides data origin authentication. The integrity of data provides reliable services to the users.

Authentication

Authentication is a process which enables the entities to verify themselves using their identities. The credentials of a particular device are stored in a server. When the device needs to communicate the credentials are verified and only the authenticated

Figure 1. Loss of Integrity

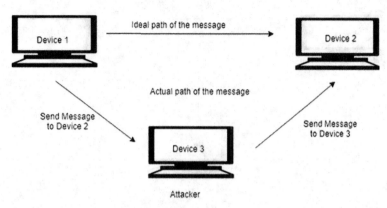

device can communicate. There are many forms of authentication such as entity authentication and message authentication. Ubiquitous connectivity of devices will the IoT exaggerate authentication problem.

Confidentiality of Data

Confidentiality of data prevents the disclosure of data to unauthorized persons. The data can be viewed by a person only after his credentials are validated and ensured that he is the authorized person.

Figure 2. Verifies the identity of the device

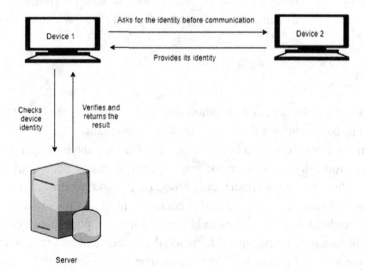

Figure 3. Loss of Confidentiality

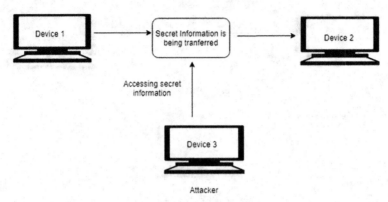

Non-Repudiation

The non-repudiation ensures that a certain device or user cannot deny the action what they have performed. It is one of major security goal for IoT applications as all are sensitive data transmission.

LIGHTWEIGHT SECURITY FRAMEWORK CONSIDERING THE KEY ELEMENTS FOR IOT ARCHITECTURE

An architecture framework is a combination of devices, gateway or access points, server, application domain. These models represent how these devices are connected in the system and also shows the flow of data inside the network. Some of the factors need to be considered while framing a secured architecture which is described as follows:

Network

IoT network is a collection of distributed sensors that collect data from the external environment based on certain factors such as temperature, sound, and pressure. Data from the sensor needs to be communicated among the nodes in the network for further processing. The network may be centralized or decentralized so that the security factors are also distributed based on the architecture of a network. In a centralized framework, a single node acts as the head of the network. As all the devices or node of IoT are lightweight devices the computational complexity is very less. In case of a decentralized network, the authentication process takes place based on the levels of hierarchy. The communication is also possible only through lightweight protocols such as MQTT. IoT is similar to the conventional network except in the point of human intervention i.e. the network will be connected with anywhere, anytime with anything. Thus, a network created with the above-given features can provide security to the network.

Storage Server

IoT devices require a storage server such as cloud since they cannot store the data in their memory due to low memory capacity. Since billions of data are stored in the cloud there may be leakage of data or data access by unauthorized users. To protect the data, it needs to be encrypted. Encryption and authentication of data need to be made with minimal operations for the lightweight device. Heavy computational algorithms cannot be processed. In a resource-constrained environment like IoT security data, the code can be multicast. While multicasting the data, a secret key has to be generated and shared among the members of the group. Since all data need not have the same level of security it can be provided based on their required level of efficiency.

IoT Architecture

Let us now discuss about the reference architecture for IoT. The reference architecture consists of 3 layers, the Physical layer, The Data Layer, The Network Layer, and the application layer. The Vertical layer is added to provide security to the User.

The Physical Layer

The physical Layer consists of the Sensors, Actuators and other so-called things that are connected to the internet. The Device Discovery and Communication have to be taken care of by this physical Layer. It also needs to ensure Device Management. Things on the internet can be identified with the help of tags. Each of the sensor, Actuator, and Tag would require a Driver component in the physical layer in order to carry out the Device Discovery and Device Management functionalities of the Layer. The Device Discovery takes care of the registration and deregistration of devices in the network. The Device Communication ensures connectivity with the devices using the corresponding Driver Component.

The Data Layer

The sensors and the things might produce millions of Data at any particular time. The Data Layer has to do data collection from the sensors/Things, perform suitable analytics on the data and finally send the processed data for the actuators for decision making. The Data Management in this layer has ensured that the computing power and the used technologies are ready to perform analytics on the larger datasets which are important for real-time applications.

The Network Layer

The network layer receives processed data from the Data Layer and determines optimal routes to transmit the information via the network. For IoT, the networks would be heterogeneous meaning it connects various devices and involves various communication technologies like Bluetooth, mobile networks, Zigee and Wi-Fi. The internet uses Standardised protocols like 6LoWPAN, IPv6 to provide networking capabilities. The most common topologies that could be adopted for the network are Star or Mesh topologies. Mesh network though complex than star network but the Mesh are more robust than the Star network.

The Application Layer

Application layer receives the data transmitted from the network layer and uses the data to provide required Servers for services and for the applications. It Connects the User to the Things. MQTT, CoAP, XMPP are application layer Protocols. While choosing an application layer protocol one must ensure that Bandwidth, latency, and reliability are to be considered.

Figure 4. IoT security architecture layers

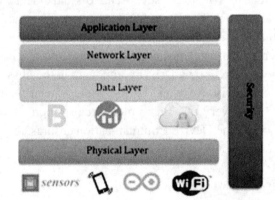

SECURITY THREATS, ATTACKS, AND VULNERABILITIES

Vulnerability

It addresses the weakness in a system which can be used by the intruder to access unauthorized data and perform the attacks. There are a variety of areas of IoT such as system hardware, software which are vulnerable. Hardware vulnerabilities are very difficult to fix. Rather software vulnerabilities can be identified in operating systems, communication protocols. Researchers have identified a number of vulnerabilities in all kinds of IoT applications.

Threats

A threat is any kind of action that causes harm to the network. Its source of origination varies from natural sources to artificial sources. In the case of natural threats, backup and recovery are the only sources to provide a solution. Threats caused by humans or other artificial resources can be of various categories. Since IoT has a large number of ubiquitous devices the number of threats also increase.

Attacks

Attacks are a kind of threat that disrupts the usual operations by a system. It can also allow an unauthorized user to access the data. Attackers exploit vulnerabilities of the network and achieve their own goals. Attacks include active and passive attacks. Active attacks monitor the data traffic and modify the data. Passive attack silently captures the network traffic without modifying the data. Some of the attacks of that can exploit the IoT network are described as follows:

- **Physical Attacks:** IoT includes ubiquitous devices which are most prone to physical attacks. The hardware or the devices or tampered by the attackers.
- **Denial-of-Service (DoS):** It is a kind of attack that makes a network resource unavailable to its intended users. Since it has limited computational resources, they are subjected to DoS attack.

IOT APPLICATIONS

Looking at the enormous growth in the new technologies, it is highly impossible to predict all the IoT based applications. (Maksymyuk, 2017). Here are few of them for discussion.

Smart Home

Many industries are getting into developing platforms to integrate IoT with building automation, entertainment, healthcare monitoring, energy monitoring in home environments. Using IoT applications, homes can act in a smart and intelligent way. Interesting applications of IoT in smart homes are smart lighting, smart environment and media, air control and central heating, energy management and security.

Smart City

The most awaited vision of almost every country. The whole world is looking out for the establishment of the smart city via IoT. Smart City aims at exploiting the most advanced communication technologies to support added-value services for the administration of the city and for the citizens. Some of the examples of the smart city are improved traffic management, improvement in infrastructure, the introduction of smart Building with green energy, smart retail shopping, smart waste management etc.

Smart Farming

Smart farming will become the important application field in the predominantly agricultural-product exporting countries. It is an important business case for the Internet of Things because it fits into various categories like mobility, industry or health. Remotely the crops could be monitored easily and reduce the manual work done by the farmers. It has become a revolution in farming. It has to be implemented on a large scale to increase the yield and monitoring and maintenance of the crops. Agricultural Internet of Things increases crop productivity and enhances the activities like crop water management, integrated pest management or control, food protection and safety, Unmanned Aerial Vehicle's (UAV) Sensors, carbon nanotube, wireless sensor monitoring.

Smart Grids

Smart grids are a special form of innovation in the Internet of Things. Smart grid promises to use the information about the behaviors of electricity suppliers and consumers in an automated fashion to improve the efficiency, reliability, and economics of electricity. It helps customers to reduce the amount of electricity used and save electricity to a specific amount. This helps customers to effectively use electricity.

Smart Supply Chain

Supply chains have been getting smarter for some years already. Solutions for tracking goods while they are on the road or getting suppliers to exchange inventory information have been on the market for years. So, this field has more scope in the upcoming years.

Wearables

Wearables are the most important innovation in recent days. Most of the **health-related** problems can be identified and controlled to a certain extent by using wearables. Wearable watches or smart watches are used to monitor a person's pulse rate, heartbeat etc.., Many companies have released smart watches which includes Apple, Sony Smart B Trainer, the Myo gesture control, or LookSee bracelet.

Healthcare

Internet of Things has made a revolution in the medical field too. Many automated machines have been developed to diagnose a patient and continuous monitoring of the patient's health can be done using certain devices like wearables. Using such devices, the doctor can monitor the patient remotely and the data collected by the devices are sent to the doctor for further analysis. Some of the activities in healthcare that has been automated are Open APS-closed-loop insulin delivery, continuous glucose monitoring system, activity trackers during cancer treatment, connected inhalers, ingestible sensors, connected contact lenses, depression- fighting Apple watch app, coagulation testing, Arthritis-Apple's research kit.

Connected Transportation

Connected transportation involves vehicles with Wi-Fi or other sensors to enable Internet connectivity during travel. The connected car is probably the most prevalent example. Many cities have begun smart transportation initiatives to optimize their public transportation routes, create safer roads, reduce infrastructure costs, and alleviate traffic congestion as more people move into cities. It uses sensors inside the connected vehicles to track them by GPS. And drivers can use the car's dashboard to reserve public parking spaces in the city.

Defense

The defense system's need is high connectivity, getting real-time information and knowing situational awareness. All this is possible with a connected technology (Internet of things) that can make soldiers more powerful, efficient and effective. Some of its achievements include battle field situational awareness, proactive equipment maintenance, monitor war fighter's health, remote training, real-time fleet management, efficient inventory management.

CONCLUSION

Thus, we have provided a solution to security issues of IoT by developing a secure architectural framework for IoT having different layers – the physical, the data layer, the network layer and the application layer, each taking care of the security aspects.

REFERENCES

Condoluci, M., Araniti, G., Mahmoodi, T., & Dohler, M. (2016, April). Enabling the IoT Machine Age With 5G:Machine-Type Multicast Services for Innovative Real-Time Applications. *IEEE Access: Practical Innovations, Open Solutions*, *4*, 5555–5569. doi:10.1109/ACCESS.2016.2573678

Maksymyuk, S. D., Brych, M., Satria, D., & Jo, M. (2017). An IoT based monitoring framework for software defined 5G mobile networks. *11th International Conference on Ubiquitous Information Management and Communication, Proceedings*. 10.1145/3022227.3022331

Section 3
Emerging Trends and Methods for Cyber Forensics

Chapter 9

The Role of Artificial Intelligence in Cyber Security

Kirti Raj Bhatele
RJIT, India

Harsh Shrivastava
RJIT, India

Neha Kumari
RJIT, India

ABSTRACT

Cyber security has become a major concern in the digital era. Data breaches, ID theft, cracking the captcha, and other such stories abound, affecting millions of individuals as well as organizations. The challenges have always been endless in inventing right controls and procedures and implementing them with acute perfection for tackling with cyber attacks and crimes. The ever-increasing risk of cyber attacks and crimes grew exponentially with recent advancements in artificial intelligence. It has been applied in almost every field of sciences and engineering. From healthcare to robotics, AI has created a revolution. This ball of fire couldn't be kept away from cyber criminals, and thus, the "usual" cyber attacks have now become "intelligent" cyber attacks. In this chapter, the authors discuss specific techniques in artificial intelligence that are promising. They cover the applications of those techniques in cyber security. They end the discussion talking about the future scope of artificial intelligence and cyber security.

DOI: 10.4018/978-1-5225-8241-0.ch009

INTRODUCTION

Is artificial intelligence less than our intelligence. (Jonze, S., 2017)

"Intelligence" is only the property that distinguishes human from anything else on this planet. The idea of having that Intelligence in man-made machines is quite fascinating although the machines can't have that inherited intelligence. Instead of natural human intelligence, the scientific, philosophical and other communities working for understanding human mind started pondering over this "Why can't machines think?" As a result of multidisciplinary efforts in areas of cognitive science, neuroscience and computer science, this idea of creating "Artificial Intelligence" began to attract the attention of researchers around the world. Around the 1960s and 70s, researchers started expecting very high from AI Research, but it was pretty much in vain without any breakthroughs.

We can define Artificial Intelligence as the scientific field that tries to understand and model human intelligence. Many Researchers have their own understanding of AI such as quoting Peter Norvig and Stuart Russel's Artificial Intelligence: A Modern Perspective "Artificial Intelligence is the study of agents that exist in the environment and perceive and act".

There has been an effort for decades to create such systems that can understand, think, learn, and behave like humans. We'll discuss some of the important approaches for AI that has pushed AI research further (Russell, S., J., & Norvig, P., 2000).

Historical Attempts

Warren McCulloch and Walter Pitts in 1943, for the first time, attempted to create an intelligent system. They proposed a model of the Artificial networked neural structure and claimed that if this structure would be defined properly, then it could learn like the human brain.

Recently after some year, Alan Turing published "Computer Machinery and Intelligence "in which he explored the idea of "Artificial Intelligence". In his work, he also proposed "Turing test" as a test to measure the machine's ability to exhibit intelligence. The setup for the test requires a natural language generating a machine, an evaluator (which is human) and a human. The evaluator will converse (interact) with the machine and the human and try to identify the machine based on the conversation. Both the machine and human will try to persuade evaluator that he or she is interacting with a human on the other side. If the evaluator fails to distinguish machine conversation from the human conversation, then the machine will be considered intelligent.

John McCarthy coined the term "Artificial Intelligence" in 1956. Two years later, he invented LISP, a high-level AI programming language for use in AI programs. In the next section we'll discuss one of the most widely adopted AI approaches historically, then we'll discuss the current and the best date approach to AI (Pattern Recognition).

Knowledge or Rule-Based Approach

In Knowledge-based AI systems, we try to embed the knowledge of human experts for their decision-making. Here the idea is to equip the system with the knowledge required for a task, for example - medical diagnosis, and the rules to infer insights from the knowledge to take a decision. This way all the decisions that KBAI system takes will be affected solely by the knowledge base created by the human expert in the concerned field. Therefore, KBAI systems are also known as Expert Systems. So, the general architecture of KBAI system consists of a Knowledgebase and an inference engine. Inference engine generally has IF-ElSE rules for inference from the knowledge base. The first knowledge-based system was MYCIN. It was written for medical diagnosis. The central Idea of knowledge-based systems was to represent knowledge explicitly through IF-ElSE rules (Russell, S., J., & Norvig, P., 2000).

Representation of Knowledge is the core task for developing an AI system. The rule-based knowledge representation is heavily used for the development of IBM Watson.

Pattern Recognition Approach

Pattern recognition is another approach to Artificial Intelligence. It is based on data unlike knowledge base in rule-based approach. It tries to learn the knowledge from data itself. We just need data for and machine learning algorithm (section 2) to discover the patterns from the data. These patterns will derive the decisions of the system in an unknown environment. Here is the modern definition of pattern recognition (Bishop): The field of pattern recognition is concerned with the automatic discovery of regularities in data through the use of computer algorithms and with the use of these regularities to take actions such as classifying the data into different categories. Pattern recognition has been the best approach to Artificial Intelligence. Machine Learning is the best approach to pattern recognition. In the next section we are going to dive in it (Russell, S., J., & Norvig, P., 2000).

MACHINE LEARNING

Machine intelligence is the last invention that humanity will ever need to make (Bostrom, N., 2015)

In 1959, Arthur Samuel coined the name "Machine Learning". According to him, "Machine learning is the field of study that gives the computer the ability to learn without being explicitly programmed". This captures the core idea. Unlike earlier approaches where we were trying to define a bulk of rules to derive insight from knowledge, machine learning develops such systems which learn those rules themselves from the data. This approach is closer to natural learning. For an example, a kid learns to identify an apple after he/she is shown a lot of examples of apples. Similarly, we give the machine a lot of data and the machine by itself develop an intuition for the data. In the words of Tom Mitchell, "A computer program is said to learn from experience E with respect to some class of tasks T and performance measure P if its performance at tasks in T, as measured by P, improves with experience E." Those algorithms that allow machines to learn are called the Machine learning algorithm. Generally, machine learning algorithms can be classified into two categories - Supervised Learning and unsupervised learning (Russell, S., J., & Norvig, P., 2000). There are also some other kinds of machine learning like Reinforcement learning etc. Those are beyond the scope of this chapter.

Supervised Machine Learning

In supervised learning, the data is labeled. Let's say, we want the system to learn to distinguish cats' images from other images. We will write a program which should take input as an image and should output whether or not it's a cat (i.e. 1 for cat and 0 for non-cat). To accomplish this task, we first need to train the machine. What this means is we'll first show the machine that this is cat image, this is noncat image and so on for a large number of images. Then we'll evaluate its performance on the images It has never seen. If the performance is not up to our expectation then, we'll train it on more data. The data used for training is known as "training set" and the data used for testing the trained system or "Model" is known as "Testing set". The examples of images in data are known as "Sample". For each sample, we have a corresponding true label in the supervised learning setup. The problem we discussed is called "Classification", the classes being only two i.e. Cat and Non-cat. When there are two classes, its known as "Binary Classification" and if there are more than two classes, its known as "Multi-class classification problem".

Unlike Classification problem, in regression we want our system to predict "continuous values". For example, predicting House prices in a locality. What data we need to collect in this setup? We'll try to collect data on the parameters that affect the house prices such as House size, no of rooms in a house etc. The parameters are known as "Features" in machine learning terminology. Here also, we'll have actual prices of the samples in the training set but not in the test set (obviously it's the data we test our system on). Another regression example could be predicting stock market prices. Another classification example could predict whether the person has cancer or not. You got the idea (Russell, S., J., & Norvig, P., 2000).

Unsupervised Learning

In Unsupervised learning, we don't provide the sample's true label or value. The data is unlabeled. The purpose of the unsupervised learning algorithm is to find the structure in the input data. Its goal is to discover hidden patterns from the data. It tries to cluster the data into characteristically separate groups (Russell, S., J., & Norvig, P., 2000). This task is known as Clustering. Let's try to understand how this is useful. A book selling company wants to improve its sales. It has a huge amount of data about the purchase history of its customers. The company feeds that data to a "Cluster" learning algorithm which outputs 5 segments of customers to the company and the company finds out that some 1st segment likes romantic genre book, 2nd like x genre book and so on. With this insight, the company can personalize its offering according to the market segments. Clustering techniques have used in Astrophysics, Computer science, etc.

General Machine Learning Pipeline

We are going to give a brief overview of the general steps that we go throw when building machine learning based solutions to the problems.

"Understanding the problem" statement is first and the most important step in an ML project. This may seem a trivial but actual problem and how you are going to model it in a way that it could become a machine learning task gets sometimes difficult for some problems. Also, a deep understanding of the problem will help somewhat for sure while taking a decision in designing ml pipeline.

Next step is to "collect enough data" for your problem. If the task is to classify emails into spam and non-spam, then collect lots of emails with their true labels. Collected data should be similar to data that your trained system will see when deployed (Russell, S., J., & Norvig, P., 2000).

As now a good number of samples are collected so it's time to prepare it for machine learning. Yes, raw data can't be directly fed to learning algorithms. Raw data can be too much noisy, biased, incorrect, missing etc. And so, we need to transform it so that it becomes useful for learning. This step is called "Data Preparation". Things like error correction, filling, normalization and more all happen in this step. Then we randomize the data and split it into training and testing set. Well, assume that the data is prepared, let's move forward.

Next step is to "select the learning model". There are so many machine learning models developed for a particular problem. In this step, we select some models based on the data. In this step, we explore the data and get some intuition about its structure. Then we chose a set of models to try on the data. For example, for classification, there many models like support vector machines, logistic regression etc.

It's time for "training" the model. We have enough data and a learning model. We'll train each learning model we selected for training on the training set. In training, the model tries to learn the best "weights" for each feature for predicting the label with the highest accuracy. Here a weight represents the importance of the feature in predicting the label.

After the model has come up with the best weights, we'll "evaluate" its performance on the unseen data. We'll run the trained models on testing set and note down the accuracy of prediction of each model. Only the best model with the highest accuracy will be selected.

In the next step, we'll tune the best model to increase its performance. There are some parameters in a model for example learning rate (how smooth the model learns) and some others. In this step, the goal is to discover the best combination of different parameters of the model. Those best parameters will then be used for prediction in the real world.

Now we'll deploy the model in the real world. The system will be maintained to keep up the accuracy same as it had at the beginning (Russell, S., J., & Norvig, P., 2000).

CYBER SECURITY

One of the main cyber-risks is to think they don't exist. The other is to try to treat all potential risks. Fix the basics, protect first what matters for your business and be ready to react properly to pertinent threats. Think data, but also business services integrity, awareness, customer experience, compliance, and reputation (Nappo, S., 2017).

Consider a set i.e., (Artificial Intelligence, Machine Learning, Block Chain, Deep Learning, Big Data Analysis, Data Science, Internet of Things etc.). This set consists some of the most thrilling and talked off technologies today. In this era of exponentially increasing expansion of the Internet and heavy workloads in the fields enclosed in the above set, cyber-security becomes a big question?

Cyber term means 'related to the culture of the computer, information technology or/and virtual reality'. This makes clear that we are talking about the security of computers, networks, information etc. Moving on to the clearer definition, cybersecurity refers to the various measures/techniques for the protection of inter-connected networks, software, hardware and data from cyber-attacks (unauthorized access and damage). While looking at the computing context both securities of cyberspace and physical space is equally important. Application security, information security, network security, operational security, etc. are some of the elements of cybersecurity, which harmonize the entire information system. This design is giving an intuition of a multilayer protection system spread all over the system involving various elements of the system and it is one of the successful defense mechanisms available.

Role of Cybersecurity

Nowadays the crowd is more frequently falling prey to cyber-attacks due to the evolutionary nature of risks in the cyberspace. Pathways are constructed through malignant and offensive activities, which give unauthorized access to predators (hackers and crackers) on computer systems or networks. These activities are called cyber threats. Predators work on the bugs and faults in the system or network to establish these pathways. There are numerous cyber threats like ransomware, virus, worms, Trojans, spyware/adware, attack vectors, social engineering, Man in The Middle (MITM) and many more (Panimalar, A., Giri, P.U. & Khan, S., 2018).

Everybody possess some valuable assets and confidential data which are under their authority and when an outsider gets access to those assets and data, they can cause extreme harms. Taking cyberspace into consideration, these accesses without the consent of the owner can be the results of one or more cyber threats. Here cybersecurity comes into play. It ensures the availability, confidentiality, and integrity of your system or network and helps it to work efficiently without compromising with the security.

Principles of Cyber Security (Principles Forming the Base for Cybersecurity)

To ensure the three important goals of cybersecurity, i.e., availability, confidentiality and integrity, some simple but effective principles can be followed.

1. **Focus on Prior Systems:** Stabilizing the degree of availability, confidentiality, and integrity of resources comes under biggest challenges and hence it is

achieved by focusing on the vital systems and providing best protection shield to it whereas other methods are applied for the protection of less-prior systems.

2. **Different Users, Different Level of Accessibility:** What data is accessible by whom should be based on what type of user he is, and no single person should get access to all the data and information. This means minimum privileges to particular responsibility. Hence the change in responsibility is directly proportional to change in privileges.

3. **Provision of Independent Defense (Protocols):** Several authentication protocols for a single job is a far better idea than a single protocol. It highly reduces the risk of successful cyber-attacks and the basic principle is increasing the work of the attacker as he has to perform numerous tasks to break through several protection layers.

4. **Backups:** Failures can occur but planning the consequences after failure can reduce extreme harms to the system, network or individual. This is a highly effective technique and is in practices in various fields.

Keeping records of all breaches: Cybersecurity staffs should keep the records of all the breaches and these should constantly be studies and protection measures should be generated. This process should be a rapid one because hackers are not waiting; they are increasing their skills as well as improving cyber-attack tools (Panimalar, A., Giri, P.U. & Khan, S., 2018).

A Modern Warfare (Warfare in Cyberspace)

The world has experienced wars in the past which has never been a pleasant experience. These inhuman activities never proved to be fruitful for any of the parties, but still, these activities continue and are now taking the benefits of the modern technologies. These days warfare grooms itself in the cyberspace and the term used to describe it is cyber warfare but there is no fixed definition for cyberwarfare; Richard A. Clarke defines it as "actions by a nation-state to penetrate another nation's computers or networks for the purposes of causing damage or disruption".

Threats leading to Cyberwarfare:

1. **Espionage:** The act of spying on bodies for political or military reasons.
2. **Sabotage:** Deliberate disruption of things especially due to political reasons.
3. **Propaganda:** Cyber propaganda refers to the biasing of information in directions which highly influence public interests.

All these things are nowadays performed in the cyber world giving rise to cybercrimes which gradually grows and leads to cyber-terrorism. Dealing with cyber terrorism is a tough task and can be achieved by either a reduction in cybercrime or introducing highly secured systems. Modern technologies from the above set can be used to design intelligent systems which can secure it.

Modern Challenges in Cybersecurity

Cyber Security is a shared responsibility, and it boils down to this: In Cyber Security the more systems we secure, the more secure we all are (Johnson, J., 2014).

After having the basic idea about how intensely cyber world is impacting every single entity starting from individual level, organizational level to national-international levels, let us dive into the complications fabricated by the technologies mentioned in the set from the previous section, i.e., {Artificial Intelligence, Machine Learning, Block Chain, Deep Learning, Big Data Analysis, Data Science, Internet of Things, etc.}. Are these technologies causing threat to cyber security? If yes, why?

Heavy technical works in the set field are going on to create products and services for mankind; In this long run of economic benefits and work convenience, the two basic necessities, privacy and protection are compromised. All these crafts and developments are leading to highly growing dependence on Internet, complex digital systems and clouds-based computation which are recently bombing technologies and consist of many loop holes that has not only increased the number of cyber-attacks but also the diversity in them.

The reason threats couldn't be countered is the lack of trusted and standard computing platforms and infrastructures. Challenges can be of different forms; their sources can be diverse, and they could be at different levels. Let's us visualize them from few different perspectives.

1. **Technologies:** Technologies is spreading everywhere every single day and predators (cyber criminals) are constantly spying in search of loopholes. The constantly increasing rate of cyber-crimes is generating 3.5 million new jobs in the field of cyber security, which will remain unoccupied. Elevations in new technologies in half a decade have increased the security requirements about three hundred and fifty (350) times, an enormous rise.
2. **User:** Technologies are not only the challenges to cyber security, but user at large scales are also one. The habit of users of doing things without thinking and sometimes unawareness of threats associated with the facilities they use are some common reasons behind the same. We could also not ignore the involvement of some user in malicious activities and irresponsible behavior of few people at higher authorities. Many a times, it is just one click of user, which makes all the disasters.

3. **Financial Expenditure:** While considering the scenario of cyber security, enhancement in the technologies, products and services are just one face of it and many a times we could not see the other one, the expenditure in these enhancements. People and organizations only expend on cyber security when they become victim of cyber-attacks. Investment in cyber security considering future threats is an obsolete practice giving invitations to predators (cyber criminals).

Evolving Computer Networks (Challenges by Complex Computer Networks)

Evolution of computer networks is increasing their complexity and these complexities are challenging cyber security. There are users and organizations those who don't have records of the assets they have directly or indirectly tied to the network and due to lack of information of assets it's hard to ensure security in these complex networks. Security in depth (multilayer protection) is a tedious task in complex computer networks.

Internet of Things (IoT Arising Challenges for Cyber Security)

Starting form homes, markets, institutions to big offices, all of these places are filled with variety of electronic gadgets and Internet of Things keeps all of these gadgets connected. Working of these connections in gadgets is primarily dependent on user's private/confidential data and these connections generate huge amounts of data and process it using internet. The main challenge is the poor mechanism for authentication and improper encryption of these large chunks of data. Analysis of efficiency versus security aspects of IoT implies the inverse dependence of security on efficiency. 70% of the IoT devices are vulnerable to cyber-attacks.

Block Chain (Block Chain Technology and Challenges Associated)

The astonishing development in crypto currency like bit coin and Ethereum has revolutionized the payment systems. It offers irreversible, quick and cheap transactions and good exchange values. Medical record management, decentralized access control and identity managements are some of the future goals associated with block chain technology. And here comes the security aspect, cyber security experts have to raise the level of principles as well as the techniques for ensuring security from cyber-attacks.

Botnets (Modern Threat)

Large collection of devices (IoT devices, servers, personal computers, mobile phones connected to internet) infected by same malware is called Botnet. Cyber predators monitor these infected devices and attacks on these systems are mostly through emails or frauds based on clicks. Botnet word is derived from robot and network. Here it means that devices in the infected network become robot/slave of the attackers.

Lack of Talents (Demand Versus Availability of Cyber Security Experts)

Many studies have revealed that due to lack of talents there is a misbalance in the demand and availability of cyber security experts. With the exponential growth of cyber threats, demand for skilled and experienced cyber security experts has also exponentially increased but their availability is a big question.

According to a survey by Leviathan Security Group it has been found that:

1. 16% of the organizations felt only half of their applicants are qualified
2. 53% of them said finding a qualified applicant can take at least six months, in case they find one.
3. 32% of them find it difficult to fill the positions of cyber experts.
4. Reasons behind this lack of cyber experts can be the under-investments on cyber education, growth in cyber-attacks, demand of experienced experts and less participation of women in cyber security field.

AI COMES TO RESCUE

With the increasingly important role of intelligent machines in all phases of our lives--military, medical, economic and financial, political--it is odd to keep reading articles with titles such as whatever Happened to Artificial Intelligence? This is a phenomenon that Turing had predicted: that machine intelligence would become so pervasive, so comfortable, and so well integrated into our information-based economy that people would fail even to notice it (Kurzweil, R., 2005).

Cyber-attacks have become more pervasive and diverse due to ubiquitous connected computers, cloud and mobile technologies. Volumes of connected devices provide cyber criminals with plenty of access points to attack on. In addition, the access points are security deficient. Rise of IOT has caused a wave of cyber-attacks that has expanded wider than ever. Topics on cyber frauds are not rare in news and media.

Traditional methods for cyber security require tremendous human efforts to identify the threats, extract properties of threats and encode properties of threats into software to detect the threats. Moreover, conventional methods are not as sophisticated as present days cyber-attacks.

In earlier days, AI and cyber security were not related in any way. But over time, the boundaries became blurred. The CAPTCHA ((Completely Automated Public Turing test to tell Computers and Humans Apart) is a very good example of the connection of AI and cyber-security. In this test, user is asked to type the letter in a masked image or with some other deformation. Traditional cyber-security techniques are primarily called as "Signature based techniques". Our focus is to discuss Machine learning based techniques but after a brief overview of signature-based techniques.

Signature Based Techniques

Signature based techniques are those approaches of information security which detects the cyber-attacks or malwares [section 7] by matching certain signature (at least a byte sequence of code) of the instance of malware in question with the database of signatures of malwares stored. The database has known malicious programs and they are called as "blacklists". The signature-based techniques assume that the malicious software can be described using the signatures (also called as malicious patterns). This method fails completely in case of new attacks or malwares, for which known patterns or signatures are not available. Unfortunately, the current scenario is against these techniques of signature detection. Still it can be used on the beginning level. Nonetheless signature-based techniques have once been one of the most common malware detection techniques. This technique has the following disadvantages:

1. **Susceptible to Evasion:** The signature patterns are commonly known since they are used for deriving signatures for malware or attacks. They can be easily duped by the hackers by techniques like inserting no-ops and code reordering (obfuscation).
2. **Zero Day Attacks:** Since the signature-based malware detection systems are built on the basis of known malware, they are not able to detect new and unknown malware, or even the variants of known malware. Thus, without accurate signatures, they cannot effectively identify polymorphic malware. Therefore, signature-based detection does not provide zero-day protection. Moreover, since a signature-based detector uses a separate signature for each malware variant, the database of signatures grows at an exponential rate (Shabtai, A., Menahem, E., & Elovici, Y., 2011).

Machine Learning Based Approach

Signature based approaches have a number of drawbacks. Recently due to availability of high compute power and enormous data, machine learning has been on rise. It has entered into almost every business and industry. There is hardly any area of work machine learning has not been used where human intelligence required. Cyber world is no exception. In almost all the conferences being organized on cyber security, you will find researchers, industrialists, businessmen, security experts, analysts and everyone speaking about the applications of machine learning in cyber security. Some might argue that AI will replace the human analysts. The truth is we are not at that stage yet. AI is for sure and asset for human analysts. Combined efforts of human and machine will surely help us fight with cyber-criminals with more excellence that separates efforts.

Data is enormous whether its firewall logs, user activities logs or network packets, it's difficult for human analysts to analyze it properly. This is where machine intelligence comes into picture. Armed with rapid and trustworthy analysis provided by machine learning can be used to take informed decisions by the organizations.

In general, we are trying to detect anomalies in cyber security. Both supervised and unsupervised machine learning techniques are used in this direction. It should be noted that the former approaches are more promising. For the purpose of understanding application of supervised learning, we can consider the problem of malware identification or classification of malicious files - where we want to detect malware or malicious files. We need to have an enormous amount of data for training. The data should have malware - label pairs. The data is then broken into training and testing data. This problem falls into category of classification in machine learning. Consider another problem of network traffic log, we'll cluster them into two groups "Normal logs" and "infected logs". Clustering will eventually output two clusters. We'll discuss these techniques in detail in coming sections. Machine learning based techniques extract the most important feature for the problem on their own and surprisingly for human it's very hard to extract such features. This is why machine learning based techniques are superior to other methods.

Network Intrusion Detection Using AI

Act of getting access to computer networks without the consent of the owner is known as Network Intrusion. Intrusion can be of two types, physical or logical. Physical intrusion involves the physical presence of intruder trying to access your computer system whereas in logical intrusion the intruder's gains access to the computer system via network. Network Intrusion is a deliberate act, which is performed to utilize network resources or/and threatening the network or/and data (Chatzigiannakis, V et.al, 2004).

Network intrusion can be divided into five different stages:

1. **Gathering Information of the Target:** In this stage intruders collect information about each and every aspect of the target. They try to comprehend their target and its strong and weak points. This information includes email addresses, open-source details, details of the network, etc. To smoothly contrive attack, they even try to knowledge about the all functionalities of the various devices in the network and spent time in finding the vulnerable points for exploitation.
2. **Inceptive Exploitation:** In this stage begins the intrusion activities. Exploitation of networks is done by infecting the frequently used websites by the victim. Water holing, phishing, SQL injection are some more ways to threaten the network and gain more control over it. Intruders patiently perform exploitations to avoid chances of getting caught.
3. **Establish Persistence:** Intruders continues their malicious activities without getting in ears of the victim. There is a rapid increase in undetected exploitation activities which include peeping into the scripts and discovering run keys.
4. **Malware Installation:** This is the stage of doing the original work by installation of malwares in the network starting with less harmful ones to the powerful ones.
5. **Penetrating Deep Into Network:** Gradually intruders gain access all over the network and now they can exploit whatever they want. They fulfill their intension and leave the network.
6. **Removal of Traces:** Some intruders who are concerned about detection of intrusion ties to remove their traces before leaving the network (Iftikhar, B., Alghamdi, A., S. 2009).

This is how the whole process of network intrusion takes place. What are the different attacks used in network intrusion?

1. **Trojans:** Trojans do not replicate itself rather it appears to useful. It follows the path of Denial of Service (DoS) attack. It erases stored data and constructs pathways for the attackers. Source of Trojans are online file repositories and archives.
2. **Worms:** Unlike Trojans worms replicate itself but without altering the user approved program files. Its abrupt replication ultimately consumes all the network resources (such as bandwidth, CPU cycles) leading to the unavailability of resources for the user approved programs/tasks. Some worms also try to

extract confidential information from important files. Sources of worms can be Internet Relay Chat protocol or attachments send via emails.

3.   **Buffer Overflow Attack:** Attacks where some special parts of the network memory is targeted and over-writing in done on it; these overwritten set of code are many a times part of the attack and are executed during the attack. Networks with large buffer size and no checking codes are more prone to this attack (Iftikhar, B., Alghamdi, A., S., 2009).

4.   **Traffic Flooding:** It is also a type of Denial of Service attack and its targets are web servers. Attacks know how to control and manage Transmission Control Protocol (TCP) connections and it order to orchestrate attack a lot of TCPs are generated aiming to stop the server and hamper its performance.

5.   **Asymmetric Routing:** In asymmetric routing, the packets travel through one route from source to destination and different one from destination to source. Here the attackers plan to packets to bypass some critical sections of the network as well as the intrusion detectors.

6.   **Protocol Specific Attack:** Network activities involve some protocols (examples: ARP, IP, TCP, UDP, ICMP, etc.) and some of them unknowingly leaves loop holes for network intrusion. Example, In Address Resolution Protocol (ARP) there is not message authentication process inviting Man in the Middle attack.

Network Intrusion detection systems monitors the network and analyze its traffic to protect system from network-based threats. Generally, A NIDS reads incoming and outgoing packets from access points in a network and tries to recognize the patterns of the threats in disguise of normal packets. When a network threat is discovered it sends notifications to the administrator about the security of the network.

An example of a NIDS would be installing it on the subnet where firewalls are located in order to catch someone who is trying to break into the firewall.

Machine Learning Based Network Intrusion Schemes

There are several methods proposed for Network intrusion detection. Machine Learning based methods have got an edge over all traditional methods for the reason that they are robust, very functional and improved.

Network intrusion detection system tries to find the anomalous activity in the network. The core task is to classify various network data packets or activities into - Normal and abnormal or anomalous. This can be clearly adapted to a classification task in supervised machine learning. Particularly, it's a binary classification task, classes being - Normal and Anomalous. To model it into a machine learning problem, we need to have a dataset of network activities samples. People have already gathered such datasets such as datasets provided by Cyber Range Lab of the Australian Centre for Cyber Security (ACCS) and other similar organizations. In this dataset, a hybrid of real modern normal activities and attack behaviors were generated. This dataset contains total forty-seven features and also contains over 2 million sample data. Not all the features are important for the task, so feature selection is performed where we select only the features correlated with Target variable (i.e. Label variable). Now that we have prepared data, we'll apply three approaches to this task: Logistic regression, Support vector machine and Decision Trees.

Logistic Regression

Logistic regression is known to be the simplest machine learning technique for classification. Logistic regression tries to come up with a straight line to separate the anomalous activities and normal activities, this is why it can be thought of as learning an equation of line: $y' = mx + c$. Here y' is the predicted output for the sample x, m is the slope of the line and c is the y-intercept. This is also called as score function. It maps input features to output labels. The values of y' can be very large and very small, we won't be able to decide which class does the sample xi belongs to and so for that purpose we'll pass the score to the sigmoid function $y' = sigmoid(y')$. Sigmoid (y') is equal to $1/1+e^{-y'}$. This function takes the value and scales it in between 0 and 1. Thus if the sigmoid outputs above 0.5, the class is positive (or Normal) and if its below 0.5, the class is negative (anomalous). So, our final equation for logistic regression is: $y' = sigmoid(mx + c)$. Due to sigmoid function used, Logistic regression is also known as sigmoid regression. Now to measure, how good and bad the predication of the learning algorithms is, we'll define cost function as:

$$\text{Cost}(y', y) = -\log(y') \text{ if } y = 1 \tag{1}$$

$$-\log(1-y') \text{ if } y = 0, \text{ here } y \text{ is the true label.} \tag{2}$$

The cost represents how large the error. The goal is to minimize the cost. We can see that the we have to find the best possible values of m and c that will minimize the cost. To minimize the cost, we'll use optimization algorithms. Gradient descent is generally used and so we'll use it in our problem.

Repeat until convergence

{

$$m = m - \alpha \partial \partial m \text{ Cost } (m) \tag{3}$$

}

At running this algorithm for a hundred of times, we'll see that optimized value of m is found. This m is then used for future prediction.

Support Vector Machines

Here is another classical linear classifier which more robust and power than Logistic regression. We'll try to give a brief overview of this technique. The score function in svm is similar to logistic regression. The cost function is a bit different and more complex, so we will avoid writing here. Basically, it tries to learn as straight-line boundary which is a farthest as possible from the sample points. The margin (distance from the sample) it learns is large and thus it is also known as Large margin classifier. We can use other optimization techniques along with Gradient descent such as Minibatch gradient descent or stochastic gradient descent for SVM. The SVM allows flexibility in learning non-linear decision boundaries by incorporating a nonlinear function as score function, polynomial being the most common choice. After a good number of iterations of optimization, we can find the best parameters with the least error possible by this learning algorithm. Now we'll give a slight look out third technique "Decision Trees".

Decision Trees

As the name suggests, Decision Tree uses a tree-like model of decisions. Although it's a commonly used tool in data mining for deriving a strategy to reach a particular goal, it is widely used in machine learning, which will be the main focus of this section. A decision tree is drawn upside down with its root at its top. Every internal node in a tree is a binary condition. It splits into two branches that meet another node. The branches are yes-no branches. The last nodes that don't split into branches are known as decision nodes. Decision nodes determines which class does the sample belong. There are many advantages of decision tree-based learning like:

1.   Easy to understand, interpret and visualize
2.   It learns linear as well as non-linear relationships
3.   It implicitly performs feature selection and extraction.

Now that we have applied all these three Learning algorithms, we will keep the model which has provided us the best accuracy. We'll then search for improved parameters for that model so that we can get more accurate results. This is called grid search. Now we'll use learned parameters on the unseen data for prediction.

Malware Detection Using AI

Malware is comprised of words 'malicious' and 'software'. Simply malware can be considered a piece of code designed to cause harm to the computers, data/ information and networks. The harms associated with malware can take place only after the installation or implantation of these malicious codes. Objectives behind these malwares are spying and stealing of confidential data, providing system control to intruders and poor performance or mal functioning of the infected systems. Following are some malwares:

1. **Virus:** Its full form is Vital Information Resources Under Seize. This malware replicates itself and this process is done via placing its codes into programs and modifying them. Its activation depends on opening of program by the user. Spreading through the user email, corrupting data, data loss, erasing data from hard-disk are some of the damages caused by virus.
2. **Worms:** Refer the previous section.
3. **Trojans:** Refer the previous section.
4. **Rootkits:** Attackers can gain continuous access to root-level using rootkit without recording its presence. It is the result of direct attack such as exploitation of known vulnerability or password. It conceals itself in the Operating System.
5. **Remote administration tools:** These pieces of software allow attackers to control infected system and give the privileges to perform all the possible tasks on the system. Their detection is difficult as they don't appear on the running programs list and many a times expected to be a benign as they were originated for legitimate use.
6. **Botnets:** Refer section 4.
7. **Spyware:** Malwares that tries to collect data about the usage of the infected device keeps records of key strokes and all activities taking place in the system. Adware, data theft, botnets, key loggers and net-worms are all part of this malware (Panimalar, A., Giri, P.U. & Khan, S., 2018).

Effects of malware on computers system:

1. It can cause slowing down of connections and computer tasks; some can even crash your system.
2. Frequent display of error messages and problem in shutting down or restarting.
3. Hijacking of browsers for redirection to malicious sites.
4. Theft of identity and confidential data.
5. Misuse of email for exchange of spam.
6. Creating path for intruders to have control over the system and resources.

Malware Detection

Malware detection system is used to determine whether a program is malicious or not. Malware comes in several forms as discussed earlier. Earlier detection systems for particular malware like for virus, antivirus systems were developed. Recently the focus has shifted towards general malware detection systems. Though it's harder but it would be universal tools to fight with these threats. Malware detector is used as a tool of defense against the malware. The quality of particular detector depends on the technique employed in its development.

Generally, malware detection techniques fall into three categories:

1. Signature based techniques,
2. Behavior based techniques and
3. Specification based techniques.

We have already discussed Signature based techniques. The Behavior based detection techniques analyze behavior of particular program which is suspicious of containing threats for the system. The specification-based techniques are modifications associated with behavior-based techniques. Suppose a behavior-based technique has a high false alarm rate, then some specification is made in the detection scheme (Yu, W., Zhang, N., Fu, X., &Zhao, W., 2010).

Malware Detection Using Machine Learning

Malware detection is also the task of classification. All the methods discussed earlier (Logistic Regression, Support Vector Machines and Decision Trees) are equally applicable in this case. In this section we'll just give you a brief introduction to another technique for classification which land us into the era of deep learning. In Machine Learning, A human analysts creates features that he thinks will be very useful for prediction, but in deep learning the model itself extracts the important features from the data. The model here is "Artificial Neural Networks". The idea of ANN is inspired form the biological neuron. Although we don't exactly know how actually our mind works, but Researcher came up with an innovative model of learning inspired from human brain. This mathematical model is now a days a buzz word and it's the best algorithm for supervised machine learning given its data requirement is fulfilled. Yes, Deep learning approach requires millions of millions of data (Zolkipli, M., F., &Jantan, A., 2010).

ANN is built upon the bricks of linear classifier like logistic regression. The classical Neural Network can be imagined as layers stacked together. In each layer, many logistic units are present and the output from each unit of previous layer is connected as input in each unit of present layer. The first layer from the left is known as Feature layer and the last layer is known as output layer. The last layer has only one unit as we want to classify into two classes. The computation flows from left to right and the similar to other approaches; The cost function is calculated and optimized using an optimizer. Check references for digging deeper. Neural Networks are the most powerful machines learning approach we have ever discovered.

FUTURE ASPECTS AND SCOPE

Researchers predict that by 2020, artificial intelligence technologies will be implemented in almost all new software products and services, which will inevitably bring a sea change the way we work, live and do business. Though AI is in its infancy, it has shown to the world its infinite potential in performing task efficiently and accurately in an array of industries from manufacturing, retail, education to healthcare and cyber security.

As always, a coin has two faces. AI is no exception. People have shown their worries for destructive use of AI. A report from The Guardian warns "As AI capabilities become more powerful and widespread, we expect the growing use of AI systems to lead to the expansion of existing threats, the introduction of new threats and a change to the typical character of threats,". Fortunately, the discussion on AI still ends up with bright face of AI.

No doubt, if AI is implemented and trained with proper care, it can improve cyber security in many ways. It can protect against the cyber-attacks in real time with lesser resources. As cyber threats are constantly evolving, data is bursting new patterns that are hard to capture and analyze for human analyst can be crunched down by a machine learning technique in seconds. Equipped with power of deep analysis provided by Machine learning, Human analysts can focus on interpreting the results and devising novel techniques for fighting with criminals proactively. Therefore, using Deep learning and machine learning in defense systems will surely take cyber security to a new level of intelligence.

REFERENCES

Bai, J., Wu, Y., Wang, G., Yang, S. X., & Qiu, W. (2006). *A very distinctive intrusion detection model based on multilayer self-organizing maps and principal part analysis. In Advances in Neural Networks*. Springer.

Barika, F., Hadjar, K., & El-Kadhi, N. (2009). Artificial neural network for mobile IDS resolution. Security and Management Journal, 271–277.

Bostrom, N. (2015), *TED Talk on Artificial Intelligence*. Retrieved from https://en.tiny.ted.com/talks/nick_bostrom_what_happens_when_our_computers_get_smarter_than_we_are

Chatzigiannakis, V., Androulidakis, G., & Maglaris, B. (2004). A Distributed Intrusion Detection Prototype Using Security Agents. In *Proceedings of Workshop of the HP Open View University Association*. University of Evry.

Iftikhar, B., & Alghamdi, A. S. (2009). Application of artificial neural network within the detection of dos attacks. *Proceedings of the ordinal international conference on Security of knowledge and networks*, 229–234.

Johnson, J. (2014). *Remarks by Secretary of Homeland Security Jeh Johnson at the White House Cybersecurity Framework Event*. Retrieved from https://www.dhs.gov/news/2014/02/12/remarks-secretary-homeland-security-jeh-johnson-white-house-cybersecurity-framework

Jonze, S. (2017). *28 Best Quotes About Artificial Intelligence*. Retrieved from https://www.forbes.com/sites/bernardmarr/2017/07/25/28-best-quotes-about-artificial-intelligence

Kivimaa, J., Ojamaa, A., & Tyugu, E. (2008). Pareto-Optimal state of affairs Analysis for the selection of Security Measures. *Proceedings of Military communications conference, MILCOM 2008*.

Kivimaa, J., Ojamaa, A., & Tyugu, E. (2009). *Graded Security accomplished System. In Lecture Notes in engineering* (Vol. 5508, pp. 279–286). Springer.

Kurzweil, R. (2005). *The Singularity is near*. Penguin Group.

Lunt, T. F., & Jagannathan, R. (1988). An example amount of your time Intrusion-Detection accomplished System. Proceedings of IEEE conference on Security and Privacy.

Nappo, S. (2017). *Goodreads.* Retrieved from https://www.goodreads.com

Panimalar, A., Giri, P.U. & Khan, S. (2018). Artificial Intelligence Techniques in Cyber Security. *International Research Journal of Engineering and Technology, 5*(3).

Preda, M. D., Christodorescu, M., Jha, S., & Debray, S. (2008). A Semantics-Based Approach to Malware Detection. *ACM Transactions on Programming Languages and Systems, 30*(5), 1–54. doi:10.1145/1387673.1387674

Russell, S. J., & Norvig, P. (2000). *Artificial Intelligence: A Modern Approach.* Prentice Hall.

Salvador, P., Nogueira, A., França, U., & Valadas, R. (2009). Framework for Zombie Detection Using Neural Networks. *Proceedings of The Fourth International Conference on Internet Monitoring and Protection ICIMP.* 10.1109/ICIMP.2009.10

Shabtai, A., Menahem, E., & Elovici, Y. (2011). F-Sign: Automatic, Function-Based Signature Generation for Malware. *IEEE Transactions on Systems, Man and Cybernetics. Part C, Applications and Reviews, 41*(4), 494–508. doi:10.1109/TSMCC.2010.2068544

Tang, Y., & Chen, S. (2007). An Automated Signature-Based Approach against Polymorphic Internet Worms. *IEEE Transactions on Parallel and Distributed Systems, 18*(7), 879–892. doi:10.1109/TPDS.2007.1050

Tang, Y., Xiao, B., & Lu, X. (2011). Signature Tree Generation for Polymorphic Worms. *IEEE Transactions on Computers, 60*(4), 4. doi:10.1109/TC.2010.130

Yu, W., Zhang, N., Fu, X., & Zhao, W. (2010). Self-Disciplinary Worms and Countermeasures: Modeling and Analysis. *IEEE Transactions on Parallel and Distributed Systems, 21*(10), 1501–1514. doi:10.1109/TPDS.2009.161

Zolkipli, M. F., & Jantan, A. (2010). Malware Behavior Analysis: Learning and Understanding Current Malware Threats. *Second International Conference on Network Applications, Protocols and Service IEEE,* 218-221. 10.1109/NETAPPS.2010.46

KEY TERMS AND DEFINITIONS

Artificial Intelligence: A machine's ability to make decisions and perform tasks that simulate human intelligence and behavior.

Block Chain: A block chain is a perfect place to store value, identities, agreements, property rights, credentials, etc. Once you put something like a Bit coin into it, it will stay there forever. It is decentralized, disinter mediated, cheap, and censorship-resistant.

Botnet: It is an infected computer terminal which can be used a platform to launch various attacks like DDoS attacks, Spamming, mining of bit coins, etc.

DDoS Attack: DDoS stands for distributed denial of service. In this type of an attack, an attacker tends to overwhelm the targeted network in order to make the services unavailable to the intended or legitimate user.

Deep Learning: The ability for machines to autonomously mimic human thought patterns through artificial neural networks composed of cascading layers of information.

Machine Learning: A facet of AI that focuses on algorithms, allowing machines to learn without being programmed and change when exposed to new data.

Malware: Malware stands for malicious software. Malware intended to infiltrate and damage or disable computers.

Supervised Learning: A type of machine learning in which output datasets train the machine to generate the desired algorithms, like a teacher supervising a student.

Chapter 10
Techniques for Analysis of Mobile Malware

Gopinath Palaniappan
Centre for Development of Advanced Computing (CDAC), India

Balaji Rajendran
Centre for Development of Advanced Computing (CDAC), India

S. Sangeetha
National Institute of Technology Tiruchirappalli, India

NeelaNarayanan V
VIT University, India

ABSTRACT

The rapid rise in the number of mobile devices has resulted in an alarming increase in mobile software and applications. The mobile application markets/stores too have created a fundamental shift in the way mobile applications are delivered to users, with apps being added and updated in thousands every day. Even though research progresses have been achieved towards detection and mitigation of mobile security, open challenges still remain and also keep evolving in this area. Several studies reveal that mobile application markets/stores do harbor applications that are either vulnerable or malicious in nature, leading to compromises of millions of devices. This chapter (1) captures the attack surface of mobile devices, (2) lists the various mobile malware analysis techniques, and (3) lays the ground for research on mobile malware by providing mobile malware dataset resources, tools for malware analysis, patent landscaping for mobile malware detection, and a few open challenges in malware analysis.

DOI: 10.4018/978-1-5225-8241-0.ch010

INTRODUCTION

The count of the Mobile devices is increasing dramatically day-by-day. Mobile devices have raised above from just being a digital device or a smartphone, in fact they have turned into a platform for convergence of our personal and digital life because of their rich computing capabilities and its wide range of features such as easier communication, more than one internet connectivity mechanisms, the storage including multimedia and so on. The ubiquitous presence of mobile devices can be understood from the statistics in Figure 1 below. The mobile devices remain online continuously by seamlessly connecting through mobile data or the closest available Wi-Fi, and keeps downloading and uploading data intermittently, increasing the complexities in protecting the data.

There exist several Mobile device vendors who deliver their devices bundled with major mobile operating systems such as Android (by Google), iOS (by Apple) and others. However recent times has seen mentionable increase in the number of Android-based Mobile devices when compared to other mobile operating systems (Figure 2).

The ubiquitous nature of mobile devices has resulted in drastic rise in the number of applications in the mobile market, complicating mobile security further (Imran Ashraf, 2012). These applications are an add-on to the features and capabilities of the mobile devices. They also make the life of the users better by providing them with the functionalities such as financial transactions, entertainment, shopping, games,

Figure 1. Sales of smartphone shipments across the globe from 2009 to 2017 and projections for 2018 to 2022
(Source: The Statistics Portal: www.statista.com)

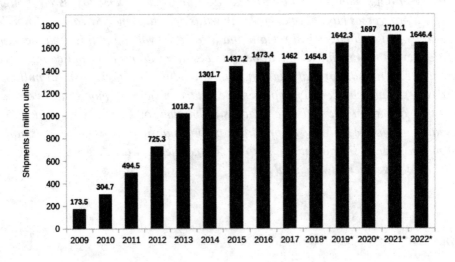

Figure 2. Global mobile OS market share in sales to end users from 1st quarter 2009 to 2nd quarter 2018
(Source: The Statistics Portal: www.statista.com)

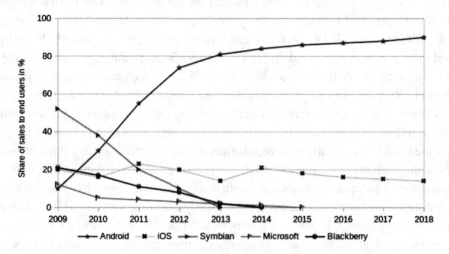

personal health tracking and so on, on their own personal mobile devices, regrettably not every application does what it seems to do, and perhaps it is difficult for users to detect a well-crafted application or forgery that withdraw data surreptitiously apart from its listed function. The mobile applications can be easily accessed, downloaded and installed by the users on to their devices from the openly available through third party and official app stores such as App Store and Google Play provide and maintained by Apple and Google respectively. However, the easily available and installable apps do come with equally severe security risks, vulnerabilities and threats.

Mobile devices are susceptible to various types of attacks (Figure 3): physical, over the network, via a vulnerability exploit of the underlying Operating System or the installed applications, or via malware.

Figure 3. Attack surface of mobile devices

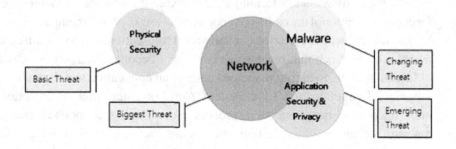

195

The physical security of a mobile device is a basic threat related to loss of device, theft of device or temporary physical access. It can be ensured by facility to locate device, backup, passcode and other protection mechanisms. The Network-based attacks are possible because of: (a) general protocol vulnerabilities, (b) design issues affecting mobile OS, and (c) excessive use of untrusted networks. The App-level vulnerabilities are: (a) plain HTTP, (b) certificate pinning, (c) HTTP request hijacking. And finally, the maliciously vulnerable apps which can successfully breach the application security or privacy, or device security is the Malware.

Mobile Malware is a threat changing its nature continuously and escaping detection, and so it needs to be considered as a high priority to always keep we equipped to detect and mitigate it. Mobile malware keeps changing its nature by using newer and evolving techniques like polymorphism, encrypted command and control communications, code obfuscation, obfuscated payloads, stealthy programming techniques, distributed architectures, dynamically changing domain and IP addresses and others. Moreover, because of the increased funding and increased interests in malicious applications by several crime organizations, developers sweat it out to keep coming up with newer ideas for malware creation. These state-of-the-art techniques keep malware unnoticed or undetected for weeks, months and even years (Geetha, S., & Phamila, A. V., 2016).

MALWARE DELIVERY METHODOLOGIES

To detect and mitigate malware attacks, one should be aware of the methodologies by which a malware is delivered to a mobile device (Amro, B., 2017):

1. **Repackaging:** The disassembling of popular benign application for adding malicious code into it and reassembling it, is repackaging. This is the most common technique used by malware developers to plagiarize legitimate applications to create the malicious applications. By this repackaging, popular apps become carriers of malware. Repackaging is done with the help of popular reverse-engineering tools, few of them are listed under section VI.

2. **Stealth Techniques:** Stealth techniques are to exploit the software vulnerabilities for code obfuscation of the malicious code in order to escape from being identified by the anti-malware applications or software. Obfuscation tries to disguise the malicious code such that reverse engineering it becomes challenging. Code obfuscation refers to hiding malicious code in an application which retaining its original functionality. Live-System Anti-Forensics, process injection, hook injection, library injection, process camouflaging are popular stealth malware techniques based on dynamic loading, native code (JNI) execution,

code encryption, key permutation and java reflection API (Adrienne Porter Felt, Dawn Song & David Wagner, 2012).

3. **Drive-By Download:** A download which was not intended for but happens because either the user had triggered it without knowing the consequences or without the knowledge of the user. When a user visits a website knowingly or unknowingly and that contains malicious content which gets automatically downloaded onto the device. This unintentional download of malware in the background is referred to as drive-by download. The downloaded software may be a malware by itself or may be a repackaging of a benign application with a malware in it.

4. **Dynamic Payloads:** An encrypted malicious payload gets downloaded onto a device in an application. This payload is then extracted and decrypted to execute the malicious code within it.

Lee Neely (2016) discusses the ubiquitous nature of mobile devices, reviews the services and practices involved in securing and protecting mobile devices and also provides a checklist for Mobile threat protection. The Table 1 below lists the requirements for Mobile threat protection by identifying seven categories of it and their associated priorities.

MALWARE ANALYSIS TECHNIQUES

The art of malware dissection in order to identify it, classify it and understand its working is known as Malware analysis. The very purpose of Malware analysis is to find it and to defeat or eliminate it. With millions of malware or malicious programs in the wild, and new and newer are encountered every day, malware analysis is critical for all Mobile devices and networks. Malware analysis first began by developing signatures for hosts and networks, because, the physical malware attack surface are the hosts and the networks. When an application is identified to be a malware using the available detection techniques, a signature representation of the application is generated, where a signature is nothing but a unique hash representation of the malware application, next time if an application with similar signature is found, it is classified as a malware. Similarly, a signature is generated for the sequence of network packets which resulted in a malware, so that any repetition of the signature in the network packets categorizes the software being received or transmitted as a malware. The host-based signatures were used to identify malware or malicious code present or entering into a device. These signatures are often compared with activities such as file creation or modification or specific changes happening at the registry or log. The network signatures are compared with those generated by monitoring

Table 1. Checklist for mobile threat protection by SANS

Priority	Installation	End-User Experience	Threat Detection			Management and Administration	Other
			Network Threats	Malware	Device Vulnerabilities		
High	• support app download from public stores • overall ease of installation	• low impact on device battery usage • display detected threats and mitigation options • app maintains end User's privacy	• SSL stripping and decryption attack detection • Rogue networks detection • automatic mitigation on detected network threats	• detection of malicious apps based on its properties • detect repackaged/ fake apps • ability to block malicious app installation • Detect malicious profiles on iOS devices	ability to identify device OS vulnerabilities	• provide visibility on detected threats and vulnerabilities • provide an overall risk estimate per device • provide the option to define an organization-level compliance policy • reporting	• Enterprise Mobility Management (EMM) integration • Security Information and Event Management (SIEM) integration
Medium		low data usage	content manipulation attack	Detect iOS malware	• ability to identify jail-broken or rooted devices • ability to prompt end users to upgrade their device OS version	provide forensic capabilities on identified threats	
Low							provide a third-party API for retrieving device security information

the packets of the network traffic for detection of transmission of malicious packets. Therefore, malware analysis helps create signatures, but not network signatures, also that the performance and effectiveness of signature-based approach is usually for known malware in transit. Hence, categorically there exist two malware analysis techniques namely, Static Analysis Techniques and Dynamic Analysis Techniques.

Static Analysis Techniques

Static analysis techniques use the code of an application to identify the code as a malware or benign without even having to execute the application (Jan Arends, 2018). Static analysis is the basic step in studying malware, it is the process of analysing a disassembled or decompiled application or executable binary file without actually executing it (Figure 4). Static Analysis can be performed in various ways as listed below, and can involve any combination of the following procedures:

1. **File Identification**: It involves identifying the format of the file and extracting file metadata which can provide us with useful information.
2. **Fingerprinting**: This involves producing a unique cryptographic hash value of the file and its environmental artefacts and comparing it with fingerprints generated earlier for malicious files.
3. **String Extraction**: This involves extraction of embedded artefacts such as dependencies with external libraries, calls to APIs, error handling, network transactions, IRC channels, Command & Control server, directory and file names, compiler and its version etc.
4. **Anti-Virus Scanning**: Most anti-virus scanners are populated with signatures of malware that were detected in the past. If a file under inspection contains a well-known malware then most of the anti-virus scanners will be able to detect with the signatures, they have with them.
5. **Disassembly and Decompilation**: The final step of static analysis if the previous steps fail to yield the results, is to disassemble the code and investigate the machine/assembly code or decompile (reverse the machine code to its high/ middle-level code) to retrieve the source code and investigate the same for its maliciousness.

The static analysis techniques are classified into the following categories depending on the type of source code analysis they perform:

Signature-Based Approach

In the signature-based approach, a unique signature for existing malware is created by extracting semantic patterns and other meta-features from its code. If the signature of a program matches any one among the set of signatures of the existing malware then it too is classified as a malware. This approach for malware detection is very fast, however, it identifies only the existing malware and fails to identify new malware variants, and also it compels for frequent updating based on the frequency of release of newer malware. Moreover, a malware can easily hide from being detected by this approach by code obfuscation or stealth techniques as discussed in section III.

Permission-Based Analysis

The access rights of the applications are decided based on the permissions it requests. Because an application is installed on devices owned by users, these applications need few permissions to execute themselves on the device and to achieve few of their functionalities. The developers must mention the permissions required by the applications for the resources and justify the requirement. 'Default Deny' is the principle followed for granting permissions to applications requesting access user's data or device, that may affect the system security, and so the User is prompted to grant the requested permissions to an application, in order to access the desired and required resources, during the installation process. It should also be understood that not all those declared and requested permissions are necessarily needed permissions for the applications functionality. Permission-based detection is the fastest in application scanning and identifying malware but with high rate of false-positives and also this technique does not analyse other files which may contain the malicious

Figure 4. Stages in static analysis

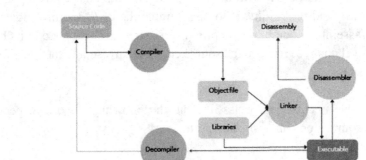

code. Also, that, only a very slight difference in permissions exists between malicious and benign applications, hence, permission-based methods require second pass and support from other techniques to provide detect malware efficiently.

Virtual Machine Analysis

A virtual machine is the software layer which facilitates execution of an application by translating its source code into the underlying operating systems machine language. It is used to analyse the bytecode of a particular application for its behaviour by deriving its control flow and data flow and investigating it for mischievous functionalities performed by malicious code in malware applications. The major drawback of virtual machine analysis is that the analysis is performed at the level of the assembly code or machine language and therefore it consumes enormous time, storage space and power/battery.

The main advantages of Static program analysis are:

- It can find weaknesses in the code at its exact location
- It reaches all corners of the software to judge all possible behavioural scenarios
- It can find unique defects such as unreachable code, unused variables, uncalled functions and boundary value violations
- It is more reliable for checking a software for reliability, security and conformance to coding best practices
- It is a safer technique because it does not need the software to be executed
- It can determine zero-day vulnerabilities/malware

Dynamic Analysis Techniques

Dynamic analysis analyses the software while it is actually executing, this can overcome the obfuscation techniques which intervene during static analysis. The various segments of dynamic analysis based on the methodology are listed below:

1. **Monitoring**: This involves keeping track of the processes, their threads, system or API calls, file system, its registry and the network. These monitoring details are then combined together to study the order and relationship between them to extract meaningful information or hostile behaviour, if found.
   a. To explore all the processes related to a program gives important insights to the functionality. We need to investigate the processes that are running, created or terminated while a program or process of a program is executing.

For example, a program killing an anti-virus process is almost sure to be classified as a malware. This kind of process monitoring has an anti-technique known as 'process replacement', which involves overwriting the memory space of an already executing process with a malicious program, so that the malicious program gets the same privileges as that of the process it had replaced. This can be overcome by analysis of the memory image.

b. The APIs and system calls are well documented across all platforms. The APIs and system call for user-mode and kernel-mode are clearly demarcated in popular Operating Systems, and so keeping track of the calls to these APIs and system calls and judging the pattern can help classify software. Analysing these calls can help us identify the correlation of individual function calls that operate on the same object and so on. Therefore, keeping track of these APIs and system calls and corresponding parameters provide better chances to determine the type of behaviour of the software. For example, any network functionality required by an app is possible only through system calls to operating system, which cater networking functionality.

c. Keeping a check on interactions of the executing software with the underlying file system, the logging system and the registry, helps us double check our results obtained by monitoring of the APIs and system calls.

d. Almost all modern malicious programs require at least minimal Internet access. To determine network interactions of a program, we need to host network services mimicking DNS, monitor DNS health at few critical nodes and links, email, IRC, file servers and execute our programs on those services (Tejaswini Yadav C.Y., Balaji Rajendran & Rajani P (2014). This can help us determine interactions via Command and Control (C&C) or IRC server too.

2. **Heap Abstraction**: This is a technique of memory forensics. Often unprecedented behaviour is attached to a functionality which persists in memory for unusually prolonged period. Such behaviour can be determined continually acquiring the execution space in the memory by copying it into a non-volatile memory and analyse it for lifetime of objects, variables and functions.

3. **Debugging**: A software capable of examining the execution (debugging) of another program is a debugger. The debugger steps through each and every execution step of a program being debugged, it may even step-over to skip a step and can pause at specified breakpoints.

Dynamic analysis examines an application during its execution time and then classifies according to one of the following techniques based on the behaviour of the detection mechanisms (Pandey, S. K., & Mehtre, B., 2014).

Anomaly-Based Analysis

Anomaly-based analysis also referred to as behavioural analysis is based on keeping a watch on the executing applications and their behaviour. The behaviour is judged based on few parameters that include battery consumption, CPU usage, network traffic, system logs, etc., and generates signatures for malware behaviour.

Taint Analysis

Taint analysis involves keeping track of the multiple sources of sensitive data to identify data leakage. In other words, the purpose of taint analysis is to track the flow of private and sensitive data between and within programs. It works by tainting sensitive data at its source, keep a watch on it and propagate the taint information and issue warning if tainted data reaches a destination. Taint analysis can be performed statically on the source code or dynamically on the app execution environment by monitoring the tainted data. But it does not generate a control flow graph for control flow tracking.

Emulation Based Analysis

Emulation based technique performs dynamic analysis of applications based on Virtual Machine Introspection on user behaviour parameters such as touches, clicks and gestures etc. The anti-malware cannot detect emulation-based analysis happening because in this technique the monitoring happens from outside the execution environment.

The main advantages of Dynamic analysis are:

- It can get over the anti-techniques for Static Analysis
- It can determine runtime behaviour of the software to be investigated
- It takes far lesser time than Static Analysis techniques

Hybrid Analysis

Hybrid Analysis is performing Static Analysis and Dynamic Analysis simultaneously, even though techniques remain the same as listed individually under Static Analysis and Dynamic Analysis (Xu, L., Zhang, D., Jayasena, N., & Cavazos, J., 2017). A comparison of the features considered for static analysis, dynamic analysis and hybrid analysis is done in Table 2.

The Figure 5 depicts the Mobile Malware features under different categories of Mobile Malware Analysis discussed above.

Supplementary Analysis Techniques

A combination of Data Mining and Machine-learning techniques are supplementary to Static and Dynamic Malware analysis techniques (Souri, A., & Hosseini, R., 2018). The following figure (Figure 6) exhibits applying machine learning algorithms on the features extracted from malware signatures database and those extracted from monitoring of application execution using data mining techniques to classify an application as malware or benign. Using these supplementary techniques such as

Table 2. Comparison of different features of Mobile applications

Features	Advantages	Disadvantages
Static features	Feature extraction is easier	stealth techniques and code obfuscation may hide features or provide false features
Dynamic features	Lesser features than static features, but more comprehensive	• feature extraction is relatively difficult when compared to extracting static features • complete coverage of code can't be guaranteed using these feature • requires root privilege on the device to extract features
Hybrid features	It is the comprehensive collection of features because it is a combination of both the static and dynamic features	complex extraction process because it needs to extract both the static and dynamic features

Figure 5. Mobile malware features

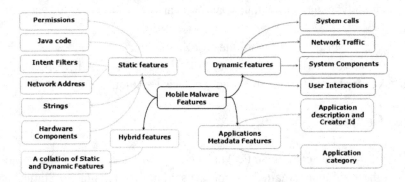

204

Figure 6. Using supplementary techniques on feature extracted using Static Analysis and Dynamic Analysis

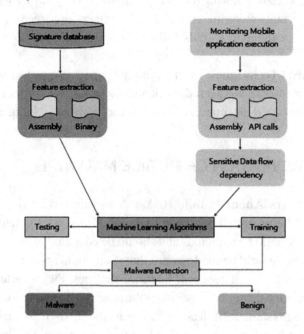

data mining, Machine-learning and Deep-learning, we can improve the precision, performance and speed of the Malware analysis techniques to a great extent (Kateryna Chumachenko, 2017).

MALWARE EVASION TECHNIQUES

Malware creators constantly keep a watch on the evolving mobile security techniques and propose newer techniques to counter its detection. Such counter techniques avoid the detection of malicious code and are called evasion techniques. Most of the evasion techniques will be based on one of the following listed below:

1. **Anti-Security Techniques:** These techniques keep scanning the device environment for anti-malware, anti-virus, firewall, and other such security and protection programs, and assists the malware from being detected by those programs.
2. **Anti-Sandbox Techniques:** Sandboxing is a technique used to demarcate each running program and its required resources from those of others. By this, it can be ensured that benign applications executing on the device remain unharmed

by unverified/malicious programs on the computer system. These anti-sandbox techniques keep monitoring the changes at the registry keys, files, or processes related to virtual environments and decide their counter-measures for the same so that automatic analysis fails and reporting on the behaviour of malware is avoided.

3. **Anti-Analyst Techniques:** In this technique, a monitoring tool is used to avoid detection of reverse engineered applications. This involves nullifying the effect of signature-based detection and other static analysis techniques.

TIPS FOR PREVENTION OF MOBILE MALWARE

1. **Educate Users About Mobile Risks:** A mobile device too is a computer and should be protected and used like one. Users must understand that the applications could be malicious and should be educated to always consider the source. Users should be made aware that if an application is asking for more privileges than what it needs for its functionalities, they should not install it.

2. **Prevent Jailbreaking:** Jailbreaking is the process of gaining root/full access to the operating system and its features, meaning there exist no security limitations. Limiting the number of root-enabled devices can prevent jailbreaking.

3. **Security Features of Wi-Fi Networks to be Considered:** Generally, Wi-Fi networks are insecure. Such networks should develop acceptable use policies, provide VPN technology, and compel that users should be provided connectivity only through secure tunnels.

4. **Keep the Device Operating Systems Up-To-Date:** The device operating systems require frequent updating with patches which may be major or minor security fixes. Keeping the operating system updated with the latest patches reduces the device vulnerability to potential exploits.

5. **Install Applications From Trusted Sources Only:** The users should install applications only from trusted sources like Google play, Apple store etc. The companies can also maintain their own applications stores encouraging their employees to download and install from it.

6. **Install Anti-Malware:** The users should be educated about the need for anti-malware software and encouraged to have them installed on their devices.

7. **Bring-Your-Own-Device (BYOD) Policies:** Enforcing BYOD should ensure that (a) an employee is able to access required resources and (b) the employee is able to access only his/her authorized resources.

Table 3. Tools for malware analysis

1.	**Mobile Security Framework (MobSF)** is an all-in-one open-source mobile application for automated penetration-testing, also capable of performing static and dynamic analysis. It can be used for effective and fast security analysis of zipped source code, binaries and applications of Android and iOS platforms. MobSF also has an API Fuzzer using which it can perform Web API Security testing. *Accessible at*: https://github.com/MobSF/Mobile-Security-Framework-MobSF
2.	**AndroL4b** provides tools for reverse engineering and malware analysis of Android applications to assist security researchers. It is an android security virtual machine based on ubuntu-mate. *Accessible at*: https://kalilinuxtutorials.com/androl4b-2/
3.	**CobraDroid** is a custom build of the Android operating system developed for being used in research by application security analysts and mobile malware analysts. *Accessible at*: https://thecobraden.com/projects/cobradroid/
4.	**Android Malware Analysis Toolkit** is a Linux distribution focused on Mobile Malware Analysis for Android. *Accessible at*: http://www.mobilemalware.com.br/amat/index.html
5.	**DroidBox** performs dynamic analysis of Android applications, on various parameters, such as, network interactions of the device, file operations, cryptographic operations, broadcast receives, services started, java classes loaded, SMS sent, phone calls made and a few others. *Accessible at*: https://github.com/pjlantz/droidbox
6.	**Drozer** (formerly Mercury) helps searching for security vulnerabilities in Android apps and devices. Drozer interacts with the Dalvik VM of Android, checks inter-component interactions of apps and the service API calls to the underlying OS. Using weasel (MWR's advanced exploitation payload) drozer can act as a Remote Access Tool (RAT), thus entertaining remote or cloud-based device scanning for devices. *Accessible at*: https://labs.mwrinfosecurity.com/tools/drozer/
7.	**CuckooDroid** has the capabilities of performing dynamic analysis of Android applications. It is an extension an open-source software, Cuckoo Sandbox, which captures suspicious file operations in an automated dynamic testing model. *Accessible at*: https://cuckoo-droid.readthedocs.io/en/latest/
8.	**Inspeckage** (Android Package Inspector) is a tool offering dynamic analysis of Android applications. It clings onto to the function calls to the Android API and keeps track of the behaviour by monitoring them for an anomaly. *Accessible at*: https://resources.infosecinstitute.com/inspeckage-dynamic-assessment-tool-android/#gref
9.	**iVerify-oss** is for iOS devices, it inspects the device at boot-time when no other code is running. It validates the integrity of the device by collecting smallest of the modifications in the device. *Accessible at*: https://github.com/trailofbits/iverify-oss
10.	**Androguard** is a reverse-engineering tool that can be used for performing malware analysis on Android mobile applications. *Accessible at*: https://androguard.readthedocs.io/en/latest/index.htm
11.	**APKTool** is a collection of tools to allow reverse-engineering of Android .apk files. It includes Smali and Baksmali which are popular android disassembler and assembler. *Accessible at*: https://forum.xda-developers.com/showthread.php?t=1755243
12.	**Smali/Baksmali** is an android assembler/disassembler. It can assemble or disassemble the dex format used by the Android's Java VM implementation, dalvik. *Accessible at*: https://github.com/JesusFreke/smali
13.	**dex2jar** converts APKs to Java jar files for decompilation. *Accessible at*: https://github.com/pxb1988/dex2jar
14.	**JD-GUI** is an effection Java decompiler working. It is a standalone application with a rich GUI to display the Java sources from CLASS files. *Accessible at*: http://jd.benow.ca/
15.	**Jadx**, one of a new breed of Android decompilers. *Accessible at*: https://github.com/skylot/jadx
16.	**ProGuard** and **DexGuard**, which are obfuscators. ProGuard ships with Android SDK. *Accessible at*: https://www.guardsquare.com/en/products/dexguard
17.	**Keyczar**, which is used for public/private key encryption. *Accessible at*: https://github.com/google/keyczar

MOBILE MALWARE DATASETS

Researcher, Developers, and Engineers wanting to conduct research and carry out experiments in the area of Mobile Malware Analysis and Detection, can find datasets available for free access from the websites listed in Table 4.

Table 4. Mobile malware datasets

Name of the Dataset	Location (URL)
AndroMalShare	http://sanddroid.xjtu.edu.cn:8080/#home
Kharon Malware Dataset	http://kharon.gforge.inria.fr/dataset/
AMD Project	http://amd.arguslab.org/
AAGM Dataset	http://www.unb.ca/cic/datasets/android-adware.html
Android PRAGuard Dataset	http://pralab.diee.unica.it/en/AndroidPRAGuardDataset
AndroZoo	https://androzoo.uni.lu/
iOS-malware	https://github.com/ashishb/ios-malware

Table 5. Indian IPR in mobile malware

1. **Invention title:** System and method for the Detection of Malware	
Application number: 1426/CHENP/2011	**Publication date:** 06/01/2012
Description: The idea is about provisioning an interactive disassembler of the binary file which performs a static analysis, by investigating the instruction sequence and indicating threatening instruction sequences by labelling them, and request for one or more other assembly language sequences from the binary file.	
2. **Invention title:** A standalone portable device for detecting and removing virus or malware or spyware	
Application number: 831/MUM/2013	**Publication date:** 30/01/2015
Description: The idea is of a portable standalone virus removing device comprising of Field Programmable Gate Array (FPGA) and Application Specific Integrated Circuit (ASIC). The device reads the entire file system and searches and identifies malicious executable files with extensions that belong to virus or malware or spyware and pre-emptively deletes such files without repairing or attempting to repair the files in order to achieve much faster execution.	
3. Invention title: System and method for bidirectional trust between downloaded applications and mobile devices including a secure charger and malware scanner	
Application number: 1230/KOLNP/2014	**Publication date:** 15/08/2014
Description: The idea is of a device which can act as a mobile charger-cum-malware scanner. The algorithms perform forensic and behavioural analysis on the mobile being charged using the proposed device.	
4. **Invention title:** Methods and systems for detecting fake user interactions with a Mobile device for improved Malware protection	
Application number: 201747021913	**Publication date:** 07/07/2017
Description: The idea is for a computing device processor configured with executable instructions to implement methods of detecting and responding to fake user interaction events. The processor can determine whether a user interaction event is a fake by analysing raw data generated by one or more hardware drivers in conjunction with user interaction event information generated or received by high level operating system.	

PATENT LANDSCAPING IN MOBILE MALWARE IN INDIA

Even though continuous progress is happening in the area of Mobile Malware Detection and Analysis, there are lot many open challenges existing and evolving with time. Hence keeping open the scope for many more patents in the said domain. Table 5 captures few of the Indian patents in the area of Mobile Malware.

FEW OPEN CHALLENGES IN MOBILE MALWARE

Most of the security issues related to Mobile such as information leakage, privilege escalation, repackaged apps, denial of service (DoS) attack, colluding, computation power usage, all these are possible using malware residing on a mobile. Therefore, preventing or detecting such malware by analysing them continues to remain as research challenge due to newer techniques continuously evolving. To counter this we need to sharpen our existing analysis techniques and supplement them with newer techniques to improve their performance and precision.

In the static and signature-based analysis techniques, statically extracted features such as configuration files, API and system calls, sequence of instructions and so on, are used. As such, extraction of these static features is quite easily feasible, but stealth techniques and code obfuscation techniques make extraction of these features a complex task. Hence there exists scope for research in enhancing static and signature-based analysis techniques to overcome the hindrances listed above.

The dynamic analysis is done using an environment created with a set of rules and policies based on behaviour implemented in it. An intelligent application aware of those set of rules and policies can come equipped with the capability of evading such environment. There exist challenges in coming up with more versatile dynamic analysis environments.

As static, dynamic or hybrid analysis techniques are not complete solutions by themselves, we can seek help of supplementary techniques such as data mining and machine learning to enhance their capabilities in malware detection and analysis.

REFERENCES

Amro, B. (2017). Malware Detection Techniques for Mobile Devices. *International Journal of Mobile Network Communications & Telematics, 7*(4/5/6),01-10. doi:10.5121/ijmnct.2017.7601

Arends. (2018). *Malware Analysis - Tools and Techniques* (Report). Academic Press.

Ashraf. (2012). *Mobile Banking Security- a security model* (Report). Academic Press.

Chumachenko. (2017). *Machine Learning Methods for Malware Detection and Classification* (Thesis). Academic Press.

Felt, A. P., Chin, E., Hanna, S., Song, D., & Wagner, D. (2011, October). Android permissions demystified. In *Proceedings of the 18th ACM conference on Computer and communications security* (pp. 627-638). ACM.

Geetha, S., & Phamila, A. V. (2016). Combating security breaches and criminal activity in the digital sphere. Hershey, PA: Information Science Reference. doi:10.4018/978-1-5225-0193-0

Harbour. (n.d.). *Stealth Secrets of the Malware Ninjas*. Academic Press.

Neely. (2016). *Mobile Threat Protection: A Holistic Approach to Security Mobile Data and Devices* (Report). Academic Press.

Pandey, S. K., & Mehtre, B. (2014). A Lifecycle Based Approach for Malware Analysis. *2014 Fourth International Conference on Communication Systems and Network Technologies*. 10.1109/CSNT.2014.161

Souri, A., & Hosseini, R. (2018). A state-of-the-art survey of malware detection approaches using data mining techniques. *Human-centric Computing and Information Sciences*, *8*(1), 3. doi:10.118613673-018-0125-x

Tejaswini Yadav, Rajendran, & Rajani. (2014). An Approach for Determining the Health of the DNS. *International Journal of Computer Science and Mobile Computing, 3*(9).

Xu, L., Zhang, D., Jayasena, N., & Cavazos, J. (2017). HADM: Hybrid Analysis for Detection of Malware. *Proceedings of SAI Intelligent Systems Conference (IntelliSys) 2016 Lecture Notes in Networks and Systems*, 702-724. doi:10.1007/978-3-319-56991-8_51

Chapter 11

Intelligent Malware Detection Using Deep Dilated Residual Networks for Cyber Security

Abijah Roseline S.
VIT Chennai, India

ABSTRACT

Malware is the most serious security threat, which possibly targets billions of devices like personal computers, smartphones, etc. across the world. Malware classification and detection is a challenging task due to the targeted, zero-day, and stealthy nature of advanced and new malwares. The traditional signature detection methods like antivirus software were effective for detecting known malwares. At present, there are various solutions for detection of such unknown malwares employing feature-based machine learning algorithms. Machine learning techniques detect known malwares effectively but are not optimal and show a low accuracy rate for unknown malwares. This chapter explores a novel deep learning model called deep dilated residual network model for malware image classification. The proposed model showed a higher accuracy of 98.50% and 99.14% on Kaggle Malimg and BIG 2015 datasets, respectively. The new malwares can be handled in real-time with minimal human interaction using the proposed deep residual model.

DOI: 10.4018/978-1-5225-8241-0.ch011

INTRODUCTION

Microsoft windows are the first desktop operating systems with a market share of 82.7% (Statista portal). MacOSX, Linux, Chrome OS, and other unknown operating systems show very less market share as shown in figure 1. The attackers target the widely used Windows OS for achieving their goals. The wider use of computer systems and internet raises the number of security threats such as malware day by day. Cybersecurity is one of the significant areas in this information world with its useful strengths in the everyday aspect of human activities at various levels. Cyber-attacks are uncommonly growing, resulting in greater amounts of data loss and financial loss to individuals or large organizations. Malware is one among the cyber-attacks which are currently sophisticated, stealthy and unknown to users. Security researchers take serious efforts to develop robust detection systems to identify known, as well as unknown malware. The cyber world happens to contain an excessive amount of data which are handled by machine learning applications.

Malware detection and identification of new malware are some of the cybersecurity challenges. Malware with different intents shows different behaviors. The advent of malware detection systems led to the development of detection avoidance mechanisms by the attackers. Although malware authors develop new malware rarely, most of the current malware are variants of existing malware. The previously written malware is slightly changed in any part of the code using any of the obfuscation techniques such as semantic nop insertion, code reordering, etc. Since new malware are similar in some characteristic to previous malware, they can be categorized into different families. But, they did not fulfill the aim of dealing with new zero-day and obfuscated malware with no false positives. Hence, it is necessary to classify malware into various classes or families for robust and intelligent detection of new malware.

Figure 1. The market share of the desktop OS between the years 2013-2018 at the global level

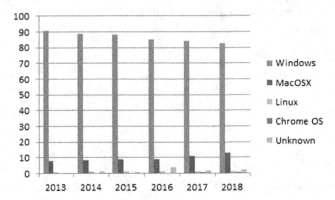

With the spread of new and unseen malware, traditional methods are not sufficient to cope with. Such traditional methods like signature-based methods are sufficient for previously known malware. But, they are not feasible solutions for advanced malware threats. To deal with such advanced threats, advanced machine learning techniques are devised. Particularly, deep learning techniques are more effective than conventional machine learning techniques for pattern recognition applications. Deep learning methods mimic human nervous systems by learning data through abstract and complex representation. The aim of the work is to train the deep learning model to effectively classify and detect the samples in the test dataset file into one of 9 categories (malware families).

The malware classification problem definition and detection solutions are described in the first section. A literature survey describing a review of the various works done for malware classification and detection is given in section 2. The variant deep learning methodologies were discussed in section 3. The proposed method is explained in detail in section 4. The malware dataset details are discussed in section 5. The comparison of various machine learning techniques is done and the effectiveness of the proposed model is evaluated and results are discussed in section 6. The final section concludes with the summary of the chapter.

PROBLEM STATEMENT

A set of samples is given as input to the system. The training data with features is denoted as X and each sample is labeled from $X_i \ldots \ldots X_n$. Each sample with its distinct features is identified as malware or benign and labeled as $Y_i \ldots \ldots Y_n$. The training phase involves training the available data using any machine learning algorithm such as support vector machines, decision trees, neural networks, etc. The searching of the best model among a set of algorithms is performed by estimating the rate of correctly classified samples. Thus, training can be referred to as learning the best features that best classify the data samples. After training a model, the model is applied for detection of new samples.

Machine Learning and Malware Detection

Machine learning plays a vital role in cyber security applications like malware classification. The identification of a file as benign causes no harm if it is executed, whereas the execution of malware files impacts the system or connected networks. Current systems take advantage of deep learning models which results in very low false positive rates and false negative rates. The cyberspace in the early days was comparatively less prone to malware threats. So simple signature and rule-based methods were sufficient for malware detection. At present, as the cyberspace is becoming wider and wider, huge numbers of malware are monitored every day and the traditional methods are insufficient to aid detection. Machine learning techniques are employed to achieve cognitive malware classification and detection.

Machine learning learns the data with the known samples and helps identify the new and unknown samples. Unsupervised and supervised learning are two different approaches to machine learning which are capable of performing different tasks. Unsupervised learning is an approach where only a dataset is given without any target class labels to which the sample belongs to. Supervised learning approach contains the data and the target labels. The aim of a security researcher is to fit the model that results in correctly identifying the newly arriving samples. Supervised learning comprises two steps. First, training and fitting a model on the dataset with malware and benign samples. Then, the trained model is used to predict the new samples.

The requirements for robust machine learning based malware detection include large typical datasets, clearly explainable trained model, low false positive rate and highly adaptive model to cope with attacks. The performance of the proposed model depends on the training data. The features that are significant for malware detection are identified by having a large training data. The dataset should contain all cases which make efficient real-world malware detection. Thus, the data collection task is a very critical step for detection using machine learning.

The machine learning models are black box models where we give an input training data X and we get an output Y. The complex process that happens after the input is given is hidden. This hidden information is important while checking any issues in the proposed model. Thus the proposed model should be clearly explainable.

The false positive rate (i.e., detection of benign as malware wrongly) should be less or zero. For malware detection, it is very sensitive that wrong classification leads users to serious dangers. The models are designed and tuned to achieve low false positive rates by checking during execution without completely retraining the model.

Malware writers develop techniques or programs to escape detection. The new class of malware varies from the known malware used in training. The benign files are also being developed newly which are not used in training. The model should detect the benign files also correctly. Machine learning techniques are more challenging when data is changed with new samples. The model should be highly adaptive by having an updated dataset and appropriate retraining of models.

Deep Learning

Deep learning is an advanced part of machine learning. The deep neural network is an artificial brain that mimics the working of the human brain. The larger amount of data given to deep learning model is comprehensive for correct detection of new samples. Artificial intelligence has shown advancement in cyber security challenges using the deep learning models. Machine learning models show false positive rates that are considerably higher compared to the current deep learning models. Dealing with new malware is still a challenge for the machine learning solutions. Deep learning based malware detection shows higher detection rates with very less false positives.

Deep learning is a significant machine learning method where the low-level features of data are extracted to a high level of abstraction. Deep learning (Kim et al., 2017; Ni et al., 2018) has shown remarkable development over the traditional signature and rule-based methods and also the typical machine learning models. Cybersecurity researchers employ deep learning techniques for detecting malware from low-level data. Deep learning techniques (Le et al., 2018) have achieved the best results in the computer vision area, mainly for image recognition tasks. The generalization property is the key to detection of new unseen samples. Deep learning techniques generalize well than traditional machine learning based techniques.

Machine learning based malware detection is based on feature engineering tasks. Machine learning techniques such as support vector machines, decision trees, random forests, etc. (Jeon et al., 2018; Jerlin et al., 2018; Kumara et al., 2018; Li et al., 2018; Rieck et al., 2011; Santos et al., 2013; Schultz et al., 2001; Tesauro et al., 1996) are used for classification of malware and benign and if it is a malware, to which family it belongs to. Features are a key to perform machine learning classification task. Deep learning based models do not require feature engineering. These deep network models are able to learn from raw data and so they are successfully applied to computer vision. With this idea, the deep dilated residual network is trained on the raw binary data of the input file to detect whether the file is a malware file or a benign file.

RELATED WORK

X. Hu et al. (2016) presented the design, development, and evaluation of a novel machine learning classifier trained on multifaceted content features such as instruction sequences, strings, section information, and other malware features. The system extracted an aggregated feature vector from each malware code based on opcode representation and knowledge from antivirus software. The proposed system classified unknown malware samples accurately and efficiently. A random forest classifier was then trained and optimized to learn the unique features that best discriminate malware families. The combination of hashing kernel that reduced the dimensionality of feature vectors and an optimal probability assignment method was employed to achieve scalability and accuracy. The system classified more than 10,000 malware samples with higher accuracy.

Yann LeCun et al. (2015) described deep learning technique where computational models consist of more number of processing layers to learn data with multiple levels of abstraction. Deep convolutional networks are used in the areas of image, video, speech and audio processing. Recurrent networks are used in serial data such as text and speech.

Sanjeev Das et al. (2016) proposed hardware based online malware detection approach called GuardOL using processor and Field-Programmable Gate Array (FPGA). A frequency-centric model was proposed for feature construction using system call patterns of known malware and benign traces. The proposed method constructs feature using the high-level semantics of malware. A machine learning technique based on multilayer perceptron was developed in FPGA and classifier was trained to exploit these features. The trained classifier classified the unknown samples based on early prediction at runtime. The method achieved high accuracy, fast detection, less power consumption, and flexibility with new malware samples. The early prediction was one of the main advantages and the method detected malware samples with low false positives.

Razvan Pascanu et al. (2015) presented a hybrid method which learned the language of malware from executed code and extracted time-based features. The combination of Echo State Networks (ESNs) and Recurrent Neural Networks (RNNs) with a higher-level classifier was presented to extract the features and was trained with an unsupervised approach. The performance of the proposed model is higher by employing ESN for the recurrent model, MaxPooling for non-linear sampling, and logistic regression for classification.

Razvan Benchea et al. (2014) proposed a detection system which comprised of simple mathematical operations and a confined Boltzmann machine, showing a better detection rate of the one side perceptron. The system modified the perceptron algorithm and combined with existing features. The analysis is performed on a substantial dataset, consisting of 3 million files. The method consumes more memory and testing time. The proposed algorithm ensured that there were no false positives in the training step and maintained an increased detection rate.

S. Banin et al. (2018) presented a study on the low-level features for multinomial malware classification. Memory access patterns are used for classification of ten malware families and ten malware types. The proposed method performs well for classifying malware families than malware types. Extensive feature selection reduces data dimensionality without any loss and does not affect classification performance. From millions of features, 50,000 features were extracted, out of which 29 features are selected. This leads to comparatively reliable models. Future work focuses on the evaluation of other models using the proposed system for handling new or unseen samples.

G. E. Dahl et al. (2013) proposed a malware classification system based on random projections and neural networks. Random projections are used to reduce the original input space. The proposed system trained large neural networks over 2.6 million samples. The system achieved a 43% reduced error rate in comparison with the logistic regression approach. In a single layer neural network, the two class error rate is 0.49% and for an ensemble of neural networks, the two class error rate is 0.42%. The number of random projections and hidden layers needed for performance improvements is studied. The addition of hidden layers did not show any improvement in accuracy.

Machine learning techniques have some limitations such as high feature engineering overhead, good expertise, etc.

Q. Hai et al. proposed a malware detection method based on behavior logs using deep learning. The proposed method is a combination of convolutional neural network and recurrent network. The proposed method achieved an accuracy of 98.75% compared to other conventional methods.

H. Yan et al. (2018) proposed a combined classification method called Pairwise Rotation Invariant Co-occurrence Local Binary Pattern - Term Frequency-Inverse Document Frequency Transform (PRICoLBP-TFIDF). The proposed PRICoLBP-TFIDF was compared with some binary-based features such as GIST, n-grams, RP, NN and LBP on three datasets. The proposed feature showed a higher accuracy of 98.6%, whereas other features showed low accuracy for a small number of samples. The proposed method achieved better linear separability among malware families and more adaptive to obfuscation. The limitations of the proposed method are vulnerability to adversarial techniques, and non-adaptive for unsupervised learning. The linear separability improvement could be achieved by extending it to sparse subspace clustering.

J. Fu et al. (2018) proposed a robust and fine-grained classification system using visualization approach. Malware is visualized as colored images and global features are extracted. The local features were extracted from code and data sections. The combination of global and local features is used for classifying malware using the random forest, K-nearest neighbor and support vector machine. The proposed system achieved an accuracy of 97.5% for 7087 samples belonging to 15 malware families. The fine-grained classification is performed with low computational complexity.

The detection and classification of malware is a challenging task. There is no perfect solution to tackle this problem. The best way to solve this problem is to use hybrid methods which include signature-based and machine learning based methods.

Malware Analysis

Malware analysis can be done in several ways, such as static analysis, dynamic analysis, and image-based (vision) analysis. Static analysis is a technique which allows analyzing a code by organizing it as a control flow graph. The dynamic analysis allows analyzing the behavior of malware code by running it in any virtual or controlled environments. Recent research is going on with image-based malware analysis (Nataraj et al., 2013). Visualization is an effective and simple technique for analyzing and classifying malware into their respective families.

Static Malware Analysis

As the name suggests, static analysis is the analysis that is done without the execution of the sample. Static analysis is a safe approach because the samples are not executed. The samples are identified prior to real-world execution. The techniques adopted by malware authors to avoid detection are called detection avoidance techniques. Obfuscation techniques, encryption techniques, usage of high-level languages, etc. cause a drawback in static analysis. Considering these issues, dynamic detection is brought into the scene.

Dynamic Malware Analysis

Deep learning methods are used to identify the behavior of the files. The behavior log contains the activities of the system as a sequence. Malware detection is done by monitoring the behavior log and the sequence of events are converted into binary vectors. The proposed model is trained using the deep dilated residual network to recognize benign and malicious files.

Image-based Malware Analysis

Malware can be visualized (Han et al., 2015; Kim et al., 2017; Nataraj et al., 2011; Ni et al., 2018) and classified using image processing and pattern recognition techniques. A malware binary is first converted to an 8-bit vector, which is converted into a grayscale image. Thus, malware is represented as grayscale images and given as input to the classifier. The malware image patterns belonging to the same family are similar in terms of texture and shape. The distinct sections of a malware code appear with the varied textures of the corresponding malware image. The figure shows the structure of a malware image of Adialer.C sample with various sections. The sections include .text, .rdata, .data, .rsrc which exhibit different textures in the image. The similarity of malware belonging to the same class is depicted below. The width of the images varies with the size of the file. For instance, if the file size is less than 10 KB, the image width is 32. If the file size exceeds 1000 KB, the image width is 1024. Likewise, file sizes between 10 KB and 1000 KB with different ranges show variations in the width of the corresponding images.

A recent work (Nataraj et al., 2011) on image-based malware classification showed the higher accuracy of 98% on a malware image dataset with 9458 samples belonging to 25 malware families. The texture features were computed using GIST and malware classification is performed using K-Nearest Neighbor classifier with Euclidean distance. The system is robust to some obfuscation techniques like section encryption. The computational time for classification is significantly very less (1.4 seconds) compared to the conventional methods for malware analysis.

L. Nataraj et al. (2013) proposed a system called SARVAM, a content-based Search And RetrieVAl of Malware which finds the similar variant of malware under query. The image signature is obtained using the input file executable as a whole. This approach could easily allow the attacker to encrypt or obfuscate any of the code sections. Also, the structural similarity of malware variants is calculated, but the identification of functionally similar malware variants with different structures was challenging. An efficient detection system analyzes the sections of the code and detects the functionally similar malware variants.

METHODOLOGY

Dilated Convolutions

Deep networks contain multiple stacked layers which represent the features. The network depth has significantly grown larger for very deep models. A drawback of very deep models is training accuracy degradation. This is due to the large training errors by the addition of more layers. The problem of degradation is resolved using

Figure 2. Adialer.C malware image variants

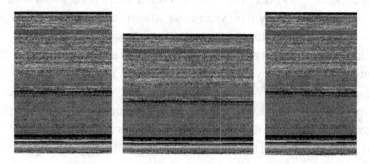

the deep residual learning model (He et al., 2016). Deep residual networks show good optimization when compared with the conventional deep networks showing high training error as the depth increases. The results are better compared to other deep models. The deep residual model is proven to be generic for image recognition problems and could be used for malware and benign classification.

Convolutional neural network (CNN) models (Kabanga et al., 2017; Kamundala et al., 2018) are popularly used in image analysis and classification problems. By CNN, the spatial resolution of the internal layers gradually reduces until reduced feature maps for the images are obtained. This reduced spatial information leads to inaccurate classification accuracy. The drawbacks of the CNN model are overcome by dilated convolutions. Yu and Koltun (2015) employed dilated convolutions as an extension to a residual learning model. The residual model increases the output resolution using a subset of inner layers by dilation. The resolution of output feature maps is widened without decreasing the receptive field of the independent neurons. Considering these ideas, the proposed deep Dilated Residual Network model (DRN) is used for malware classification and detection with inputs as malware images. Dilated residual networks do not require deeper layers and work with reduced complexity. Without fine-tuning, the weakly supervised localization problem found in sections of malware class image patterns is addressed, thereby achieving top-1 accuracy in classifying malware variants.

Deep Dilated Residual Networks

The detailed analysis of malware image is done using dilated residual networks. Deep dilated residual network (Yu et al., 2017) model is based on CNNs where high spatial resolution is maintained throughout the output layers. This characteristic feature exhibits high predictive accuracy in classifying malware images. The image localization problem is addressed using this deep learning model by achieving useful output activations. Downsampling for achieving limited memory may lead to loss of useful information in image classification. CNNs reduce spatial resolution using downsampling but degrade the model's performance. This issue is addressed by dilated residual networks. The downsampling layer is removed from residual networks and is replaced by the expansion (dilated) convolution, maintaining the spatial resolution of the feature map.

Deep dilated residual networks (DRNs) need not require deeper layers. It works by generating a subset of layers using dilations. The model complexity is less for dilated residual networks. Without fine-tuning, DRNs show better accuracy for weakly supervised scenarios. For instance, a 101 layered residual shows performed less compared to a 42 layer DRN. The network architectures (Yu et al., 2017) consist of five sets of layers. The first layer in each set performs downsampling by calculating the convolution filter at even rows and columns. This reduces the resolution output by a factor of 2 for each dimension. Each set of layers is denoted as S_l^i for $l = 1, 2,$ 3, 4, 5, where each layer in the set may be denoted as S_l^i. Let f_l^i be the filter for each layer S_l^i. Each layer consists of multiple feature maps. The output of S_l^i is given by,

$$\left(S_l^i * f_l^i\right)(m) = \sum\nolimits_{a+b=m} S_l^i\left(a\right) f_l^i\left(b\right)$$

where m is the feature map in the set S_l^i and a and b are the two features mapped.

For increasing resolution in the higher layers of the network, if the subsampling is removed from the inner layers, the receptive field in the successive layers gets reduced consistently. As the resolution increases, the receptive field gets reduced. This results in the loss of significant information for the model to predict accurately. This limitation is resolved with a better approach using dilated convolutions (Nataraj et al., Oct, 2011)[25]. In this approach, the receptive field increases as the resolution increases. The units in the dilated layers retain the same receptive field as corresponding units in the actual model.

Consider the last two sets S_4^i and S_5^i of the convolutional layers. The output resolution of S_4^i is doubled without affecting the receptive field units. But all the successive layers are affected due to their reduction of receptive fields by a downsampling factor of 2. Thus, the 2-dilated convolutions are given by,

$$\left(S_4^i * 2f_4^i\right)(m) = \sum\nolimits_{a+2b=m} S_4^i\left(a\right) f_4^i\left(b\right)$$

The final set S_5^i is given by,

$$\left(S_5^i * 2f_5^i\right)(m) = \sum\nolimits_{a+2b=m} S_5^i(a) f_5^i\left(b\right)$$

Dilated residual networks downsample the input image by a factor of 8. For example, if the resolution of the input image is 224×224, the output resolution of the final set S_5^i is 28×28. The global average pooling results with reasonable resolution to improve the classifier predictive accuracy.

PROPOSED SYSTEM

The proposed approach uses deep dilated residual networks for learning distinct patterns from malware images. The proposed system is capable of generalization and allows the detection of newly arriving malware. The main challenge is to classify a given malware image as to which malware family it belongs to. The input to the system is the raw malware samples in binary format. The sample is then converted into gray scale image. Malware images for variant families are generated.

The DRN model is used for feature extraction and classification. DRN consists of many convolutional layers involving residual connections. These layers are capable of extracting low-level, mid-level and high-level features from the malware images. The output of the final 2D convolutional layer is transformed to 1D vector. These 1D vectors act as the input to Fully Connected (FC) Layer containing several neurons. The n number of neurons in FC layer is equal to n number of classes. This FC layer performs classification and outputs are predicted. The images are correctly classified to their respective classes. The proposed system model is depicted in figure 3. The algorithm for the proposed model is summarized in Algorithm 1.

Algorithm 1

Proposed Malware Classification and Detection

Input: Training set X, Test set Y
Output: Benign class $\rightarrow B_i$ and Malware class $\rightarrow M_i$, where i is any integer representing the class which the sample belongs to
Step 1: Convert raw samples from X and Y to gray-scale images.
Step 2: Initialize the DRN model.

Figure 3. Proposed system model

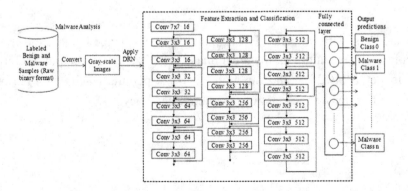

Step 3: Extract the features and train the proposed classifier model for the training and testing set.

Step 4: Output the predictions as B_{i-0} or $M_{i=1,2,3,...n}$, where $i=1,2,3,...n$ are the n number of malware families

Step 5: Evaluate the performance of DRN on the datasets.

DATASETS

The proposed system is tested on two datasets, namely, Kaggle Malimg dataset and BIG 2015 dataset. The Malimg dataset (Nataraj et al., 2011) consists of 9,339 malware samples from 25 different malware families. The number of malware samples that belong to each family is shown in Table 1. Nataraj et al. converted malware binaries into an 8-bit vector composing a matrix, $M \in R^{\{m \times n\}}$. The matrix is visualized as a grayscale image with values ranging [0, 255], with 0 representing black and 1 representing white.

The BIG 2015 dataset (Ronen et al., 2018) provided by Microsoft consists of nine malware variants with varying content and characteristics. The dataset includes 21741 known samples belonging to any of the nine malware families, of which 10868 are taken for training and 10873 are taken for testing. The size of the dataset is almost a half terabyte in uncompressed form. Each malware sample is uniquely identified using a hash value and the class to which a malware belongs is represented using integers from 1 to 9 (nine malware classes). The names of nine malware classes include Ramnit, Lollipop, Kelihos_ver3, Vundo, Simda, Tracur, Kelihos_ver1, Obfuscator.ACY, and Gatak. Table 2 shows the distribution of kaggle samples and their respective samples.

For every malware sample, the data include hexadecimal representation of the file's binary content and ASM file containing metadata such as strings, function calls, instruction sequences, registers, etc. The hexadecimal file consists of the byte count, address, record type and data. An assembly program consists of various sections such as data section, bss section, text section, rsrc section, rdata section, idata section, edata section, reloc section.

RESULTS AND DISCUSSION

The experiments were carried out on Kaggle Malimg dataset and BIG 2015 dataset for classification and detection of malware images. The Malimg dataset contains images for malware variants, whereas the BIG 2015 dataset contains byte and asm

Table 1. Malware families of kaggle malimg dataset

No.	Family	Family Name	No. of Variants
1	Dialer	Adialer.C	122
2	Backdoor	Agent.FYI	116
3	Worm	Allaple.A	2949
4	Worm	Allaple.L	1591
5	Trojan	Alueron.gen!J	198
6	Worm:AutoIT	Autorun.K	106
7	Trojan	C2Lop.P	146
8	Trojan	C2Lop.gen!G	200
9	Dialer	Dialplatform.B	177
10	Trojan Downloader	Dontovo.A	162
11	Rogue	Fakerean	381
12	Dialer	Instantaccess	431
13	PWS	Lolyda.AA 1	213
14	PWS	Lolyda.AA 2	184
15	PWS	Lolyda.AA 3	123
16	PWS	Lolyda.AT	159
17	Trojan	Malex.gen!J	136
18	Trojan Downloader	Obfuscator.AD	142
19	Backdoor	Rbot!gen	158
20	Trojan	Skintrim.N	80
21	Trojan Downloader	Swizzor.gen!E	128
22	Trojan Downloader	Swizzor.gen!I	132
23	Worm	VB.AT	408
24	Trojan-Downloader	Wintrim.BX	97
25	Worm	Yuner.A	800

files. So, the files are first converted to image files which are used for executing deep learning models such as CNN, ResNet and DRN. Then, the data was trained and validated using different classification models such as K-Nearest Neighbor, Random Forest, Support Vector Machine (SVM), Neural Network, Convolutional Neural Networks, Residual Networks, and the proposed DRN model. The accuracies achieved by various machine learning models are shown in Table 3. It has been observed that the proposed model gives highest accuracy of 98.50% and 99.14% for Malimg and Kaggle BIG 2015 datasets respectively. The existing models have

Table 2. Malware families of kaggle BIG 2015 dataset

No.	Family Name	No. of Variants
1	Ramnit	1541
2	Lollipop	2478
3	Kelihos ver3	2942
4	Vundo	475
5	Simda	42
6	Tracur	751
7	Kelihos ver1	398
8	Obfuscator ACY	1228
9	Gatak	1013

shown good accuracy, but our proposed model has even outperformed them. Our proposed model is appropriate for malware classification as it reduces the model complexity issue of CNN with good predictive accuracy.

CONCLUSION

In this chapter, a deep dilated residual network model for malware classification and detection system is presented. The system uses a recent technique of visualizing malware as grayscale images and the pattern identification leads to the classification of malware into their respective families. The visual representation of malwares is

Table 3. Results of various classification models on kaggle malimg and BIG 2015 datasets

S. No	Classification Model	Accuracy (in %)	
		Malimg Dataset	BIG 2015 Dataset
1	K-Nearest Neighbor (Nataraj et al., 2011; Yan et al., 2018)	97.18	96.60
2	Random Forest (Zhou et al. 2016)	95.26	96.82
3	SVM (Yan et al., 2018)	90.45	94.60
4	Neural Network (Yan et al., 2018)	93.70	95.50
5	CNN (Yu et al., 2015; Yu et al., 2017)	98.28	93.86
6	ResNet (Yu et al., 2015)	96.08	98.35
7	DRN	98.50	99.14

time consuming compared to other malware analysis methods. The proposed system is validated on two datasets, Kaggle Malimg and BIG 2015 malware datasets. The system is compared with other existing systems and the effectiveness of the proposed system is studied. The system outperforms the existing systems in terms of accuracy and computational time. The localization problem is addressed by using dilated model, thus focusing on local sections of various image patterns. The chapter employs an effective deep learning technique for building intelligent solutions to counter future threats.

REFERENCES

Banin, S., & Dyrkolbotn, G. O. (2018). Multinomial malware classification via low-level features. *Digital Investigation, 26*, S107–S117. doi:10.1016/j.diin.2018.04.019

Benchea, R., & Gavriluṭ, D. T. (2014, July). Combining restricted Boltzmann machine and one side perceptron for malware detection. In *International Conference on Conceptual Structures* (pp. 93-103). Springer. 10.1007/978-3-319-08389-6_9

Dahl, G. E., Stokes, J. W., Deng, L., & Yu, D. (2013, May). Large-scale malware classification using random projections and neural networks. In *Acoustics, Speech and Signal Processing (ICASSP), 2013 IEEE International Conference on* (pp. 3422-3426). IEEE. 10.1109/ICASSP.2013.6638293

Das, S., Liu, Y., Zhang, W., & Chandramohan, M. (2016). Semantics-based online malware detection: Towards efficient real-time protection against malware. *IEEE Transactions on Information Forensics and Security, 11*(2), 289–302. doi:10.1109/TIFS.2015.2491300

Fu, J., Xue, J., Wang, Y., Liu, Z., & Shan, C. (2018). Malware Visualization for Fine-Grained Classification. *IEEE Access: Practical Innovations, Open Solutions, 6*, 14510–14523. doi:10.1109/ACCESS.2018.2805301

Garcia, F. C. C., Muga, I. I., & Felix, P. (2016). *Random forest for malware classification*. arXiv preprint arXiv:1609.07770.

Gibert, D. (2016). *Convolutional neural networks for malware classification* (Doctoral dissertation). Dept. of Computer Science, UPC.

Hai, Q. T., & Hwang, S. O. (n.d.). An efficient classification of malware behavior using deep neural network. *Journal of Intelligent & Fuzzy Systems*, 1-14.

Han, K. S., Lim, J. H., Kang, B., & Im, E. G. (2015). Malware analysis using visualized images and entropy graphs. *International Journal of Information Security, 14*(1), 1–14. doi:10.100710207-014-0242-0

He, K., Zhang, X., Ren, S., & Sun, J. (2016). Deep residual learning for image recognition. In *Proceedings of the IEEE conference on computer vision and pattern recognition* (pp. 770-778). IEEE.

Hu, X., Jang, J., Wang, T., Ashraf, Z., Stoecklin, M. P., & Kirat, D. (2016). Scalable malware classification with multifaceted content features and threat intelligence. *IBM Journal of Research and Development, 60*(4), 6–1. doi:10.1147/JRD.2016.2559378

Jeon, D., & Park, D. (2018). Real-time Malware Detection Method Using Machine Learning. *The Journal Of Korean Institute Of Information Technology, 16*(3), 101–113. doi:10.14801/jkiit.2018.16.3.101

Jerlin, M. A., & Marimuthu, K. (2018). A New Malware Detection System Using Machine Learning Techniques for API Call Sequences. *Journal of Applied Security Research, 13*(1), 45–62. doi:10.1080/19361610.2018.1387734

Kabanga, E. K., & Kim, C. H. (2017). Malware images classification using convolutional neural network. *Journal of Computer and Communications, 6*(01), 153–158. doi:10.4236/jcc.2018.61016

Kamundala, E., & Kim, C. (2018). CNN Model to Classify Malware Using Image Feature. *KIISE Transactions On Computing Practices, 24*(5), 256–261. doi:10.5626/KTCP.2018.24.5.256

Kim, H., Kim, J., Kim, Y., Kim, I., Kim, K. J., & Kim, H. (2017). Improvement of malware detection and classification using API call sequence alignment and visualization. *Cluster Computing*, 1–9.

Kumara, A., & Jaidhar, C. D. (2018). Automated multi-level malware detection system based on reconstructed semantic view of executables using machine learning techniques at VMM. *Future Generation Computer Systems, 79*, 431–446. doi:10.1016/j.future.2017.06.002

Le, Q., Boydell, O., Mac Namee, B., & Scanlon, M. (2018). Deep learning at the shallow end: Malware classification for non-domain experts. *Digital Investigation, 26*, S118–S126. doi:10.1016/j.diin.2018.04.024

LeCun, Y., Bengio, Y., & Hinton, G. (2015). Deep learning. *Nature, 521*(7553), 436.

Li, H. Z. M., Wu, T., & Yang, F. (2018). *Evaluation of Supervised Machine Learning Techniques for Dynamic Malware Detection*. Academic Press.

Narayanan, B. N., Djaneye-Boundjou, O., & Kebede, T. M. (2016, July). Performance analysis of machine learning and pattern recognition algorithms for malware classification. In *Aerospace and Electronics Conference (NAECON) and Ohio Innovation Summit (OIS)* (pp. 338-342). IEEE. 10.1109/NAECON.2016.7856826

Nataraj, L., Karthikeyan, S., Jacob, G., & Manjunath, B. S. (2011, July). Malware images: visualization and automatic classification. In *Proceedings of the 8th international symposium on visualization for cyber security* (p. 4). ACM.

Nataraj, L., Kirat, D., Manjunath, B. S., & Vigna, G. (2013, December). Sarvam: Search and retrieval of malware. *Proceedings of the Annual Computer Security Conference (ACSAC) Worshop on Next Generation Malware Attacks and Defense (NGMAD)*.

Nataraj, L., Yegneswaran, V., Porras, P., & Zhang, J. (2011, October). A comparative assessment of malware classification using binary texture analysis and dynamic analysis. In *Proceedings of the 4th ACM Workshop on Security and Artificial Intelligence* (pp. 21-30). ACM. 10.1145/2046684.2046689

Ni, S., Qian, Q., & Zhang, R. (2018). Malware identification using visualization images and deep learning. *Computers & Security*, *77*, 871–885. doi:10.1016/j.cose.2018.04.005

Pascanu, R., Stokes, J. W., Sanossian, H., Marinescu, M., & Thomas, A. (2015, April). Malware classification with recurrent networks. In *Acoustics, Speech and Signal Processing (ICASSP), 2015 IEEE International Conference on* (pp. 1916-1920). IEEE. 10.1109/ICASSP.2015.7178304

Rieck, K., Trinius, P., Willems, C., & Holz, T. (2011). Automatic analysis of malware behavior using machine learning. *Journal of Computer Security*, *19*(4), 639–668. doi:10.3233/JCS-2010-0410

Ronen, R., Radu, M., Feuerstein, C., Yom-Tov, E., & Ahmadi, M. (2018). *Microsoft Malware Classification Challenge*. arXiv preprint arXiv:1802.10135

Santos, I., Brezo, F., Ugarte-Pedrero, X., & Bringas, P. G. (2013). Opcode sequences as representation of executables for data-mining-based unknown malware detection. *Information Sciences*, *231*, 64–82. doi:10.1016/j.ins.2011.08.020

Schultz, M. G., Eskin, E., Zadok, F., & Stolfo, S. J. (2001). Data mining methods for detection of new malicious executables. In *Security and Privacy, 2001. S&P 2001. Proceedings. 2001 IEEE Symposium on* (pp. 38-49). IEEE. 10.1109/SECPRI.2001.924286

Singh, A. (2017). *Malware Classification using Image Representation* (Doctoral dissertation). Indian Institute of Technology Kanpur. Retrieved from https://www.statista.com/statistics/218089/global-market-share-of-windows-7/

Tesauro, G., Kephart, J., & Sorkin, G. (1996). Neural networks for computer virus recognition. *IEEE Expert*, *11*(4), 5–6. doi:10.1109/64.511768

Yan, H., Zhou, H., & Zhang, H. (2018). Automatic Malware Classification via PRICoLBP. *Chinese Journal of Electronics*, *27*(4), 852–859. doi:10.1049/cje.2018.05.001

Yu, F., & Koltun, V. (2015). *Multi-scale context aggregation by dilated convolutions.* arXiv preprint arXiv:1511.07122

Yu, F., Koltun, V., & Funkhouser, T. A. (2017, July). *Dilated Residual Networks* (Vol. 2). CVPR.

Zhou, B., Khosla, A., Lapedriza, A., Oliva, A., & Torralba, A. (2016). Learning deep features for discriminative localization. In *Proceedings of the IEEE Conference on Computer Vision and Pattern Recognition* (pp. 2921-2929). IEEE.

Chapter 12
Security Framework for Smart Visual Sensor Networks

G. Suseela

iD https://orcid.org/0000-0002-9162-7444
VIT University, India

Y. Asnath Victy Phamila
VIT University, India

ABSTRACT

Due to the significance of image data over the scalar data, the camera-integrated wireless sensor networks have attained the focus of researchers in the field of smart visual sensor networks. These networks are inexpensive and found wide application in surveillance and monitoring systems. The challenge is that these systems are resource deprived systems. The visual sensor node is typically an embedded system made up of a light weight processor, low memory, low bandwidth transceiver, and low-cost image sensor unit. As these networks carry sensitive information of the surveillance region, security and privacy protection are critical needs of the VSN. Due to resource limited nature of the VSN, the image encryption is crooked into an optimally lower issue, and many findings of image security in VSN are based on selective or partial encryption systems. The secure transmission of images is more trivial. Thus, in this chapter, a security frame work of smart visual sensor network built using energy-efficient image encryption and coding systems designed for VSN is presented.

DOI: 10.4018/978-1-5225-8241-0.ch012

INTRODUCTION

The contemporary advancements in CMOS technology, multimedia systems together with communication technologies empowered image communication over resource constrained Visual Sensor Network (VSN). The image communication is more significant than scalar data communication, hence it has attained wide applications like critical infrastructure monitoring, habitat monitoring, surveillance, traffic monitoring, industrial control systems, smart home systems and many more. Recently (Paek, Hicks, Coe, & Govindan, 2014) has reported the bird nest monitoring system at the James San Jacinto Mountain Reserve and the system assisted the biologists to study the life of birds during the nesting spell to unbox the biological interrogations connected to the laying, incubation and hatching of eggs and way of life of the new born nestlings in the nests. Yet quite a lot of new commercial applications which require visual support are emerging out embedded VSN.

In Visual Sensor Network the VS nodes are deployed in places where they can be used to monitor and sense environmental conditions by collaborating and communicating with each other over the wireless communication channels. Smart cameras which are capable of processing the sensed images onboard can be connected to Visual Sensor Networks. Typically, Visual Sensor Networks are built with resource-limited devices. These networks are resource restricted systems with limited memory, processing speed, computational power and bandwidth. Visual Sensor Networks are autonomous systems capable of capturing, processing and communicating the image in difficult-to-access regions without exclusive network infrastructure in

Figure 1. VSN architecture and senor mote architecture

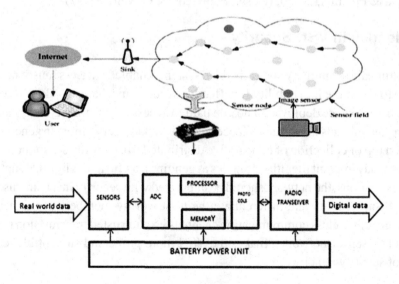

adhoc fashion. The typical VSN architecture and Senor Mote architecture are shown in Figure 1 (Suseela & Phamila, 2016). Generally, wireless networks prefer energy efficient computation and communication for better lifetime of the network. As images contain more redundancies, processing and communicating the image data will consume more energy. Hence for the increased active lifetime of the network image processing algorithms exclusively developed for energy efficiency and low resource utilization must be adopted in VSN. The inherent nature of visual data in the form of images is self-descriptive. Therefore, the secrecy and privacy protection are more essential in wireless communication networks, as wireless links are more prone to security threats by nature (Gonalves & Costa, 2015).

VISUAL SENSOR NETWORK SECURITY REQUIREMENT

In these modern days, VSNs are gaining more attention by both private and public communities and security becomes a prominent issue to address. The visual data are more sensitive than scalar data when an image data is meddled the information content of the transmitted image will be revealed abruptly; while tampering the scalar numeric data will not unveil the meaning of it is and symbolize just as a number. The visual data are easily understood by a human, they will not conceal the privacy features of the image and reveal the genteel clues about time, location information etc. The VSN is predisposed and can be dismayed to compromise the network task or to acquire unauthorized admission to pertinent information. The key security requirements for Visual Sensor Networks are data integrity, confidentiality, authenticity, freshness, localization, controlled access and privacy preservation (Suseela & Phamila, 2016), (Costa, Figuerêdo & Oliveira, 2017).

Challenges in VSN Security

As multimedia technology and embedded systems enabled wireless sensor networks endure to grow, the inevitability for effective security mechanisms also grows. The sensor networks are deployed in hostile hard to access environments for tracing and tracking the subjects under surveillance without human intervention. In general, VSN made on top of collection of cooperative distributed trust worthy sensor nodes. The attackers may implant illegitimate nodes as genuine trustful nodes by node capturing. In such situations, the network should be integrated with security mechanisms which validate, substantiate and differentiate the trust worthy members of the network. The nature of wireless communication channels i.e., untrusted transmission medium of wireless sensor networks, makes the VSN more prone and susceptible to many types of security attacks.

Almost all the applications of VSN require secure transmission without jeopardizing resource scarcity. Due to inherent resource limited nature and volume of pixel data produced by VSN makes the customary cryptographic algorithms like AES-Advanced Encryption Standard, DES-Data Encryption Standard, IDEA -International Data Encryption Algorithm and modern algorithms designed using hash function are MD-5, SHA-1 are inapplicable. Thus security in VSN poses more challenges than any other wireless network and scalar WSN. Thus, the limitations mandate the development of light weight security algorithms to protect the image/ video data along with compression algorithms.

Image Cryptography

In general, secured image communication is guaranteed with cryptography algorithms. The paradigm of encrypting visual data is known as visual cryptography (VC). VC is classified into two types namely symmetric and asymmetric based on cryptographic key sharing technique adapted among the communicating entities (Gonalves & Costa, 2015).

In symmetric cryptographic systems, a single key is used for both encryption and decryption. This makes system modest but key distribution is transmitted over the channel may be trapped. Some of the classical symmetric cryptographic algorithms are AES, DES, IDEA, MD-5, SHA-1.

Asymmetric cryptographic systems are popularly known as Public Key Cryptography (PKC). PKC algorithms use different keys for encryption and decryption. The key used by all nodes for encryption is called a public key. Each node has their own reserved key for decryption which is not shared with any other node in the network called private key. Some of the prominently used asymmetric cryptographic algorithms in communication networks are Rabin's scheme, Rivest, Shamir and Adelman (RSA), Digital Signature Algorithm (DSA) Elliptic curve cryptography (ECC), Pretty Good Privacy (PGP). But PKC levies more computational overhead in generating, distributing and managing the keys. Hence PKC is not reasonable for resource restricted VSN. Many researchers have reported the incompatibility of PKC in VSN due to resource scarcity imposed on VS nodes.

IMAGE COMPRESSION IN VSN

A large amount of redundancies present in image data will consume more energy of the network. The transceiver is the most energy hunger component in any wireless network. The redundancies must be reduced by energy efficient image compression algorithms before transmission for better network lifetime. Hence to reduce redundancy and to reduce communication cost low bitrate and low energy consuming compression algorithms must be employed. There are a lot of such energy efficient image compression and coding algorithms are reported in the literature. The various image compression algorithms proposed for VSN can be broadly categorized into transform based, non-transform based and hardware based solutions. (Mammeri, Hadjou, & Khoumsi, 2012) suggested that the transform based solutions are very much suitable for low bitrate requirement for VSN. The transform stage of the compression algorithm de-correlates the most significant data portions from the insignificant data portions of the image. The low bitrate compression is achieved by coding only the most significant coefficients of the transform matrix. The non-transform-based solutions eliminate the complexity of the transform stage, but they could not meet the low or very low bitrate requirement, in other words, these systems could not offer high compression efficiency (DuranFaundez, Lecuire, & Lepage, 2011). Hardware based solutions are also realized in FPGA (Field Programmable Gate Arrays), ASIC (Application-Specific Integrated Circuits) but are bit expensive than software-based solutions.

Transform Based Image Compression Algorithms for VSN

The transform-based solutions are mostly based on DCT (Discrete Cosine Transform) and DWT (Discrete Wavelet Transform). The DCT's small tiling style of processing is very much appropriate for the light weight processor of the smart camera attached VS node. The true DCT in its original form involves lot of complex floating point operations and more number of multiplication operations. Thus true DCT is not suitable for resource restricted VS node as such they are. There are lot of low complexity multiplier-less integer DCTs are evolved in the literature. These systems carry out DCT transform using only addition and shift operations. The various multiplier less DCT computational complexity are shown in Table 1 (Suseela & Phamila, 2018). The DWT based compression algorithms are more superior to DCT with respect to image quality. The DWT requires full frame processing which is not feasible in VSN. There are few line based DWT algorithms, in which the decomposition is done by considering a few lines at a stage. The lined based processing reduced the memory requirement of DWT approaches still the computational complexity remained the same and not reduced as expected.

Table 1. Computational complexity of multiplier less DCT architectures

DCT Type	1D-Transform		2D-Transform	
	Add	Shift	Add	Shift
Cordic Loeffler	38	16	608	256
BinDCT-C1(k=8)	42	23	672	368
BinDCT-C7(k=8)	28	9	448	144
BinDCT-C8(k=8)	24	5	384	80
DTT (k=4)	26	14	312	168
BinDCT-C7(k=2)	19	6	190	60
BinDCT-C8(k=2)	12	1	120	10

SECURED IMAGE COMPRESSION SYSTEMS AND THEIR SUITABILITY IN VSN

Compression and encryption both are indispensable in image communication. Secured image compression is a key need in VSN, as the pure compressed image without any security association may drop the information content over unreliable wireless channel and pure encryption system without compression will consume more resources of the network like transmission energy, bandwidth, and memory. The joint compression and encryption systems are broadly categorized into three types based on the order of image processing. Namely, (i) Compression - Encryption Systems(CES), (ii) Encryption - Compression Systems (ECS) and (iii) Simultaneous Compression – Encryption (SCE). In the first two categories namely ECS and CES, the compression and encryption processes are implemented as two discrete stages. The output of the compression or encryption system is pipelined to the encryption or compression system. Due to the linearity unveiled in incorporating these two systems, an attacker can effortlessly break the cryptosystem without demurring compression methodology. In the SCE category, the encryption and compression are combined in a single stage to realize the simultaneous compression- encryption.

Compression - Encryption Systems (CES)

Generally, encryption is performed on the compressed data. The CES systems are good as the compression algorithms take away the redundancy exists in the image data. Also, the compressed image will show a more uniform distribution of characters. The CES systems are anticipated to improve coding efficiency. These systems will reduce the computational load of encryption system as encryption algorithm is applied only to the compressed image and the storage requirement is also reduced. However, the attacker may catch the hints about the encrypted image by size information as encryption is carried out on the compressed data. In some of the works based on compression then encryption the compression efficiency was unfavorable. Li and Lo suggested a CES cryptosystem based on orthogonal transform and RC4 (Li & Lo, 2015). Their system was able to achieve better compression ratio and image quality however, the statistical analysis of the encrypted image reveals that the encryption system is not sufficiently strong as histogram plot is not uniform and correlation plot of neighboring pixels of the encrypted image is not widely dispersed.

Encryption - Compression Systems (ECS)

In ECS systems compression is performed on encrypted image data. The difficulty in Joint compression and encryption is that the compression algorithms may disturb or alter the data fidelity present in the raw image. In order to preserve the fidelity encryption algorithm is employed first then compression is followed. The ECS systems focus more on image security than compression. The work proposed by Zhou et al have stated that the encryption then compression systems have significantly deprived the compression performance than the state of the art compression algorithms which accept unencrypted input (Zhou, Gong, Pei, & Liao, 2015). Moreover, as encryption is employed at first on the image data and then compression is followed, most of the pixel data might be omitted by the compression system. The computational resources energy will be wasted or overspent. Thus, in resource-deprived VSN as energy efficient computation is more stringent, adapting encryption then compression based ECS systems are not workable.

Simultaneous Compression- Encryption (SCE)

Simultaneous compression and encryption systems are aimed to decrease the computational resources like computational cost and time. Referring to simultaneous encryption and compression using chaos and Chinese remainder theorem reported in the year 2013 (Zhu, Zhao, & Zhang, 2013), even though it could offer good compression efficiency of 4:1 with very good entropy, correlation the system is not strong enough to withstand the plaintext attack. Thus this category of compression and encryption systems also are not able to offer good compression efficiency and a strong cryptosystem.

Thus all the three categories of joint encryption systems are not able to provide high compression efficiency along with a robust security system. The linearity existing between the encryption and compression must be tightly coupled for stronger image encryption system and efficient compression system.

PARTIAL OR SELECTIVE IMAGE ENCRYPTION SYSTEMS IN VSN

The image encryption and decryption process are usually a complex and expensive task. The resource-deprived nature of VSN may not afford such expense. As energy efficient processing is an important design goal, security in VSN is less desired or pursued as an optimally lower issued yet it is highly necessitated. The volume of image data is vast and difficulty of affording security mechanisms further challenges the VSN. Generally, encryption is applied to the whole image but to exclude the computational overhead and to reduce the computational cost, encryption is applied only to a selected portion of the image called selective or partial image encryption. Selective encryption offers a reasonable level of security while reducing the complexity. The image transformations like DCT, DWT, KLT (Karhunen Loeve Transform) will segregate the significant and insignificant data of the image. To ensure the security it is sufficient to encrypt only significant coefficients of the transformed image (Wickramasuriya, Datt, Mehrotra & Venkatasubramanian, 2004). Also, the significant portion of the image which needs to be secured is determined by image processing tools like a background or foreground subtraction, edge detector etc. These techniques will give the most significant portion of the image like a face of a human.

Limitations of Selective Encryption

The aim of the partial encryption systems is to reduce the computational cost along with warranting an acceptable level of security. For the resource-deprived VSN the partial encryption systems will involve additional computational resource for determining the significant or sensitive portion of the image to be ciphered as they must apply image analyzing tools like edge detector, foreground or background subtraction model etc. (Khan, Ahmad, Javaid & Saqib, 2017), (Nandhini, & Radha, 2017). Execution of these tools is also accountable for energy consumption and memory consumption. Yet another limitation is unencrypted image portions may give more hint about the image like time, location information to the attacker. Hence low energy consuming low bitrate resource efficient image coding techniques along with highly secured full encryption system are to be developed exclusively for low power and resource-deprived environments like VSN. Thus the problem is still open to the researchers for novel solutions in the future.

Chaotic Image Encryption Systems

Chaotic systems are dimensional nonlinear dynamic systems that are proficient of producing complex and unpredictable behavior. Initially, chaos has been employed in various research domains like physics, biology, mathematics etc. Applying the chaotic systems for image encryption is a great contribution in improving the security of the image data. The chaotic systems are well suited for creating the pseudo-randomness and offered adequate cryptographic properties. Chaos-based image encryption systems have acknowledged significant attention because of the typical features of chaos like the ease of generation, dynamical, random-like behavior, sensitivity to initial conditions (butterfly effect), deterministic and periodicity. The well-known chaotic systems in the literature are Arnold's cat map, Logistic map, Tent map, Bakers' map, Lorenz system, FLT (Fibonacci Transform). These maps can be used as image scramblers for shuffling the pixels in the image. A strong encryption system is realized by two stages namely confusion and diffusion. The confusion stage is associated with pixel permutation or pixel shuffling by the image scramblers based on a chaotic map. The diffusion stage is essential as confusion does not alter the pixel values of the image. Thus a histogram plot will reveal the information content scrambled over the encrypted image. The histogram of the plain image and encrypted image will be similar. At the diffusion stage, the pixel values are modified using reversible techniques. The chaotic systems like 2D-Arnolds cat map, FLT systems are very much suitable for resource-constrained VSN. These systems require very less mathematic operations. The Arnolds cat map requires only two additions, four multiplications, and two division modulo per pixel block. As VSN is embedded with lightweight processor, chaotic systems permit low memory operation by block processing. The chaotic system requires more memory space and more memory cycles. This problem is greatly eradicated by Duran Faundez et al. and made the chaotic systems adaptable in VSN (DuranFaundez, Lecuire, & Lepage 2011).

The Arnold transform for block shuffling the pixel block at the spatial location (a, b) is given as

$$
\begin{bmatrix} as \\ bs \end{bmatrix} = \begin{bmatrix} 1 & 1 \\ 1 & x+1 \end{bmatrix}^m \begin{bmatrix} a \\ b \end{bmatrix} \mod W
\tag{1}
$$

where 1), (as, bs) is the new position of the pixel block at (a, b),

$$W = \frac{width\ of\ the\ image}{size\ of\ the\ pixel\ block}$$ and 'm' is the number of rotations key and the typical

value of x =1.

SECURITY FRAMEWORK FOR SMART VISUAL SENSOR NETWORK

Generally, the VSN is deployed in hard to access regions. The data communicated in VSN is data intensive. The VSN will produce an enormous amount of visual data. The networking and automation of camera embedded VSN is topical prevailing expansion in Sensor networks, leading to the establishment of smart camera VSN. These networks are capable of adapting energy aware computations. The compression algorithms amended in VSN have a great part in reducing the network traffic. According to the bitrate requirement of the application or privilege of the communication, the image compression will take part at various bitrates like low, medium and very low bitrate. The different operations involved in secure transmission can be implemented individually in VSN. But each module requires separate implementation, administration procedures, this further complicates the resource-deprived VSN system in terms of network traffic in controlling and coordinating these individual units. Henceforth a security framework for smart VSN is depicted in Figure 2 which assures basic security requirement. It is framed by integrating three central units involved secure transmission. They are sensing unit, image processing subsystem, and communication subsystem. Each subsystem contains several modules which can be made adaptive in such a way appropriate for various applications.

The sensor unit may contain a heterogeneous type of sensor including low-cost imaging sensors and scalar sensor like pressure, temperature, light sensors etc. The imaging sensors are capable of capturing and storing the image from time to time. The image processing subsystem is an integration of a compression unit, a security unit, and a coding unit. The joint compression and encryption system may be of the category CES, ECS, and SES based on the application requirement. The bitrate requirement unit decides the number of bits to be transmitted based on the parameters priority of the communication, network traffic, residual energy of the node, QoS etc. According to the bit rate, the energy-aware compression unit may offer different compression ratio from high bitrate to very low bitrate.

Figure 2. Security framework for smart VSN

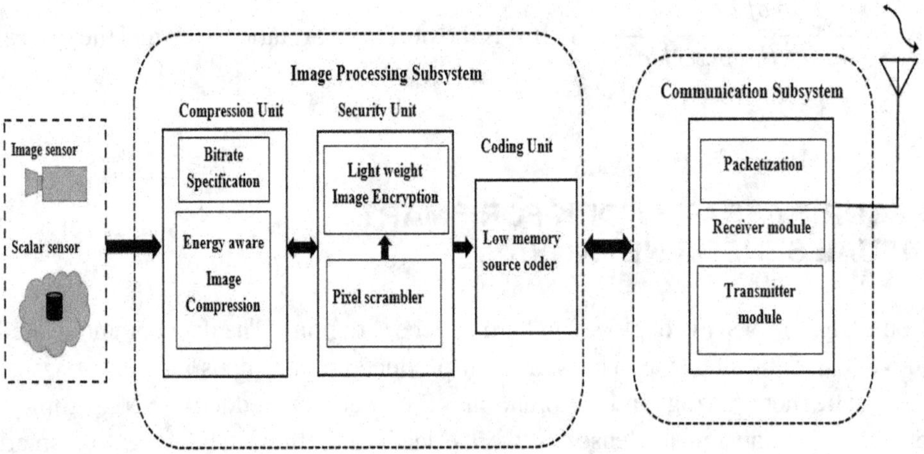

PERFORMANCE ANALYSIS METRICS OF THE SECURED IMAGE COMPRESSION SYSTEMS

This section discusses some of the performance analysis and metrics used for evaluating the compression combined encryption systems. The compression performance is evaluated using image quality at reconstruction by Peak Signal to Noise Ratio (PSNR) and Structural Similarity Index Measure (SSIM) and compression efficiency by Bit rate (BR). The strength of the cryptographic system is largely analyzed by brute-force analysis, statistical analysis, and differential analysis. As energy-efficient computing is an important design goal of the resource-constrained VSN, some of the tools used for energy consumption analysis is also discussed.

Performance metrics of Compression Algorithm

1. **Peak Signal to Noise Ratio (PSNR):** It is the metric which determines the amount of error present in the reconstructed image with reference to the raw image. The unit of PSNR is decibels (dB). PSNR is defined as,

$$PSNR = 10\log_{10} \frac{x^2 MN}{\sum_{x=1}^{M}\sum_{y=1}^{N}\left[I\left(x,y\right) - R\left(x,y\right)\right]^2} \qquad (2)$$

where x is the highest pixel value, for an 8-bit grey scale image x is 255. I and R are the raw images and the decompressed image respectively.

2. **Structural Similarity Index Measure (SSIM):** SSIM is based human visual system perceptual model, it defines the degree of image quality degradation perceived by the compressed image in the view of its structural details from the uncompressed raw image.

$$SSIM\left(i,j\right) = \frac{2\mu_i\mu_j + K1}{\mu_i^2 + \mu_j^2 + K1} \frac{2\sigma_{ij} + K2}{\sigma_i^2 + \sigma_j^2 + K2} \tag{3}$$

where μi and μj are the sample means of raw image i and reconstructed image j, σi, σj are the variances of i, j, and σij is the cross-covariance between i and j. The K1=0.01 and K2=0.03. The constants K1 and K2 will slacken the effect of the weak divisor.

3. **Bit Rate (BR):** Bit rate denotes the minimum number bits allocated by compression system to represent single pixel value and it is measured in bits per pixel (bpp). BR lesser than 0.5bpp is considered as low bitrate appropriate for energy efficient transmission in VSN. Transmission energy is greatly reduced at this bitrate.

Security Analysis Metrics

As per the theory of cryptography, an encryption system must be strong enough to withstand various attacks. The attacks that can be made on the encrypted images are categorized into brute-force attacks, statistical attacks, differential attacks. The harshness of the crypto-system against brute-force attacks is studied by key sensitivity analysis, key space analysis, noise, and cropping attack analysis. The ruggedness of the encryption system against statistical attacks is verified by global Shannon's entropy, Local Shannon's entropy, correlation analysis, and histogram analysis. A good encryption algorithm must have large key space and very good sensitivity to small change in encryption key to having tolerance over brute-force attack. The intruders will try to crack the encryption system by constructing a minor change in the plain image and attempt to investigate the association exists between the encrypted images of before and after alteration of the plain image. The process of injecting or diffusing some changes in the plain image and attempting to bring out the correlation among the encrypted images by studying the differential behavior of the encryption system is called the differential attack. The resistivity of the encryption system against differential attacks is examined by the metrics Number Pixel Change Rate (NPCR) and Unified Average Change in pixel Intensity (UACI).

Brute-Force Attack Analysis

1. **Key Space Analysis:** Key space is defined as a set of all possible entirely different keys that are used by the encryption system. The key length must be large because the keys are guessed on trial and error basis. Therefore the key space must be extremely large enough to make the brute force attack impracticable.

2. **Key Sensitivity Analysis:** This analysis determines the sensitivity of the keys used in an encryption system. For a very small change in the key values, the encryption system should produce a significantly great change in the encrypted image. To prove the key sensitivity the encrypted image with the modified key should be decrypted with the correct key. If the decrypted image is totally meaningless from the original plain image and could not convey any significant useful information visually, then the crypto-system is considered to be very much sensitive to the key value changes and strong against brute force attacks. Similarly, if there is a small change is associated in the decryption key, the decryption system should offer a totally different image and should not convey the information content of the plain image.

3. **Noise Attack Analysis:** It is expected that image could be contaminated with noise over the communication channel while transmission or the intruders may inject the additive noise over the communication channel, for making the communication unserviceable. An encrypted image containing noise must preserve at least the overall information content of the plain image and convey approximately significant information content at the decryption. The additive noise WG (White Gaussian noise) influences the encrypted image EI_1 and generates the noise added image EI_2. On decrypting EI_2, The information content should be preserved to a certainty and visually recognizable. The noise model is as follows,

$$EI_2 = EI_1 + WG \tag{4}$$

Figure 3 shows the typical noise attack analysis and decrypted images conveys some meaning with respect to the original image.

4. **Cropping Attack:** The intruders may steal some portion of the encrypted image and allowed to transmit over the network. The occlusion of the cipher can affect the decrypted images greatly. The sturdiness and the sustainability of the encryption system against cropping attacks must be studied. The data loss can crucially affect the decrypted image. The cropping attack is carried out by

Figure 3. Typical noise attack analysis (a) Original Lena, (b) Noise added encrypted image (c) Decrypted image

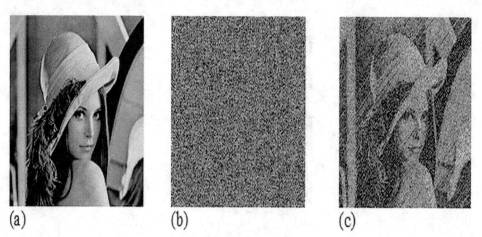

(a)   (b)   (c)

occluding some portion of the encrypted image, and the image is decrypted. The decrypted image should convey the information content greatly. Figure 4 shows the typical cropping attack on the encrypted Lena image and decrypted images conveys some meaning with respect to the original image.

Statistical Analysis

As per Shannon's information theory, a crypto-system can be easily broken by reviewing the statistical properties of the encrypted data. Therefore, the robustness against statistical attacks is very imperative in evidencing the strength of the security system.

Correlation Analysis

The correlation among the pixel data is a very important statistical feature. The pixel in the plain image is strongly correlated with the neighboring pixels and convey meaningful information. An efficient encryption system must de-correlate the adjacent pixels very well to avoid information leakage by statistical analysis. The correlation analysis is carried out by picking up a few thousands of pair of adjacent pixels randomly from the plain and encrypted image independently along all the directions namely horizontal, vertical and diagonal. The correlation is defined as

Figure 4. Results of robustness test on cropping attack: (a) Lena image and (b) Encrypted Image (c) 3.8% occluded image (d) decrypted the image

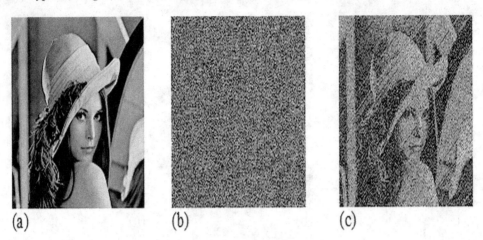

(a)   (b)   (c)

$$correlation = \frac{covariance(x,y)}{\sqrt{d(x) \times d(y)}} \qquad (5)$$

where, $covariance(x,y) = \dfrac{1}{N}\sum_{i=1}^{N}\left(x_i - \mu(x)\right)\left(y_i - \mu(y)\right)$, μ (t) – sample mean

and $d(t) = \dfrac{1}{N}\sum_{i=1}^{N}\left(t_i - \mu(t)\right)^2$, N is the total number of pixels used for the correlation

analysis.

If the correlation coefficient is closer to one then the association among the data is said to be strongly correlated. Thus the plain image will have a high correlation with correlation coefficient closer to one. If the association among the data is weak, the correlation coefficient will be closer to zero.

Thus the correlation coefficient of pixels of the pseudo-random generated encrypted image should be closer to zero justifying the weak correlation or association among the neighboring pixels.

A typical scatter plot of correlation distribution of plain and encrypted images of Barbara is shown in Figure 5. The narrow distribution of the plots of the plain image illustrates that the pixels are highly correlated and the wide distribution of the encrypted image instinctively confirms the weak correlation amongst the neighboring pixels in all the directions.

Figure 5. Correlation distribution scatters plot of pixels (a) horizontal (b) vertical and (c) diagonal directions of the plain image. Correlation distribution plot of pixels in the neighbourhood of (d) horizontal (e) vertical and (f) diagonal directions of the encrypted image.

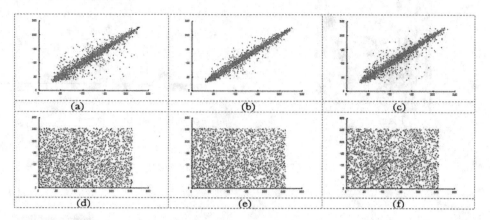

Histogram Analysis

Histogram is a graphical representation of the distribution of pixel values against gray levels in an image. The histogram plot of the encrypted image should be flat denoting the uniform distribution along almost all the gray levels. The typical histogram of plain Lena image, pixel block shuffled image and encrypted image are shown in Figure 6. It is inferred that the encrypted image using image scrambler changes only the positions of the pixels, thus the histogram of the encrypted image remains the same as the plain image. The histogram plot of the encrypted image should be uniform, such that the encryption system must homogenize the plain image for stronger encryption as shown in Figure 6.

Global Entropy Analysis

As per Shannon the entropy of a system producing 2^n symbols with equal probability is n (Shannon CE, 1949). An encryption system should conceal the structural information of the entire image to avoid information leakage. The randomness of the security system is measured by entropy. As it is calculated for the entire image it is known as global entropy. For a grey image with 2^8 grey levels, entropy must be closer to 8 bits and can reach the maximum of 8 for ideal encryption.

Figure 6. (a)Histogram of the plain image (Lena) (b) Histogram of permuted image (c) Histogram of encrypted image (d) Histogram of plain image (Peppers) (e) Histogram of permuted image (f) Histogram of the encrypted image.

Plain image

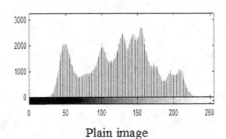

Plain image

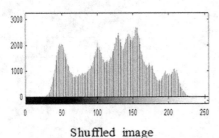

Shuffled image

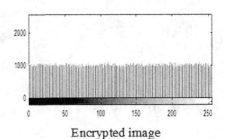

Encrypted image

The entropy H(s) is as

$$H(s) = -\sum_{n=0}^{255} p(k) * \log p(k) \tag{6}$$

where p(n) is the probability of each pixel in the encrypted image.

Local Shannon Entropy

The local Shannon entropy is computed by arbitrarily picking some non-overlapping pixel blocks of size k x k of the encrypted image. The entropy is figured for all the local blocks independently and mean of the entropy of all the n blocks is measured as local Shannon entropy. The Local Shannon Entropy is defined as

$$H_{LSE}(S) = \sum_{i=1}^{n} \frac{H(S_i)}{n} \tag{7}$$

Differential Analysis

The NPCR and UACI are the two parameters used to determine resistivity against differential attacks. These metrics are computed between two encrypted images in which their respective plain images differ at least by single pixel. A binary matrix D(x, y) is set to 1, If C1(x, y) = C2(x, y) otherwise D(x, y) is set to 0. The NPCR and UACI are defined as

$$NPCR = \sum_{x=1}^{M}\sum_{y=1}^{N}D(x,y) * \frac{100\%}{M * N} \tag{8}$$

$$UACI = \left[\sum_{x=1}^{M}\sum_{y=1}^{N}\frac{|C1(x,y) - C2(x,y)|}{255}\right] * \frac{100\%}{M * N} \tag{9}$$

The ideal values of NPCR should be range 96%-99% and 100% for ideal encryption. The UACI of the encryption system should be in the range 33%-36% for battling the differential attack.

Energy Consumption Analysis

The sensor motes widely used in smart camera equipped VSN test beds and by research community are mostly based on AdvanticSys, Atmel microcontrollers. The TelosB motes are built with TI MSP430 microcontroller operating at 8 MHz ChipCon CC2420 radio module (Amiri, 2010). The Mica2 mote is built with Atmel 128 microprocessor operating at 8 MHz with CC1000 radio module. The energy consumption of the sensor mote is broadly subdivided into computation energy and communication energy.

The Mica2 and TelosB sensor mote specification are shown under Table 2.

Computation Energy Analysis

The computation energy can be estimated or determined approximately by simulations. The WSim, COOJA, WinAVR, AVR Studio are the various simulator tools used for analyzing energy consumption of the algorithm at the target platform (Teng, Zheng, & Dong, 2008). The simulators WSim, WinAVR, AVR Studio will offer the number of clock cycles, code size, and data size for the codes simulated under them. While the COOJA simulator of the Contiki OS offers a power trace tool of the code being

Table 2. Mica 2 and TelosB sensor mote specification

Mote	Mica2	Telosb
Processor	Atmega128	MSP430
Data rate	38.4Kbps	250 kbps
Radio	CC1000	CC2420
Processor [mW]	22mW	3 mW in active mode
Transmit [mW]	69mW	35 mW
Operating frequency	8MHZ	6 MHz

simulated on it (Dunkels, Eriksson, Finne & Tsiftes, 2011). The power trace file further examined for energy consumption of the system. The execution time can be obtained from the number of clock cycles consumed. The energy spent by the microcontroller is computed based on the energy model as given in Equation (11).

$$Execution\,time = \frac{number\,of\,clock\,cycle}{clock\,frequency} \tag{10}$$

$$Energy = Power \times Execution\,Time \tag{11}$$

Communication Energy Analysis

The communication energy is hardware specific, the communication cost includes transmission energy and reception energy. The transmission energy is more than the reception energy. The transmission energy over the radio modules CC1000 and CC2420 are computed theoretically as follows.

Transmission energy and reception energy per bit over the distance 'd' under CC1000 (Heinzelman, Chandrakasan, & Balakrishnan, 2002)

$$E_{Tran} = E_{elec} + \varepsilon_{fs} \cdot d^2, d < d_0 \tag{12}$$

$$E_{Recv} = E_{elec} \tag{13}$$

where $E_{elec} = 50 \times 10^{-3} \mu J$ /bit, $\varepsilon_{fs} = 10 \times 10^{-6} \mu J$ /bit/m^2, $\varepsilon_{amp} = 0.0013\ 10^{-6} \mu J$ /bit/m^4 and distance $d_0 = 87$ m.

The transmission energy per bit over the radio module CC2420 is computed by considering the current consumption and voltage specifications from the datasheet of the TelosB node and the time to transmit a packet sized 128 bytes over 250 kbps data rate IEEE 802.15.4 using Equation 14.

$$E_{Tran} = \left(time \times Voltage \times Current\right) / 1024J \tag{14}$$

The transmission energy E_{Tran} represents the cost of single bit transmission. The energy for transmitting an image ($E_{I\,Tran}$) is computed by

$$E_{ITran} = \text{Number of bits transmitted} \times E_{Tran} \tag{15}$$

CONCLUSION

VSNs have established due to the fusion of Micro-electro Mechanical Systems (MEMS), multimedia technologies along with wireless communication technologies. Visual Sensor Networks have been engaged in sensitive and data-intensive applications like visual surveillance and monitoring applications. Secured image transmission becomes complicated due to resource limitations imposed on the processing node. This complicated scenario could be simplified by employing hardware friendly low complexity image cryptographic algorithms and resource efficient coding algorithms. A security framework for smart VSN has been presented in this chapter. Which ensures a strong cryptosystem by allowing full image encryption with energy efficient computations. Thus the research direction in secured visual communication in WSN moves from nominal partial encryption to the development of energy efficient and strong encryption systems.

REFERENCES

Costa, D. G., Figuerêdo, S., & Oliveira, G. (2017). Cryptography in Wireless Multimedia Sensor Networks: A Survey and Research Directions. *Cryptography*, *1*(1), 4. doi:10.3390/cryptography1010004

Dunkels, A., Eriksson, J., Finne, N., & Tsiftes, N. (2011). *Powertrace: Network-level power profiling for low-power wireless networks*. Academic Press.

Duran-Faundez, C., Lecuire, V., & Lepage, F. (2011). Tiny block-size coding for energy-efficient image compression and communication in wireless camera sensor networks. *Signal Processing Image Communication*, *26*(8-9), 466–481. doi:10.1016/j.image.2011.07.005

Gonalves, D., & Costa, D. (2015). A Survey of Image Security in Wireless Sensor Networks. *Journal of Imaging,* 4-30.

Heinzelman, W. B., Chandrakasan, A. P., & Balakrishnan, H. (2002). An application-specific protocol architecture for wireless microsensor networks. *IEEE Transactions on Wireless Communications, 1*(4), 660–670. doi:10.1109/TWC.2002.804190

Khan, M. A., Ahmad, J., Javaid, Q., & Saqib, N. A. (2017). An efficient and secure partial image encryption for wireless multimedia sensor networks using discrete wavelet transform, chaotic maps and substitution box. *Journal of Modern Optics, 64*(5), 531–540. doi:10.1080/09500340.2016.1246680

Li, P., & Lo, K. T. (2015, December). Joint image compression and encryption based on alternating transforms with quality control. In Visual Communications and Image Processing (VCIP), 2015 (pp. 1-4). IEEE. doi:10.1109/VCIP.2015.7457867

Mammeri, A., Hadjou, B., & Khoumsi, A. (2012). A survey of image compression algorithms for visual sensor networks. *ISRN Sensor Networks, 2012.*

Moslem. (2010). *Measurements of energy consumption and execution time of different operations on Tmote Sky sensor nodes.* Academic Press.

Nandhini, S. A., & Radha, S. (2017). Efficient compressed sensing-based security approach for video surveillance application in wireless multimedia sensor networks. *Computers & Electrical Engineering, 60,* 175–192. doi:10.1016/j.compeleceng.2017.01.027

Paek, J., Hicks, J., Coe, S., & Govindan, R. (2014). Image-based environmental monitoring sensor application using an embedded wireless sensor network. *Sensors (Basel), 14*(9), 15981–16002. doi:10.3390140915981 PMID:25171121

Shannon, C. E. (1949). Communication theory of secrecy system. *The Bell System Technical Journal, 28*(4), 656–715. doi:10.1002/j.1538-7305.1949.tb00928.x

Suseela, G., & Phamila, Y. A. V. (2016). Visual sensor networks: Critical infrastructure protection. In *Combating Security Breaches and Criminal Activity in the Digital Sphere* (pp. 263–282). IGI Global.

Suseela, G., & Phamila, Y. A. V. (2018). Low-complexity low-memory energy-efficient image coding for wireless image sensor networks. *Imaging Science Journal, 66*(2), 125–132. doi:10.1080/13682199.2017.1385175

Teng, G., Zheng, K., & Dong, W. (2008, October). A survey of available tools for developing wireless sensor networks. In *Systems and Networks Communications, 2008. ICSNC'08. 3rd International Conference on* (pp. 139-144). IEEE. 10.1109/ICSNC.2008.15

Wickramasuriya, J., Datt, M., Mehrotra, S., & Venkatasubramanian, N. (2012). Privacy protecting data collection in media spaces. *Proceedings of the 12th Annual ACM International Conference on Multimedia - MULTIMEDIA '04, 1.* doi:10.1145/1027527.1027537

Zhou, N. R., Hua, T. X., Gong, L. H., Pei, D. J., & Liao, Q. H. (2015). Quantum image encryption based on generalized Arnold transform and double random-phase encoding. *Quantum Information Processing, 14*(4), 1193–1213. doi:10.100711128-015-0926-z

Zhu, H., Zhao, C., & Zhang, X. (2013). A novel image encryption–compression scheme using hyper-chaos and Chinese remainder theorem. *Signal Processing Image Communication, 28*(6), 670–680. doi:10.1016/j.image.2013.02.004

ADDITIONAL READING

Sajjad, M., Muhammad, K., Baik, S. W., Rho, S., Jan, Z., Yeo, S. S., & Mehmood, I. (2017). Mobile-cloud assisted framework for selective encryption of medical images with steganography for resource-constrained devices. *Multimedia Tools and Applications, 76*(3), 3519–3536. doi:10.100711042-016-3811-6

Wu, Y., Zhou, Y., Saveriades, G., Agaian, S., Noonan, J. P., & Natarajan, P. (2013). Local Shannon entropy measure with statistical tests for image randomness. *Information Sciences, 222,* 323–342. doi:10.1016/j.ins.2012.07.049

Zhang, L. Y., Liu, Y., Pareschi, F., Zhang, Y., Wong, K. W., Rovatti, R., & Setti, G. (2018). On the security of a class of diffusion mechanisms for image encryption. *IEEE Transactions on Cybernetics, 48*(4), 1163–1175. doi:10.1109/TCYB.2017.2682561 PMID:28368843

KEY TERMS AND DEFINITIONS

Chaotic Systems: Chaotic systems are time dynamic system whose state will vary with time. Based on time there are two types of chaotic systems namely, discrete chaotic systems and continuous chaotic systems.

Differential Attack: The intruders try to break the encryption system by injecting minimum changes into an image. They attempt to study the statistical correlation that exists between the encrypted images of original and modified image.

Entropy: Entropy is a measure of amount of uncertainty or disorder present in the system within the possible probability distribution. The entropy and amount of unpredictability are directly proportional to each other.

Image Compression: The process of removing the redundancies present among the pixels of the image and reducing the size of image in compact form for efficient storage and transmission.

Image Cryptography: The image cryptography is one of the practice employed for securing the information content of the image using strong encryption algorithms.

Image Transform: Image transform is a two-dimensional signal processing technique which decorrelates the data very well allows an image analyzer to work directly on the significant and insignificant components of the data.

Secured Transmission: Secure transmission refers to transfer of data from source to destination over the communication channel meeting out the basic security requirements like confidentiality, data integrity, authenticity, etc., ensuring that the information coded in the transmitted data is not seeped in the transit.

Selective Encryption: The process of encrypting only the most significant and sensitive portion of the data is known as selective or partial encryption.

Section 4
Techniques for Countering Cyber Attacks

Chapter 13
Blockchain Technology Is a Boost to Cyber Security:
Block Chain

Sowmiya B.
SRM Institute of Science and Technology, India

Poovammal E.
SRM Institute of Science and Technology, India

ABSTRACT

The information in any real-time application is needed to be digitalized across the world. Since digitalization of data happens, there comes the role of privacy. Blockchain could address the security challenge that happens in the any real sector. There are a few more challenges that prevail in the industry such as integrity in data, traceability of stored records, and interoperability among organizations that share information. This chapter says what blockchain is and applications in which blockchain technology could solve the existing challenges where they lack security, privacy, integrity, and interoperability.

INTRODUCTION

In the last few years, the major concern is about moving to the online world safely. The unauthorized access of data, program among the network is quite common. In spite of using various conventional ways of protecting online data, still, hackers are smart to intrude into the network. Figure 1 shows the traditional way of protecting online data against the cyber-attacks.

DOI: 10.4018/978-1-5225-8241-0.ch013

Figure 1. Traditional Techniques used against the cyber threat

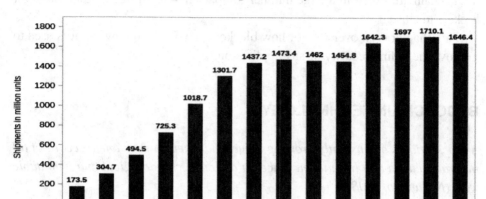

By looking at some of the recent cyber-attacks it seems like things get only worse day by day around the world.

BACKGROUND

Massive Cyber Security Attacks Of 2018

- A massive DOS attack with 1.35TB per second of traffic hitting the popular website 'Github'.
- On a single day, 3 billion yahoo email address got affected.
- 150 million people personal information was hacked by gaining access to certain files in a U.S. website application.

A very high level of dependency on the internet platform only leads to these types of cyber-attacks. Centralization of control, lack of integrity information that we are getting, the trust of quality in data is also some of the problems that need to be addressed.

So to answer all these problems an impenetrable technology called "BLOCKCHAIN" can be used to protect personal information data from attacks and improve cybersecurity across platforms.

The reason for the existing cyber-attacks is because they are partially decentralized. Implementing blockchain technology would fully decentralized DNS; the contents in the chain are stored in a large number of nodes making it nearly impossible for hackers to attack.

This chapter is an overview of how blockchain works and how can it is used to improve the online security of any application.

BLOCKCHAIN TECHNOLOGY

A blockchain is a constantly growing ledger that keeps a permanent record of all the transactions that have taken place, in a secure, chronological and immutable way. (Nakamoto, 2008).

A blockchain is a ledger where it keeps track of all the transaction made permanently. That means once a transaction is made you can't pull it out. It is recorded permanently (Nakamoto, 2008).

Every transaction is recorded in a ledger one after other i.e.) chronological order.

As shown in figure 2 a group of the block together forms a blockchain network. Each block contains basically three values,

1. Data
2. Previous block hash value
3. Current block hash value

Figure 2. Creation of a blockchain network

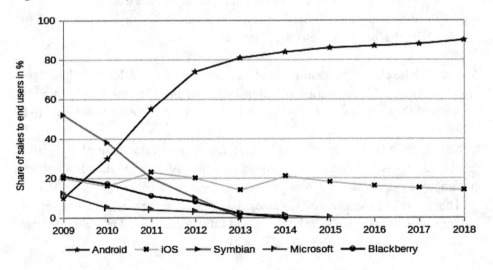

Figure 3. How a genesis block looks

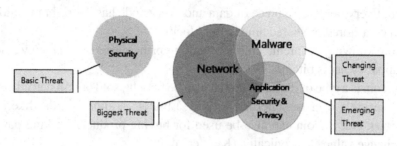

Figure 3 shows that always the Previous Block hash value in a genesis block is all zero's since that is the very first block created. The Hash values for each block are generated using the hash function. The hashing technique is explained briefly in the upcoming section.

HOW TO UPDATE A DATA IN A BLOCK?

In a blockchain, if a node needs to update a particular piece of data in a transaction to a block, it has to add a new transaction on top of the previous transaction on the block. Since even a small dot or comma gets added to the data the hash value gets changed. Using this technique, it is easy for the system to detect which block contains incorrect or false data.

KEY FEATURES OF BLOCKCHAIN

- A decentralized storage platform for secured transactions
- Chronological order
- Immutable
- No intermediaries
- Easy fraud identification
- Stable data

The biggest advantage of using blockchain is, for instance, a hacker tries to tamper with a block; the whole system analyzes every single block of data to find the one that differs from the rest. The system eliminates this type of block and identifies it as false (ArunaSri et. al, 2018).

The blockchain technology has no single point authority or single point storage location. Every node has a piece of data and every node has the right to validate or verify a data stored or shared among the blocks

Before knowing the architecture or working principle of blockchain we need to know about "what is bitcoin"?

A bitcoin is a type of digital asset that can be bought, sold or transferred between parties' securely over the internet. Buying a bitcoin is more similar like buying gold, silver, etc. Bitcoin can also be used for buying products, making payments and exchange value electronically. (King et. al, 2012)

"There is no physical form for a bitcoin either as coin form or paper form"

When you send a bitcoin to someone directly (i.e.) another party there is no need for a bank, third-party authentication or even a credit or debit card. Just you simply send the bitcoin over the internet it will reach the person instantly in a secured mode. To achieve this bitcoin uses four components digital signature, the blockchain, distributed network, and mining.

A blockchain is inherently immutable because once recorded, data cannot be changed without the subsequent alteration of hash values in all nodes connected in the blockchain. In other words, for changing the past records majority of the users should agree and willing to spend resources to update all subsequent block of a chain.

TYPES OF BLOCKCHAIN

Permission-Less Blockchain

In Permission-less type of blockchain, there is no need for authorizing the transaction.
In the below-given scenario,

Luke wants to build an app where anyone can voice their opinion about political parties. Now Luke wants to protect the privacy of the contributors

In Luke situation, we can use a permission-less blockchain. Anyone anywhere would be able to contribute their opinion on the app. No authority can remove their opinion, it will be permanently recorded.

Public Permissioned Blockchain

In Public Permissioned type of blockchain, the person is chosen for sanctioning a transaction. The person chosen can be a higher authority, government officials, institutional heads or a person assigned.

In the below-given scenario,

Eliza wants to sell diamond jewelry in a public chain; she wants the members in the chain to know about the cost, quality of stone, design pattern, etc.

Eliza can assign a person to write about the diamond jewelry but the members in the blockchain are able to view the data and don't have the permission to write anything. The data is however permanently recorded (Christian, 2017).

Private Permissioned Blockchain

The private Permissioned blockchain is similar to the Public Permissioned blockchain except for the public view of transaction data is restricted.

In the below-given scenario,

John works in a business firm and also he involves in business transactions with two starts up enterprises. They involve in a regular transaction with each other.

In such a case john need not reveal his business transaction as public. The data is however permanently recorded. Every transaction is tallied instantaneously. Here when they transmit with each other, they don't have to maintain a separate a ledger (Christian, 2017).

HASHING

The inclusion of cryptographic functions is used as a hash in each block which makes it difficult for hackers to get into the blockchain network and alter the records stored in the ledger. The most popularly used cryptographic function for hashing is SHA256/SHA512 because it generates unique hash value each and every time. Once in 6 million times, the hash value gets repeated.

BASIC FIVE FEATURES OF SHA256

These five features make each transaction stored in the blockchain a secured one.

1. **It is One Way:** The hash is once created it can't be reversed again
2. **Deterministic**: All the time for the same input data it gives the same output data.

3. **Fast Computation:** It takes only a very less amount of time to encrypt the data into a hash.
4. **Avalanche Effect:** If the input changes slightly and the output changes significantly.
5. **Must Withstand Collision:** (for more details→ pigeon hole concept)

DISTRIBUTED NETWORK

The blockchain uses a distributed network which further enhances the immutability and also ensures reliability. This is possible because everyone in the node stores the same copy of the transactions, which makes extremely difficult for the malicious attackers to modify the record stored in all nodes. The greatest advantage of blockchain there is no centralization of data storage and single point of control.

In figure 4, let us assume the blockchain consist of 4 nodes and all the transactions are recorded in the ledger. The first four transactions are successfully recorded in all nodes. In the fifth transaction, an intruder tries to change the transaction hash value (red color transaction). The remaining nodes will check that there is a change in hash value in node 2 and intimate it to node 2.

MINING

In a blockchain network, there are a group of people who are called "Miners". The role of miners is to process and confirm transactions.

Figure 4. Solution to an attack in distributed blockchain network

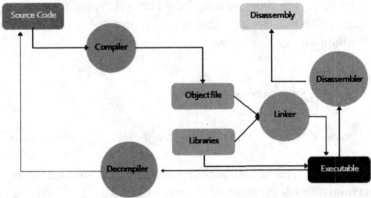

Steps Involved in Mining

- Miners need powerful blockchain mining computers to solve and confirm real-world transactions.
- The miners will choose the left out transaction from the "Mempool" based on the value assigned for the transaction for verifying it as shown in figure 5.
- Once the verification process is over within 72 hours a transaction should be added to a block.
- If the transaction is not mined again is sent back to the Mempool.
- Miners who successfully completed the mining process are rewarded with bitcoins.

CONSENSUS

Consensus algorithm is used to achieve reliability agreement on a single data value among distributed network where unreliable nodes are present. To accept a valid transaction 51% of consensus is required (Lakshmi et. al 2017; Zibin 2017).

Consensus algorithm support many real-world systems including Google's PageRank, load balancing smart grids, clock synchronization and drone control.

Figure 5. Steps involved in the Mining process

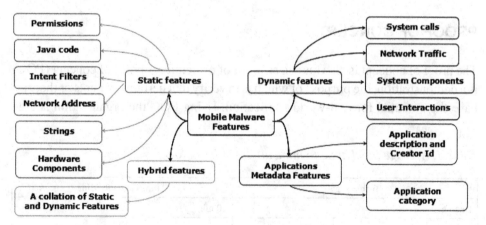

PROOF OF WORK

As already mentioned in steps involved in mining the miners need to verify a valid transaction. To do so, the miners should solve a mathematical puzzle known as proof of work. Once the miner finds the solution to the puzzle he/she announces in public around the network and gets the reward (Bach, 2018). The average time taken by the miners to solve the puzzle is shown in table 1.

Technically speaking solving a mathematical puzzle is nothing but finding the nonce value. In other terms, we call the mining process as inverse hashing, so the cryptographic hash algorithm of block data results in less than a given threshold. This threshold is called difficulty.

PROOF OF STAKE

Proof of stake is a similar algorithm as proof of work to mine the transaction unlike the miner is decided in a deterministic way by analyzing the wealth, also defined as a stake.

No reward is given for the miner instead the miner takes the transaction fee (Bach, 2018).

Some other common consensus algorithms are

- Byzantine fault tolerance algorithm (PBFT)
- Delegated proof of stake algorithm (DPOS)

PROOF OF CONCEPT

The proof of concept is also known as proof of principle. A proof of concept (POC) is a demonstration, the purpose of which is to verify that certain concepts or theories have the potential for real-world application. Using POC the organization is able

Table 1. Average block time to mine an individual block

Technology	Time Taken to Mine
Bitcoin	10 min
Ethereum	15 sec
Ripple	3.5 sec

to get the internal feedback about the products and service they provide which help to reduce unnecessary risk and help the stakeholder to make changes in the early stage itself (Bach, 2018).

APPLICATIONS OF BLOCKCHAIN

Money Transactions

One of the greatest applications of blockchain is transmitting money and storing information without the help of banks. Because everyone started thinking that bank third-party agents who perform money transactions with a huge amount of transaction fees and also takes hours and weeks together for validating the transactions (Mahdi et. al 2018).

Supply Chain Management

Over a hundred years ago, supply chains were relatively simple because commerce was local, but they have grown incredibly complex. Throughout the history of supply chains, there have been innovations such as the shift to haul freight via trucks rather than rail or the emergence of personal computers in the 1980s that led to dramatic shifts in supply chain management (Mahdi et. al 2018). It's incredibly difficult for customers or buyers to truly know the value of products because there is a significant lack of transparency in the current system. In a similar way, it's extremely difficult to investigate supply chains when there is suspicion of illegal or unethical practices. They can also be highly inefficient as vendors and suppliers try to connect the dots on who needs what, when and how. Blockchain can increase the efficiency and transparency of supply chains and positively impact everything from warehousing to delivery to payment.

Power

The blockchain can be used for transferring solar power to neighbors. The application enables the users to buy and sell the renewable energy resource by counting the electrons and posting it in the blockchain (Mahdi et. al 2018, Lo3ENERGY, n. d).

Healthcare

A trend followed in healthcare is slowly moving the data and services digitally due to the availability of entire patient medical history in real time but the problem is a lack of security. To address the problem the Permissioned/Permissionless blockchain can be used (Mahdi et. al 2018).

The blockchain is used in the healthcare sector for maintaining the patient records safely on the internet, to check the fake medicine, for clinical research purpose, claim and billing management system, etc.

Real Estate

To maintain all sort registration in real estate business using the traditional method is more expensive and also requires a huge amount of labor-intensive operation. In real Estate business transaction for record keeping purpose, one of the secured platforms is blockchain.

Sweden government partners with ChromaWay Company (Mahdi et. al 2018). Here, they aim to test the possibility of a blockchain based land registry.

Tourism

Whether you like it or not, Travel agencies provide traditional paper tokens, coupons, discount and other sorts of loyalty rewards to their customers. Blockchain allows companies to make use of the new digital format into their customer services programs, creating their own Blockchain loyalty tokens and coins for their customers.

Webjet is an Australian based online booking site that allows stock of empty hotel rooms to be efficiently tracked and traded (Zibin 2018; Webjet n. d.).

Transport

Image how difficult it would be to search and locate a secure parking space in a crowded area. The blockchain brings a solution to this. The parking owners can rent their long-term parking space when they are not in use for them (Zibin 2018; Parkgene n. d).

Even though the driverless cars need not require drivers to park the car but it needs to pay the parking fees to park the car. So the blockchain car wallet could be to transmit the parking fees without using a bank transaction.

Government

The traditional way to vote in a country is through a paper-based system or e-voting via a machine in a polling station or i-voting through a web browser. There is always security threat about the voting system whether the data is secured and defend against potential attacks. By using the blockchain concept in e-voting platform we can ensure a transparent and verifiable election around the globe (Zibin 2018).

CONCLUSION

The blockchain is simple technology in a distributed network where the data is independently verified and audited by all actors in the network. A new revolutionary way to create a system that is free from attacks or free from reliance on any centralized trusted entity to dictate trust. The blockchain technology would guarantee in helping in critical areas where data need to be preserved and prone from attacks. Above all blockchain is been currently used in finance offers but it could be effectively used in a business startup to existing all real-time applications.

REFERENCES

Miraz & Ali. (2018). Applications of Blockchain Technology beyond Crypto currency. *Annuals of Emerging Technologies in Computing, 2*(1).

Arabaci. (2018). *Blockchain consensus mechanisms- the case of natural disasters July 2018 basics.* Retrieved from https://pdfs.semanticscholar.org/0afd/a615470760dd1cd661fe4b5f7d3e9b39cdf3.pdf

Bach, Mihaljevic, & Zagar. (2018). Comparative analysis of blockchain consensus algorithms. *Information and Communication Technology Electronics and Microelectronics (MIPRO) 41st International Convention on*, 1545-1550.

Cachin & Vukolić. (2017). *Consensus Protocols in the Wild.* IBM Research.

King, S., & Nadal, S. (2008). *Bitcoin: Peer-to-peer crypto-currency with proof-of-stake.* (Unpublished)

Nakamoto, S. (2008). *Bitcoin: A peer-to-peer electronic cash system*. Academic Press.

Sankar, Sindhu, & Sethumadhavan. (2018). *Survey of consensus protocols on blockchain applications*. Academic Press.

Sri & Bhaskari,. (2018). A study on blockchain technology. *International Journal of Engineering & Technology, 7*(2), 418-421.

Zheng, Xie, Dai, Chen, & Wang. (2017). An Overview of Blockchain Technology: Architecture, Consensus, and Future Trends. *IEEE 6th International Conference on Big Data*.

Chapter 14
Secured Information Exchange Using Haptic Codes

B. Rajesh Kanna
VIT Chennai, India

ABSTRACT

This chapter discloses an invention related to methods and systems to provide secure and custom information exchange code for the users of haptic or kinesthetic communication devices in a variety of applications. The proposed information exchange codes are named as "haptic codes," where it maps several touch interactive locations into a single information exchange code. Thus, the proposed haptic code facilitates the representation of different notions to unique information exchange character/digit/symbol. A method has been invented to design eight such codes from the intuitive touch gestures (ITG) of user, each of which uses double-touch on arbitrary location within the touch pad/screen without shifting hand position on every touch. Hand position may or may not be the same after the generation of every ITG. Haptic codes are made secure by incorporating a new cryptographic system, which employs polar graph for encoding and decoding such locations using polar curves as shareable keys. Therefore, haptic codes can be exchanged for secure communication and read by devices that supports to touch.

FIELD OF INVESTIGATION

The present invention relates to development of information exchange code for short and secured communication using human finger gestures on haptic or kinesthetic communication device. These new information exchange codes are named as custom

DOI: 10.4018/978-1-5225-8241-0.ch014

haptic code. To enhance the security of such haptic codes graphical key based encryption and decryption system is also incorporated particular to kinesthetic communication.

PRIOR ART

In an Information communication system, coding schemes to represent data or Coding is the vital and fundamental scheme in any information exchange process, it requires language and its characters must be represented as unique code. Code is nothing but a unique number associated with every character so as to facilitate the information exchange unambitious between sender and receiver. There are quite a few standards existing in the literature to represent text, special character in communications equipment, and other devices. The Binary Coded Decimal (BCD) is a 4-bit code and each decimal digit is represented by 4 binary digits. Extended binary coded decimal interchange code (EBCDIC), is an 8-bit code, can represent 256 characters to represent English alphabets and numerals. ASCII stands for American standard code for information interchange (S. Tabirca et al, 1998). It was published in 1968 by ANSI (American National Standard Institute) (C. V. Krishna et al, 2016). It is the most widely used coding scheme for personal computers. The 7-bit code can represent 128 characters. An 8-bit code can represent 256 characters and to represent graphic symbols. ASCII, EBCDIC are character encoding based on the English alphabet. Unicode is an industry standard to represent and manipulate text expressed in most of the world's writing systems. Indian script codes for information interchange (ISCII) code are characters required in the ten Brahmi based Indian scripts.

In earlier 1990, key boards were the major form input device involved in information exchange system. Hence, the entire standard tried to allocate a number to each key on the keyboard that can be traded as code for communication system. All those standards are prompt to map a number to unique character for their preferred linguistics/language, it leads to one to one mapping for a character. Table 1, shows few ASCII codes for few English uppercase character and its associated decimal / hexadecimal / binary codes.

Table 1. ASCII coding of English alphabets

Character	A	B	. . . .	Y	Z
Decimal	65	66	. . . .	89	90
Hex	41	42	. . . .	59	5A
Binary	01000001	01000010	. . . .	01011001	01011010

Due to this one to one map, secured communication modality has always been at the forefront of research and development in information communication technologies With a myriad of requirements in the form of encryption, non-standard code, robustness and power requirement etc., Secured communication presents a ripe challenge for a blend of research problems. Seldom is the problem viewed holistically in order to develop an end-to-end secure communication system. Hence, cryptography has been employed for information security to protect information from accidental or unauthorized disclosure while sending and receiving information through means of such standard electronic codes.

Apart from keyboard as an input device, now-a-days other means of interactions are very popular in the form of touch screen, is an input as output device. Any user can give input or control through simple or multi-touch gestures by touching top of an electronic visual display. Though, several control activities has been assigned through simple or multi-touch gestures by touching the screen with a special stylus or one or more fingers. Although, haptic interfaces have been widely used for emotional communication between users over distance (D. Tsetserukou et al 2010, E. Gatti et al 2013), no information exchange code has been attempted as of now for such haptic interfaces (M. Chen et al 2011, M. A. Eid et al 2016).

Here, I invented a method to define/establish few exchange codes which corresponds to well-defined multi-touch actions (reviewed detailed in the description) for fast and secured communication system among haptic based devices. These new information exchange codes are named as custom haptic code; it provides many representations to denote a single character, whereas the existing code provides one to one map between characters.

DESCRIPTION OF INVENTION

In this work, novel haptic based codes have been proposed, which facilitates representation of different notions for a unique code. Here, I attempted to define eight intuitive touch gestures (ITG), each of which uses double-touch on arbitrary location within the touch pad/screen without shifting hand position on every touch. Hand position may or may not be the same after the generation of every ITG. The touch positions of each ITG are further projected onto an imaginary convex polygon (CP) logically placed to bind the gesture within the overall boundary of the touch pad/screen. The orientation and dimension of CP is considered as the geometrical private key for information exchange between the users. The projected coordinate is represented as custom code and used for data communication.

These ITGs are arranged to spell out the security code message, orders and brief reports during any means of communications. By means of proposed ITG, a minimalist haptic language is developed in order to relay important communications in the form of touch gestures. These gestures are geometric and location independent in nature, it means single touch gestures at different locations on the screen will map onto a single semantic in order to formulate message. This is unlike traditional cryptography where information is represented using unique symbols or character sets and every symbol denote the unique notion. The language directly translates into a haptic feedback system at the receiver end which increases secrecy as only the actuator configuration at the receiver and user perception of the haptic feedback can decipher the messages.

At the MAC layer, encoder and decoder modules guarantee message delivery over long distances. The haptic code, I propose takes this limitation into account while formulating the message. Our use of multiple gestures for the same semantic nullifies the need for traditional encryption and decryption, as this many to one mapping itself makes deciphering the message near impossible. The representation of ITG is obscure and very difficult to interpret and denotes various pairs of 0-dimensional flats in Euclidean or polar space with lesser dimension for single symbol. It facilitates the development of use of a custom minimalistic haptic language over a secured network.

Proof of Concept

Let "P" be the 2D flat surface on any multi-touch screen wherein (L, W) indicates the bottom - right corner of "P" and top-right corner (0,0) indicates the origin of "P". A single point touch on the surface P, called as a point gesture location, is represented by the Cartesian coordinates (x,y).

Table 2. Haptic codes associated with angle formed by multi-touch

Angle Formed by Directional Gesture (θ)	Haptic Code Associated to "θ"
$360° - \Delta\theta \leq \theta; 0° + \Delta\theta$	A
$045° - \Delta\theta \leq \theta; 45° + \Delta\theta$	B
$090° - \Delta\theta \leq \theta; 90° + \Delta\theta$	C
$135° - \Delta\theta \leq \theta; 135° + \Delta\theta$	D
$180° - \Delta\theta \leq \theta; 180° + \Delta\theta$	E
$225° - \Delta\theta \leq \theta; 225° + \Delta\theta$	F
$270° - \Delta\theta \leq \theta; 270° + \Delta\theta$	G
$315° - \Delta\theta \leq \theta; 315° + \Delta\theta$	H
where $\Delta\theta$ is 22.5°	

Definition of Haptic Code

Let "F" be the first gesture point location denoted by (xf, yf), followed by "S", a second gesture point location on P denoted by (xs,ys). From these multi-touch gesture points F and S, then define a vertical line lv by joining the points (xf, yf), and (xf, 0) denoted as initial line and another line ls between the points (xf, yf), (xs,ys) denoted as terminal line. Let "θ" be the angle formed between initial line and terminal line in clockwise direction.

$$\angle \; lv \; ls = \theta$$

By considering the directional pattern of each two-touch gestures and obtained value of "θ", eight unique codes has been assigned and are labeled as {A,B,C,D,E,F,G,H }, tabulated in table 2. Hence, a pair of single touch F followed by S will produce any one haptic code.

Time Complexity Analysis to Penetrate Haptic Code

The penetration attempts to generate a code from malicious activity requires two one point touches "F" and "S" on flat surface P with its size L_x W. Single touch location can be represented as pair 'x_i' and 'y_i' and are two separate variables on "P".

Therefore to identify the first touch "F", typically it requires maximum of W * L attempts, if the selection of point locations are happened sequentially from top to bottom and left to right. Since both W and L are independent variables then time complexity is O (W*L). Further, assume that the value of W will never be greater than L. Thus, it can also write the bound of the complexity as $O(L^2)$. The time complexity to penetrate the first touch location (tft) as well the second touch (tst) is quadratic. Hence the overall time complexity (tl) is polynomial time complexity.

$$tl = tft + tst$$

$$tl = O(n^2)$$

Haptic Code Encoding

- **Plain Text:** To represent a haptic code it requires two gesture point locations (x_f, y_f) and (x_s, y_s) are referred in rectangular coordinate. Herein, the plain text represents those positions in polar form and are labeled as (r_f, θ_f), (r_s, θ_s) respectively.

- **Encryption Key:** Here the key is Graphical Pre-shared key (GPSK), specified as a plane polar curve by defining "f" as a function of "ϕ" resulting the curve points of the form f(ϕ),ϕ). Various types of curves can be described by various polar equations with different values of radius and angle. The GPSK has three components specified polar curve equation, predefined value of "r" and "ϕ". GPSK can describe familiar Cartesian shapes such as circle or ellipses as well as some unfamiliar shapes such as cardioid, limaçon, lemniscate, polar rose, Archimedean spiral, and etc. with various parameters
- **Encryption:** The encryption of the plane text is the mapping of single point touch location in two-dimensional space of a domain into another domain using map function;

$$w = f(z);$$

where f(z) is function defined by the GSPK. The GSPK relates to the mapping of surface onto another surface so that all the angles between intersecting curves remains unchanged.

- **Ciphertext:** The resultant polar coefficients (rf$_c$, θf$_c$) and (rs$_c$, θs$_c$) obtained after the encryption process is cipher texts for the selected point gestures. Further, this polar representation are converted into rectangular space and labeled as cipher text for first and second point gestures F1(x,y), S1(x,y) respectively.

Haptic Interface: Sender

1. Map the appropriate Haptic code from consecutive two single point touch co-ordinates and display in sender
2. Convert the screen co-ordinate of first and second touch locations into normalized device co-ordinate value
3. Transform the corresponding elements of first touch two-dimensional normalized device coordinate "x" and "y" into polar coordinates F_theta and F_rho.
4. Transform the corresponding elements of second touch two-dimensional normalized device coordinate "x" and "y" into polar coordinates S_theta and S_rho.
5. Select conformal transformation from pre-shared key or mappings and construct forward transformation over F_theta, F_rho, S_theta and S_rho.
6. Apply Euclidean transform over the forwarded conformal transformed values
7. Send the transformed Euclidean distance value to receiver

Figure 1. Secured Information exchange system (SIES) using haptic codes

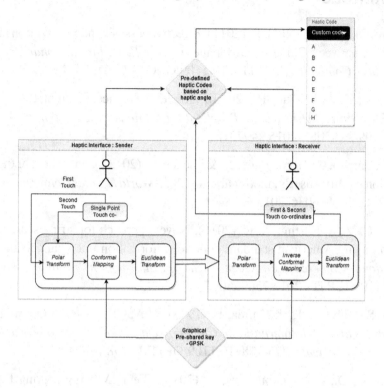

Haptic Interface: Receiver

1. Transform the corresponding elements of received Euclidean co-ordinate into polar coordinates
2. Select conformal transformation from pre-shared key or mappings and construct inverse transformation to obtain F_theta, F_rho, S_theta and S_rho.
3. Transform the corresponding elements of first touch two-dimensional normalized device coordinate "x" and "y" from polar coordinates F_theta and F_rho.
4. Transform the corresponding elements of second touch two-dimensional normalized device coordinate "x" and "y" from polar coordinates S_theta and S_rho.
5. Obtain actual screen co-ordinate of first and second touch locations from normalized device co-ordinate and screen resolutions
6. Map the appropriate Haptic code for the obtained single point touch co-ordinates and display in Receiver

REFERENCES

Chen, M., Okada, S., & Nitta, K. (2011). Effectiveness of haptic interaction in online negotiation between Chinese and Japanese. *2011 IEEE International Conference on Granular Computing*, 111-114. 10.1109/GRC.2011.6122577

Eid, M. A., & Al Osman, H. (2016). Affective Haptics: Current Research and Future Directions. *IEEE Access: Practical Innovations, Open Solutions*, 4, 26–40. doi:10.1109/ACCESS.2015.2497316

Gatti, E., Caruso, G., Bordegoni, M., & Spence, C. (2013). Can the feel of the haptic interaction modify a user's emotional state? *2013 World Haptics Conference (WHC)*, 247-252. 10.1109/WHC.2013.6548416

Krishna, C. V., & Karthik, S. R. (2016). Novel approach for string searching and matching using American standard code for information interchange value. *2016 International Conference on Recent Trends in Information Technology (ICRTIT)*, 1-5. 10.1109/ICRTIT.2016.7569550

Tabirca, S., Tabirca, T., & Ciurea, E. (1998). Is ASCII Code An Optimal Code? *Proceedings of the 6th International Conference on Optimization of Electrical and Electronic Equipments*, 775-778. 10.1109/OPTIM.1998.708044

Tsetserukou, D., & Neviarouskaya, A. (2010). iFeel_IM! Augmenting Emotions during Online Communication. *IEEE Computer Graphics and Applications*, 30(5), 72–80. doi:10.1109/MCG.2010.88 PMID:24807416

Chapter 15
Real–Time ECG–Based Biometric Authentication System

Jagannath Mohan
VIT Chennai, India

Adalarasu Kanagasabai
SASTRA University (Deemed), India

Vetrivelan Pandu
VIT Chennai, India

ABSTRACT

Security plays an important role in present day situation where identity fraud and terrorism pose a great threat. Recognizing human using computers or any artificial systems not only affords some efficient security outcomes but also facilitates human services, especially in the zone of conflict. In the recent decade, the demand for improvement in security for personal data storage has grown rapidly, and among the potential alternatives, it is one that employs innovative biometric identification techniques. Amongst these behavioral biometric techniques, the electrocardiogram (ECG) is being chosen as a physiological modality due to the uniqueness of its characteristics which integrates liveness detection, significantly preventing spoof attacks. The chapter discusses the overview of existing preprocessing, feature extraction, and classification methods for ECG-based biometric authentication. The proposed system is intended to develop applications for real-time authentication.

DOI: 10.4018/978-1-5225-8241-0.ch015

INTRODUCTION

Biometric advances offer superior security systems over conventional authentication techniques, similar to secret word based ones, given the way that the biometric highlight could be a special physiological characteristic that continuously shows and, contingent upon the strategy utilized, may not be obvious to other individuals. In any case, one concern is that a few biometric strategies have certain equipment and reaction time prerequisites that make them improper for portable gadgets and cards (Boriev et al., 2015).

Finger impression may be a prevalent biometric method and has been utilized for over 100 a long time completely different applications, counting authentication on cell phones. The utilization of cards for monetary exchanges or secure get to has gotten to be irreplaceable within a recent couple of decades. This prominence has to been gone with by security concerns. Conventional cards don't bolster authentication and thus are not unequivocally related to their proprietor. Money related educate have attempted to address this issue through the presentation of PINs (Individual Confirmation Numbers) and incorporated circuits on cards. These highlights stay as it were valuable for contact cards. This has diminished the number of breaches, but detached assaults (Stick burglary or signature producing) are as yet hazardous (Poree et al., 2016).

Portable gadgets such as smartphones and PDAs have turned out to be crucial contraptions for various capacities. Clients are ending up more comfortable with putting away profoundly private data, for example, messages, photographs, and other delicate records on such gadgets. The well-known versatile login strategies depend on numerical or graphical secret codes. These systems are helpless against uninvolved assaults actuated by people observing from a distance to see the gadget screen or the tracking of the fingers with the objective of taking the secret code (Miakotko, 2017).

Conventional authentication has demerits as they can be spoofed by an assailant that captures the personality cleared out by clients on security. This has been illustrated with commercial frameworks that utilize finger impression authentication (Joy et al., 2016). Electrocardiogram (denoted to as ECG or EKG) techniques have the benefits of concealing the biometric highlights during authentication. Electrocardiography records the electrical activity of the heart over a specific timeframe with the help of electrodes placed on the human body (Biel et al., 2001). The electrodes locate the modest electrical changes from the body by heartbeats produced by the heart. There are three fundamental segments to an ECG (Louis et al., 2016). To begin with is the P wave, which acts the depolarization of atria, second is the QRS complex which acts the ventricular depolarization and final is T wave, which appears the ventricular repolarization. The ECG is separated into the following morphological features (Figure 1).

- **PR Interval:** Time difference between the beginning of the P and QRS wave.
- **P Wave:** Corresponds to atrial depolarization.
- **PR Segment:** Time difference between the beginning and end of the Q and P wave.
- **QRS Complex:** Corresponds to ventricular depolarization.
- **ST Segment:** Time difference between the beginning and end of T and S wave.
- **T Wave:** Corresponds to ventricular repolarization.
- **QT Interval:** Time difference between the QRS complex and the T wave.

Later a long time has seen a developing intrigued in ECG based biometric recognition technique, especially in conflict zones. In any case, complex equipment is required to acquire this signal, making it difficult to actualize in versatile gadgets. Current ECG authentication algorithms are intended to work in portable conditions given the way that they require protracted ECG signals or have to be combined with other biometric modalities in order to accomplish reliable outcomes (Pinto et al., 2017). Consequently, frameworks and strategies that empower ECG based biometric authentication to stay profoundly alluring. The proposed real-time ECG based biometric authentication system is shown in Figure 2.

Figure 1. The typical ECG waveform with its common intervals and point of measurement are depicted

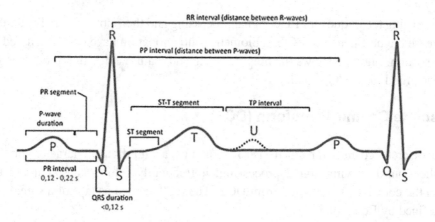

Figure 2. The proposed system for real-time ECG based biometric authentication

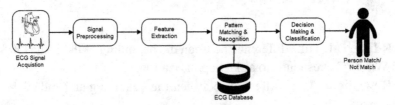

Figure 3. The typical preprocessing and features extracted from the raw ECG signal

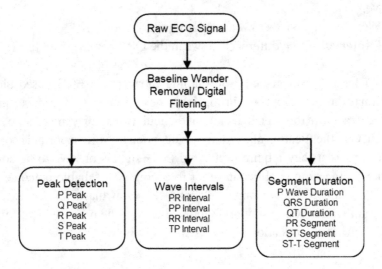

Signal Processing

The existing techniques for ECG signal processing and their potential to essentially increase the pertinence of ECG in biometric authentication have been discussed in this section. Figure 3 shows the preprocessing and feature extraction process from the acquired raw ECG signal.

Discrete Cosine Transform (DCT)

The discrete cosine transform (DCT) contains a significant characteristic for applications involving signal processing; it frequently reforms a signal exactly from the coefficients obtained from DCT. The DCT named as (x_{ct}) of a signal (x_i) is defined by Equation (1).

$$
x_{ct}\left(k\right) = \begin{cases} \dfrac{1}{\sqrt{N}}\displaystyle\sum_{n=0}^{N-1} x_i\left(n\right), & k = 0 \\[4ex] \sqrt{\dfrac{2}{N}}\displaystyle\sum_{n=0}^{N-1} x_i\left(n\right)\cos\left[\dfrac{\pi\left(2n-1\right)k}{2N}\right], & k = 1,\dots,N-1 \end{cases}
\tag{1}
$$

Note that, x_{ct} and x_i have the same sizes of N samples. The DCT additionally offers energy compaction. In addition, the cosine bases of the DCT are orthogonal to each other (Martis et al., 2013).

Baseline Wander

The baseline wander of the ECG signal is considered to be one of the concerns in detecting peaks. For instance, due to the wander, the T peak can be higher than R peak, and it is identified as an R peak. The low frequency wanders of the ECG signal can be triggered by breathing or muscle artifact. The drift of the baseline with breath can be characterized as a sinusoidal component and the frequency of breath included to the ECG signal. The deviation could be reconstructed by ECG amplitude modulation by the sinusoidal component that is included to the baseline. These noises ought to be removed before extracting the features from the raw ECG signal. The noise removal can be refined by allowing the ECG signal through a filter having a cut-off frequency as a function of the noise frequency.

Digital Filtering

Despite the fact that the raw ECG signal is getting filtered from the baseline wander, a few high-frequency artifacts from leads, equipment, and interfaces persist. All imperative data of the ECG signal is found between 0.05Hz to 100Hz. Such cut-off frequencies can be effectively digitally filtered with the help of infinite impulse response (IIR) Butterworth filters (Proakis and Manolakis, 2007). The transfer function of an IIR filter is specified in Equation (2).

$$
H\left(z\right) = \frac{\displaystyle\sum_{i=0}^{P} b_i z^{-i}}{1 + \displaystyle\sum_{j=1}^{Q} a_j z^{-j}}
\tag{2}
$$

where a and b are coefficients of the IIR filter, and z is the signal to be filtered.

FEATURE EXTRACTION

From the filtered ECG signal, the P-QRS-T waves would appear in one cardiac cycle in a better way from the raw ECG signal. The feature extraction process defines the peaks and intervals in the ECG signal for consecutive investigation. The peaks and intervals value of P-QRS-T segment decides the functioning of the heart of each individual.

Peak Detection

The filtered signal is handled advance to extract the ECG features such as P, Q, R, S and T peaks, which are considered as one of the highlights for authenticating an individual. In literature, a scope of methodologies has been investigated to extract these features (Mehta and Lingayat, 2008; Pan and Tompkins, 1985). The alternative method is detecting large R peaks. Be that as it may, due to the absence of repetitive excess data, the R peak prompts numerous errors and timing vulnerabilities (Peter et al., 2016). The Pan–Tompkins algorithm (PTA) is applied for real-time QRS detection (Figure 4). This algorithm extracts the QRS complex from the filtered ECG signal and is appropriate for resource-constrained gadgets. This algorithm is likewise considered reliable in the occurrence of abnormal ECGs, for instance, arrhythmias (Patel et al., 2012). It plays out filtering phases and examination stages for the feature extraction process.

Figure 4. ECG signal and detected peaks after the Pan-Tompkins algorithm

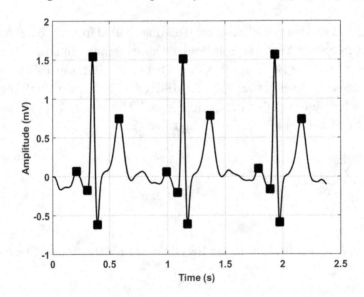

Wave Intervals

The fundamental approach, cross-correlation technique compares the features derived from the DCT coefficients for the intervals such as PR, PP, RR and TP, which is spared within the database that facilitated in the server, with following successive intervals. Along these lines, if the correlated outcome is over 95% (Derval et al., 2014), an individual is assessed to be an authorized one; otherwise, they are assessed as an unauthorized individual. This procedure is restricted to 10 s, at that point the entire procedure will start again.

Segment Duration

Sornomo (1987) examined a probability method dependent on the statistical analysis for low and high-frequency sections of the ECG signal. The QRS complex is estimated from the initial onset to the final end. The ST segment taking after the QRS complex is the time, at which the whole ventricle gets depolarized and generally relates to the ventricular action potential. The ST segment is imperative within the analysis of ventricular ischemia or hypoxia on the grounds that under those conditions, the ST segment can become either down or raised up. When the limit of QRS complex is realized each beat that is categorized in two gatherings, one comprises of the QRS complex and other with the P, ST-T and T segments.

Haar Wavelet Transform (HWT) Features

The Haar wavelet transform (HWT) is used to extract the wavelet features. The multi-resolution investigation process is done by separating input signals into high and low-frequency portions, at that point partitioning the low-frequency portion again using iteration method. The wavelet coefficients in Level (1,2) and Level (3,4) are impacted by frequency interference and the baseline conversions respectively (Ali, 2014).

CLASSIFICATION

The decision-making process involves the classification procedures out of which few popularly existing methods are depicted in Figure 5.

Correlation Coefficient

The correlation coefficient technique is broadly utilized within the authentication systems. It provides a statistical index that establishes the linear relationship between two variables. By computing the relationship between two features, it can be examined whether the two features are taken from the same class or not. Consider the two datasets A_i and B_i, and the correlation coefficient (C_c) between them is defined as in Equation (3) (Dai et al., 2015).

$$C_c = \frac{\sum_i \left(A_i \left(B_i - \bar{B} \right) - \bar{A} \left(B_i - \bar{B} \right) \right)}{\sqrt{\left(\sum_i \left(A_i - \bar{A} \right)^2 \right) \left(\sum_i \left(B_i - \bar{B} \right)^2 \right)}} \tag{3}$$

where A and B are the means of the datasets A_i and B_i.

Logistic Regression

Logistic regression is a discriminative model that can be applied to accomplish classification. It applies the sigmoid function to allot perceptions to a discrete group. The range of the sigmoid function is confined to [0, 1], in this way the logistic regression can be seen as the probability that the perception has a place with the

Figure 5. Signal analysis and classification methods

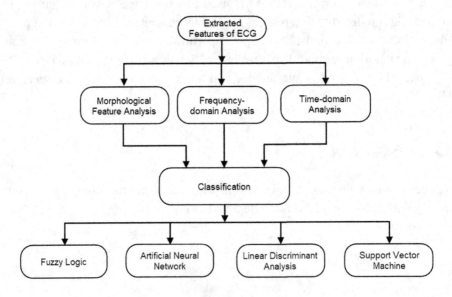

positive group. The input given to the sigmoid function is a linear combination of ECG features. The coefficients are called as weights, and the logistic regression takes the best weights that augments the execution, i.e., limits the error of the classifier (Miguel-Hurtado et al., 2016).

Fuzzy Logic

The neural network weighted fuzzy membership functions could be an administered fuzzy neural network that classifies classes with aid of the boundary sum of weighted fuzzy membership functions that were trained from input set. It comprises the input layer, hyperbox layer, and output layer. The input layer consists of N nodes and each node is associated with one input feature set. The number of nodes present in the hyperbox layer is attained by multiplying the number of nodes of the input layer and the output layer. The number of hyperboxes is equal to the number of nodes in the output layer. The membership functions have three linguistic variables which are large, medium and small. The data that is entered through the consequences of the fuzzy membership function is evaluated through the boundary sum of this variable (Lim, 2009). Each ECG biometric feature that is extracted through Haar wavelets was coordinated to one input node to derive authenticated and unauthenticated class nodes in the output layer. The procedures of training the acquired ECG signal from the user and those that are present in the database are recorded in the network, and authentication is the point at which a person's ECG is categorized through the outcomes of the trained fuzzy membership functions (Lim et al., 2006).

k-Nearest Neighbors (k-NN)

The k-nearest neighbors (k-NN) is an algorithm that can be applied for classification problems. During the prediction stage, k-NN calculates the distance between each training point and the new perception. This algorithm allocates a label to the new perception by selecting the class shared by most of the k nearest points. Accordingly, "training" stage is not present, which makes the algorithm design simple. In predicting a new label, k-NN has to implement over the whole training set, which makes it difficult when there is a presence of large datasets. The level of performance can be influenced by the parameter k. When k is small, the model becomes liable to overfitting, as the prediction is made dependent only on a few neighbors, which is profound to noise specific to the chosen training set. When k is high, the model gives less importance to the region of the new perception and more emphasis on the general frequency of the samples. In cases, when k equals the number of training points would drive k-NN to dependably forecast the label that corresponds to the most frequent class (Dakhil and Ibrahim, 2018).

Support Vector Machine (SVM)

The support vector machine (SVM) is predominantly used as a classification algorithm by finding the hyperplane that isolates the positive and negative class observations in the feature space. Optimization is carried out on the variables of the hyperplane to yield the highest margin between the nearest data point and the isolating hyperplane (Jayaram et al., 2015). The resulting hyperplane is applied to perform classification on new data points. The classification problems offer when data points are not linearly separable. SVMs can moderate this issue by utilizing a method called the Kernel Trick. Kernel functions contain polynomials, the sigmoid function, and the radial basis function. Kernel functions can be utilized to transform the input space into a higher dimensional space, which eventually allows the observations to be linearly separable. As the number of dimensions increases, the risk of overfitting also increases.

Artificial Neural Network (ANN)

The artificial neural network (ANN) is another classification technique which is performed by optimizing the training set present in the neural system. The two phases such as learning and testing phases are present in the operation of ANN (Badri, 2010). The learning phase involves adjusting the weights of the neural system to be tuned out to the training dataset. The optimal size for the dataset is based on many factors such as the total number of layers, the number of hidden units in the middle layers, and a number of units in the output layers. This plays out the important extraction from a noisy training set to attain better occurrence of depiction. The learning limits a cost function in perspective of the error signal, concerning system parameters (weights), with the true objective that the real response of each output neuron tracks the objective response. A typically employed for the cost function is the mean square error rule, described as the mean square estimation of the sum squared error.

Linear Discriminant Analysis (LDA)

The principal component analysis (PCA) and linear discriminant analysis (LDA) are generally utilized for biometric classification. The LDA, also called Fisher discriminant analysis, is defined by the transformation. The eigenvectors of LDA are known as "fisherfaces". The LDA transformation is emphatically subjected to the number of classes (c), the number of samples (n), and the original space dimensionality (d). Probably, there are nearly c-1 non-zero eigenvectors. The c-1 non-zero eigenvectors are considered as the upper bound of the discriminant space dimensionality. It is impractical to ensure this condition in numerous real-time applications. Therefore, an intermediate transformation is required to decrease the dimensionality of the space (Samik and Saurabh, 2016).

CONCLUSION

This paper provides a general discussion of most frequently used processing and classification methods in real time ECG based biometric authentication system. This review is useful for appropriate use of existing methods as well as the scope of the invention of new methods. This ECG based authentication also helps in detecting liveness, significantly preventing spoof attacks. The proposed system would provide a solution to develop applications for real-time authentication.

This research received no specific grant from any funding agency in the public, commercial, or not-for-profit sectors. However, the research was supported by the Vellore Institute of Technology (VIT) Chennai for providing us the e-Journal facilities.

REFERENCES

Ali, A. I. (2014). Iris recognition using Haar wavelet transform. *Journal of Al-Nahrain University*, *17*(1), 80–86.

Badri, L. (2010). Development of neural networks for noise reduction. *The International Arab Journal of Information Technology*, *7*(3), 289–294.

Biel, L., Pettersson, O., Philipson, L., & Wide, P. (2001). ECG analysis: A new approach to human identification. *IEEE Transactions on Instrumentation and Measurement*, *50*(3), 808–812. doi:10.1109/19.930458

Boriev, Z. V., Sokolov, S. S., & Nyrkov, A. P. (2015). Review of modern biometric user authentication and their development prospects. *Proceedings of the IOP Conference Series. Materials Science and Engineering*, *91*(1). doi:10.1088/17578 99X/91/1/012063

Dai, M., Zhu, B., Zheng, G., & Wang, Y. (2015). A method of ECG identification based on the weighted correlation coefficient. *Proceedings of the Chinese Conference on Biometric Recognition*, 633-640. 10.1007/978-3-319-25417-3_74

Dakhil, I. G., & Ibrahim, A. A. (2018). Design and implementation of fingerprint identification system based on k-NN neural network. *Journal of Computer and Communications*, *6*(03), 1–18. doi:10.4236/jcc.2018.63001

Derval, N., Bordachar, P., Lim, H. S., Sacher, F., Ploux, S., Laborderie, J., ... Jaïs, P. (2014). Impact of pacing site on QRS duration and its relationship to hemodynamic response in cardiac resynchronization therapy for congestive heart failure. *Journal of Cardiovascular Electrophysiology*, *25*(9), 1012–1020. doi:10.1111/jce.12464 PMID:24891271

Jayaram, M. A., Prashanth, G. K., & Taj, S. (2015). Classification of ear biometric data using support vector machine. *British Journal of Applied Science and Technology*, *11*(1), 1–10. doi:10.9734/BJAST/2015/19509

Joy, Y. H., Jeon, S. Y., Im, J. H., & Lee, M. K. (2016). *Security analysis and improvement of fingerprint authentication for smartphones. In Lecture Notes in Electrical Engineering* (Vol. 354, pp. 71–77). Singapore: Springer.

Lim, J. S. (2009). Finding features for real-time premature ventricular contraction detection using a fuzzy neural network system. *IEEE Transactions on Neural Networks*, *20*(3), 522–527. doi:10.1109/TNN.2008.2012031 PMID:19179246

Lim, J. S., Wang, D., Kim, Y.-S., & Gupta, S. (2006). A neuro-fuzzy approach for diagnosis of antibody deficiency syndrome. *Neurocomputing*, *69*(7-9), 969–974. doi:10.1016/j.neucom.2005.06.009

Louis, W., Komeili, M., & Hatzinakos, D. (2016). Continuous authentication using one-dimensional multi-resolution local binary patterns (1DMRLBP) in ECG biometrics. *IEEE Transactions on Information Forensics and Security*, *11*(12), 2818–2832. doi:10.1109/TIFS.2016.2599270

Martis, R. J., Acharya, U. R., Lim, C. M., & Suri, J. S. (2013). Characterization of ECG beats from cardiac arrhythmia using discrete cosine transform in PCA framework. *Knowledge-Based Systems*, *45*, 76–82. doi:10.1016/j.knosys.2013.02.007

Mehta, S., & Lingayat, N. (2008). Detection of P and T-waves in electrocardiogram. *Proceedings of the World Congress on Engineering and Computer Science*, 22-24.

Miakotko, L. (2017). *The impact of smartphones and mobile devices on human health and life*. Retrieved from http://www.nyu.edu/classes/keefer/waoe/miakotkol.pdf

Miguel-Hurtado, O., Guest, R., Stevenage, S. V., Neil, G. J., & Black, S. (2016). Comparing machine learning classifiers and linear/logistic regression to explore the relationship between hand dimensions and demographic characteristics. *PLoS One*, *11*(11), e0165521. doi:10.1371/journal.pone.0165521 PMID:27806075

Pan, J., & Tompkins, W. J. (1985). A real-time QRS detection algorithm. *IEEE Transactions on Biomedical Engineering*, *32*(3), 230–236. doi:10.1109/TBME.1985.325532 PMID:3997178

Patel, A. M., Gakare, P. K., & Cheeran, A. (2012). Real time ECG feature extraction and arrhythmia detection on a mobile platform. *International Journal of Computers and Applications*, *44*, 40–45.

Peter, S., Reddy, B. P., Momtaz, F., & Givargis, T. (2016). Design of secure ECG-based biometric authentication in body area sensor networks. *Sensors (Basel)*, *16*(4), 570. doi:10.339016040570 PMID:27110785

Pinto, R. J., Cardoso, S. J., Lourenço, A., & Carreiras, C. (2017). Towards a continuous biometric system based on ECG signals acquired on the steering wheel. *Sensors (Basel)*, *17*(10), 2228. doi:10.339017102228 PMID:28956856

Porée, F., Kervio, G., & Carrault, G. (2016). ECG biometric analysis in different physiological recording conditions. *Signal, Image and Video Processing*, *10*(2), 267–276. doi:10.100711760-014-0737-1

Proakis, J. G., & Manolakis, D. G. (2007). *Digital Signal Processing: Principles, Algorithms, and Applications*. New York: Pearson Education.

Samik, C., & Saurabh, P. (2016). Photoplethys-mogram signal based biometric recognition using linear discriminant classifier. *Proceedings of the 2nd International Conference on Control Instrumentation Energy & Communication (CIEC)*, 183-187.

Sornomo, L. (1987). A model based approach to QRS delineation. *Proceedings of the Computers and Biomedical Research*, 526–540. 10.1016/0010-4809(87)90024-3

ADDITIONAL READING

Abo-Zahhad, M., Ahmed, S. M., & Abbas, S. N. (2014). Biometric authentication based on PCG and ECG signals: Present status and future directions. *Signal, Image and Video Processing*, *8*(4), 739–751. doi:10.100711760-013-0593-4

Balakirsky, V. B., Ghazaryan, A. R., & Han Vinck, A. J. (2007). Testing the independence of two non–stationary random processes with applications to biometric authentication. *In Proceedings of the International Symposium on Information Theory* (pp. 2671-2675), France. 10.1109/ISIT.2007.4557622

Bhattacharyya, D., Ranjian, R., Alisherov, F., & Choi, M. (2009). Biometric authentication: A review, *International Journal of u- and e-Service. Science and Technology*, *2*(3), 13–28.

Boumbarov, O., Velchev, Y., Tonchev, K., & Paliy, I. (2011). *Face and ECG based multi–model biometric authentication. Advanced Biometric Technologies* (pp. 67–86). InTech; doi:10.5772/21842

Camara, C., Peris-Lopez, P., & Tapiador, J. E. (2015). Human identification using compressed ECG signals. *Journal of Medical Systems*, *39*(11), 1–10. doi:10.100710916-015-0323-2 PMID:26364201

Fang, S. C., & Chan, H. L. (2009). Human identification by quantifying similarity and dissimilarity in electrocardiogram phase space. *Pattern Recognition*, *42*(9), 1824–1831. doi:10.1016/j.patcog.2008.11.020

Jain, A. K., Ross, A. A., & Nandakumar, K. (2011). Introduction to Biometrics. New York, NY, USA: Springer Science+Business Media, LLC. doi:10.1007/978-0-387-77326-1

Kyoso, M., & Uchiyama, A. (2001). Development of an ECG identification system. *In Proceedings of the 23rd Annual International Conference of the IEEE Engineering in Medicine and Biology Society* (vol. 4, pp. 3721-3723), Istanbul, Turkey.

KEY TERMS AND DEFINITIONS

Authentication: A process in which the credentials provided are compared to those on file in a database of authorized users' information on a local operating system or within an authentication server. If the credentials match, the process is completed, and the user is granted authorization for access. The permissions and folders returned define both the environment the user sees and the way he can interact with it, including hours of access and other rights such as the amount of allocated storage space.

Biometry: A measurement and statistical analysis of people's physical and behavioral characteristics. The technology is mainly used for identification and access control, or for identifying individuals that are under surveillance. The basic premise of biometric authentication is that everyone is unique and an individual can be identified by his or her intrinsic physical or behavioral traits. (The term "biometrics" is derived from the Greek words "bio" meaning life and "metric" meaning to measure.)

Electrocardiography: The process of recording the electrical activity of the heart over a period of time using electrodes placed on a patient's body. These electrodes detect the tiny electrical changes on the skin that arise from the heart muscle depolarizing during each heartbeat. It is commonly a non-invasive procedure for recording electrical changes in the heart. The record, which is called an electrocardiogram, shows the series of waves that relate to the electrical impulses which occur during each beat of the heart. The results are printed on paper or displayed on a monitor. The waves in a normal record are named P, Q, R, S, and T and follow in alphabetical order. The number of waves may vary, and other waves may be present.

Feature Extraction: In machine learning, feature extraction starts from an initial set of measured data and builds derived values (features) intended to be informative and non-redundant, facilitating the subsequent learning and generalization steps, and in some cases leading to better human interpretations. Feature extraction is a dimensionality reduction process, where an initial set of raw variables is reduced to more manageable groups (features) for processing, while still accurately and completely describing the original data set.

Signal Acquisition: It is a process of sampling signals that measure real world physical conditions and converting the resulting samples into digital numeric values that can be manipulated by a computer. Data acquisition systems, abbreviated by the acronyms DAS or DAQ, typically convert analog waveforms into digital values for processing. The components of data acquisition systems include: Sensors converts physical parameters to electrical signals. Signal conditioning circuitry converts sensor signals into a form that can be converted to digital values. Analog-to-digital converters convert conditioned sensor signals to digital values.

Signal Processing: It concerns the analysis, synthesis, and modification of signals, which are broadly defined as functions conveying information about the behavior or attributes of some phenomenon. Signal processing techniques are used to improve signal transmission fidelity, storage efficiency, and subjective quality, and to emphasize or detect components of interest in a measured signal.

Template Matching: It is the act of checking a given sequence of features for the presence of the constituents of some pattern. In contrast to pattern recognition, the match usually has to be exact: "either it will or will not be a match."

Chapter 16
Digital Healthcare Security Issues:
Is There a Solution in Biometrics?

Punithavathi P.
VIT Chennai, India

Geetha Subbiah
VIT Chennai, India

ABSTRACT

Digital healthcare system, which is undergoing transformation phase to provide safe, swift, and improved quality care, is experiencing diverse problems. The serious threats to the digital healthcare system include misidentification of patients and healthcare-related frauds. Biometrics is a cutting-edge scientific field which overcomes the weaknesses of password-based authentication methods while ensuring a friction-free user experience. It enables unprecedented authentication capabilities based on human characteristics that cannot be replicated by fraudsters. The growing demand for biometrics solutions in digital healthcare system is mainly driven by the need to combat fraud, along with an initiative to preserve privacy of the patient besides with healthcare safety. This chapter examines how biometric technology can be applied to the digital healthcare services.

DOI: 10.4018/978-1-5225-8241-0.ch016

EVOLUTION OF DIGITAL HEALTHCARE

Digital healthcare is the combination of both digital and genomic technologies with healthcare and society such that the efficiency of healthcare delivery is enhanced, and medicines are made more personalized and precise. The health problems and challenges faced by patients have been addressed simultaneously by both information and communication technologies. Digital healthcare involves both hardware and software solutions and services, including web-based analysis, email, telemedicine, text messages, mobile phones and applications, and clinic or remote monitoring sensors. Commonly, digital healthcare involves development of interconnected health systems to improve the use of computational technologies, computational analysis techniques, smart devices, and communication media to aid patients and healthcare professionals manage health risks and illnesses, as well as promote health and well-being.

In simple words, the growth of Internet of Things (IoT) (Gubbi, Buyya, Marusic, & Palaniswami, 2013) has revolutionized healthcare domain too. The multi-disciplinary digital healthcare involves many stakeholders, including researchers, clinicians, and scientists with a wide range of expertise in engineering, healthcare, public health, social sciences, health economics and management. Several personal healthcare tools like wearable sensors are the most popular elements of the healthcare domain. These wearables can be a device to measure physical parameters such as pulse, blood pressure, muscle exertion, blood oxygen, etc., or a sweat biosensor embedded on smartwatch to measure biochemical parameters such as hydration levels, body electrolytes, etc.

India Brand Equity Foundation has estimated that there are currently 930 million mobile users, 360 million internet users, and half a billion new smartphone users projected in the next five years. With these developments, it has been assessed that India will be a money-spinning market for sensors and mobile-based apps, especially in healthcare. Soon the doctor may be just a click away.

The digital healthcare is the confluence of healthcare and technology which are pivot elements in improving the efficiency of the healthcare management. The digital healthcare applications are still in budding stage in India while significant inroads have been made in the use of digital health and healthcare IT initiatives globally. The "E-health" (National Health Portal of India, n.d.) initiatives under the Government of India's "Digital Healthcare Program" aimed at addressing the healthcare gap in the country are slowly but surely revolutionizing the public health scenario in the country. Coupled with the large number of start-ups that are driving the penetration of technology in the healthcare sector, this joint public private focus on digital is paving the way to the future.

Cloud based services are gaining traction in the digital healthcare community. The combination of reliability, cost effectiveness and security has prompted many healthcare organizations to move data to the cloud for storage and analysis. New cloud opportunities are arising in promoting collaboration among care givers and in analysing large data sets (e.g. genomics). A GI cloud initiative under "MeghRaj" Policy (National Cloud of India, n.d.), Ministry of Electronics and Information Technology, Government of India, proves to be a cutting edge in providing seamless digital health services to rural people of India.

THREATS TO DIGITAL HEALTHCARE

In the United States (US), healthcare is one of the biggest industries in trillion dollar club. The US has spent more on healthcare per person than any other nation in 2011 (Biometric Identification in Healthcare, n.d.), as per the World Health Organization (WHO). This trillion-dollar industry has always been under threat from malicious intruders as shown in Figure 1, compared to other sectors with huge economy.

The healthcare fraud consumes $80 billion a year in the US, as shown in Figure 2, according to an estimate by Federal Bureau of Investigation (FBI). Currently threats are even coming from the internet other than usual healthcare fraud like duplicate claims, fake billing, etc.

A study conducted by NTA in 2002 on 500 participants with approximately 21 passwords each, has revealed that about 81% of the participants use same password and about 30% of the participants write their passwords in a file. In 2017, "WannaCry"

Figure 1. Data Breaches in Various Industries

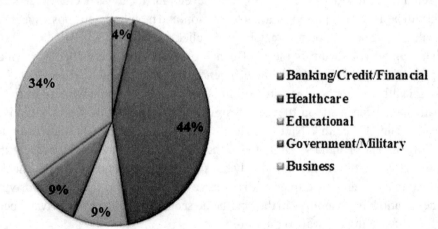

Figure 2. Impacts of healthcare data breaches during the period of 2015-2019

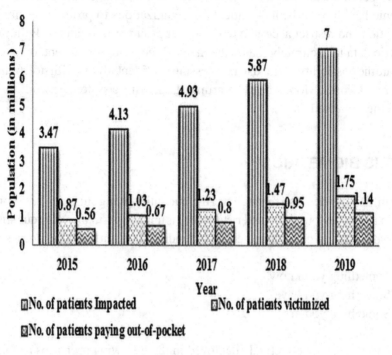

☐No. of patients Impacted ☐No. of patients victimized

☐No. of patients paying out-of-pocket

malware (What is Wannacry Ransomware, n.d.) attack badly affected the hospitals of several nations. Due to this attack, several computers and devices were left encrypted. It has become evident that the higher the dependency on information technology, the higher is the cyber-attack on healthcare facility mainly the patient records. The healthcare facilities have several operational challenges like patient identification and patient record maintenance.

The hazards of stolen health care data to name a few are financial loss, inaccurate medical records and, thus, misdiagnosis. In last four years, there has been a steep increase of criminal intrusions into health care systems have risen 100% in the past four years, according to a recent Ponemon report (https://www.ponemon.org/library). In several incidents improper identification of patients has led to death of patients. A severe warning has been given by FBI to ward of serious cyber threats during mandatory migration to electronic health records. The FBI has emphasized the rise of "malicious actors" who target on medical device fields and health care data.

At a broader level, biometric authentication solutions prevent patients from becoming victims of medical identity theft. And unlike other types of identity theft (i.e. credit card), medical identity theft victims are rarely notified by their healthcare provider about suspicious account activity. Given the highly-sensitive nature of electronic health records, it is critical for organizations to properly secure patient information and restrict access to only a select group of individuals. By leveraging biometric data to accurately match the medical record to the patient, organizations eliminate the possibility of fraudsters accessing confidential data with stolen employee cards or passwords. Moreover, cybercriminals entering a system network are unable to steal the protected data.

WHAT IS BIOMETRICS?

The term "Biometrics" is a means to verify or identify living subjects. The biometrics is physical or behavioural characteristic which is unique, permanent and quantitatively measurable identity of each and every individual. In a nut shell biometrics is:

1. "Something you know"
2. "Something you have"
3. "Something you are"

Biometrics can be effectively deployed in the following scenarios as follows:

1. **Verification/Authentication:** Is a one-to-one matching scenario to verify the claim "I am Mr. /Mrs. ...."
2. **Identification:** Is one-to-many matching scenario to answer the question "Who am I?"

The functions of four major components of biometric system are as follows:

1. **Scanner:** Scanning and capturing digital image/features of alive person's biometric characteristic
2. **Feature Extractor:** Creating template from captured raw biometric data
3. **Matcher:** Matching previously created/stored biometric template with a query template
4. **User Interface:** Communicating the match result

There are two stages in biometric system process – enrolment and matching.

- **Enrolment:** It is the process of capturing the biometric sample of an individual (e.g., using a sensor for fingerprint, camera for face recognition, microphone for speech recognition, camera for iris recognition). The unique features are then extracted from the biometric sample to create a template and store it in database.

- **Matching:** It is the process of matching a query template acquired from user during authorization grant with the template stored in database. A matching score is generated based on a determination of the common elements between the two templates. The threshold value for generating matching score is determined by the system designers based upon the convenience requirements of the system and security level.

BIOMETRIC MODALITIES

Biometrics enables automated identification or verification of individuals based on their unique traits. Biometric modalities can be classified as follows:

Physiological/Static Biometrics

Static biometrics refers to inherent physiological traits of an individual such as fingerprint, iris, hand-geometry, Deoxy-ribo Nucleic Acid (DNA), ears and other traits as shown in Figure 3. These attributes are acquired by each and every human during birth. In practice it is very hard to replicate them. Hence these attributes are highly reliable when used for identification.

Behavioural/Dynamic Biometrics

Dynamic behavioural characteristics can be related to the behavioural characteristics of an individual. The examples include walking gait, voice, keystroke dynamics, mouse dynamics, etc. as shown in Figure 4. Brainwave signals are one among the latest dynamic behavioural area currently being explored. It is used to determine a person's mental state. These biometric traits ensure a high level of accuracy when tested in real time. Dynamic biometrics proves to be an active trait among the behavioural biometrics and they can be easily tracked in real time using emerging technologies. Several security experts prefer applied dynamic biometrics for verification purposes because of the fact that the process of acquiring static biometrics is a time-consuming process. The static biometrics is susceptible to several threats too.

Figure 3. Physiological biometrics

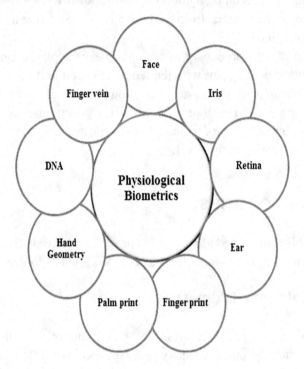

Selection of Biometric Modality

The process of selecting an appropriate biometric modality depends on the following factors:

1. Based on the nature of environment in which verification or identification process is performed
2. Based on the user profile, requirements for matching accuracy and throughput
3. Based on the cost and capabilities of the system
4. Based on the cultural issues which affects user acceptance

The comparison of between different biometric technologies is shown in Table 1. It also rates the performance of the metrics.

Figure 4. Behavioural biometrics

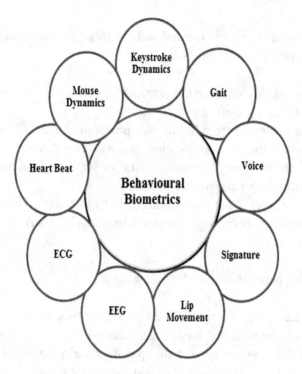

Table 1. Comparison of popular biometric modalities

Biometric Modality	Accuracy	Uniqueness	Failure-to-Enrol Rate	Record Size	Universality	Durability
Face	M	M	L	H	H	M
Fingerprint	H	M	M	M	H	H
Hand Geometry	L	L	L	L	M	M
Iris	M	H	L	M	M	H
Signature	L	M	L	M	M	M
Vein	M	H	L	M	H	H
Voice	L	M	M	H	H	L

(https://fas.org/irp/agency/dod/dsb/biometrics.pdf)
*H- High, M- Medium, L- Low

WHY BIOMETRICS?

The healthcare identification is secured and enhanced by biometric technology. It is evident from the following claims:

1. Authenticating the patient in the provider's location will prevent card sharing and patient identity theft
2. Provider is prevented from billing for "phantom claims" or services when a patient is not at the provider location on the service date
3. Managing and verifying "encounter data" or services from providers so that data for setting of managed care rates
4. Checking the level of potential fraud called "upcoding" by creating an "audit trail" comprising check in and check out times for comparison against type of service provided

The additional benefits will be the following:

1. Providers can verify if a patient is eligible at the time of service so that faster payments can be collected for services rendered
2. Costs and risks associated with the 'pay & chase' programs can be reduced hence attempt to recoup inaccurate and fraudulent payments
3. Patient safety is increased by reducing medical errors due to mismatch or incomplete records
4. Unique patient and provider master index are provided to ensure that patient records in multiple provider locations are linked accurately
5. Secured authentication of patients and providers; and protection of patient identity and patient health care information go hand-in-hand
6. Biometrics can be employed to verify if an individual requesting for a particular treatment is eligible in cases where the individuals' eligibility for certain services changes often
7. Inventory theft can be reduced. For instance providing accurate audit trails detailing the way in which the individual has accessed the inventory

BIOMETRICS VS. TOKENS/PASSWORDS/SMART CARDS

With their increasingly frustrating parameters (warnings like password must be at least 12 characters long, should contain a capital letter, a number, a special character, and cannot contain a word, name, or a place), passwords can easily be forgotten, forcing developers to include a password reset feature that can be bypassed through simple social engineering or a brute force attack. The hackers can easily tap into a user terminal's Bluetooth or Wi-Fi connection and "sniff" network traffic to swipe both locally stored passwords as well as passwords that unsuspecting users are typing in when checking their bank account balance, for instance. Concisely, passwords represent an antiquated system of authentication, one that has no place in the world of internet, where the stakes and risks of both monetary and identity theft are among the greatest.

The front lines of security are identity management and access control. The insiders are separated from outsiders accurately by identifying the users and controlling what they do within your systems. The traditional tool for this task – the password – is apparently inadequate for the job. The emerging alternative solution is biometrics.

Passwords are the most common user authentication methods. It is comprised of a sequence of alphanumeric characters typed through a keypad or keyboard. For instance we largely use the Personal Identification Number (PINs) in bank applications. The followings claims prove that the password and PIN have not been an effective method:

1. Mostly the users choose date of birth of them or their partner, telephone number, names, children/pets, and other obvious choices. This has prone to be susceptible to guessing attacks. A test has shown that there is 90% chance of guessing the password correctly and gaining access to a system
2. The users tend to write the passwords on a sheet of paper for future use. In such case the password is revealed to the external world easily. A poll conducted in United Kingdom has revealed that nearly one out of three people write down the PIN for their bank card. It has also been estimated that about one out of five people have been unable to withdraw money from an automatic teller machine due to the reason that they have been unable to remember their PIN
3. An imposter may steal the password just by observing the owner entering it into a system
4. In case if an owner wants to grant certain privilege to a colleague or a friend, the password is deliberately lent thus causing password breach

The user is not required to remember the password or PIN just by putting it into a Smart Card or Magnetic Strip Card. On the other hand the system can track the log details of the person at certain point of time. It becomes impossible to determine if the card has been used by an authorized user or an imposter. It becomes evident that the smart cards or other tokens are robust against the problems arisen by claims 1 and 2 but are susceptible to the claims 3 and 4.

The only way to solve all the above problems is to use biometrics. This is an efficient way to guarantee the presence of the owner at the place where a transaction is made. It is very difficult to counterfeit the biometric characteristics. The biometrics cannot be forgotten or lent like smart cards.

BIOMETRICS IN DIGITAL HEALTHCARE

The term "healthcare biometrics" refers to biometric applications in doctors' offices, hospitals, or for use in monitoring patients. This can include access control, identification, workforce management or patient record storage. Biometrics in healthcare often takes two forms: providing access control to resources and patient identification solutions. Many hospitals and healthcare organizations are currently deploying biometric security architecture. Secure identification is critical in the healthcare system, both to control logical access to centralized archives of digitized patients' data, and to limit physical access to buildings and hospital wards, and to authenticate medical and social support personnel.

There is also an increasing need to identify patients with a high degree of certainty. Identity verification solutions based on biometric technology can provide identity assurance and authentication, thereby lowering healthcare fraud instances, while increasing privacy and security. Biometric technology can add operational efficiencies to the healthcare system that reduce costs, reduce fraud, and increase patient satisfaction by reducing medical errors. As electronic health records and personal health records become more commonly used, biometrics are being utilized as an authentication mechanism by medical facilities, patients and insurers.

The primary focus of using biometrics in healthcare sector is for providing solutions to staff authentication and patient identification. The biometrics can also be combined with smart cards or passwords to secure access to sensitive patient records and to assist with patient registration requirements. A research study performed by Biometrics Research Group, Inc. (n.d.) has revealed that by 2020, the phase value of biometric solutions in the healthcare market will reach up to a value of US$5 billion. Biometric use will reflect the growing demand for healthcare fraud prevention, along with the need to improve patient privacy and healthcare safety.

The Government of India has planned to make the healthcare plan accessible through Aadhaar which is the world's largest biometric database, governed by the Unique Identification Authority of India (UIDAI, n.d.) and is currently used to authenticate delivery of social services including school attendance, natural gas subsidies to India's rural poor, and direct wage payments to bank accounts. In its first budget, the government has allocated $340 million to speed up the Aadhaar registration process. The government's objective is now to enrol the citizens with Aadhaar. UIDAI has already enrolled about 700 million people and issued unique identification numbers to 650 million. The introduction of universal healthcare to India's citizens will arguably be the most ambitious use of the biometric database. The process of linking healthcare services in India would help in keeping a check on any fraudulent insurance claims or ghost beneficiaries.

Biometrics for Authenticating Healthcare Practitioner/Patient

To prevent any errors which could mean the difference between life and death, there is a pressing need to find a highly accurate method to secure critical healthcare information and prevent any errors. Biometric modalities like fingerprints, face, iris, voice, etc., can be used to uniquely identify individuals from an entire population even in case of twins. The usage of biometric identification systems in hospitals will increase security and privacy as well as accuracy of patient identification. The patient safety is thus ensured.

Government regulations mandate the tracking of electronic records each time a physician or healthcare professional accesses a patient's record. Such tracking is extremely important to maintain confidentiality of patient data and avoid any cases of medical fraud. Implementing fingerprint authentication makes it extremely convenient for medical personnel to access patient data with a simple fingerprint swipe. It ensures that the person accessing the record is definitely who they claim to be and also have the right to see the patient's record. Any mismatch can be flagged instantly and notified to the appropriate authorities that some intruder is trying to access the secure medical records.

Biometrics for Patient Identification

When patients are not identified correctly, bad things happen. Critical health information can be linked to a duplicate medical record or the wrong record. This affects patient safety, data integrity, and healthcare costs. Inaccurate patient identification costs the average hospital several million per year from denied claims and that's just the tip of the iceberg. Patient safety and lives are also at risk when data is matched to the wrong patient or missing from the patient record. Biometric patient identification offers numerous advantages over manual identification of patient record in Master Patient Index (MPI). These are:

1. **Accuracy:** Biometrics offers unmatched accuracy. The whole process from capture to authentication is digitized. There is no human element of error

involved in matching the scanned biometric of a new patient against the stored records and is fully automated. This results in high accuracy. Overlays and duplicate medical records cannot happen with biometric patient identification.

2. **Reliability:** Biometrics technologies such iris recognition, fingerprint matching etc., have evolved to very high standards. The False Acceptance Ratio (FAR) and False Rejection Ratio (FRR) occur at very low and insignificant levels. The results of matching against the database are consistent and reliable.

3. **Speed:** Automatic scans and high-speed matching lead to quick authentication in a few seconds. This is a major improvement over manually going through all the MPI records with similar data and trying to identify the correct one.

4. **Patient Enrolment and Admission Process is Streamlined:** The process of patient enrolment and admission becomes fast and hassle free as a simple biometric scan is all it takes to identify and admit a patient.

5. **Security:** Biometric patient identification eliminates medical identity thefts. Instances of medical identity thefts have caused huge financial losses to patients and healthcare providers alike. There are certain stringent Health Insurance Portability and Accountability Act (HIPAA) standards (https://www.hhs.gov/hipaa/for-professionals/security/laws-regulations/index.html) around the same.

Biometrics for Workforce Management in Hospital

Authentication implies identification and access control for premises and system networks while monitoring includes surveillance, time, and attendance. The market is mainly driven by the need for organizations to adopt biometric workforce management to replace traditional security systems. These include identity cards, passwords and keys that are traditionally used to record clock in and clock out.

Market segmentation of biometrics in workforce management by application

1. Identification
2. Access control
3. Monitoring

Biometric access control systems restrict unauthorized access, thus ensuring safety of employees and mitigating the risk of tampering important data. People are granted access only when their identity is confirmed by the information stored in the database of the enterprise.

Biometrics for Financial Sector in Digital Healthcare

One area where biometrics has begun to take hold is healthcare insurance. A study by the Ponemon Institute (https://www.ponemon.org/library) found nearly 1.5 million Americans to be victims of medical identity theft. Healthcare fraud is estimated to cost between $70 billion and $255 billion a year, accounting for as much as 10% of total US healthcare costs. Many insurers are using biometrics to help reduce billing fraud by eliminating the sharing of medical insurance cards between patients, or by making it more difficult for a person to assume another's identity. For example, as an alternative to paper insurance cards, a biometric iris scan can immediately transport proof of a patient's physical presence at a healthcare facility.

Biometric technology is also assisting healthcare insurers with compliance and data integrity standards — in particular with those set by the HIPAA. For example, in addition to adhering to requirements for automatic logoff and user identification, insurers must implement additional safeguards that include PINs, passwords and some method of biometrics. Fingerprint biometrics helps hospitals to ensure compliance to government regulations such as the HIPAA and other such laws worldwide that mandate protection of patient privacy. With fingerprint authentication, only those who are authorised can access patient data. Every time a patient record is accessed, a concrete audit trail is created that helps to ensure compliance and ensures true accountability. Thus patients and healthcare professionals can feel very secure and confident about the privacy of their healthcare data with fingerprint technology.

Biometrics in Public Health Surveillance

The new trend is driven by the need for early detection of surreptitious biological attacks. The trend is likely to accelerate because evidence is accumulating and these new approaches are successful. They can detect outbreaks earlier than existing methods and even identify outbreaks that have previously gone unnoticed. This trend has important implications for researchers and developers in clinical informatics because it is creating new design requirements for clinical information system.

Biometrics in Remote Patient Monitoring

Bioelectrical signals especially, the Electro Cardio Gram (ECG) and the Electro Encephalo Gram (EEG) are emerging biometric identities. Unlike anatomical biometric identities that have two-dimensional data representation, the ECG or EEG is physiologically low-frequency signals that have one-dimensional data representation. Using the ECG or EEG signals as biometric may offer the following characteristics:

universality, measurability, uniqueness, and robustness. Universality refers that each (live) individual must possess the ECG or EEG signals. Measurability refers that the ECG or EEG signals can be recorded using electrodes placed on the body surface near to the particular organ (e.g., chest, hands, and legs for the ECG and along the scalp for the EEG) as shown in Figure 5.

The biological information of a person genetically governed from deoxyribonucleic acid or ribonucleic acid proteins. Eventually, the proteins are responsible for the existence of uniqueness in the certain body parts. Similarly, the organs like heart and brain are composed of protein tissues called myocardium and glial cells, respectively. Therefore, the electrical signals evoked from these organs show uniqueness among individuals. Last but not the least, the replay or reproduction of the ECG or EEG signals is very difficult until the same individual is not called for the re-enrolment. Therefore, the proposed methods using the ECG or EEG as biometric are sufficiently non-vulnerable to spoof attacks. Consequently, the fact of using the ECG or EEG signals as biometric modalities yields an assurance that the biometric data is coming from the legitimate individual who is indeed present during the enrolment. It is an essential condition for the perfect working of a practical biometric system.

Figure 5. Architecture of remote patient monitoring system (http://iot4health.utu.fi/?p=53)

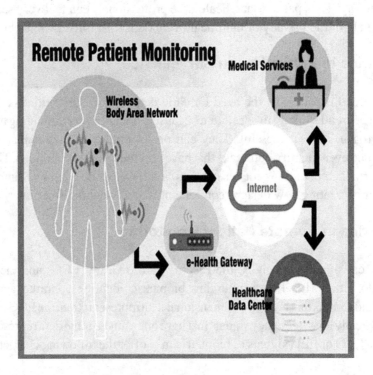

CONCLUSION

A blooming digital health care sector should be able to provide world class service to all people. The vision of the digital healthcare should be imparting secure and reliable health care service. The healthcare data should be accessible whenever required by authorized personnel alone. Biometrics plays a vital role in authenticating the medical personnel and controlling/managing the workforce. The most pressing challenge of healthcare industry in today's society is patient safety. The elimination of medical identity theft and prevention of duplicate medical records stand out as two of the main culprits which jeopardize the integrity of the healthcare industry. Biometrics plays a key role in combating the healthcare data breaches. The root cause of several problems in healthcare industry is generally inaccurate patient identification. This costs millions of dollars per year including legal and administrative expenses and liabilities. This problem can be rectified only through the adoption of biometric technology. The biometric template can be directly linked to an electronic medical record for accurate credentialing on subsequent visits. This ensures that no duplicate medical records can be created, and the right care is delivered to the right patient.

REFERENCES

Biometric Identification in Healthcare. (n.d.). Retrieved from https://www.bayometric. com/biometric-identification-in-the-healthcare-sector/

Biometrics Research Group Inc. (n.d.). Retrieved from https://in.linkedin.com/ company/biometrics-research-group-inc-

2013 . Data Breaches. (2013). Retrieved from http://www.idtheftcenter.org/ITRC-Surveys-Studies/2013-data-breaches.html

Digital Health: A Review. (n.d.). Retrieved from https://www.accenture.com/us-en/ insight-revenue-risk-healthcare-provider-cyber-security-inaction

Gubbi, J., Buyya, R., Marusic, S., & Palaniswami, M. (2013). Internet of Things (IoT): A vision, architectural elements, and future directions. *Future Generation Computer Systems*, *29*(7), 1645–1660. doi:10.1016/j.future.2013.01.010

Indian Express. (2016). Retrieved from http://indianexpress.com/article/technology/ tech-news-technology/digital-health-wearables-health-apps-smartwatch-health-apps-2797787/

Iot4Health. (n.d.). Retrieved from http://iot4health.utu.fi/?p=53

National Health Portal of India. (n.d.). Retrieved from https://www.nhp.gov.in/e-health-india_mty

NIC, National Cloud of India. (n.d.). Retrieved from https://cloud.gov.in/

Ponemon Institute. (n.d.). *Research studies and White paper*. Retrieved from https://www.ponemon.org/library

Report of the defense science board task force on defence biometrics. (2007). Retrieved from https://fas.org/irp/agency/dod/dsb/biometrics.pdf

Summary of HIPAA Security Rule. (n.d.). Retrieved from https://www.hhs.gov/hipaa/for-professionals/security/laws-regulations/index.html

UIDAI. (n.d.). Retrieved from https://uidai.gov.in/

What Is WANNACRY Ransomware. (n.d.). Retrieved from https://www.thesun.co.uk/tech/3562470/wannacry-ransomware-nhs-cyber-attack-hackers-virus/

Compilation of References

2013 . Data Breaches. (2013). Retrieved from http://www.idtheftcenter.org/ITRC-Surveys-Studies/2013-data-breaches.html

Al Fahdi, M., Clarke, N. L., & Furnell, S. M. (2013). Challenges to digital forensics: A survey of researchers and practitioners attitudes and opinions. *Proceeding in IEEE conference in Information Security for South Africa*, 1-8. 10.1109/ISSA.2013.6641058

Ali, A. I. (2014). Iris recognition using Haar wavelet transform. *Journal of Al-Nahrain University*, *17*(1), 80–86.

Allen, W. H. (2005). Computer Forensics. *IEEE Security and Privacy*, *3*(4), 59–62. doi:10.1109/MSP.2005.95

Alrajeh, N. A., Khan, S., & Shams, B. (2013). Intrusion detection systems in wireless sensor networks: A review. *International Journal of Distributed Sensor Networks*, *9*(5), 167575. doi:10.1155/2013/167575

Alsheikh, M. A., Lin, S., Niyato, D., & Tan, H. P. (2014). Machine learning in wireless sensor networks: Algorithms, strategies, and applications. *IEEE Communications Surveys and Tutorials*, *16*(4), 1996–2018. doi:10.1109/COMST.2014.2320099

Amro, B. (2017). Malware Detection Techniques for Mobile Devices. *International Journal of Mobile Network Communications & Telematics*, *7*(4/5/6),01-10. doi:10.5121/ijmnct.2017.7601

An Introduction to the Internet of Things (IoT). (2013). Lopez Research LLC. Retrieved from https://www.cisco.com/c/dam/en_us/solutions/trends/iot/introduction_to_IoT_november.pdf

Antic, B., Letic, D., Culibrk, D., & Crnojevic, V. (2009). K-means based segmentation for real-time zenithal people counting. *16th IEEE International Conference on Image Processing (ICIP)*. 10.1109/ICIP.2009.5414001

Arabaci. (2018). *Blockchain consensus mechanisms- the case of natural disasters July 2018 basics*. Retrieved from https://pdfs.semanticscholar.org/0afd/a615470760dd1cd661fe4b5f7d3e9b39cdf3.pdf

Arends. (2018). *Malware Analysis - Tools and Techniques* (Report). Academic Press.

Ashraf. (2012). *Mobile Banking Security- a security model* (Report). Academic Press.

Bach, Mihaljevic, & Zagar. (2018). Comparative analysis of blockchain consensus algorithms. *Information and Communication Technology Electronics and Microelectronics (MIPRO) 41st International Convention on*, 1545-1550.

Badri, L. (2010). Development of neural networks for noise reduction. *The International Arab Journal of Information Technology, 7*(3), 289–294.

Bai, J., Wu, Y., Wang, G., Yang, S. X., & Qiu, W. (2006). *A very distinctive intrusion detection model based on multilayer self-organizing maps and principal part analysis. In Advances in Neural Networks*. Springer.

Banin, S., & Dyrkolbotn, G. O. (2018). Multinomial malware classification via low-level features. *Digital Investigation, 26*, S107–S117. doi:10.1016/j.diin.2018.04.019

Bannan. (2016). *The IoT threat to privacy*. Retrieved from https://techcrunch.com/2016/08/14/the-iot-threat-to-privacy/

Barandiaran, J., Murguia, B., & Boto, F. (2008). Real-Time People Counting Using Multiple Lines. *Ninth International Workshop on Image Analysis for Multimedia Interactive Services*, 159-162. 10.1109/WIAMIS.2008.27

Barika, F., Hadjar, K., & El-Kadhi, N. (2009). Artificial neural network for mobile IDS resolution. Security and Management Journal, 271–277.

Bellekens, X. J., Tachtatzis, C., Atkinson, R. C., Renfrew, C., & Kirkham, T. (2014, September). A highly-efficient memory-compression scheme for GPU-accelerated intrusion detection systems. In *Proceedings of the 7th International Conference on Security of Information and Networks* (p. 302). ACM. 10.1145/2659651.2659723

Benchea, R., & Gavriluţ, D. T. (2014, July). Combining restricted Boltzmann machine and one side perceptron for malware detection. In *International Conference on Conceptual Structures* (pp. 93-103). Springer. 10.1007/978-3-319-08389-6_9

Biel, L., Pettersson, O., Philipson, L., & Wide, P. (2001). ECG analysis: A new approach to human identification. *IEEE Transactions on Instrumentation and Measurement, 50*(3), 808–812. doi:10.1109/19.930458

Biometric Identification in Healthcare. (n.d.). Retrieved from https://www.bayometric.com/biometric-identification-in-the-healthcare-sector/

Biometrics Research Group Inc. (n.d.). Retrieved from https://in.linkedin.com/company/biometrics-research-group-inc-

Bird, N., Masoud, O., Papanikolopoulos, N., & Isaacs, A. (2005). Detection of Loitering Individuals in Public Transportation Areas. *IEEE Transactions on Intelligent Transportation Systems, 6*(2), 167–177. doi:10.1109/TITS.2005.848370

Boriev, Z. V., Sokolov, S. S., & Nyrkov, A. P. (2015). Review of modern biometric user authentication and their development prospects. *Proceedings of the IOP Conference Series. Materials Science and Engineering, 91*(1). doi:10.1088/1757899X/91/1/012063

Bostrom, N. (2015), *TED Talk on Artificial Intelligence*. Retrieved from https://en.tiny.ted.com/talks/nick_bostrom_what_happens_when_our_computers_get_smarter_than_we_are

Brown, L. M., Senior, A. W., Tian, Y., Connell, J., Hampapur, A., Shu, C., ... Lu, M. (2005). Performance Evaluation of Surveillance Systems under Varying Conditions. *Proc. IEEE PETS Workshop*, 1-8.

Butun, I., Morgera, S. D., & Sankar, R. (2014). A survey of intrusion detection systems in wireless sensor networks. *IEEE Communications Surveys and Tutorials, 16*(1), 266–282. doi:10.1109/SURV.2013.050113.00191

Cachin & Vukolić. (2017). *Consensus Protocols in the Wild*. IBM Research.

Cady, F. (2017). *The Data Science Handbook*. John Wiley & Sons. doi:10.1002/9781119092919

Canny, J. (1986). A Computational Approach to Edge Detection. *IEEE Transactions on Pattern Analysis and Machine Intelligence*, 679-698.

Cao, P., & Wang, Z. (2004). Efficient top-k query calculation in distributed networks. In *Proc. of ACM PODC*. ACM. 10.1145/1011767.1011798

Casey, E. (2011). *Digital evidence and computer crime: Forensic science, computers, and the internet*. Academic Press.

Chatzigiannakis, V., Androulidakis, G., & Maglaris, B. (2004). A Distributed Intrusion Detection Prototype Using Security Agents. In *Proceedings of Workshop of the HP Open View University Association*. University of Evry.

Chen, B. (2010). *Energy Efficient Top-K Query Processing in Wireless sensor network. Canberra, ACT, Australia, October 26 30, Toronto*. Ontaria, Canada: ACM.

Chen, B., Liang, W., & Yu, J. X. (2010). *Online Time Interval Top-k Queries in Wireless Sensor Networks. Management*. MDM.

Cheng, J., Jiang, H., Liu, J., Liu, W., & Wang, C. (2011). On Efficient Processing of Continuous Historical Top-k Queries in Wireless Sensor Networks. *IEEE Trans. Vehicular Technology, VOL., 60*(5), 2363–2367. doi:10.1109/TVT.2011.2148203

Cheng, S., Li, J., & Yu, L. (2012). Location Aware Peak Value Queries in Sensor Networks. *Proceeding IEEE INFOCOM*, 486-494. 10.1109/INFCOM.2012.6195789

Chen, M., Okada, S., & Nitta, K. (2011). Effectiveness of haptic interaction in online negotiation between Chinese and Japanese. *2011 IEEE International Conference on Granular Computing*, 111-114. 10.1109/GRC.2011.6122577

Chen, S., Xu, H., Liu, D., Hu, B., & Wang, H. (2014). A vision of IoT: Applications, challenges, and opportunities with China perspective. *IEEE Internet of Things Journal*, *1*(4), 349–359. doi:10.1109/JIOT.2014.2337336

Cho, Y., Son, J., & Chung, Y. D. (2008). POT: An Efficient Top-K Monitoring Method for Spatially Correlated Sensor Readings. *Proc. Fifth Workshop Data Management for Sensor Networks (DMSN '08)*, 8-13. 10.1145/1402050.1402053

Chumachenko. (2017). *Machine Learning Methods for Malware Detection and Classification* (Thesis). Academic Press.

Clough, J. (2015). *Principles of Cyber Crimes*. Cambridge University Press.

Condoluci, M., Araniti, G., Mahmoodi, T., & Dohler, M. (2016, April). Enabling the IoT Machine Age With 5G:Machine-Type Multicast Services for Innovative Real-Time Applications. *IEEE Access: Practical Innovations, Open Solutions*, *4*, 5555–5569. doi:10.1109/ACCESS.2016.2573678

Conti, M., Dehghantanha, A., Franke, K., & Watson, S. (2018). *Internet of Things security and forensics: Challenges and opportunities*. Academic Press.

Costa, D. G., Figuerêdo, S., & Oliveira, G. (2017). Cryptography in Wireless Multimedia Sensor Networks: A Survey and Research Directions. *Cryptography*, *1*(1), 4. doi:10.3390/cryptography1010004

Dahl, G. E., Stokes, J. W., Deng, L., & Yu, D. (2013, May). Large-scale malware classification using random projections and neural networks. In *Acoustics, Speech and Signal Processing (ICASSP), 2013 IEEE International Conference on* (pp. 3422-3426). IEEE. 10.1109/ICASSP.2013.6638293

Dai, M., Zhu, B., Zheng, G., & Wang, Y. (2015). A method of ECG identification based on the weighted correlation coefficient. *Proceedings of the Chinese Conference on Biometric Recognition*, 633-640. 10.1007/978-3-319-25417-3_74

Dakhil, I. G., & Ibrahim, A. A. (2018). Design and implementation of fingerprint identification system based on k-NN neural network. *Journal of Computer and Communications*, *6*(03), 1–18. doi:10.4236/jcc.2018.63001

Das, S., Liu, Y., Zhang, W., & Chandramohan, M. (2016). Semantics-based online malware detection: Towards efficient real-time protection against malware. *IEEE Transactions on Information Forensics and Security*, *11*(2), 289–302. doi:10.1109/TIFS.2015.2491300

DeFranco, J. F. (2013). *What Every Engineer Should Know About Cyber Security and Digital Forensics*. CRC Press. doi:10.1201/b15581

Deirmenjian, J. M. (1999). Stalking in cyberspace. *The Journal of the American Academy of Psychiatry and the Law*, *27*, 407–413. PMID:10509940

Derval, N., Bordachar, P., Lim, H. S., Sacher, F., Ploux, S., Laborderie, J., ... Jaïs, P. (2014). Impact of pacing site on QRS duration and its relationship to hemodynamic response in cardiac resynchronization therapy for congestive heart failure. *Journal of Cardiovascular Electrophysiology*, *25*(9), 1012–1020. doi:10.1111/jce.12464 PMID:24891271

Digital Health: A Review. (n.d.). Retrieved from https://www.accenture.com/us-en/insight-revenue-risk-healthcare-provider-cyber-security-inaction

Dunkels, A., Eriksson, J., Finne, N., & Tsiftes, N. (2011). *Powertrace: Network-level power profiling for low-power wireless networks.* Academic Press.

Duran-Faundez, C., Lecuire, V., & Lepage, F. (2011). Tiny block-size coding for energy-efficient image compression and communication in wireless camera sensor networks. *Signal Processing Image Communication*, *26*(8-9), 466–481. doi:10.1016/j.image.2011.07.005

Edson. (2016). Ecolab uses cloud computing to save freshwater on the ground. *Microsoft Internet of Things.* Retrieved from https://blogs.microsoft.com/iot/2016/04/05/ecolab-uses-cloud-computing-to-save-freshwater-on-the-ground/#XMQgmhjSRmdtDQ7B.99

Eid, M. A., & Al Osman, H. (2016). Affective Haptics: Current Research and Future Directions. *IEEE Access: Practical Innovations, Open Solutions*, *4*, 26–40. doi:10.1109/ACCESS.2015.2497316

Ellison, L., & Akdeniz, Y. (1998, December). *Cyber-stalking: The Regulation of Harassment on the Internet. Criminal Law Review,* 29–48.

Felt, A. P., Chin, E., Hanna, S., Song, D., & Wagner, D. (2011, October). Android permissions demystified. In *Proceedings of the 18th ACM conference on Computer and communications security* (pp. 627-638). ACM.

Finch, E. (2001). *The Criminalisation of Stalking: Constructing the problem and Evaluating the solution.* London: Cavendish Publishing. doi:10.4324/9781843142638

Finch, E. (2002). Stalking: A Violent Crime or a Crime of Violence? *Howard Journal*, *41*(5), 422–433. doi:10.1111/1468-2311.00256

Fu, J., Xue, J., Wang, Y., Liu, Z., & Shan, C. (2018). Malware Visualization for Fine-Grained Classification. *IEEE Access: Practical Innovations, Open Solutions*, *6*, 14510–14523. doi:10.1109/ACCESS.2018.2805301

Gandhi, B. M. (2017). *Indian Penal Code* (4th ed.). Eastern Book Company.

Garcia, F. C. C., Muga, I. I., & Felix, P. (2016). *Random forest for malware classification.* arXiv preprint arXiv:1609.07770.

Gatti, E., Caruso, G., Bordegoni, M., & Spence, C. (2013). Can the feel of the haptic interaction modify a user's emotional state? *2013 World Haptics Conference (WHC)*, 247-252. 10.1109/WHC.2013.6548416

Ge, T., Zdonik, S., & Madden, S. (2009). Top-k Queries on Uncertain Data: On Score Distribution and Typical Answers. SIGMOD'09, 375-387.

Geetha, S., & Phamila, A. V. (2016). Combating security breaches and criminal activity in the digital sphere. Hershey, PA: Information Science Reference. doi:10.4018/978-1-5225-0193-0

Gibert, D. (2016). *Convolutional neural networks for malware classification* (Doctoral dissertation). Dept. of Computer Science, UPC.

Gillespie, A. A. (2002). Child protection on the Internet - challenges for criminal law. *Child and Family law Quarterly Journal*, 411-412.

Gonalves, D., & Costa, D. (2015). A Survey of Image Security in Wireless Sensor Networks. *Journal of Imaging*, 4-30.

Graevenitz, G. (2007). Biometric authentication in relation to payment systems and ATMs. *DuD Datenschutz Und Datensicherheit*, 681-683.

Granja, F. M., & Rafael, G. D. R. (2017). The preservation of digital evidence and its admissibility in the court. *International Journal of Electronic Security and Digital Forensics*, *9*(1), 1–18. doi:10.1504/IJESDF.2017.081749

Gubbi, J., Buyya, R., Marusic, S., & Palaniswami, M. (2013). Internet of Things (IoT): A vision, architectural elements, and future directions. *Future Generation Computer Systems*, *29*(7), 1645–1660. doi:10.1016/j.future.2013.01.010

Gunjan, V. K., Kumar, A., & Avdhanam, S. (2013, September). A survey of cybercrime in India. In *Advanced Computing Technologies (ICACT), 2013 15th International Conference on* (pp. 1-6). IEEE.

Hacking, I. (1983). *Representing and intervening* (Vol. 279). Cambridge, UK: Cambridge University Press. doi:10.1017/CBO9780511814563

Hai, Q. T., & Hwang, S. O. (n.d.). An efficient classification of malware behavior using deep neural network. *Journal of Intelligent & Fuzzy Systems*, 1-14.

Han, K. S., Lim, J. H., Kang, B., & Im, E. G. (2015). Malware analysis using visualized images and entropy graphs. *International Journal of Information Security*, *14*(1), 1–14. doi:10.100710207-014-0242-0

Hara, T., Hagihara, V., & Nishio, S. (2010). Data Replication for Top-k Query Processing in Mobile Wireless Sensor Networks. *IEEE International Conference on Sensor Networks, Ubiquitous, and Trustworthy Computing*, 115-122. 10.1109/SUTC.2010.25

Harbour. (n.d.). *Stealth Secrets of the Malware Ninjas*. Academic Press.

Heinzelman, W. B., Chandrakasan, A. P., & Balakrishnan, H. (2002). An application-specific protocol architecture for wireless microsensor networks. *IEEE Transactions on Wireless Communications*, *1*(4), 660–670. doi:10.1109/TWC.2002.804190

He, K., Zhang, X., Ren, S., & Sun, J. (2016). Deep residual learning for image recognition. In *Proceedings of the IEEE conference on computer vision and pattern recognition* (pp. 770-778). IEEE.

Hossain, M. M., Fotouhi, M., & Hasan, R. (2015, June). Towards an analysis of security issues, challenges, and open problems in the internet of things. In *Services (SERVICES), 2015 IEEE World Congress on* (pp. 21-28). IEEE. 10.1109/SERVICES.2015.12

Household Use of Information Technology. (2007-08). *Australian Bureau of Statistics.* Retrieved from http://www.abs.gov.au

Hu, X., Jang, J., Wang, T., Ashraf, Z., Stoecklin, M. P., & Kirat, D. (2016). Scalable malware classification with multifaceted content features and threat intelligence. *IBM Journal of Research and Development*, *60*(4), 6–1. doi:10.1147/JRD.2016.2559378

Iftikhar, B., & Alghamdi, A. S. (2009). Application of artificial neural network within the detection of dos attacks. *Proceedings of the ordinal international conference on Security of knowledge and networks*, 229–234.

Ilyas, I., Beskales, G., & Soliman, M. (2008). A Survey of Top-k Query Processing Techniques in Relational Database Systems. ACM Computing Surveys, 40.

Indian Express. (2016). Retrieved from http://indianexpress.com/article/technology/tech-news-technology/digital-health-wearables-health-apps-smartwatch-health-apps-2797787/

Iot4Health. (n.d.). Retrieved from http://iot4health.utu.fi/?p=53

Jayaram, M. A., Prashanth, G. K., & Taj, S. (2015). Classification of ear biometric data using support vector machine. *British Journal of Applied Science and Technology*, *11*(1), 1–10. doi:10.9734/BJAST/2015/19509

Jeon, D., & Park, D. (2018). Real-time Malware Detection Method Using Machine Learning. *The Journal Of Korean Institute Of Information Technology*, *16*(3), 101–113. doi:10.14801/jkiit.2018.16.3.101

Jerlin, M. A., & Marimuthu, K. (2018). A New Malware Detection System Using Machine Learning Techniques for API Call Sequences. *Journal of Applied Security Research*, *13*(1), 45–62. doi:10.1080/19361610.2018.1387734

Jiang, H., Cheng, J., Wang, D., Wang, C., & Tan, G. (2012). A General Framework for Efficient Continous Multidimensional Top-k Query Processing in Sensor Networks. *IEEE Transactions on Parallel and Distributed Systems*, *23*(9), 1668–1680. doi:10.1109/TPDS.2012.69

Jiang, H., Cheng, J., Wang, J., Wang, C., & Tan, G. (2011). Continuous Multi-Dimensional Top-k Query Processing in Sensor Networks. *Proceedings - IEEE INFOCOM.*

Jiang, H., Jin, S., & Wang, C. (2010). Parameter-Based Data Aggregation for Statistical Information Extraction in Wireless Sensor Networks. IEEE Trans. *Vehicular Technology, VOL.*, *59*(8), 3992–4001. doi:10.1109/TVT.2010.2062547

Johnson, J. (2014). *Remarks by Secretary of Homeland Security Jeh Johnson at the White House Cybersecurity Framework Event.* Retrieved from https://www.dhs.gov/news/2014/02/12/remarks-secretary-homeland-security-jeh-johnson-white-house-cybersecurity-framework

Jonze, S. (2017). *28 Best Quotes About Artificial Intelligence.* Retrieved from https://www.forbes.com/sites/bernardmarr/2017/07/25/28-best-quotes-about-artificial-intelligence

Joy, Y. H., Jeon, S. Y., Im, J. H., & Lee, M. K. (2016). *Security analysis and improvement of fingerprint authentication for smartphones. In Lecture Notes in Electrical Engineering* (Vol. 354, pp. 71–77). Singapore: Springer.

Jun, C., & Chi, C. (2014, January). Design of complex event-processing ids in internet of things. In *Measuring Technology and Mechatronics Automation (ICMTMA), 2014 Sixth International Conference on* (pp. 226-229). IEEE. 10.1109/ICMTMA.2014.57

Kabanga, E. K., & Kim, C. H. (2017). Malware images classification using convolutional neural network. *Journal of Computer and Communications, 6*(01), 153–158. doi:10.4236/jcc.2018.61016

Kakad, Sarode, & Bakal. (2012). A Survey on Query Response Time Optimization Approaches for Reliable Data Communication in Wireless Sensor Network. *International Journal of Wireless Communications and Networking Technologies, 1*(2), 31-36.

Kakad, S., Sarode, P., & Bakal, J. (2013). Analysis and Implementation of Top k Query Response Time Optimization Approach for Reliable Data Communication in Wireless Sensor Networks. *International Journal of Engineering and Innovative Technology, 3*(2), 201–211.

Kamundala, E., & Kim, C. (2018). CNN Model to Classify Malware Using Image Feature. *KIISE Transactions On Computing Practices, 24*(5), 256–261. doi:10.5626/KTCP.2018.24.5.256

Kaswan, A., Tomar, A., & Jana, P. K. (2018). An efficient scheduling scheme for mobile charger in on-demand wireless rechargeable sensor networks. *Journal of Network and Computer Applications, 114*, 123–134. doi:10.1016/j.jnca.2018.02.017

Khan, M. A. (2016). A survey of security issues for cloud computing. *Journal of Network and Computer Applications, 71*, 11–29. doi:10.1016/j.jnca.2016.05.010

Khan, M. A., Ahmad, J., Javaid, Q., & Saqib, N. A. (2017). An efficient and secure partial image encryption for wireless multimedia sensor networks using discrete wavelet transform, chaotic maps and substitution box. *Journal of Modern Optics, 64*(5), 531–540. doi:10.1080/09500340.2016.1246680

Kim, H., Kim, J., Kim, Y., Kim, I., Kim, K. J., & Kim, H. (2017). Improvement of malware detection and classification using API call sequence alignment and visualization. *Cluster Computing*, 1–9.

King, S., & Nadal, S. (2008). *Bitcoin: Peer-to-peer crypto-currency with proof-of-stake.* (Unpublished)

Kivimaa, J., Ojamaa, A., & Tyugu, E. (2008). Pareto-Optimal state of affairs Analysis for the selection of Security Measures. *Proceedings of Military communications conference, MILCOM 2008.*

Kivimaa, J., Ojamaa, A., & Tyugu, E. (2009). *Graded Security accomplished System. In Lecture Notes in engineering* (Vol. 5508, pp. 279–286). Springer.

Krishna, C. V., & Karthik, S. R. (2016). Novel approach for string searching and matching using American standard code for information interchange value. *2016 International Conference on Recent Trends in Information Technology (ICRTIT)*, 1-5. 10.1109/ICRTIT.2016.7569550

Kumara, A., & Jaidhar, C. D. (2018). Automated multi-level malware detection system based on reconstructed semantic view of executables using machine learning techniques at VMM. *Future Generation Computer Systems*, *79*, 431–446. doi:10.1016/j.future.2017.06.002

Kumar, S. N. (2015). Review on network security and cryptography. *International Transaction of Electrical and Computer Engineers System*, *3*(1), 1–11.

Kurzweil, R. (2005). *The Singularity is near.* Penguin Group.

Kyaw, A. K., Chen, Y., & Joseph, J. (2015, November). Pi-IDS: evaluation of open-source intrusion detection systems on Raspberry Pi 2. In *Information Security and Cyber Forensics (InfoSec), 2015 Second International Conference on* (pp. 165-170). IEEE.

LeCun, Y., Bengio, Y., & Hinton, G. (2015). Deep learning. *Nature, 521*(7553), 436.

Lee. (2016). Fathym's IoT-enabled WeatherCloud enhances driver safety during inclement weather. *Microsoft Internet of Things.* Retrieved from https://blogs.microsoft.com/iot/2016/12/09/fathyms-iot-enabled-weathercloud-enhances-driver-safety-during-inclement-weather/

Le, Q., Boydell, O., Mac Namee, B., & Scanlon, M. (2018). Deep learning at the shallow end: Malware classification for non-domain experts. *Digital Investigation, 26*, S118–S126. doi:10.1016/j.diin.2018.04.024

Lewis, J. A. (2002). *Assessing the risks of cyber terrorism, cyber war and other cyber threats.* Washington, DC: Center for Strategic & International Studies.

Li, H. Z. M., Wu, T., & Yang, F. (2018). *Evaluation of Supervised Machine Learning Techniques for Dynamic Malware Detection.* Academic Press.

Li, P., & Lo, K. T. (2015, December). Joint image compression and encryption based on alternating transforms with quality control. In Visual Communications and Image Processing (VCIP), 2015 (pp. 1-4). IEEE. doi:10.1109/VCIP.2015.7457867

Liang, W., Chen, B., & Xu, J. (2008). Response Time Constrained Top-k Query Evaluation in Sensor Network. *14th IEEE International Conference on Parallel and Distributed Systems*, 575-782. 10.1109/ICPADS.2008.65

Lianh, W., Chen, B., & Yu, J. X. (2010). *Top-k Query Evaluation in Sensor Networks Under Query Response Time Constraint.* Canberra, Australia: School of Computer Science, Australian National University.

Liao, W., & Huang, C. (2012). An Efficient Data Storage Scheme for Top-k Query in Wireless Sensor Networks. *IEEE Network Operations and Management Symposium (NOMS)*, 554-557.

Lim, J. S. (2009). Finding features for real-time premature ventricular contraction detection using a fuzzy neural network system. *IEEE Transactions on Neural Networks*, *20*(3), 522–527. doi:10.1109/TNN.2008.2012031 PMID:19179246

Lim, J. S., Wang, D., Kim, Y.-S., & Gupta, S. (2006). A neuro-fuzzy approach for diagnosis of antibody deficiency syndrome. *Neurocomputing*, *69*(7-9), 969–974. doi:10.1016/j.neucom.2005.06.009

Liu, X., Xu, J., & Lee, W. C. (2010). A Cross Pruning Framework for Top-k Data Collection in Wireless Sensor Networks. *Proc. Int'l Conf. Mobile Data Management.* 10.1109/MDM.2010.41

Louis, W., Komeili, M., & Hatzinakos, D. (2016). Continuous authentication using one-dimensional multi-resolution local binary patterns (1DMRLBP) in ECG biometrics. *IEEE Transactions on Information Forensics and Security*, *11*(12), 2818–2832. doi:10.1109/TIFS.2016.2599270

Luca, C., Steffen, W., & Wojciech, M. (2017). The Future of Digital Forensics: Challenges and the Road Ahead. *IEEE Transactions on Security and Privacy*, *1*, 12-17.

Lunt, T. F., & Jagannathan, R. (1988). An example amount of your time Intrusion-Detection accomplished System. Proceedings of IEEE conference on Security and Privacy.

Mai, H., & Kim, M. (2011). Processing Continuous Top-k Data Collection Queries in Lifetime-Constrained Wireless Sensor Networks. ICUIMC'11, Seoul, South Korea. doi:10.1145/1968613.1968631

Maksymyuk, S. D., Brych, M., Satria, D., & Jo, M. (2017). An IoT based monitoring framework for software defined 5G mobile networks. *11th International Conference on Ubiquitous Information Management and Communication, Proceedings.* 10.1145/3022227.3022331

Malhotra, B., Nascimento, M., & Nikolaidis, I. (2011). Exact Top-k Queries in Wireless Sensor Networks. IEEE Transactions on Knowledge and Data Engineering, 23(10). doi:10.1109/TKDE.2010.186

Mammeri, A., Hadjou, B., & Khoumsi, A. (2012). A survey of image compression algorithms for visual sensor networks. *ISRN Sensor Networks, 2012*.

Martis, R. J., Acharya, U. R., Lim, C. M., & Suri, J. S. (2013). Characterization of ECG beats from cardiac arrhythmia using discrete cosine transform in PCA framework. *Knowledge-Based Systems*, *45*, 76–82. doi:10.1016/j.knosys.2013.02.007

Mattern, F., & Floerkemeier, C. (2010). From the Internet of Computers to the Internet of Things. In K. Sachs, I. Petrov, & P. Guerrero (Eds.), Lecture Notes in Computer Science: Vol. 6462. *From Active Data Management to Event-Based Systems and More.* Berlin: Springer. doi:10.1007/978-3-642-17226-7_15

McAfee. (2018). *Mobile threat report.* Author.

Mehare, T. M., & Bhosale, S. (2017). *Design and Development of Intrusion Detection System for Internet of Things.* Academic Press.

Mehta, S., & Lingayat, N. (2008). Detection of P and T-waves in electrocardiogram. *Proceedings of the World Congress on Engineering and Computer Science*, 22-24.

Miakotko, L. (2017). *The impact of smartphones and mobile devices on human health and life.* Retrieved from http://www.nyu.edu/classes/keefer/waoe/miakotkol.pdf

Miguel-Hurtado, O., Guest, R., Stevenage, S. V., Neil, G. J., & Black, S. (2016). Comparing machine learning classifiers and linear/logistic regression to explore the relationship between hand dimensions and demographic characteristics. *PLoS One*, *11*(11), e0165521. doi:10.1371/journal.pone.0165521 PMID:27806075

Miraz & Ali. (2018). Applications of Blockchain Technology beyond Crypto currency. *Annuals of Emerging Technologies in Computing*, *2*(1).

Moslem. (2010). *Measurements of energy consumption and execution time of different operations on Tmote Sky sensor nodes.* Academic Press.

Musiclab, B. (2006). *P2P Application.* Retrieved from http://www. bearshare. com

Nakamoto, S. (2008). *Bitcoin: A peer-to-peer electronic cash system.* Academic Press.

Nandhini, S. A., & Radha, S. (2017). Efficient compressed sensing-based security approach for video surveillance application in wireless multimedia sensor networks. *Computers & Electrical Engineering*, *60*, 175–192. doi:10.1016/j.compeleceng.2017.01.027

Nappo, S. (2017). *Goodreads.* Retrieved from https://www.goodreads.com

Narayanan, B. N., Djaneye-Boundjou, O., & Kebede, T. M. (2016, July). Performance analysis of machine learning and pattern recognition algorithms for malware classification. In *Aerospace and Electronics Conference (NAECON) and Ohio Innovation Summit (OIS)* (pp. 338-342). IEEE. 10.1109/NAECON.2016.7856826

Nataraj, L., Kirat, D., Manjunath, B. S., & Vigna, G. (2013, December). Sarvam: Search and retrieval of malware. *Proceedings of the Annual Computer Security Conference (ACSAC) Worshop on Next Generation Malware Attacks and Defense (NGMAD).*

Nataraj, L., Karthikeyan, S., Jacob, G., & Manjunath, B. S. (2011, July). Malware images: visualization and automatic classification. In *Proceedings of the 8th international symposium on visualization for cyber security* (p. 4). ACM.

Nataraj, L., Yegneswaran, V., Porras, P., & Zhang, J. (2011, October). A comparative assessment of malware classification using binary texture analysis and dynamic analysis. In *Proceedings of the 4th ACM Workshop on Security and Artificial Intelligence* (pp. 21-30). ACM. 10.1145/2046684.2046689

National Health Portal of India. (n.d.). Retrieved from https://www.nhp.gov.in/e-health-india_mty

Neely. (2016). *Mobile Threat Protection: A Holistic Approach to Security Mobile Data and Devices* (Report). Academic Press.

Nelson, B., Phillips, A., & Steuart, C. (2014). *Guide to computer forensics and investigations*. Cengage Learning.

NIC, National Cloud of India. (n.d.). Retrieved from https://cloud.gov.in/

Niedermayer, J., Nascimento, M., & Renz, M. (2010). Exploiting Local Node Cache in Top-k Queries within Wireless Sensor Networks. ACM GIS '10, 434-437. doi:10.1145/1869790.1869855

Nieminen, J., Savolainen, T., Isomaki, M., Patil, B., Shelby, Z., & Gomez, C. (2015). *Ipv6 over bluetooth (r) low energy* (No. RFC 7668).

Ni, S., Qian, Q., & Zhang, R. (2018). Malware identification using visualization images and deep learning. *Computers & Security*, *77*, 871–885. doi:10.1016/j.cose.2018.04.005

OASIS Standard. (2014). *MQTT version 3.1. 1*. Retrieved from http://docs. oasis-open. org/ mqtt/mqtt/v3

Offences, C. (2001). *Model Criminal Code Officers Committee*. Retrieved from https://catalogue. nla.gov.au/Record

Online Statistics of Communication and Digital Economy. (2008). *Australian Government archive*. Retrieved from http://www.archive.dbcde.gov.au/2008

Paek, J., Hicks, J., Coe, S., & Govindan, R. (2014). Image-based environmental monitoring sensor application using an embedded wireless sensor network. *Sensors (Basel)*, *14*(9), 15981–16002. doi:10.3390140915981 PMID:25171121

Pandey, S. K., & Mehtre, B. (2014). A Lifecycle Based Approach for Malware Analysis. *2014 Fourth International Conference on Communication Systems and Network Technologies*. 10.1109/ CSNT.2014.161

Panimalar, A., Giri, P.U. & Khan, S. (2018). Artificial Intelligence Techniques in Cyber Security. *International Research Journal of Engineering and Technology, 5*(3).

Pan, J., & Tompkins, W. J. (1985). A real-time QRS detection algorithm. *IEEE Transactions on Biomedical Engineering*, *32*(3), 230–236. doi:10.1109/TBME.1985.325532 PMID:3997178

Parag & Khanna. (2016). *The Evolution of Technology*. Retrieved from http://bigthink.com/ hybrid-reality/the-evolution-of-technology

Pascanu, R., Stokes, J. W., Sanossian, H., Marinescu, M., & Thomas, A. (2015, April). Malware classification with recurrent networks. In *Acoustics, Speech and Signal Processing (ICASSP), 2015 IEEE International Conference on* (pp. 1916-1920). IEEE. 10.1109/ICASSP.2015.7178304

Patel, A. M., Gakare, P. K., & Cheeran, A. (2012). Real time ECG feature extraction and arrhythmia detection on a mobile platform. *International Journal of Computers and Applications, 44*, 40–45.

Peter, S., Reddy, B. P., Momtaz, F., & Givargis, T. (2016). Design of secure ECG-based biometric authentication in body area sensor networks. *Sensors (Basel), 16*(4), 570. doi:10.339016040570 PMID:27110785

Piccardi, M. (2004). Background subtraction techniques: A review. *IEEE International Conference on Systems, Man and Cybernetics (IEEE Cat. No.04CH37583).*

Pinto, R. J., Cardoso, S. J., Lourenço, A., & Carreiras, C. (2017). Towards a continuous biometric system based on ECG signals acquired on the steering wheel. *Sensors (Basel), 17*(10), 2228. doi:10.339017102228 PMID:28956856

Pollitt, M. (2010). A history of digital forensics. *Proceedings of International Conference on Digital Forensics*, 3-15.

Ponemon Institute. (n.d.). *Research studies and White paper.* Retrieved from https://www.ponemon.org/library

Pongle, P., & Chavan, G. (2015). Real time intrusion and wormhole attack detection in internet of things. *International Journal of Computers and Applications, 121*(9).

Porée, F., Kervio, G., & Carrault, G. (2016). ECG biometric analysis in different physiological recording conditions. *Signal, Image and Video Processing, 10*(2), 267–276. doi:10.100711760-014-0737-1

Preda, M. D., Christodorescu, M., Jha, S., & Debray, S. (2008). A Semantics-Based Approach to Malware Detection. *ACM Transactions on Programming Languages and Systems, 30*(5), 1–54. doi:10.1145/1387673.1387674

Proakis, J. G., & Manolakis, D. G. (2007). *Digital Signal Processing: Principles, Algorithms, and Applications.* New York: Pearson Education.

Purcell, R., Pathe, M., & Mullen, P. E. (2000). *Stalkers and Their Victims.* New York: Cambridge University Press.

Purcell, R., Pathe, M., & Mullen, P. E. (2004). Stalking: Defining and prosecuting a new category of offending. *International Journal of Law and Psychiatry, 27*(2), 157–169. doi:10.1016/j.ijlp.2004.01.006 PMID:15063640

Re, C., Dalvi, N., & Suciu, D. (2007). Efficient Top-k Query Evaluation on Probabilistic Data. ICDE. doi:10.1109/ICDE.2007.367934

Report of the defense science board task force on defence biometrics. (2007). Retrieved from https://fas.org/irp/agency/dod/dsb/biometrics.pdf

Residential Telephone Service Survey. (2007). *Statistics Canada.* Retrieved from http://www.statcan.gc.ca

Rieck, K., Trinius, P., Willems, C., & Holz, T. (2011). Automatic analysis of malware behavior using machine learning. *Journal of Computer Security, 19*(4), 639–668. doi:10.3233/JCS-2010-0410

Rolls-Royce and Microsoft collaborate to create new digital capabilities. (2016). Microsoft Internet of Things. Retrieved from https://customers.microsoft.com/en-us/story/rollsroycestory

Ronen, R., Radu, M., Feuerstein, C., Yom-Tov, E., & Ahmadi, M. (2018). *Microsoft Malware Classification Challenge.* arXiv preprint arXiv:1802.10135

Russell, S. J., & Norvig, P. (2000). *Artificial Intelligence: A Modern Approach.* Prentice Hall.

Salvador, P., Nogueira, A., França, U., & Valadas, R. (2009). Framework for Zombie Detection Using Neural Networks. *Proceedings of The Fourth International Conference on Internet Monitoring and Protection ICIMP.* 10.1109/ICIMP.2009.10

Samik, C., & Saurabh, P. (2016). Photoplethys-mogram signal based biometric recognition using linear discriminant classifier. *Proceedings of the 2nd International Conference on Control Instrumentation Energy & Communication (CIEC),* 183-187.

Sankar, Sindhu, & Sethumadhavan. (2018). *Survey of consensus protocols on blockchain applications.* Academic Press.

Santos, I., Brezo, F., Ugarte-Pedrero, X., & Bringas, P. G. (2013). Opcode sequences as representation of executables for data-mining-based unknown malware detection. *Information Sciences, 231,* 64–82. doi:10.1016/j.ins.2011.08.020

Schultz, M. G., Eskin, E., Zadok, F., & Stolfo, S. J. (2001). Data mining methods for detection of new malicious executables. In *Security and Privacy, 2001. S&P 2001. Proceedings. 2001 IEEE Symposium on* (pp. 38-49). IEEE. 10.1109/SECPRI.2001.924286

Sforzin, A., Mármol, F. G., Conti, M., & Bohli, J. M. (2016, July). RPiDS: Raspberry Pi IDS—A Fruitful Intrusion Detection System for IoT. In *Ubiquitous Intelligence & Computing, Advanced and Trusted Computing, Scalable Computing and Communications, Cloud and Big Data Computing, Internet of People, and Smart World Congress (UIC/ATC/ScalCom/CBDCom/IoP/SmartWorld), 2016 Intl IEEE Conferences* (pp. 440-448). IEEE.

Shabtai, A., Menahem, E., & Elovici, Y. (2011). F-Sign: Automatic, Function-Based Signature Generation for Malware. *IEEE Transactions on Systems, Man and Cybernetics. Part C, Applications and Reviews, 41*(4), 494–508. doi:10.1109/TSMCC.2010.2068544

Shamshirband, S., Amini, A., Anuar, N. B., Kiah, M. L. M., Teh, Y. W., & Furnell, S. (2014). D-FICCA: A density-based fuzzy imperialist competitive clustering algorithm for intrusion detection in wireless sensor networks. *Measurement, 55,* 212–226. doi:10.1016/j.measurement.2014.04.034

Shannon, C. E. (1949). Communication theory of secrecy system. *The Bell System Technical Journal*, 28(4), 656–715. doi:10.1002/j.1538-7305.1949.tb00928.x

Siegel, L. J., & McCormick, C. R. (2010). *Criminology in Canada: Theories, patterns, and typologies*. Nelson Education.

Silberstein, A., Braynard, R., Ellis, C., Munagala, K., & Yang, J. (2006). A sampling-based approach to optimizing top-k queries in sensor networks. *Proc. ICDE*, 68–80.

Singh, A. (2017). *Malware Classification using Image Representation* (Doctoral dissertation). Indian Institute of Technology Kanpur. Retrieved from https://www.statista.com/statistics/218089/global-market-share-of-windows-7/

Singh. (2016). *IoT Security-Issues, Challenges and Solutions*. Retrieved from https://internetofthingswiki.com/iot-security-issues-challenges-and-solutions/937/

Sivabalakrishnan, M., & Manjula, D. (2009). An Efficient Foreground Detection Algorithm for Visual Surveillance System. *International Journal of Computer Science and Network Security*, 9(5), 221–227.

Sivabalakrishnan, M., & Manjula, D. (2010). Adaptive Background subtraction in dynamic environments using fuzzy logic. *International Journal on Computer Science and Engineering*, 2(2), 270–273.

Sivabalakrishnan, M., & Manjula, D. (2010). Adaptive background subtraction using fuzzy logic. *IJMIS International Journal of Multimedia Intelligence and Security*, 1(4), 392–401. doi:10.1504/IJMIS.2010.039239

Sivabalakrishnan, M., & Manjula, D. (2010). Fuzzy Rule-based Classification of Human Tracking and Segmentation using Color Space Conversion. *International Journal of Artificial Intelligence & Applications IJAIA*, 1(4), 70–80. doi:10.5121/ijaia.2010.1406

Sivabalakrishnan, M., & Manjula, D. (2010). Human Tracking Segmentation using color space conversion. *International Journal of Computer Science Issues*, 7(5), 285–289.

Sivabalakrishnan, M., & Manjula, D. (2010). RBF Approach to Background Modelling for Background subtraction in Video Objects. *International Journal of Computer Science and Research*, 1(1), 35–42.

Sivabalakrishnan, M., & Manjula, D. (2011). Background extraction using improved mode algorithm for visual surveillance applications. *IJCSE International Journal of Computational Science and Engineering*, 6(4), 275–282.

Sivabalakrishnan, M., & Manjula, D. (2011). Novel Segmentation Method using improved edge flow vectors for people tracking. *Journal of Information and Computational Science*, 8(8), 1319–1332.

Sivabalakrishnan, M., & Manjula, D. (2012). Performance analysis of fuzzy logic-based background subtraction in dynamic environments. *Imaging Science Journal, 60*(1), 39–46. doi:10.1179/17 43131X11Y.0000000008

Smith, P. K., Mahdavi, J., Carvalho, M., Fisher, S., Russell, S., & Tippett, N. (2008). Cyberbullying: Its nature and impact in secondary school pupils. *Journal of Child Psychology and Psychiatry, and Allied Disciplines, 49*(4), 376–385. doi:10.1111/j.1469-7610.2007.01846.x PMID:18363945

Sornomo, L. (1987). A model based approach to QRS delineation. *Proceedings of the Computers and Biomedical Research*, 526–540. 10.1016/0010-4809(87)90024-3

Souri, A., & Hosseini, R. (2018). A state-of-the-art survey of malware detection approaches using data mining techniques. *Human-centric Computing and Information Sciences, 8*(1), 3. doi:10.118613673-018-0125-x

Sri & Bhaskari,. (2018). A study on blockchain technology. *International Journal of Engineering & Technology, 7*(2), 418-421.

Summary of HIPAA Security Rule. (n.d.). Retrieved from https://www.hhs.gov/hipaa/for-professionals/security/laws-regulations/index.html

Suseela, G., & Phamila, Y. A. V. (2016). Visual sensor networks: Critical infrastructure protection. In *Combating Security Breaches and Criminal Activity in the Digital Sphere* (pp. 263–282). IGI Global.

Suseela, G., & Phamila, Y. A. V. (2018). Low-complexity low-memory energy-efficient image coding for wireless image sensor networks. *Imaging Science Journal, 66*(2), 125–132. doi:10.1 080/13682199.2017.1385175

Swanson, C. R., Chamelin, N. C., Territo, L., & Taylor, R. W. (2003). *Criminal investigation.* Boston: McGraw-Hill.

Tabirca, S., Tabirca, T., & Ciurea, E. (1998). Is ASCII Code An Optimal Code? *Proceedings of the 6th International Conference on Optimization of Electrical and Electronic Equipments*, 775-778. 10.1109/OPTIM.1998.708044

Tang, J., Wang, Z., Sung, Y., Du, C., & Zhou, Z. (2014). Top-k Queries in Wireless Sensor Networks Leveraging Hierarchical Grid Index. *Eighth International Conference on Innovative Mobile and Internet Services in Ubiquitous Computing*, 381-386. 10.1109/IMIS.2014.51

Tang, Y., & Chen, S. (2007). An Automated Signature-Based Approach against Polymorphic Internet Worms. *IEEE Transactions on Parallel and Distributed Systems, 18*(7), 879–892. doi:10.1109/TPDS.2007.1050

Tang, Y., Xiao, B., & Lu, X. (2011). Signature Tree Generation for Polymorphic Worms. *IEEE Transactions on Computers, 60*(4), 4. doi:10.1109/TC.2010.130

Tejaswini Yadav, Rajendran, & Rajani. (2014). An Approach for Determining the Health of the DNS. *International Journal of Computer Science and Mobile Computing, 3*(9).

Teng, G., Zheng, K., & Dong, W. (2008, October). A survey of available tools for developing wireless sensor networks. In *Systems and Networks Communications, 2008. ICSNC'08. 3rd International Conference on* (pp. 139-144). IEEE. 10.1109/ICSNC.2008.15

Tesauro, G., Kephart, J., & Sorkin, G. (1996). Neural networks for computer virus recognition. *IEEE Expert, 11*(4), 5–6. doi:10.1109/64.511768

Toyama, K., Krumm, J., Brumitt, B., & Meyers, B. (1999). Wallflower: Principles and practice of background maintenance. *Proceedings of the Seventh IEEE International Conference on Computer Vision*, 255-261. 10.1109/ICCV.1999.791228

Tsetserukou, D., & Neviarouskaya, A. (2010). iFeel_IM! Augmenting Emotions during Online Communication. *IEEE Computer Graphics and Applications, 30*(5), 72–80. doi:10.1109/MCG.2010.88 PMID:24807416

UIDAI. (n.d.). Retrieved from https://uidai.gov.in/

Understanding the Internet of Things (IoT). (2014). *Connected Living, GSMA*. Retrieved from https://www.gsma.com/iot/wp-content/uploads/2014/08/cl_iot_wp_07_14.pdf

Vacca, J. R. (2005). *Computer Forensics (Computer Crime Scene Investigation)*. Hingham, MA: Charles River Media.

Van, N. T. T., & Thinh, T. N. (2015, November). Accelerating anomaly-based IDS using neural network on GPU. In *Advanced Computing and Applications (ACOMP), 2015 International Conference on* (pp. 67-74). IEEE. 10.1109/ACOMP.2015.30

What Is WANNACRY Ransomware. (n.d.). Retrieved from https://www.thesun.co.uk/tech/3562470/wannacry-ransomware-nhs-cyber-attack-hackers-virus/

Wickramasuriya, J., Datt, M., Mehrotra, S., & Venkatasubramanian, N. (2012). Privacy protecting data collection in media spaces. *Proceedings of the 12th Annual ACM International Conference on Multimedia - MULTIMEDIA '04*, 1. doi:10.1145/1027527.1027537

Witkin, A. (1983). Scale-Space Filtering. *Proceedings 8th International Joint Conference*, 1019-1022.

Wood, L. A. (2001). Cyber-Defamation and the Single Publication Rule. *BUL Rev., 81*, 895.

Wu, M., Xu, J., Tang, X., & Lee, W. C. (2007). Top-k Monitoring in Wireless Sensor Network. *IEEE Transactions on Knowledge and Data Engineering, 19*(7), 962–976. doi:10.1109/TKDE.2007.1038

Xu, L., Zhang, D., Jayasena, N., & Cavazos, J. (2017). HADM: Hybrid Analysis for Detection of Malware. *Proceedings of SAI Intelligent Systems Conference (IntelliSys) 2016 Lecture Notes in Networks and Systems*, 702-724. doi:10.1007/978-3-319-56991-8_51

Yan, H., Zhou, H., & Zhang, H. (2018). Automatic Malware Classification via PRICoLBP. *Chinese Journal of Electronics, 27*(4), 852–859. doi:10.1049/cje.2018.05.001

Yeo, M., Seong, D., Park, J., Ahn, M., & Yoo, J. (2013). An energy-efficient sequence-aware top-k monitoring scheme in wireless sensor networks. *International Journal of Distributed Sensor Networks*, 1–13.

Yu, F., & Koltun, V. (2015). *Multi-scale context aggregation by dilated convolutions.* arXiv preprint arXiv:1511.07122

Yu, F., Koltun, V., & Funkhouser, T. A. (2017, July). *Dilated Residual Networks* (Vol. 2). CVPR.

Yu, W., Zhang, N., Fu, X., & Zhao, W. (2010). Self-Disciplinary Worms and Countermeasures: Modeling and Analysis. *IEEE Transactions on Parallel and Distributed Systems*, *21*(10), 1501–1514. doi:10.1109/TPDS.2009.161

Zarpelão, B. B., Miani, R. S., Kawakani, C. T., & de Alvarenga, S. C. (2017). A survey of intrusion detection in Internet of Things. *Journal of Network and Computer Applications*, *84*, 25–37. doi:10.1016/j.jnca.2017.02.009

Zhang, Z. K., Cho, M. C. Y., Wang, C. W., Hsu, C. W., Chen, C. K., & Shieh, S. (2014). IoT Security: Ongoing Challenges and Research Opportunities. *2014 IEEE 7th International Conference on Service-Oriented Computing and Applications*, 230-234. 10.1109/SOCA.2014.58

Zhang, X., Zhou, L., Zhang, T., & Yang, J. (2014). A novel efficient method for abnormal face detection in ATM. *2014 International Conference on Audio, Language and Image Processing.* 10.1109/ICALIP.2014.7009884

Zhao, K., & Ge, L. (2013). A Survey on the Internet of Things Security. *2013 Ninth International Conference on Computational Intelligence and Security*, 663-667. 10.1109/CIS.2013.145

Zheng, Xie, Dai, Chen, & Wang. (2017). An Overview of Blockchain Technology: Architecture, Consensus, and Future Trends. *IEEE 6th International Conference on Big Data.*

Zhou, B., Khosla, A., Lapedriza, A., Oliva, A., & Torralba, A. (2016). Learning deep features for discriminative localization. In *Proceedings of the IEEE Conference on Computer Vision and Pattern Recognition* (pp. 2921-2929). IEEE.

Zhou, N. R., Hua, T. X., Gong, L. H., Pei, D. J., & Liao, Q. H. (2015). Quantum image encryption based on generalized Arnold transform and double random-phase encoding. *Quantum Information Processing*, *14*(4), 1193–1213. doi:10.100711128-015-0926-z

Zhu, C., Yang, L., Shu, L., Leung, V., Hara, T., & Nishio, S. (2015). Insights of Top-k Query in Duty-Cycled Wireless Sensor Networks. *IEEE Transactions on Industrial Electronics*, *62*(2), 1317–1328. doi:10.1109/TIE.2014.2334653

Zhu, H., Zhao, C., & Zhang, X. (2013). A novel image encryption–compression scheme using hyper-chaos and Chinese remainder theorem. *Signal Processing Image Communication*, *28*(6), 670–680. doi:10.1016/j.image.2013.02.004

Zion China uses Azure IoT, Stream Analytics, and Machine Learning to evolve its Intelligent Diabetes Management Solution. (2017). *Microsoft Internet of Things*. Retrieved from http://customers.microsoft.com/en-us/story/zionchina

Zolkipli, M. F., & Jantan, A. (2010). Malware Behavior Analysis: Learning and Understanding Current Malware Threats. *Second International Conference on Network Applications, Protocols and Service IEEE*, 218-221. 10.1109/NETAPPS.2010.46

About the Contributors

S. Geetha received the B.E., from the Madurai Kamaraj University, M.E., and Ph.D. degrees in Computer Science and Engineering from Anna University, Chennai, in 2000, 2004 and 2011 respectively. She has 14+ years of teaching experience. Currently, she is a professor at School of Computing Science and Engineering at VIT-University, Chennai Campus. She has published more than 50 papers in reputed IEEE International Conferences and refereed Journals. She joins the review committee for IEEE Transactions on Information Forensics and Security and IEEE Transactions on Image Processing, Springer Multimedia Tools and Security, Elsevier – Information Sciences. She was an editor for the Indian Conference proceedings of ICCIIS 2007 and RISES-2013. Her research interests include multimedia security, intrusion detection systems, machine learning paradigms and information forensics. She is a recipient of University Rank and Academic Topper Award in B.E. and M.E. in 2000 and 2004 respectively. She is also a pride recipient of the "Best Academic Researcher Award 2013" of ASDF Global Awards.

Asnath Victy Phamila is an Associate Professor in School of Computing Science and Engineering, Vellore Institute of Technology, Chennai Campus, India. She holds M.E and Ph.D degree in Computer Science and Engineering from Anna University, India. Her research area includes Image Processing, Wireless Sensor Networks, Network Security and Deep Learning. She has around 15 years of academic and 4 years of industry experience. She is a recipient of proficiency award from Government of Tamil Nadu, Best Team Player award from Ramco Systems and research award from VIT. She has around 40 research papers to her credit. She also serves as reviewer in reputed journals.

* * *

KirtiRaj Bhatele is an Assistant Professor in the RJIT BSF Academy Tekanpur, an institute run by the Border Security. Currently he is pursuing PhD in the field of Computer Science engineering and information technology. He has done M.Tech in Information Technology and B.E. in Information Technology from the RGPV, university. He also has PG Diploma in Cyber Law from the National law institute University Bhopal. He has teaching experience of more than eight years and has published 20 research papers and eight chapters.

Himanshu Bhatt is an engineering graduate from the Rustamji Institute of Technology, BSF Academy Tekanpur, an institute run by the Border Security. He has worked on various projects related to Cybersecurity and Internet of Things and represented the college in the National Level Hackathons. He has written various articles and Blogs on Computer Programming and Cyber Security.

Karishma Das is an engineering graduate from the Rustamji Institute of Technology, BSF Academy Tekanpur, an institute run by the Border Security. She has work on various projects related to Cyber security and Internet of Things and represented college in the National Level competitions like Hackathon. She has written various articles and Blogs on Computer Programming and Cyber Security.

Suseela G. is a PhD Research scholar at School of Computing Science and Engineering, Vellore Institute of Technology, Chennai Campus, Tamilnadu, India. She holds B.E., and M.Tech degrees in Computer Science and Engineering. She has 10 years of teaching experience. She has around 10 publications to her credit. Her areas of research include Wireless Image Sensor Network, Image Coding and security.

Umadevi K. S. is working as Associate Professor at the Department of Information Security of School of Computer sciences and engineering at Vellore Institute of Technology, Vellore. Along with vast teaching experience and mentoring, her research interests includes Personal Area Networks, Protocol Engineering, Network Virtualization, Wireless Sensor Networks, Distributed computing, Software Defined Networking, Cloud Computing, Mobile and Wireless Security and Cybersecurity.

Adalarasu Kanagasabai is an Associate Professor in the School of Electrical and Electronics Engineering at SASTRA Deemed to be University, Thanjavur, Tamil Nadu. He received the B.E. degree in Electronics and Instrumentation Engineering from University of Madras, Tamil Nadu, India, in 1998 and obtained the M.Tech. degree in Biomedical Engineering from Indian Institute of Technology Madras (IIT) Madras, Chennai. He received the Ph.D. degree in driver fatigue measurements from IIT Madras, India, in 2010. He is serving in the teaching profession for more than a decade. His areas of research are cognitive neuroscience, sleep studies, industrial human safety and ergonomics testing of vehicles.

B. Rajesh Kanna is an Associate Professor, School of Computing Science and Engineering, Vellore Institute of Technology (VIT), Chennai, India since 2012, Previously, Assistant Professor, St. Joseph's College of Engineering, Chennai, India. His research interests include digital image analysis, hypergraph based models of images, Bio-medical image processing, Haptic system and Bioinformatics. His doctoral dissertation "Development of Hypergraph based Models for Selected Image Engineering Applications has proposed two innovative models for contour-based image analysis and proved the efficiency of the models through experiments. He currently explores the incorporation of the Deep Net in microbial analysis to curb the accelerated progress against the global burden of malaria and tuberculosis. ACM SIGSOFT has chosen him as one of the researchers to receive travel scholarship to attend ACM A.M. Turing Centenary celebration held at San Francisco, California, during June 15-16, 2012. His work on parallelism in noise removal won the Best poster award at 22nd International Symposium on High-Performance Parallel & Distributed Computing, June 17-21, 2013 at New York. He has published several research papers in reputed Journals and Conferences. Pursued doctoral degree at School of Computing, SASTRA University, India under the guidance of Prof. Dr. Chandrabose Aravindan of SSN College of Engineering, Chennai, India. He received his Master degree in Computer Applications with distinction from Faculty of Engineering of Madurai Kamaraj University(MKU), India, in 2003. He graduated with Bachelors' from MKU in 1993.

Neha Kumari is Facebook PyTorch Scholar and currently serving as chief student coordinator of Computer Society of India student branch RJIT, Gwalior, MP. She has been awarded six scholarships by Central and State Government of India for her exceptional work in academia. Her area of interest is Machine Learning, Deep Learning and its applications in various fields like Computer Vision, Natural Language Processing, etc.

Deepak Dutt Mishra is an engineering graduate from the Rustamji Institute of Technology, BSF Academy Tekanpur, an institute run by the Border Security Force. He has work on various projects related to Cyber security, BlockChain and Internet of Things and represented college in the National Level competitions like Hackathons and participated in International Competitions like CodeChef's Snackdown, Google Code Jam, Facebook Hacker Cup and ACM ICPC. He has written various articles and Blogs on Computer Programming and Cyber Security.

Jagannath Mohan is an Associate Professor in the School of Electronics Engineering at Vellore Institute of Technology (VIT), Chennai, India. Prior to joining VIT, he was serving the position of Senior Project Officer at the Industrial Consultancy and Sponsored Research at IIT Madras. He obtained his Ph.D. from IIT Madras in the year 2012. He received Best Academic Researcher of the Year 2017 from the Office of the Prime Minister of the Republic of India. He received Technical Icon of the Year 2012 from the Institution of Engineering and Technology, Young Professional Society (Chennai Network), UK. His research interests include sleep research, music research, biomedical instrumentation systems, signal and image processing.

S. Muthuramalingam is an enthusiastic and energetic computer networks, wireless and mobile computing researcher who quickly grasp new ideas and concepts, and to develop innovative and creative solutions. Completed UG Degree from SASTRA, PG from MKU and PhD from Anna University.

Punithavathi P. completed Bachelor of Engineering - Computer Science in 2007, and Master of Technology - Computer Science in 2014. She has achieved University Rank for M. Tech. She has four years of teaching experience. She is pursuing Ph. D. at VIT University, Chennai. She has been awarded with prestigious Visvesvaraya PHD Scheme supported by Media Lab Asia, Ministry of electronics and Information Technology, Government of India. She is a life member of HKCBEES and IEEE. Her areas of interest include biometric template security, image processing and multimedia security.

Gopinath Palaniappan has 13 years of experience in software Research and Development. He has delivered several e-governance solution for Government of India. He has a patent filed, titled as "Safeguarding personal biometrics from being stolen at the point-of-sale". His areas of research include Malware and Program Analysis.

Vetrivelan Pandu received the M.E. degree in Embedded System Technologies from College of Engineering Guindy, Anna University, Tamilnadu, India, in 2008 and the Ph.D. degree in Information and Communication Engineering from College of Engineering Guindy, Anna University, Tamilnadu, India, in 2014. At present, he is an Associate Professor in the School of Electronics Engineering at Vellore Institute of Technology (VIT), Chennai, Tamil Nadu, India. He has published his research work in number of national and international journals and conferences. His research interests include wireless sensor networks, wireless communication and embedded systems.

Balaji Rajendran is an Internet Evangelist and has established a forum (Indian Internet Research and Engineering Forum) for promoting the development of Internet Standards in India. He is currently setting up a Centre of Excellence in DNS Security. His current interests are in the broad domain of Applications of

Cryptography, spanning Digital Signatures to Blockchain. He works with Centre for Development of Advanced Computing (C-DAC) and has more than 17+ years of R&D experience in various niche segments of IT.

S. Abijah Roseline is a full time Ph.D. scholar in School of Computing Science and Engineering, VIT University, Chennai Campus, India. She has pursued B.E., degree in Computer Science and Engineering from Vel's Srinivasa College of Engineering and Technology (Affiliated to Anna University, Chennai), India in 2008 and M.E., degree in Computer Science and Engineering from MNM Jain Engineering College (Affiliated to Anna University, Chennai), India in 2011. She has published papers in reputed International Conferences. Her research interests include Malware Analysis, Security, and Machine Learning.

Sangeetha S. is working as Assistant Professor in Department of Computer Applications, National Institute of Technology, Tiruchirappalli. She obtained her Ph.D. from National Institute of Technology, Tiruchirappalli in 2013 . Her Areas of Interest include Information Extraction, Natural language processing and Information security. She has published many papers in reputed International conferences and International Journals. She is a member of various professional societies including ACM and IEEE.

Prachi Sarode received the BE and ME degree from Savitribai Phule Pune University, MS, India in 2005 and 2010 respectively. She is currently an Assistant Professor with the Department of Information Technology, MIT College of Engineering, Pune, MS, India. And also working towards the PhD degree in Vellore Institute of Technology, Chennai, TN, India. Her current research interests include Wireless Sensor Networks and Software Modeling. She is a member of the CSI.

Harsh Shrivastava is Research Intern at Multimodal Digital Media Analysis Lab, IIIT, Delhi and currently serving at Dean of School of AI at Gwalior, MP. He has been awarded Two MP Government Fellowships ie. Vigyan Manthan Yatra Fellowship and Child Scientist Fellowship. His area of interests is Machine learning, Deep learning and its applications in various fields like computer vision, NLP, etc.

Reshmi T. R. received her PhD under the Faculty of Information and Communication Engineering at Anna University, Chennai, India. She is currently working as Senior Assistant Professor in VIT University, Chennai, India. She is an IPV6 Forum Certified Engineer (Silver) and a CCNENT Cisco certified trainer. She has authored many reputed journal article and book chapters. Her research area includes Wireless Networks, Next generation Networks, QoS, Network Security and service applications.

330

Neelanarayanan Venkataraman received his Master of Science in Computer Science from Madurai Kamaraj University, India in 1995 and PhD from IT University of Copenhagen, Denmark in 2012. Currently, he is an Associate Professor at VIT University, Chennai, India. Before joining VIT University he has worked as a Scientist at Centre for Advanced Computing (CDAC), India and as a Lecturer in Madurai Kamaraj University, India and its affiliated institutions. His areas of research include distributed computing such as grid and cloud computing, context-aware computing, network management and security, XML-based security technologies and e-communities. He has initiated a number of international research collaborations with universities in Europe, Australia and South Korea as a Research Group Coordinator and Chief Investigator at VIT University. He was instrumental for initiating joint research collaboration between VIT University and industries such as CDAC and DLink. He has published more than 35 papers in various peer-reviewed international conferences and journals. He has organised various national workshops, international conference and symposium. Currently, he is heading the Cloud Computing Research Group at VIT University, Chennai campus and six students are pursuing their PhD under his guidance. He received the research award in VIT University for the year 2015 for his achievements, exemplary commitment, dedication and motivation towards research publication during 2015–16.

Index

T

V

W

Ensure Quality Research is Introduced to the Academic Community

Become an IGI Global Reviewer for Authored Book Projects

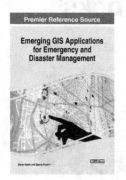

Premier Reference Source

Emerging GIS Applications for Emergency and Disaster Management

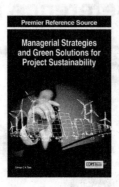

Premier Reference Source

Managerial Strategies and Green Solutions for Project Sustainability

Premier Reference Source

Comparative Approaches to Using R and Python for Statistical Data Analysis

Premier Reference Source

Solutions for High-Touch Communications in a High-Tech World

The overall success of an authored book project is dependent on quality and timely reviews.

In this competitive age of scholarly publishing, constructive and timely feedback significantly expedites the turnaround time of manuscripts from submission to acceptance, allowing the publication and discovery of forward-thinking research at a much more expeditious rate. Several IGI Global authored book projects are currently seeking highly qualified experts in the field to fill vacancies on their respective editorial review boards:

Applications may be sent to:
development@igi-global.com

Applicants must have a doctorate (or an equivalent degree) as well as publishing and reviewing experience. Reviewers are asked to write reviews in a timely, collegial, and constructive manner. All reviewers will begin their role on an ad-hoc basis for a period of one year, and upon successful completion of this term can be considered for full editorial review board status, with the potential for a subsequent promotion to Associate Editor.

If you have a colleague that may be interested in this opportunity, we encourage you to share this information with them.